Jim + Patricia —

God bless you on
"the Climb"! I
hope this helps
you read your 50
verses per day!

Scott Wade
2022

THE CLIMB
START HERE
SCOTT WADE

A PRACTICAL JOURNEY
THROUGH SCRIPTURE, BOOK 1

The Climb: Start Here

Published by:
One Stop Publications
6621 Britton Ave., Cincinnati, OH   45227
513-503-8965
www.OneStopPrintSolutions.com

This book is dedicated to my friend Sama Gilliland,
the first one who said to me,
"Hey, you ought to put these in a book!"
Thank you, Sama, for seeing possibilities where I didn't.
I hope the results are everything you thought they could be!

What people are saying about *The Climb...*

So many people who didn't grow up in the church view the Bible as an archaic and intimidating encyclopedia of content that is impossible to wade through. At the same time, those of us with a broader spiritual background never become so astute that we get beyond the need to have its key insights articulated in relevant and accessible ways. With "The Climb," Pastor Scott Wade appeals to - and heightens - the biblical engagement of, both groups— unlocking its practicality and applicability to those that have never explored its depths while coherently expressing fresh observations that will benefit and bless those who have read it and loved it for years.

- John Whitsett, Pastor

Scott's personal stories kick off many of his devotionals to bring you in while preparing you for the message. His strong use of God's Word and practical applications tie everything together making this my personal favorite of so many devotionals available. Thank you for your faithfulness in bringing such a wonderful start to each day.

- Kurt Johnson,
Southwestern Ohio Nazarene Missions President

Pastor Scott is a wonderful pastor who knows and loves people. I read his devotional writings and am amazed at how often they fit perfectly with what I am experiencing in life. Most of his material could easily be the prompting of sermons or teaching. You will get to know and love Pastor Scott Wade...I do!!!

- Bob Mahaffey,
District Superintendent, Church of the Nazarene

It isn't often you receive a devotional book that helps you achieve the goal of reading through scripture in an organized format, and in a manageable size of daily reading. Pastor Scott adds his commentary of thoughts and insights that are helpful, poignant, personal and practical. Humorous at times, and transparent always. It portrays the heart of a true pastor and friend.

- Joanne Powell,
Former Asst. Professor of Social Work, Taylor University.

The focus of "The Climb" is great for all people, regardless of their spiritual maturity. We need an intentional plan to read and digest more scripture, for The Word is "light and life" to our walk of faith. These writings are interesting, practical, helpful, and scripturally underpinned. You will find yourself pondering a thought after you're finished reading and can often share it with someone else in common conversation. Enjoy your climb!

- Larry Leckrone,
Tenured Evangelist, Church of the Nazarene

Foreword

The Climb brings back very vivid memories. The year, 1986. I was the keynote speaker for the North Carolina District Church of the Nazarene annual missions assembly. God was at work in amazing ways. Sitting in the audience was a young business man, Scott Wade. That day, through the power of the Holy Spirit, Scott heard God's call to begin his journey as a minister of the gospel.

Across the years, Scott and his capable wife, Lana, have faithfully served in ministry wherever God has led them. I have been privileged to know them well, to stay in their home, eat sumptuous meals at their table, snack on popcorn in the family room, and worship and speak in their church.

Scott writes The Climb from lessons Christ taught him on the journey. I relate to the steps he outlines. They lead us through the Bible in systematic, flexible, and practical ways. The presentations in The Climb not only give helpful nuggets of Biblical truth, but inspire us to be faithful to live in the Word on the journey. It is a good tool for small group Bible study and conversations. It is also useful for family devotional times.

I'm recommending The Climb to you because of the focus on the Bible, the integrity of the author, and the confidence that the devotionals will give momentum to your journey as you climb.

Thank you, Scott Wade, for compiling your spiritual insights to inspire us daily in our devotional reading. The climb will be more delightful.

Nina G. Gunter
General Superintendent Emerita
Church of the Nazarene

"A journey of a thousand miles begins with a single step."

What it is...

The Climb will help you take that step. Reading the Bible through is like a journey of a thousand miles - *up a mountain*! It begins with a single chapter. You can climb that mountain! Reading "A-Chapter-A-Day" as outlined in *The Climb*, you will read through the New Testament and Psalms each year and will complete the Old Testament over the course of five years.

How it began...

Many years ago, I was asked by a new Christian, "What should I read in the Bible?" I prepared a thirty day schedule of one chapter per day. Soon, I began publishing a reading schedule for the entire year, sending out daily email reminders. Then I added a few comments that I thought would help the reader understand and apply a verse or two from the chapter. That concept has evolved over time to *The Climb*.

How it works...

Each day you will be given one chapter (sometimes two for shorter chapters) from the Bible to read.

Along with the daily chapter, there is a practical devotional article and a suggested prayer that will help you internalize what you have read and establish spiritual momentum for *The Climb*.

You also will read a short selection from the book of Psalms. The longer Psalms are divided into smaller sections. You can choose to read a section each day, or you can read the Psalm in its entirety on the day it first appears. This may help you maintain continuity and context.

Not starting in January? Want to move at a slower (or faster) pace? This method is adaptable for day-by-day use. Each reading has both a date and a day number on the page. If you are reading by date, just go to the date. If you choose instead to read by the day, you can follow "Day 1," "Day 2," etc.

The most important thing to read is the daily chapter and Psalm. Read the Bible first. Then, as time permits, read the devotional article and say the prayer that follows.

This is Book 1 of the series, and it is called *Start Here*. This year the New Testament will come alive to you, and you will also begin the journey through the Old Testament, reading Genesis - Numbers.

Let's get started!

Are you afraid you will lose your focus and momentum? If you get discouraged along the way, remember what the ancient pilgrims used to say as they made The Climb to Jerusalem for the festivals:

I lift up my eyes to the hills. From where does my help come?
My help comes from the LORD, who made heaven and earth.
He will not let your foot be moved; he who keeps you will not slumber.
Behold, he who keeps Israel will neither slumber nor sleep.
The LORD is your keeper; the LORD is your shade on your right hand.
The sun shall not strike you by day, nor the moon by night.
The LORD will keep you from all evil; he will keep your life.
The LORD will keep your going out and your coming in from this time forth and forevermore

Psalm 121.1-8

Keep moving, dear friend. There is great reward for those who persevere.

— SW

THE CLIMB

START HERE

A PRACTICAL JOURNEY
THROUGH SCRIPTURE, BOOK 1

Driven by the Spirit

Daily Reading: Mark 1

> *The Spirit immediately drove him out into the wilderness. And he was in the wilderness forty days, being tempted by Satan. And he was with the wild animals, and the angels were ministering to him.* (Mark 1.12-13)

Devotional Thought: The gospel of Mark starts out, "The beginning of the gospel of Jesus Christ…" What better book to begin our journey through the Bible! Mark's style is straightforward, and he has a focus on *immediacy*. The word 'immediately' appears 35 times in the 16 chapters of the book, 9 times in this first chapter! In verse 12, we read, "The Spirit immediately drove him [Jesus] out into the wilderness." In the wilderness, Jesus encountered temptation (from Satan) and danger (from wild animals). But, he also enjoyed the presence of ministering angels!

Entering a new year feels a little like going into the wilderness, doesn't it? Political upheaval, border uncertainty, international instability, religious intolerance, and economic uncertainty - these and many other doubts crowd our minds. Other, more personal, temptations and dangers are sure to be encountered. We do not know what the new year holds, but we know that we have been driven to it. We have no choice!

We also know something else - a very important game-changer. We know that God will be with us! He has said, "I will never leave you nor forsake you" (Hebrews 13.5). Jesus himself told his disciples when he was returning to heaven, "behold, I am with you always, to the end of the age" (Matthew 28.20). Don't you imagine they were feeling a little uncertain about their future at that moment when Jesus seemed to be leaving them on their own?

So, in the new year, do not let uncertainties rule over you. Instead, remember Jesus is walking with you! Let's get in step with him *immediately*.

Prayer: Father, I do not know what the future holds, but I know that you hold the future. Help me to face the temptations and dangers of this New Year with peace and confidence. Amen.

Psalm of the Day: 1.1-6

And When...

Daily Reading: Mark 2

> *And when...* (Mark 2.2, 4, 5)

Devotional Thought: In life, there are some things that can't happen until other things happen first. A car can't go until the tank is filled with gas. A baby can't be born until the mother goes into labor. Dinner can't be eaten until the groceries are purchased and the meal is prepared. A house can't be built until the materials are purchased and delivered.

The same is true in the kingdom of heaven. When certain things happen, they open the way for other things to happen. Consider the 'and when' statements in Mark 2...

When Jesus was in Capernaum for several days, the news spread throughout the town... When some folks were hindered in their approach to Jesus, they had an opportunity to show that they would not take no for an answer... When an opening was made, those who needed Jesus were able to get to him... When faith reached out to Jesus, sins were forgiven...

Too often we as Christians adopt the philosophy that says, "Whatever will be will be." That simply is not Biblical. The Bible is clear in its call for us to decide and act. What we choose and do has an impact for good or for harm.

Stop for a moment and think, "What – in this new year – do I desire from Jesus? Are there some 'and when's' that are under my control? How can I foster an environment in which prayers can be answered, in which change can happen?" Success and progress are not automatic in our lives. God has given us the privilege and honor to partner with him. Will we do our part?

Prayer: Father, thank you for inviting me to partner with you in the fulfillment of your will for my life. Help me to believe you enough to choose and to do, to decide and to act. Help me to do so with confidence. Amen.

Psalm of the Day: 2.1-6

The Best You Can Be

Daily Reading: Mark 3

Then he went home, and the crowd gathered again, so that they could not even eat. And when his family heard it, they went out to seize him, for they were saying, "He is out of his mind." And the scribes who came down from Jerusalem were saying, "He is possessed by Beelzebul," and "by the prince of demons he casts out the demons." (Mark 3.20-22)

Devotional Thought: In high school, I testified of being called to the ministry. I clearly remember my high school gym teacher's reaction: "You're crazy! You're too talented to be a preacher!" That comment didn't necessarily cause my delay in becoming a preacher, but it did teach me a lesson I have never forgotten: People will not always understand and encourage the sacrifice and service we make for Jesus. As a matter of fact, they may call us crazy!

In Mark 3, Jesus was so happy doing his Father's will that he and his disciples were not even taking time to eat. Jesus' family thought he had lost his mind. And, when Jesus' detractors heard that, they became emboldened to accuse him - not of just being insane, but being filled with all manner of evil! (We need to be careful how we talk about our brothers and sisters in Christ with whom we disagree. Our negativity may embolden the Enemy to make a more direct attack on them...)

Circumstances and family, friends and enemies may oppose your total commitment to God. Some may even try to force you to "Choose between God and me!" That's a false choice. We can serve God with all our heart and give our very best to our family at the same time. As a matter of fact, we are at our best for our family when we are at our best for God.

This year, choose God and be the best you can be!

Prayer: Father, I commit to serve you with all my being. Help me to recognize the lies of the Enemy and to remain firm in the face of opposition. Amen.

Psalm of the Day: 2.7-12

Let the Son Shine!

Daily Reading: Mark 4

> And he said to them, "Is a lamp brought in to be put under a basket, or under a bed, and not on a stand? For nothing is hidden except to be made manifest; nor is anything secret except to come to light."
> (Mark 4.21-22)

Devotional Thought: Having just come through the Christmas season, my mind is fresh with examples of how people want to leave Christ out of Christmas. "Happy Holidays!" "Seasons' Greetings!" But, it's hard to have Christmas without Christ, unless of course we reduce it to an opportunity for unbridled consumerism – celebrated all the way from Black Friday through the after-Christmas sales!

Each year, a team of volunteers would come to the church I pastored and "**UN**decorate" the sanctuary. Garland down, wreaths packed away, trees disassembled, and lights unplugged. The sanctuary always looks so bare after the decorations are down. It seems so empty. Life is like Christmas in that way. Without Jesus, it is just plain and dark. It is empty. The good news is that we don't have to have Christmas without him and we don't have to pack him pack away with the Christmas lights!

Jesus is the light of the world. The light is shining in the darkness and the darkness cannot overcome it (John 1). He didn't come to be packed away and hidden. He came to be placed in a prominent place in our lives, in our homes, and in our world. Let Jesus have that prominent place in your life, so that the joy and peace, the hope and love of Christmas shine through your life all year long!

Prayer: Lord Jesus, come into my life and shine your light in every secret place. Search me, O God, and know my heart, try me and know my thoughts. Cleanse me and set me free to celebrate Christmas all year long. Amen.

Psalm of the Day: 3.1-8

Made for Better Things

Daily Reading: Mark 5

> *"Come out of the man, you unclean spirit!" ... Now a great herd of pigs was feeding there on the hillside, and they begged him, saying, "Send us to the pigs; let us enter them."* (Mark 5.8, 11-12)

Devotional Thought: "I'm disappointed in you. You're a better person than that!" I heard that from a 6th grade teacher after I had done something to hurt another person. It was a like a guided missile, scoring a direct hit on my heart. There were other things that turned me toward the good and toward God, but that event helped shape my life. It has stuck with me. In that interaction I came to know that I was made for better things!

In Mark 5, we read how Jesus made a trip across the Sea of Galilee with one purpose in mind: to rescue a man from a wasted life. He was possessed by a "Legion" of unclean spirits, causing him and those who loved him great pain. Jesus knew that he was made for better things. The man needed to hear the truth, and Jesus spoke it with authority: "Come out of the man, you unclean spirit!" Those spirits found a temporary 'home' in a herd of pigs.

You and I were made for better things than what this world has to offer. John described it like this: "For all that is in the world—the desires of the flesh and the desires of the eyes and pride of life—is not from the Father but is from the world. And the world is passing away along with its desires, but whoever does the will of God abides forever" (1 John 2.16-17). We were made for eternal things – for light, for love, and for life.

We don't have to live like pigs. We weren't made for that. Thank God! We were made for better things!

Prayer: Jesus, thank you for crossing over the sea that separated me from you. Thank you for saving me from sin. Help me to live in the grace and with the goodness that you provide me. Break every chain in my life, O Lord!

Psalm of the Day: 4.1-8

Who Gets Credit?

Daily Reading: Mark 6

King Herod heard of it, for Jesus' name had become known. (Mark 6:14)

Devotional Thought: In Mark 6, Jesus sends out his disciples, two by two, to bear witness to his name, to drive out unclean spirits, and to heal the sick. They were to take nothing for their journey besides a staff – no food, no change of clothes, no money, not even an extra tunic. The disciples had to trust in the Lord to provide for them as they went. These disciples followed Jesus' instructions and went out to proclaim the message of repentance, casting out demons and healing the sick.

These acts were so tremendous that King Herod heard of it. Notice that Herod didn't hear of the mighty duos of disciples performing miracles, but rather he heard because "Jesus' name had become known," (v14). The disciples were not to be credited for these miracles. These things were impossible without the power given to them by Jesus himself.

When we accomplish spiritual victories in our lives, are we willing to give Jesus the glory? Are we ready for our names to decrease in reputation so that His may increase? How tempting it would have been for those disciples to feel prideful over the things they were sent to do! Even knowing it was Jesus' power that allowed them to do those things, they still could have felt puffed up that Jesus chose them to accomplish His purposes. But we see no evidence of this in the Scripture, seeing that it was just Jesus' name that had become known to Herod. May we follow this example set by the twelve, and humbly obey the Spirit when we feel His prompting, being careful to give all glory and honor to whom it belongs.

Prayer: Lord, we are so often tempted to let the praise of others focus on us, when it is really you we should honor. Please help us to see our victories as gifts of your grace, undeserved, but given freely to us because you love us. Equip our hearts to use every opportunity to tell others of your love and mercy, giving you all of the glory. Amen.

Psalm of the Day: 5.1-6

A Friend of Sinners

Daily Reading: Mark 7

> *Some of his disciples ate with hands that were defiled, that is, unwashed.* (Mark 7.2)

Devotional Thought: Jesus faced a lot of criticism in his day. Legalistic people didn't like what he did on the Sabbath. They didn't appreciate his calling God *Father*. They didn't like the people he hung out with. All of that did not faze Jesus. So, these religious elites began to criticize his disciples as a way to get at him: "Their hands are dirty!"

It sounds a bit trite to us, but it was serious business to those Pharisees and Scribes. To them, having defiled hands when you ate meant that you yourself became defiled with the sinfulness of the heathen Gentiles. And that meant that you were unfit to worship God. To the Pharisees, you couldn't be friends with sinners and with God at the same time.

Jesus blew that up.

It is true that we can't be friends with the world – meaning the philosophy and values and immorality of the world – while being friends with God. The scripture says, "You adulterous people! Do you not know that friendship with the world is enmity with God? Therefore whoever wishes to be a friend of the world makes himself an enemy of God" (James 4.4). But it also says that Jesus was a friend of sinners (Matthew 11.19, Luke 19.7). Jesus went places and did things that offended and even shocked the religious hypocrites of his day. The question is, "Do I?" Am I willing to "get my hands dirty" in order to be a friend of sinners?

May Jesus help me to be a friend of sinners! Not a friend of sin, but of sinners!

Prayer: Lord, help me today to guard my heart and to love people like you love them. Keep me from being critical and judgmental. May I embrace those who are often rejected. Amen.

Psalm of the Day: 5.7-12

Is Anybody Hungry?

Daily Reading: Mark 8

> *I have compassion on the crowd, because they have been with me now three days and have nothing to eat. And if I send them away hungry to their homes, they will faint on the way. And some of them have come from far away.* (Mark 8.2-3)

Devotional Thought: In the gospels, we read of two instances when Jesus fed a multitude of people. On this occasion in Mark 8, Jesus said that he had compassion on them. It is so encouraging that Jesus identifies with and reaches out to the physically hungry, but I see something interesting in the latter part of verse 2: "They have been with me now three days and have nothing to eat." I wonder if that describes us sometimes. Are we walking with Jesus and going without "eating"?

There are many people in and around the church who have a testimony of knowing the Lord but who seldom if ever open the Bible. They neglect the gift of prayer. They don't realize that there are multiple opportunities to learn and grow. They are trying to survive on a Sunday morning service once a week – if that! They go "away hungry to their homes." Jesus knows that they "will faint on the way," and he has compassion on them.

"Some of them have come from far away." I have friends like that. They have turned toward Jesus from a life deep in sin and far from the church. How sad that they do not feast at the table of his love! They are unable to draw close to God because they neglect the things of God. They have no spiritual strength because they take no spiritual food. Jesus teaches me not to judge them but to have compassion on them. After all, I came from far away, and I sometimes neglect my spiritual diet.

Am I trying to follow Jesus without taking advantage of the abundance of spiritual food he provides? And, do I have compassion on the "hungry"?

Prayer: Thank you, Jesus, for having compassion on me. When I was wandering – hungry and weak – you fed me with spiritual food. Help me, O Lord, to eat my fill at your table and then to rise with compassion for the spiritually hungry. Amen.

Psalm of the Day: 6.1-5

Salt-Cured

Daily Reading: Mark 9

For everyone will be salted with fire. (Mark 9.49)

Devotional Thought: When in South Carolina, I love getting a ham biscuit. Not just any ham biscuit, but a salt-cured ham biscuit! It is delicious! There's nothing quite like southern, salt-cured ham!

Before refrigeration was available, meats were sometimes preserved through a process called salt-curing. The salt would draw out the moisture from the meat and prevent the meat from spoiling. Another process to cure meats was smoking, where the meat was preserved by exposing it to smoke that sealed it and removed the moisture from it. It was this process to which Jesus referred in Mark 9, when he said "Everyone will be salted with fire." Impurities will be removed and destinies will be set.

There are two fires that salt people. One is the fire of the Holy Spirit. John the Baptist said of Jesus, "He will baptize with the Holy Spirit and with fire." This baptism removes impurity (sin) and preserves (seals) us in Christ. The other fire that salts us is the fire of adversity. Trials and troubles of life purify us in another way. They make us focus on what is important. In this kind of purification and preservation, we — as disciples of Jesus — "lay aside every weight, and sin which clings so closely… [to] run with endurance the race that is set before us" (Hebrews 12.1).

Have you been salted with fire? Adversity is a part of life, whether we seek it or not: "Man is born to trouble as the sparks fly upward" (Job 5.7). So, do not fret if you have adversity. Instead remember it is purifying and preserving you.

The purifying, preserving fire of the Holy Spirit, however, is something you can seek. Have you prayed to be filled with the Spirit?

Prayer: Lord, when I go through the fires of adversity, help me to rely on you. Purify my soul, O God! Fill me with the Holy Spirit and fire that I might be "salted with fire." Amen.

Psalm of the Day: 6.6-10

Serving and Leading

Daily Reading: Mark 10

The cup that I drink you will drink, and with the baptism with which I am baptized, you will be baptized. (Mark 10.39)

Devotional Thought: Moms want the best for their children, don't they? They will go to great lengths to give their kids every possible opportunity to succeed. Sometimes, they even go beyond what is proper. The mother of James and John did. In love, she went beyond what was proper and asked Jesus for a special favor for her two boys: "Let them sit at your right and left hand in your kingdom." Jesus let her – and her sons – know right away: with leadership comes sacrifice, even suffering. Position attained without sacrifice is dangerous. I often quote, the unnamed Jewish rabbi who said, "To receive without giving corrodes the soul."

Without sacrifice, leadership feels like *privilege*. Instead of being focused on those led, leadership becomes all about the needs and wants of the leader. God found fault with those Old Testament shepherds: "Ah, shepherds of Israel who have been feeding yourselves! Should not shepherds feed the sheep? You eat the fat, you clothe yourselves with the wool, you slaughter the fat ones, but you do not feed the sheep" (Ezekiel 34.2-3).

Without sacrifice, leadership feels like *control*. Jesus laid down his life for his sheep. He said his sheep hear and know his voice and follow him. They are not coerced into doing his will, but rather joyfully follow the voice of love. Leadership is not about coercion, but rather about service. And, service demands sacrifice.

Jesus told that mom and those boys that his leadership would demand the ultimate sacrifice. He had a cup to drink and a baptism to undergo. If they wanted to be at his right hand in leadership, they had to be at his right hand in sacrifice.

How about you? Are you ready to drink his cup and undergo his baptism?

Prayer: Lord, I desire to sit at your right hand of service and at your left hand of sacrifice. Help me to drink your cup and undergo your baptism. Amen.

Psalm of the Day: 7.1-5

Purpose-full Living
Daily Reading: Mark 11

Go into the village in front of you, and immediately as you enter it you will find a colt tied, on which no one has ever sat. Untie it and bring it. (Mark 11.2)

Devotional Thought: As Jesus entered Jerusalem en route to the cross, he was mindful of his purpose – to lay down his life as a ransom for many (Matthew 20.28). In order to fulfill prophecy – and thus to identify himself as the Lord's Messiah – he arranged to ride into Jerusalem on a colt upon which no one had ever ridden. It was a custom of that day that an animal intended for sacred use must be 'unbroken.' This was in order that it would be broken exclusively for the purpose of the deity. And so Jesus not only identified himself as the Messiah, but also as God.

Jesus also was mindful of his purpose in another way. Instead of riding in triumphantly on a war horse, Jesus came humbly upon an animal of peace. That was to remind us that his purpose was not the overthrow of Rome. The Jewish population deeply resented Roman control and influence, but Jesus didn't come to break that grip. He came to break the power of sin! If you and I had been in Jesus' position, it would certainly have been tempting to bypass the cross and seek the crown. After all, the crowds had come to him. He was in a good position to establish an earthly political kingdom.

But, he kept his purpose in mind.

Often we are tempted to do things our own way and to seek ends of our own choosing. It is particularly tempting to do so when we are in a position of power and control. Are we, however, able to be like Jesus? Are we able to say, "Nevertheless, not my will, but yours, be done"?

What is your purpose? Are you keeping it in mind?

Prayer: Father, thank you for your wonderful plan for my life; it is a plan to prosper me and not to harm me, a plan to give me hope and a future. Please help me to keep your plan in mind and to surrender my will to yours. Amen.

Psalm of the Day: 7.6-13

Fruit Production

Daily Reading: Mark 12

> *A man planted a vineyard and put a fence around it and dug a pit for the winepress and built a tower, and leased it to tenants and went into another country.* (Mark 12.1)

Devotional Thought: in Mark 12, Jesus told a parable that offended and threatened the religious leaders. The parable has some wonderful symbolism.

- The man represents God, who is the owner of everything. God created the world to produce a family of love for himself.
- The vineyard represents this world which God created – in some sense the physical order, but even more importantly it represents the human race. Through the human race God desires to form and love his family. What a wonderful thought that he made us to love us!
- The fence represents the grace of God which preserves our lives in Christ.
- The pit and winepress represent the pressures of life that we go through. These responsibilities and disappointments, failures and successes, are shared with us in relationship with God.
- The tower is the cross of Jesus, standing above the horizon of human history. This tower reveals the loving perspective of God. It is both a place to see and a shelter under which we can live.
- The tenants are people – in particular spiritual leaders, but in essence every person – who are created to help one another discover God and his grace.
- The other country represents the fact that Jesus is in heaven right now awaiting the instruction of the Father. One day he will return and take all his children to be with him forever!

As you read this parable, remember to be faithful as a tenant to produce fruit according to God's will. The vineyard is not our own, but our Father's. He desires that we share his love – in our families, our churches, our communities, and our world.

Prayer: Father, thank you for giving me life in the vineyard. Help me to live and love so that others may find the grace of God that brings salvation. Remove from me selfishness and help me to trust you. Amen.

Psalm of the Day: 7.14-17

Wake Up!

Daily Reading: Mark 13

> *Therefore stay awake—for you do not know when the master of the house will come, in the evening, or at midnight, or when the rooster crows, or in the morning— lest he come suddenly and find you asleep.*
> (Mark 13:35-36)

Devotional Thought: Jesus told his disciples that one day "The Son of Man will come in clouds with great power and glory, and send the angels to gather His elect from the ends of the earth" (vv. 26, 27).

No one - not even the Son - knows the day or hour this will happen. While only the Father knows that time, we do know that the gospel must first be proclaimed to all nations (v. 10). Jesus gives an analogy likening His followers to the servants in charge of the master's house while He is gone. "Therefore stay awake – for you do not know when the master of the house will come, in the evening, or at midnight, or when the rooster crows, or in the morning – lest he come suddenly and find you asleep," (vv. 35-36).

Jesus is not referring to a physical sleep, but rather to a spiritual stupor. We are instructed to stay awake, to stay alert. What could this mean for us as believers?

We have likely all been through dry spells in our faith – times when we have not been in communion with God; unconcerned about His will for our lives and in the lives of those around us. This happens primarily when we are on "autopilot." Things are cruising along pretty well, and we don't really need Jesus in our everyday lives. Then we hit some turbulence and find ourselves on our knees again, pleading with the Lord about our sudden trial. When those times of turbulence come into your life, take heed and take heart. The God who loves us and has called us His children is reminding us of our constant need of Him.

Prayer: Father, we are sorry for all of the times we have tried to walk alone, without your guidance and protection. Please lead us in the way of dependence on you, that we may see the love and provision that you long to show us.

Psalm of the Day: 8.1-9

While Jesus Prays

Daily Reading: Mark 14

Sit here while I pray. (Mark 14.32)

Devotional Thought: On the eve of Jesus' arrest and suffering, he went to the Garden of Gethsemane where he prayed. As he entered the sacred space (made sacred by his presence and purpose), he instructed most of his disciples to wait at a distance: "Sit here while I pray." Those were his only instructions. They were not to do anything but sit, waiting in a position of peaceful anticipation of his return.

What a blessed thought! Jesus has gone to the right hand of the Father where he is making intercession for us. While he is there, he invites us to sit and wait for him – not to fret, not to worry, not to run looking for him. We can sit in peace, knowing that he will return with further instructions.

I am reminded of that scripture: "Be still and know that I am God" (Psalm 46.10). Whatever life may throw at us, Jesus is just out of sight, praying for us! As a matter of fact, though we cannot see him, we know that he sees us! When Jesus is praying we can have confidence that all will be well.

But there is another factor in this story. While he prayed, Jesus took his closest friends to a place even closer to the 'action.' Those he told to "watch and pray." Though Jesus was out of sight, he was closer and could respond to them more quickly.

It is a great privilege to sit in peace while Jesus prays, but how much greater to be invited to that closer place! There we have greater intimacy, greater privilege, greater knowledge, and greater responsibility. Let's go on into the garden of intimacy with Jesus!

Prayer: Jesus, thank you for the peace that we have knowing that you are even now making intercession for us at the right hand of the Father. Help us, O Lord, to go further into the garden of prayer that we might know you more. Amen.

Psalm of the Day: 9.1-6

Take Courage

Daily Reading: Mark 15

Joseph of Arimathea, a respected member of the council, who was also himself looking for the kingdom of God, took courage and went to Pilate and asked for the body of Jesus. (Mark 15.43)

Devotional Thought: On the day that Jesus was crucified, Joseph of Arimathea retrieved and buried the body of Jesus. Joseph. What was he like?

Of Arimathea… Not from Jerusalem, perhaps Joseph was not seduced by the power of that religious center. As we see in politics today, it is easy for people to fall prey to the intoxicating effects of power.

Respected and Religious… When duty called, Joseph answered. He came through the ranks of service and leadership until he found himself in a position of influence in the Jewish community. There is much to be said of doing our part, of faithfully filling a role because it needs to be done.

Seeker after Truth… Though he was faithful in the organization, Joseph was looking for something more – the Kingdom of God. He didn't assume that the human organization was the be-all, end-all. He wanted to make sure that he discovered the truth *behind* the organization.

Courageous… Since Jesus was executed as a heretic and an insurrectionist, to retrieve the body of Jesus would bring suspicion upon Joseph. He had seen what they had done to Jesus, but he stood courageous in the face of the religious and civil authorities!

Bold… Joseph did not beat around the bush. He knew that what he felt in his heart was right. It would not have been right to leave the body of Jesus on the cross. He went right 'to the top' and asked Pilate for the body.

May we learn from and live like Joseph of Arimathea!

Prayer: Father, how can we ever thank you enough for the gift of your Son? Grant us courage this day that we may honor Jesus through our service. Like Joseph, "let us go to Jesus outside the camp and bear the reproach he endured."

Psalm of the Day: 9.7-12

Who Will Roll Away the Stone?

Daily Reading: Mark 16

Who will roll away the stone for us from the entrance of the tomb?
(Mark 16.3)

Devotional Thought: Have you ever felt like those women who – on Easter morning – were going to anoint the body of Jesus? Faced with the thought of a huge stone blocking the grave, they had no plan. All they could do was take turns asking one another, "Who will roll away the stone for us?"

A legitimate question. The guards that were there wouldn't help. No one else was going. They only had their own arms and legs to put to the task. They knew that wasn't enough. But, they went anyway. Serving Jesus, they believed that somehow they would get that stone out of the way. Their trek to the tomb and their repeated questions were a type of prayer.

God came through. And he did it in even bigger ways than they imagined. He not only rolled *that* stone away, with the resurrection of Jesus he rolled the stone of death away! Jesus Christ took the battle to Satan's stronghold. Death was no match for the Son of God!

Perhaps you are facing an insurmountable task or problem. You may be asking yourself, "Why am I doing this? Why am I going through this?" Like those women on Easter morning, keep on walking. Do not shrink from the battle. Do not quit in resignation. There is great victory for the one who believes in Jesus and who keeps on going even though the situation seems hopeless! In the face of the insurmountable, God will enable you to "Mount up with wings as eagles!" And like those women, you will look up and see that the stone has been rolled back – even though it is very large.

Prayer: Lord, we know that when you came forth from the grave, you defeated death! There is no enemy that can stand against you. Help us to trust you and keep on going even in the face of the impossible. Roll away our stones, O Lord. Amen.

Psalm of the Day: 9.13-20

Power and Light Company
Daily Reading: Genesis 1

> *Let there be light...* (Genesis 1.3)

Devotional Thought: Some electric companies are called "Power and Light Company." I like that. Without power there is no light. God is in the power and light business. When he turns on the power, the lights come on! At one point in ages past, before day or night existed, God created the heavens and the earth (Genesis 1.1). Then, on the very first 'day,' God said, "Let there be light." Out of the formless void, God's creative power brought forth light, illuminating the rest of creation. And from the beginning, God separated light from darkness (v. 4). Light is good; darkness – not so much.

Darkness, however, was not only "over the face of the deep" when God created the heavens and the earth; it was also over the dry land. So God gave greater light and lesser light (day 3 of creation) to bring power and order to life.

Sometimes darkness falls over us, too. The loss of a job, the news of sickness, the death of a loved one... Many, many things bring darkness. But God is in the power and light business! He sets the greater light and the lesser light to ward off the darkness. And, even when things seem the bleakest, we can – if we look – see the stars of his eternal love blinking in the darkest heavens.

The Shepherd Psalmist was familiar with the darkness. He said, "Even though I walk through the shadow of death, I will fear no evil, for you are with me..." (Psalm 23.4) We may not be able to see our way through the darkness, but no night is so dark that God cannot see! He is with us, and ... He is in the power and light business!

Prayer: Thank you, Lord, that you are in the power and light business. From the beginning you created light to bring order to our chaos, clarity to our confusion, and hope to our despair. Help us to walk in the light as you are in the light! Amen.

Psalm of the Day: 10.1-11

Where Are You?

Daily Reading: Genesis 2-3

> *But the LORD God called to the man and said to him, "Where are you?"*
> (Genesis 3.9)

Devotional Thought: Have you ever lost one of your children? Or have you been with someone who has? Several years ago my wife and I were with my daughter and her daughters at Coney Island Park in Cincinnati. Coney Island has what is billed as "the largest flat-surface swimming pool in North America." It's over 2 acres. It holds a lot of people. And, as we discovered, it 'hides' a lot of people. Our youngest (at the time!) granddaughter got separated from us for a moment. That is scary. She was just 2 years old. Can I tell you that we were not embarrassed about screaming her name at the top of our lungs? "Adalyn!" We found her – safe and dry – but not until my daughter pierced some nearby eardrums!

Losing someone you love is a horrible feeling. God felt that in the Garden of Eden, when Adam and Eve sinned and then hid themselves from him. "Adam! Eve!" he called in desperation.

Sin separates us from God now just the same as it did Adam and Eve then. But the good news is that God is seeking each one of us. He calls our names. He searches for us in the places we are hidden. Sometimes we hide ourselves. At other times, circumstances of life hide us. But God continues to seek, to call, to find, to save. I've had friends whom God found in jail, in hospitals, in restaurants, in court, and yes, in church.

Where are you? Are you feeling separated from God? Take heart! He is calling your name.

Prayer: Jesus, thank you that you are the good Shepherd who seeks out the lost sheep. Come find me, Lord, for I need you. Use me that others may be found and rescued, too. Amen.

Psalm of the Day: 10.12-15

Give Your Best with Zest

Daily Reading: Genesis 4

> *And the Lord had regard for Abel and his offering, but for Cain and his offering he had no regard. So Cain was very angry, and his face fell.* (Genesis 4.4b-5)

Devotional Thought: After the fall of mankind into sin in Genesis 3, things just keep getting worse. In the fourth chapter, we find the account of the first people born to Adam and Eve – their two sons, Cain and Abel. Cain was a farmer and Abel tended to the sheep. They both brought offerings to the Lord, both seemingly good and acceptable offerings. But God, who knew the hearts of both men, had regard for only Abel and his offering.

When we are caught with an ulterior motive, or with nefarious purposes, we can relate to Cain's reaction. He was "very angry, and his face fell," (v 5). This is defensiveness, and it is often our first reaction to accusation as well, even when we know the accusation has merit. Sadly, Cain's response was extreme, and he killed his brother Abel.

This chapter shows us the Lord's expectations for those who love Him. We see it spelled out more clearly in Leviticus later, as God gives very specific requirements for the Israelites' offerings and worship. He expects us to give the best of what we have to Him. When we hold back, when we choose to meet our own desires and needs before giving to Him – whether it be with our time or money – the offering is not a pleasing aroma to Him. Rather, it is a reminder that there are other gods before Him: the gods of control, greed, accumulation, pride, comfort, or selfish ambition. When we give of our time, energy, and financial resources, let it be the "first fruits" that we give – the very best of what we have – to acknowledge His lordship over every aspect of our lives.

Prayer: Lord, we know we sometimes fail to give you the best of ourselves. Help us to see that all good and perfect gifts are from you, the Father of lights, and that our gifts are meant to center our hearts on you. Amen.

Psalm of the Day: 10.16-18

Relief

Daily Reading: Genesis 5

> *When Lamech had lived 182 years, he fathered a son and called his name Noah, saying, "Out of the ground that the LORD HAS CURSED, THIS ONE SHALL BRING US RELIEF FROM OUR WORK AND FROM THE PAINFUL TOIL OF OUR HANDS."* (Genesis 5.28-29)

Devotional Thought: There are many chapters in the Bible like Genesis 5 – chapters of names and genealogies, or chapters of tribes, clans, and numbers. It is tempting, as we read such chapters, to "just get through it." But, if we read carefully and thoughtfully – and most importantly if we ask the Holy Spirit to illuminate our thinking – we will almost always find something inspirational and helpful. The story about Lamech, the father of Noah, is like that.

Apart from his longevity, Lamech's story is inspirational because God gave him a son and with that son a vision. As we read in Genesis 3, the "ground" had been cursed because of Adam and Eve's sin. But with the birth of Noah, God promised relief was on the way. Noah's name sounded very similar to the word for "rest." Lamech named his son Noah, because he believed God was bringing "relief from our work and from the painful toil of our hands." Later, Noah was called by God to build an ark and to rescue not only his family but posterity as well.

Noah was a sign of One to come: Jesus! Out of the "ground" of human flesh, God brought a savior. The curse of sin reached its worst when Jesus, the Son of God, hung on the cross. The waters of death closed in on him, but he came forth from the grave! Once again, "out of the ground" of the tomb, God brought forth "relief from our work and from the painful toil of our hands!"

Thanks be to God!

Prayer: Jesus, thank you for coming to redeem us from the burden – the power and penalty – of sin. Help us to share that good news with joy and with love so that others may join us in the 'ark of safety.' Amen.

Psalm of the Day: 11.1-7

My Fellow Passengers

Daily Reading: Genesis 6-7

Keep them alive with you. (Genesis 6.19)

Devotional Thought: As God instructed Noah to build the Ark, he assured him that his sons and their wives, along with the animals he brought onto the Ark, would be kept alive. Noah was to build the Ark for that very reason: to "keep them alive." God not only wants to save us, he desires for our family and friends to be saved!

When the Apostle Paul was about to be shipwrecked with 275 others in the Mediterranean Sea, an angel appeared to him with the good news of his own salvation, and he added this: "God has graciously given you the lives of all who sail with you" (Acts 27.24b). What a great promise! God not only wants to save us, he desires for our family and friends to be saved!

Paul had earlier written these intriguing words to Christians: "the unbelieving husband is made holy because of his wife, and the unbelieving wife is made holy because of her husband. Otherwise your children would be unclean, but as it is, they are holy" (1 Corinthians 7.14). What a great promise! God not only wants to save us, he desires for our family and friends to be saved!

Think about those you love. God loves them, too. We are the vessel of God's salvation for our family and friends. That says two things to me: 1) I need to make sure that I am building my ark so that it can withstand the storms and floods of life. Only then can I "keep them alive with me." 2) I can have confidence as I pray, for "God has graciously given me the lives of all who sail with me," and if they are willing, God certainly is waiting to save them!

Prayer: Thank you, Lord, for graciously giving me the lives of those I love. As you have saved me, help me to build my life so that it will be a vessel of hope and salvation for those I love.

Psalm of the Day: 12.1-8

The Olive Branch of Peace

Daily Reading: Genesis 8

And the dove came back to him in the evening, and behold, in her mouth was a freshly plucked olive leaf. (Genesis 8.11a)

Devotional Thought: Several years ago, I had a *falling out* with a friend of mine over some issue now long forgotten. Words were exchanged and the relationship changed. As time passed, so did our anger, but there was no occasion for restoring the friendship. Consequently, neither one of us did anything. Then, almost out of the blue, I received news of a situation that caused me to reach out to my friend. I warily extended a "dove of peace" to see where it might lead. I thought, "Well, I've nothing to lose, so I might as well try." Much to my delight, my friend seemed open to returning to the relationship as it had been. My friend returned an "olive branch of peace." Since that time, we have restored the broken relationship and enjoyed wonderful fellowship. We both regained a friend. Wonderful! It is my opinion that one can never have too many friends!

5,000 years ago, God and mankind had a falling out. A flood came and covered the earth, and only eight people were saved. They floated upon the waters of the flood for many, many days – almost a year. It seemed as if the friendship might be forgotten for good. But God extended an olive leaf – the symbol of peace – in the beak of a dove. In this way, he let Noah, representing all humanity, know that the storm was over, the danger was past, and a reunion was on its way.

Perhaps you have been separated from a friend or a family member – even from God himself – and you long for the olive branch of peace. Do what I did. Do what Noah did. By faith release a dove. I think you will find that reconciliation is not only possible but already begun!

Prayer: Father, thank you for the wonderful gift of friendship. For any broken relationships in my life, help me, like you, to extend the olive branch of peace. Heal and restore those relationships I pray. Amen.

Psalm of the Day: 13.1-6

With God There's Always More

Daily Reading: Genesis 9

After the flood Noah lived 350 years. (Genesis 9.28)

Devotional Thought: I had a wonderful mentor and friend who told me of a prayer that a college professor had taught him to pray, "Lord, help me not to peak too soon." As a young man, on my way "up" in life, in energy, in skill, in opportunities, and in success, I didn't really understand that. As I have aged, however, I have come to appreciate the reality behind that prayer. I want to always be moving upward, getting closer to Christ, growing in effectiveness. My body and mind don't always cooperate, however!

As we read the account of Noah, it seems fair to say that Noah "peaked" in his life when he saved his family – and humanity! – from the flood. But, his story does not end there, does it? "After the flood Noah lived 350 years." I wonder what he did in those years. I hope the incident with his sons was not typical.

After attaining a certain stage or age or wage in life, it is easy to rest on our laurels. Like the rich man in Luke 12, it is easy to say to ourselves, "Relax! Eat, drink, and be merry!" But "after the flood" there is still a lot of living left to do! Like Abraham at 100, God may want to give us a "child" to mentor; or like Moses at 80, there may be works of deliverance for us to do; or like John in his 90's, there may be books to write and counsel to give.

You may have reached a certain level of success, but remember – with God there's always more!

Prayer: Lord, help me not to become satisfied with where I am, but grant that I may continue to grow in effectiveness and effort for you. Help me to live each of the years that are before me. May I not peak too soon. Amen.

Psalm of the Day: 14.1-3

Are You Making a Name for Yourself?
Daily Reading: Genesis 10-11

> Then they said, "Come, let us build ourselves a city and a tower with its top in the heavens, and let us make a name for ourselves, lest we be dispersed over the face of the whole earth." (Genesis 11:4)

Devotional Thought: Genesis 11 gives the account of the Tower of Babel. At this point in history, there was only one language. Even though people were multiplying and spreading, they remained unified in their nationality and language. They were now attempting to attain security and sufficiency through their building project.

What may seem innocuous to us (what's the harm in constructing a skyscraper?) was concerning to the Lord. He knew their hearts were no longer centered on him, but rather on their own fame and fortune. The intention of the tower was to "make a name" for themselves (v.4), sparing absolutely no thought for the glory of their Creator. God's response was to take away their ability to work together by confusing their language, and therefore disperse them from the city and the tower.

I cannot help but be reminded of our own natures and the pride we take in self-sufficiency. We, too, strive to build ourselves up, to make a name for ourselves – whether it's through our wealth, our reputation, our status, or even our standing before God. The reality is that we are all needy, dependent people who are completely reliant on God's grace through His redemption. May we take to heart the words of Paul to the Galatians: "May I never boast except in the cross of our Lord Jesus Christ, through which the world has been crucified to me, and I to the world," (Gal. 6:14).

Prayer: Lord, we confess that we, too, are tempted to build a name for ourselves, giving little thought to your glory and your great name. Please help us to keep our focus on Jesus and on his kingdom. Amen.

Psalm of the Day: 14.4-7

An Ounce of Prevention

Daily Reading: Colossians 1

Walk in a manner worthy of the Lord. (Colossians 1.10)

Devotional Thought: Have you heard the expression "An ounce of prevention is worth a pound of cure"?

My brother and I had a favorite uncle when we were kids. We used to spend the weekends with him. I remember one occasion when my brother and I were at his house that we made some "prank" phone calls. Just kid stuff. Well, we got caught. The people we had pranked called my uncle, but he told them, "My nephews would never do that." When confronted and we 'fessed up, he said something that was the worst of all punishments: "I guess I'm going to have to call them and tell them I was wrong about you." We had disappointed him! That broke my little boy heart! I didn't want him to be wrong about me! I wanted him to be proud of me! When the incident was over, and apologies made, my uncle went right back to being proud of us!

God is proud of us, too. We are his children. We would never want to disappoint him, would we? It would break our hearts! Sometimes we do, however, and it is good to know that when we go to him and sincerely repent, he will forgive us. He will be proud of us. That's way more than a pound of cure!

What is even better, however, is to "walk in a manner worthy of the Lord." How do we do that? By "bearing fruit in every good work and increasing in the knowledge of God; being strengthened with all power, according to his glorious might, for all endurance and patience with joy; giving thanks..." (Colossians 1.11-12) That is way more than an ounce of prevention.

Prayer: Lord, thank you that you love me so much! Help me to love you in return and to walk in a manner worthy of your great love. And when I falter, forgive me and help me to trust your mercy and receive your grace. Amen.

Psalm of the Day: 15.1-5

Shadow vs. Substance

Daily Reading: Colossians 2

These are a shadow of the things to come, but the substance belongs to Christ. (Colossians 2.17)

Devotional Thought: Do you love your church? Do you love the place where you gather to worship? Do you love your friends who you meet with there? How about the place where you sit? The songs that you sing? The sermons that your pastor preaches? I hope you answered "yes" to all those questions.

It is good to have those people, locations and ceremonies through which you can comfortably draw near to God, but we must remember, "These are but a shadow of things to come."

The Apostle Paul, in Colossians 2, had to help some folks see the difference between substance and style, between reverence and ritual, between essence in worship and preference in worship. There was a group of believers in that church who were tempted to replace genuine heartfelt worship of Christ with things from their past – either Jewish ritualism or stoic asceticism. Paul reminded them, "The substance belongs to Christ!" We occasionally need to be reminded that this world and all its forms – including our form of worship – are passing away. They are but shadows. In the end, what will matter is that we have kept Christ first in our lives. He is the substance.

Perhaps your recent experience is quite the opposite. Maybe you are feeling unsettled by recent changes in your worship experience. You don't recognize the songs; someone else is sitting in your seat; someone you love is no longer there; there is a new preacher who doesn't know what you've been through. In that situation, take heart! The substance has not changed. It is Jesus!

Prayer: Jesus, thank you for those rituals and ceremonies that help me worship you. Thank you for the places, the times and the people who are a part of that experience. I cherish them as do you. But help me to remember that they are but a shadow. You are the substance. Amen.

Psalm of the Day: 16.1-6

Ages and Stages

Daily Reading: Colossians 3

> *Seek the things that are above, where Christ is, seated at the right hand of God. Set your minds on things that are above, not on things that are on earth.* (Colossians 3.1b-2)

Devotional Thought: "What am I to do with my life? Am I to amass wealth? Am I to become powerful and popular?" The question of what we are to pursue is relevant at any age. And, depending on your life stage, it will change; depending on your circumstances, it will change.

The Apostle Paul learned that. There were times when he was free to move about and preach the gospel. In those stages of his life, he served as a church-planting missionary – going all over the Roman Empire preaching the gospel. There were other times when he was imprisoned for his faith. In those times, he gave himself to writing letters and encouraging his congregations and friends from a jail cell. A disciple of Paul, Epaphras, learned that. While he was in jail with Paul, he was "*always* struggling on your behalf in his prayers." There are seasons when all we can do is pray. There are other times, when we are sick as Epaphroditus in Philippians 2, that all we can do is get better.

With all the ages and stages of our lives we must have an overarching purpose to get us through the changes. Paul told us what that purpose is to be: "Seek the things that are above, where Christ is..." No matter where we are or what our circumstances, we are able to transform them – by transporting them – to where Christ is! Jesus said it like this, "Seek first the kingdom of God and his righteousness, and all these things will be given to you as well."

What are you seeking today? If it is Christ, then no matter your age or your stage, you will live with purpose and meaning.

Prayer: Lord Jesus, help me to seek the things that are above, to value the things that are eternal. I know that "the present form of this world is passing away" so help me to live with an eye to heaven! Amen.

Psalm of the Day: 16.7-11

Who Is One of You

Daily Reading: Colossians 4

And with him Onesimus, our faithful and beloved brother, who is one of you. (Colossians 4.9)

Devotional Thought: One of the things I love about being a pastor is to see new relationships forming. When Jim and Debbie began attending our church, I invited them to my small group, thinking how great it would be great to have them with me. I also told them about other groups/classes as well. They came to my class one time, but they "landed" with another class. That group was perfect for them. How rewarding it was to see them really become a part of that group – to learn and grow in the Lord, to connect and pray with people. Jim and Debbie are "one of them."

In Colossians 4, Paul is *re*-connecting Onesimus to that congregation. Onesimus – who had been a slave of Philemon, one of the leading members of that church – had run away from Colossae and gone to Rome. There, he met Paul and came to know Christ. (You can read his story in Philemon.) It was Paul's privilege to send Onesimus back to Colossae, back to Philemon, and back to the church – no longer as a slave, but as a brother. Was he nervous about it? You bet! Onesimus was his friend, and Paul wasn't sure how it would go. But, Paul knew it was the right thing to do.

Onesimus, who had once been a slave, was now "our faithful and beloved brother." He was "one of you." The connection was made. If church tradition is accurate, the connection was solid. Onesimus grew in the Lord until he became the Bishop of Ephesus, a city near Colossae.

Two questions arise. First, are you connected? Second, who are you connecting?

Prayer: Lord, thank you for giving me a faith family. Help me to connect with them so that I might give and receive encouragement and support. Give me eyes to see others who need to be connected as well. And help me then to do my part. Amen.

Psalm of the Day: 17.1-5

Let There Be No Strife Between Us

Daily Reading: Genesis 12-13

> Then Abram said to Lot, "Let there be no strife between you and me, and between your herdsmen and my herdsmen, for we are kinsmen. Is not the whole land before you? Separate yourself from me. If you take the left hand, then I will go to the right, or if you take the right hand, then I will go to the left." (Genesis 13:8-9)

Devotional Thought: Genesis 12 begins the account of Abram who became known as Abraham, that great patriarch of Israel. In chapter 13, Abraham, with his nephew Lot, had become quite rich in livestock. So great were their herds, the land could not support both families. To avoid conflict, Abraham suggested that they separate. Instead of exercising his right as the elder male relative and taking the best of the land for himself, he gave Lot first choice. Lot chose what appeared to be the better option, the well-watered land of the Jordan Valley.

Abraham demonstrated a selfless love toward his nephew Lot. First, he recognized the potential for discord between the two families before it became a larger problem. Second, he gave Lot the first choice of land. And third, he was content with what appeared to be the inferior land, and built an altar to the Lord to worship Him. We too should strive to be like Abraham in our relationships – humble, selfless, loving, thoughtful, and thankful. Imagine what our culture would look like if more believers chose the 'others-before-self' way of living.

Jesus was no stranger to this self-sacrificing love. He both taught it and practiced it. On one occasion, the twelve apostles were arguing with each other about which of them was the greatest. Jesus, perceiving their hearts, sat down, called them over and said, "If anyone would be first, he must be last of all and servant of all," (Mark 9:35). In other parables, His message was the same. If there was any doubt left about Jesus' sincerity, He demonstrated this sacrificial love when He died in our place, to reconcile us to the Father. Talk about practicing what you preach!

Jenny

Prayer: Lord, please help us to demonstrate selfless, sacrificial love to those around us. We know that this is how the world will know you, if we love one another the way Christ loved us. Give us the strength of spirit to be able to live selflessly in a selfish world.

Psalm of the Day: 17.6-12

The Enemy Took...

Daily Reading: Genesis 14

So the enemy took all the possessions of Sodom and Gomorrah, and all their provisions, and went their way. They also took Lot, the son of Abram's brother, who was dwelling in Sodom, and his possessions, and went their way. (Genesis 14.11-12)

Devotional Thought: In this story, we can liken 'the enemy' to sin.

Sin is greedy, stealing *possessions*. When we are controlled by sin, we spend what we have and sacrifice what we've saved, in order to satisfy sin's appetites. Sin is never satisfied with just a little, but it costs us everything. Whether they are gamblers, addicts, or materialists, I've seen many people lose everything because of the sin that controls their lives.

Sin is cruel and heartless, taking *provisions*. Think of provisions as those things that we need just to live: whether they are physical things such as food, water, clothing, and shelter, or personal things like strength, passion, love and energy. Little by little, sin robs us of the ability to cope every day. Again, I've seen people just give up because they are so deep in sin they feel that they can never escape.

Sin is impartial, ruining *people*, the innocent along with the guilty. Sin does not care who it destroys. Lot just happened to be there. He was not a part of those communities' sinful past, but he was swept up by the plundering enemy. When sin invades a life, it not only destroys that person, but it spreads to families, to churches, to communities. I've seen many spouses and children suffer because of sinful choices they had nothing to do with.

Like the people in Genesis 14, we need a savior. Someone who helps us reclaim our possessions, our provisions, and our people. Abram (Abraham) came to their rescue, but our Savior is stronger; he is perfect. It is Jesus! And, "because he continues forever.... he is able to save to the uttermost those who draw near to God through him" (Hebrews 7.24-25). Hallelujah!

Prayer: Lord Jesus, thank you that you have come to be our Savior, our Rescuer! You are stronger than sin. You completely destroyed sin at the cross! Help us to run to you! Amen.

Psalm of the Day: 17.13-15

A Binding Covenant
Daily Reading: Genesis 15

> *When the sun had gone down and it was dark, behold, a smoking fire pot and a flaming torch passed between these pieces. On that day the Lord made a covenant with Abram.* (Genesis 15.17-18a)

Devotional Thought: I've heard it said that friendships formed in a shipwreck are enduring. I'm sure that you remember the people who were with you in dark and painful trials. Through the valley of the shadow of death... through winding paths of illness... through uncertainty of job loss... through the devastation of a break-up... bonds form that are not easily broken.

In the days of the Old Testament, people formed blood covenants. In this covenant, an animal was sacrificed (signifying death), and the covenanting partners would pass through the sections of the sacrifice to indicate that they would pass through death itself together. It also symbolized that breaking the covenant was punishable by death!

That is what God symbolized in the covenant he made with Abram (Abraham) in Genesis 15. God had instructed Abraham to make a covenant sacrifice, accepting the promise of God to multiply his offspring. Then as Abraham slept during the darkness of night a smoking firepot and a flaming torch passed through the sacrifice. The smoking firepot symbolized Abraham - containing fire, but shrouded in smoke. The flaming torch symbolized God - the source of pure fire, the source of the fire in Abraham's heart. Together they passed through the pieces of death. It was "a friendship formed in a shipwreck."

Abraham has died, but God has not forgotten that covenant. While Abraham is in the company of God in heaven above, God is continuing to work out the covenant on earth below as he multiplies Abraham's descendants (children of faith) like the sand of the seashore and the stars of the sky.

Thanks be to Jesus that he has provided the sacrifice for us! Let us enter into a binding covenant with him and become a part of God's promise to Abram!

Prayer: Lord, I know that you have paid the price for my sins. I receive your free gift of forgiveness and life in Jesus' name. I commit to live in covenant relationship with you. Amen.

Psalm of the Day: 18.1-6

Running Out of Daylight

Daily Reading: Genesis 16

> *Abram was eighty-six years old when Hagar bore Ishmael to Abram.* (Genesis 16.16)

Devotional Thought: Have you ever taken things out of God's hands to hold them in your own hands? If you're like me, you probably have. And, if you're like me, you've probably made a mess of things.

Don't feel bad; Abram - commended for his great faith - was like that, too. After he had "believed the Lord, and he counted it to him as righteousness" (Genesis 15.6) and after he had accepted the promise and the covenant of God, Abram struggled to maintain his faith, to keep believing. Instead of allowing God to work things out, Abram took things into his own hands. At the behest of Sarai, Abram agreed to let Hagar, Sarai's servant, became a surrogate mother for the couple. You can understand their concern - Abram was 86 years old at the time. They were running out of daylight!

But that was not God's plan.

God's plan included the building up of Abram's faith. God wanted Abram - and all of us who would have faith in Abram's God - to know that God "is able to do far more abundantly than all that we ask or think, according to the power at work within us" (Ephesians 3.20). God desires that we know it is his hand that is at work, that we understand that "'It is not by might nor by power, but by my Spirit,' says the Lord of Hosts" (Zechariah 4.6).

Has God made a promise to you? Are you running out of daylight? Don't give up! God has not forgotten you. Don't stop believing. Let God work things out. When he makes a promise, he provides the means to fulfill it.

Prayer: Lord, help me to hear and believe your promises. And if I should ever waver in my faith, trying to work things out on my own, show me that you have not forgotten me. Amen.

Psalm of the Day: 18.7-12

Promise Keeper

Daily Reading: Genesis 17

> *When Abram was ninety-nine years old the Lord appeared to Abram and said to him, "I am God Almighty; walk before me, and be blameless, that I may make my covenant between me and you, and may multiply you greatly."* (Genesis 17:1-2)

Devotional Thought: A group called Promise Keepers was formed in 1990. The name "Promise Keepers" derives from the covenant that God fulfilled through Jesus Christ. In Christ, God kept all the promises that he made to mankind and as we rely upon him, he will help us keep our promises. In 1995, I joined several men from our church in NY to attend a Promise Keepers rally held in RFK stadium in Washington DC. More than 52,000 men were there to learn about becoming a successful modern man. There were 13 1/2 hours of preaching, praying and hymn singing on Friday night and all day Saturday. It was an awesome experience.

A covenant is a promise. Who is making the promise? It is God, El Shaddai, "God Almighty" and He will keep His promises. His promises continue to our day in the New Covenant (Heb. 9:15). Paul wrote in 2 Cor. 1:20 "For all the promises of God find their Yes in him. That is why it is through him that we utter our Amen to God for his glory." But think about our scripture focus, verses 1 and 2. Abraham is 99. It has been more than 25 years since God first made promises to him. More than 25 years of endless waiting for Abraham and Sarah and there still was no child. Do you think Abraham was getting tired of waiting? Do you think Abraham and Sarah were doubting God and His covenant promises? Have you been waiting maybe years for an answer and God has still not responded? A prayer request not yet answered? Take heart. Remember that God is a promise keeper.

Pastor Dale

Prayer: Father in heaven, I thank you for your promises and the confidence I have in you as the ultimate Promise Keeper. Help me to follow your instruction to Abraham to walk before you and be blameless. Amen

Psalm of the Day: 18.13-18

A Theopha-what?

Daily Reading: Genesis 18

He [Abraham] sat at the door of his tent in the heat of the day. He lifted up his eyes and looked, and behold, three men were standing in front of him. (Genesis 18.1-2)

Devotional Thought: I love the story of Abraham's encounter with God in Genesis 18! Theologians call this appearance of God a 'theophany,' God revealing himself in physical form. I tend to agree with them. The 'three men' before Abraham were a revelation of the Father, Son, and Holy Spirit. I thought about this particular appearance of God and realized that...

- Abraham sat at the door of his tent. Abraham was facing outward. He was in a position to see God when he showed up. Too often we get ourselves in a position where we could not see God even if he did show up. Our doubt, anger, sin, jealousy, etc. cloud our vision.
- It was the heat of the day. When life's pressures mount and the heat builds up, we need to watch for God! He will show up if we wait.
- He lifted up his eyes. There are times when we need to make a choice, to assert our will, in order to see God. I have a friend who says, "God never shows up to help me." My friend is so negative that he won't lift his eyes to see that God is there.
- He looked. We have to be willing to consider what God is saying, not just to see him, but to really think, "Hey, this might be just what I need," and then to taste and see that the Lord is good!
- God showed up! The three men appeared to a seeking Abraham. When we need him and when we look for him, God is faithful! God says, "You will seek me and find me when you seek me with all your heart!" (Jeremiah 29.13)

Do you need a theophany? Look for God in the small things of life. You will find him there.

Prayer: Father, I confess that all too often I am willing to set my gaze low. I do not see when you appear. I do not hear when you speak. Come to me, O Lord, I look for you. I wait for you. I seek you with all my heart. Amen.

Psalm of the Day: 18.19-24

Trigger Warning!

Daily Reading: Genesis 19

This fellow came to sojourn, and he has become the judge! Now we will deal worse with you than with them. (Genesis 19.9)

Devotional Thought: It has become accepted behavior in our culture to engage in sex outside marriage and in homosexual acts. But, God's Word has not changed. The truth remains today, just as unflinching as it was in the days of Lot. So many in the church, however, have adopted political and cultural expediency over the plain truth of Scripture. I sometimes wonder, "When the Son of man comes, will he find faith on earth?" (Luke 18.8)

When the messengers of God left Abraham and appeared in Sodom and Gomorrah, the sinful citizens of those towns lusted after them, pressuring them to join in their sin. Lot, however, stood in the way. The men became angry and threatened to make Lot pay dearly. That sounds so familiar!

Sin is a jealous and insecure master, angered and threatened by any opposing views. Sin will cast judgment on others but refuse to tolerate any judgment on itself. That is why you read about bakers being sued by same-sex couples and pro-life advocates being cast as anti-woman. That is why cohabitating couples will lash out at anybody questioning the wisdom of their choices. That is why the First Lady of the United States is ridiculed for reading the Lord's Prayer. That is why 'safe spaces' and 'trigger warnings' are needed on college campuses. When you think about it, it is inconsistent and even hypocritical to cast judgment on others for judging! But, there is nothing consistent and sincere about sin.

As we read in the account of Lot, this is nothing new. But, let us - as the people of God - stand upon the Word of God. Not in judgment, but in love.

Prayer: Father, thank you for giving us your Word to lead us to happy, healthy and holy living. Help us to hide your Word in our hearts that we might not sin against you. And, Lord, grant that mercy will always triumph over judgment in our hearts and attitudes. Amen.

Psalm of the Day: 18.25-30

Sin's Compounding Interest
Daily Reading: Genesis 20

> And Abraham said of Sarah his wife, "She is my sister." And Abimelech king of Gerar sent and took Sarah. (Genesis 20:2)

Devotional Thought: Afraid for his life because of Sarah's beauty, Abraham told "a little white lie." Abimelech the king took Sarah to his palace to make her his wife. Before he even touched her, God appeared in a dream and exposed the truth that Sarah was a married woman. Abimelech returned Sarah to Abraham, scolding Abraham for bringing a great sin upon his kingdom.

After seeing all of the wonderful qualities of Abraham, it seems incongruent to see this man of God lying, especially about his wife. Fear brought out the worst in Abraham, and what started as a little sin quickly compounded into a greater evil, affecting the whole kingdom of Abimelech. When we are faced with fear, we often fall into the same patterns. Fear can overcome our faith, and instead of reacting with confidence, we can find ourselves stacking sin on top of sin. It is why Jesus told his followers to "fear not." He taught in Matthew 10:28, "Do not be afraid of those who kill the body but cannot kill the soul. Rather fear him who can destroy both soul and body in hell."

Notice how something seemingly small (Abraham's white lie) turned into something far bigger. It is like this when we sin too. One lie turns into another, and another, as we desperately try to cover our tracks. Rather than turning to God in repentance, we stubbornly cling to our lie, making the consequences much worse. Or perhaps we say something unloving and hurtful, and rather than apologizing, we react with defensiveness making the situation even worse.

Let us be constantly aware of our own hearts, and of the Spirit's conviction. If we fall into sin, let us be quick to accept the Spirit's conviction and turn to God in repentance.

Jenny

Prayer: Search our hearts, Father, and see if there is any offensive way in us. Convict us through your Spirit, and lead us in the way everlasting. Help us to swallow our pride and to be quick to humble ourselves in repentance.

Psalm of the Day: 18.31-34

A Tight Spot

Daily Reading: Genesis 21

Fear not, for God has heard the voice of the boy where he is.
(Genesis 21.17)

Devotional Thought: Nothing hurts worse than when your children are hurting. I have been through some pretty hard times with my kids, and I felt just like Hagar felt when she saw her son hurting so bad - just wanting to curl up in a ball and cry. But, in those times, I found what Hagar had found. God came to us and comforted us. He drove away our fear. He assured us that he had heard the voice of our girls - just where they were. And, he brought us out to a wider place - a better place.

Hagar had been in a tight place before - one she had caused herself by her own bad attitude and cutting words. This time, however, she had done nothing wrong. It was her son, Ishmael, who had caused their crisis. Both times, however, God showed up at just the right time. The solutions were different each time, but the fact was - God had a plan.

Is someone you love in a tight spot? Are they at the end of their rope? Are you at the end of your hope for them? Do you feel like curling up in a ball and crying? Do it! God sees you. He hears you. Trust in him. He has chosen you and your loved one to know his grace and goodness. Pour out your tears and your prayers to him. You will find him close by.

Prayer: Father, thank you that you hear the voice of our cries - both ours and our children's. Thank you that your plan is to build us into your great family. When we grow weary and sad, open our eyes to see the water of life, give us strength to come out from hiding and receive your blessings. Amen.

Psalm of the Day: 18.35-45

Is Your *All* on the Altar?

Daily Reading: Genesis 22

And in your offspring shall all the nations of the earth be blessed, because you have obeyed my voice. (Genesis 22.18)

Devotional Thought: What could that have been like? To have God ask you to put your son on the altar of sacrifice? That is literally what God asked Abraham to do with Isaac. Yes, God himself provided the sacrifice - but only after Abraham displayed his complete and unwavering faith. God is, of course, totally opposed to human sacrifice, but he wanted Abraham to come to the point that nothing - absolutely nothing! - would come between him and his God. Even the promise itself (for God had made clear that it was through Isaac that the promise would be fulfilled) was not to be greater that the God who made the promise.

Because Abraham obeyed - and God intervened - God reiterated the promise and the call that he had originally given to Abraham when he set out: "In your offspring shall all the nations of the earth be blessed." We know, from this side of history, that the fulfillment of that promise came through Jesus Christ - the offspring of Abraham. All of humankind has been blessed with the offer of salvation through Jesus!

Take heart, dear brother and sister. You, too, can be a part of this wonderful plan. As you believe in God you are bearing the truth and light of Jesus to the world. The offspring of your faith means the salvation of those you love and pray for. But, we must be willing to put our all on the altar of sacrifice. Have you done that?

> *Is your all on the altar of sacrifice laid?*
> *Your heart does the Spirit control?*
> *You can only be blessed and have peace and sweet rest*
> *As you yield him your body and soul.*

Prayer: Father, thank you for the promise of your blessing. Greater than the promise to me, however, is the One who has made the promise. I yield everything to your will. Use me as you wish for your glory. Amen.

Psalm of the Day: 18.46-50

Princes and Princesses of God
Daily Reading: Genesis 23

Hear us, my lord; you are a prince of God among us. (Genesis 23.6)

Devotional Thought: Have you ever known somebody whose presence just seemed to brighten up the room? Of course, my grandchildren do that, but my mind also went to others who seem to take the blessing and peace of God with them wherever they go. There's just something special about them.

In Genesis 23, the people of Abimilech recognized something special about Abraham: he was as "a prince of God among us." Abraham's presence meant blessing and prosperity to all those in that region. They didn't want him to leave. And, when it came time for Abraham to bury his wife Sarah, they offered to give him a burial plot without cost. They really wanted to ensure that he would remain among them.

I once had an old preacher (Hey, I'm one of those now!) tell me, "Go where the people don't want you, and stay until they don't want you to leave." What is the secret of doing that? Being a "prince of God among them." Like Abraham I want to bring the blessing of God wherever I go. I want to bring love. I want to bring laughter. I want to bring peace. I want to bring freedom.

God has promised that he would bless the world through us. Are we willing participants in that blessing? Are you and I "princes and princesses of God among the people"? Do people want to be around us? Is the atmosphere lifted when we are present? Is God evident when we are on the scene? "Let your light shine before others, so that they may see your good works and give glory to your Father who is in heaven" (Matthew 5.16).

Prayer: Thank you, O Lord, that you have made your light shine upon us. Help us, O Father, to so live that our lives will shine forth with your glory that we may be princes and princesses of God among those who need your hope and light. Amen.

Psalm of the Day: 19.1-6

Don't Go Back!

Daily Reading: Genesis 24

See to it that you do not take my son back there. The Lord, the God of heaven, who took me from my father's house and from the land of my kindred, and who spoke to me and swore to me, 'To your offspring I will give this land...' (Genesis 24.6-7)

Devotional Thought: When we follow Christ, he gives us a promise, "I will never leave you or forsake you." And, "I am with you always, to the end of the age." We must be careful to pass on that promise of God's presence and blessing to our offspring. Too often, however, people are content to let their children find their own way. Abraham wouldn't think of it! He was proactive in making sure his son continued in the way of the promise.

As Abraham approached the end of his life, his thoughts turned to his posterity and legacy. He knew that the future of the promise depended on his being faithful to the end. A large part of that faithfulness was how he passed on the blessing and promise to his son, Isaac. God had 'saved' Abraham out of his past and delivered him into the glorious future. Abraham knew without doubt that the old way of life held no promise for him and his offspring. So, when it came time to find a wife for Isaac, Abraham was insistent that Isaac not return to the old ways.

Has God saved you? Are you passing that on to your children? Not just in a passive way, but in an active way? Abraham was not about to let Isaac stray from the promise. Even though Isaac was a grown man, there was too much at stake to leave it to chance. We must not leave the next generation to chance. Starting at an early age and all the rest of their lives, we need to lead our children over and over again to the Lord. Don't let them go 'back there.' The promise lies ahead, not behind!

Prayer: Father, thank you for bringing us from darkness to light, from death to life, from despair to hope. Help us, O God, to do our part to keep our children in the way of faith. In Jesus' name, amen.

Psalm of the Day: 19.7-14

41

Much Obliged...

Daily Reading: Romans 1

I am under obligation both to Greeks and to barbarians, both to the wise and to the foolish. So I am eager to preach the gospel. (Romans 1.14-15a)

Devotional Thought: One day I was talking with a friend about aging. (I am doing that more and more lately!) We discussed how we want to be around family and friends as we get older. My friend spoke of how much our friendship meant to him. I was a bit "embarrassed" by his kind words, for I know that I receive the greater blessing through the friendship.

That's the way Paul felt about the people he ministered to. He believed that he had received so much more love than he had ever given. Such was his debt to them that he said he was "under obligation." He felt that way about nearly everybody! And the obligation was not a burden to him. It was his joy!

That's a great formula for a full life, isn't it? Realizing, with a sense of joy, how much you "owe" the people around you. If neighbors would see each other that way, there would be a lot fewer Hatfields and McCoys. If couples would see each other that way, there would be a lot fewer Smith vs. Smiths. If employers and employees would see each other that way, there would be a lot less resignations and terminations. How much better our world would be if we could replace suspicion with joyful obligation!

Paul's obligation had a definite content, too. That was to "preach the gospel." What is the gospel if it is not the love of God reaching down to the sinner and outcast? So, when we are "under obligation" it is first and foremost to show the love of God to all those around us. Are you – as was Paul – eager to "preach the gospel" of love?

Prayer: Lord, thank you for loving me. Thank you also for giving me people around me who have shown me love as well. Help me to love others with your love. Amen.

Psalm of the Day: 20.1-5

Entitled

Daily Reading: Romans 2

> *Do you presume on the riches of his kindness and forbearance and patience, not knowing that God's kindness is meant to lead you to repentance?* (Romans 2.4)

Devotional Thought: We live in an entitled culture. In my work (pastoral ministry), I have the opportunity to observe people in many settings. Sometimes I even see them when they don't know I'm around. I like to 'catch' them when they're up to good! But, sometimes, to my discomfort and their embarrassment, I 'catch' people when they are up to **no** good! One of the common ways that happens is to see how they treat those who serve them.

There are some folks who are very appreciative of the service and attention they receive from wait staff, store clerks, public servants, and even family members. Others... not so much. They seem to think that they are owed something. They take for granted the services and favors they receive. They presume upon friends and family - upon the government and the church - to do for them what they 'deserve.'

Sadly, I see people who treat God that way, too. They act like spoiled children who are used to getting whatever they want. After all, they reason, God is gracious and merciful, so why shouldn't I expect it? In the words of Paul, they "presume on the riches of his kindness and forbearance and patience."

Yes, God is kind and long suffering and patient. But his purpose in that is to lead us to repentance, to give us time to respond in faith to his love, to invite us to leave behind our self-centeredness and enter into a relationship of love and reverence focused on him.

Let us not presume upon the riches of his grace. Rather, let us thank God every day for blessings received and adopt the attitude Jesus described in Luke 17.10: "We are unworthy servants. We have only done our duty."

Prayer: Help me, O Lord, to remember that if I got what I deserved it would be death. But thanks be to God for the riches of your kindness, forbearance and patience! Help me to serve you with humility and to love others as you have loved me. Amen.

Psalm of the Day: 20.6-9

Who Said Anything About Sin?
Daily Reading: Romans 3

All have sinned and fall short of the glory of God, and are justified by his grace as a gift, through the redemption that is in Christ Jesus, whom God put forward as a propitiation by his blood, to be received by faith. (Romans 3:23-25)

Devotional Thought: "All have sinned!" Hardly palatable and certainly not politically correct to today's culture. Yet Paul said it. This is utterly contrary to the "religion" we are surrounded by today. The message of our culture is that each person can define what is right and wrong for himself/herself; therefore, nobody can possibly be wrong. Sure, there are still some things we can all agree seem wrong (e.g. murder, other than the unborn), but the world offers no moral absolute that makes a thing intrinsically right or wrong. Is there even a right and a wrong? We are left guessing.

But we don't have to guess - Paul told us what the problem with humanity is: "...all have sinned and fall short of the glory of God..." The problem doesn't originate with race relations, terrorism, discrimination, poverty, education, the patriarchy, etc. The problem originated with the first sin of mankind recorded in Genesis 3, and it has been a problem for every human born ever since (with one exception).

When we read Romans 3, it should amaze us that the Lord found anything worth saving in any of us. As it is written, "None is righteous, no, not one; no one understands; no one seeks for God," (v11). In spite of what our culture would tell us, there is an absolute right and wrong. It requires a righteousness that no human being can achieve. That is why God sent His Son to live the perfect life we could never live and to die as the perfect sacrifice so that we could be "justified by his grace as a gift, through the redemption that is in Christ Jesus," (v24).

Jenny

Prayer: Lord, we thank you for the amazing grace that you poured out on us through the precious blood of Your Son. Our righteousness is like filthy rags, and yet you planned for our salvation from the conception of the world. Praise be to you for this indescribable gift!

Psalm of the Day: 21.1-7

Too Good to be True

Daily Reading: Romans 4

> *In hope he believed against hope...* (Romans 4.18)

Devotional Thought: Have you ever heard yourself or somebody else saying, "That's too good to be true"? And what do you typically find out? That it's not true! But the good news is - God isn't constrained by our expectations! When God says something is true - even when it's too good to be true - it's true!

In Romans 4, the Apostle Paul shared the story of Abraham who had received the promise of God that he would be the father of many nations with Sarah, his wife, as the mother. At one point the promise seemed too good to be true. Sarah was barren at 89 years old and he himself was 99 years old. But, Abraham "in hope believed against hope" and found out that God "specializes in things thought impossible."

Peter, imprisoned for his faith, thought it was too good to be true when an angel rescued him from his jail cell. He thought he was dreaming! Naaman, leprous and desperate, thought it was too good to be true when he was told to wash and be clean. He thought it was too easy. Some Israelites, bitten by venomous snakes, thought it was too good to be true when they were told to look at a bronze snake and live. They thought it was silly.

I have friends who have cancer, others whose relationships are severed, others who are addicted, others who need a home, others who are in financial straits, and still others who feel totally inadequate for their divine assignments. They need answers that are too good to be true. I join with them "in hope to believe against hope." If you are that way, I encourage you to "in hope believe against hope."

Prayer: Father, you specialize in things that seem impossible. You demonstrated this when you raised Jesus from the dead. I present my impossibilities to you today so that you can do what no one else can. In hope, I believe against hope. Amen.

Psalm of the Day: 21.8-13

Rock Your World!

Daily Reading: Romans 5

God's love has been poured into our hearts through the Holy Spirit who has been given to us. (Romans 5.5)

Devotional Thought: Joe and Cheryl, amazing servants of the church, came to stay with us for several months. I remember when they backed their van up to our garage. There was a lot of 'stuff' to take in. Books and clothes and food and computers. You see, when we invited them in, we invited their 'stuff.' Among that 'stuff' we found three teenagers: Jonathan, Hannah, and Becky! It rocked our world!

I have learned to pray, "Lord, I receive your Spirit." After all, Jesus told his disciples to "receive the Holy Spirit," so I figure that I don't have to ask for the Spirit. I just need to receive him. The cool thing is that when he comes, he brings his stuff with him! When I pray to receive the Spirit, I pray to receive all that stuff!

Paul mentioned one of those things that the Spirit brings with him in Romans 5: Love! But, according to Galatians 5, the Spirit also brings joy, peace, patience, kindness, goodness, faithfulness, gentleness, and self-control. That's good stuff isn't it? It rocks your world!

Now when I pray, "I receive your Spirit," I pray along with that, "I receive love." I let God's love fill my heart and my mind. "I receive joy," and let the joy of the Lord give me strength. "I receive peace," and I allow the Spirit to give me the peace of Jesus, surrendering my worries to him. "I receive patience," and I commit to show it to others. As I receive each fruit of the Spirit, I can feel my whole outlook changing.

I recommend that you receive the Spirit in a purposeful way each day... and with him that you receive all his stuff. It will rock your world!

Prayer: Father, I receive your Spirit. With your Spirit I receive love... joy... peace... patience... kindness... goodness... faithfulness... gentleness... self-control. Help me to give these gifts away today. Amen.

Psalm of the Day: 22.1-5

I Love My Boss!

Daily Reading: Romans 6

But now that you have been set free from sin and have become slaves of God, the fruit you get leads to sanctification and its end, eternal life. (Romans 6.22)

Devotional Thought: Have you ever had a 'bad boss'? Harsh? Playing favorites? Dishonest? Maybe it's not fair to say your boss is bad, but that's what it feels like. It's miserable. What did you do? Did you try to get a transfer? Quit your job? Talk to the boss' boss? Grin and bear it? Some working relationships are beyond repair; they just require a change.

Having sin as our 'boss' is that way. Sin is a harsh taskmaster. You can never do enough to satisfy sin. You never get ahead. The system seems rigged against you. As someone once said, "Sin will take you farther than you want to go, keep you longer than you want to stay, and cost you more than you want to pay." There's only one thing to do: Quit!

Through Jesus Christ, we have been set free from sin. We no longer have to satisfy its demands. We are free to be the person we were created to be. As we walk with Jesus, fully surrendered to him, our lives begin to take on his character more and more. Yes, it takes time to grow in our faith and obedience and Christ-likeness. There is a difference between purity and maturity. We are set free in a moment, but grow over the course of time.

Having a new, forgiving, caring boss, why would I ever want to check in with the old, harsh, and hateful boss? Why would I subject myself to that abuse? I wouldn't! Neither would you. If we would not do that in employment matters, why would we do it in spiritual matters?

Live in the freedom that Christ gives you!

Prayer: Jesus, thank you for setting me free from sin. Help me to live this day in that freedom, fully depending on you as my new 'boss'!

Psalm of the Day: 22.6-11

Litterbug?

Daily Reading: Romans 7

> *We serve in the new way of the Spirit and not in the old way of the written code.* (Romans 7.6b)

Devotional Thought: Several months ago, I was at a cross country meet with a friend of mine. I watched with admiration as the young runners kept up the pace and crossed the finish line. I was just as amazed, however, with something I noticed my friend doing. Many spectators had dropped water bottles, cups, and other trash around the area. My friend busied herself picking up the discarded items and placing them in the proper trash receptacle which was overflowing. She even approached an event organizer and asked for another trash liner. I commended her for it. It wasn't her trash, but she picked it up anyway. She shrugged it off, saying, "I just like to do my part."

I wondered what the litterers would have done if a police officer had been there with a sign that said, "$100 fine for littering." Not having the law compel them into being conscientious, they just threw their trash down. My friend didn't need the law. There was something inside her that just wanted to do the right thing.

Some folks try to serve God by following the rules. They may do OK as long as they feel that God is watching, but there is something missing in their motivation. Rules have their place - they help us know what the right thing is - but rules are just not good motivators.

Aren't you glad that we don't serve God in the old way of the written code? We have the Spirit who is our strength and helper. He is our motivator. Folks who serve by the rules, say "Is this enough?" Those who serve by the Spirit say, "Can I do more?" What motivates you?

Prayer: Lord, thank you for the written code which has shown me the right thing. But help me not to simply follow the rules, but instead to follow you with my whole heart. Amen.

Psalm of the Day: 22.12-19

Set On the Flesh or Submitted to God?

Daily Reading: Romans 8

The mind that is set on the flesh is hostile to God, for it does not submit to God's law; indeed, it cannot. (Romans 8.7)

Devotional Thought: Have you ever been on a diet? I guess we all are on some form of a diet, aren't we? I sometimes find myself - when my belt gets a little snug - trying to curtail my intake in order to reduce my weight. Generally what happens then is that that I think about food all the more! Especially ice cream! For some reason, I can't get ice cream off my mind in the evenings. What I have found is that the more I think about ice cream, the more I want ice cream. Setting my mind on ice cream is a sure way to eat ice cream!

Just as ice cream is hostile to weight loss, so a mind set on the flesh is hostile to God. Your flesh - that part of you that craves satisfaction - will lead you to do things that you know are not good for you - eat too much, look at the wrong things, avoid exercise, seek attention, and other things more harmful. Our flesh cannot be reasoned with. It must be 1) surrendered to God and 2) disciplined.

There is a war that takes place in the heart of a believer. Who is going to be master? Will it be my flesh or will it be the Lord? If we choose to satisfy the flesh, we find ourselves in a hostile position toward God. Maybe not right away, but an un-surrendered and undisciplined flesh will certainly rear its ugly head - and usually at the most inopportune times!

Thankfully, as Paul reveals in another letter, there is a solution: "Walk by the Spirit, and you will not gratify the desires of the flesh" (Galatians 5.16)

Are you walking by the Spirit?

Prayer: Father, forgive me for setting my mind on the things of the flesh. Help me, O Lord, to walk by the Spirit today and thus to please God.

Psalm of the Day: 22.20-24

Be an Includer

Daily Reading: Romans 9

> *Those who were not my people I will call 'my people,' and her who was not beloved I will call 'beloved.'* (Romans 9.25)

Devotional Thought: I am an 'includer' by nature. I want everybody to belong, everybody to be a part of the group. Perhaps I have the gift of hospitality. At any rate I am very sensitive to being on the outside looking in. I remember when my three kids were growing up at home, one of the things that got me the most upset was when two of them would exclude the other. "You all play together!" I can identify with the sting of being left out.

I think God is an 'includer' too! When he sees people who are left out, he says, "I'll take you!" And when he comes across someone who is unloved, he says, "I love you!" Aren't you glad that he includes you!

Ancient Israel often struggled to catch on to the concept of inclusion, adopting instead an attitude of exclusion. They saw themselves as an exclusive club. They were God's chosen people, and the rest of the world was just out of luck. They were jealous of their perceived special place in God's heart. God reminded them that he loved everybody and desired that those who were not his people would become his people.

Sometimes we in the church make the same mistake, don't we? We look at people who are still prisoners of sin and think, "What are they doing around here? I'm glad I'm not like them..." We struggle to remember that at one time we were outsiders and God included us. We forget that someone in the church reached out a welcoming hand to us.

Look for someone who is on the outside, and determine to love that person with the love of God! And more than that, include them in the fellowship of the church!

Prayer: Father, open my eyes to see those around me who are lost and lonely, suspected and rejected. Then, help me to love them and include them. In the name of Jesus, the greatest Includer of all! Amen.

Psalm of the Day: 22.25-31

Zeal with Knowledge

Daily Reading: Romans 10

> *For I bear them witness that they have a zeal for God, but not according to knowledge. For, being ignorant of the righteousness of God, and seeking to establish their own, they did not submit to God's righteousness.* (Romans 10:2-3)

Devotional Thought: In the previous chapter Paul wrote, "Behold, I am laying in Zion a stone of stumbling, and a rock of offense; and whoever believes in him will not be put to shame," (v33). The Jews - a zealous people, but without a knowledge of Christ - stumbled over the stumbling stone, as was foretold, and God's salvation was then offered to the Gentiles as well (Acts 28:27-28, also see Romans 11:11).

The Jewish people (as a whole) failed to recognize their long-awaited Messiah. Some saw and believed and were saved. Israel rejected the Cornerstone because they did not have the eyes to see Him for who He was. We may wonder how that is possible, when all of the prophecies pointed to Jesus, but without awakening from the Holy Spirit, all spiritual wisdom is folly (1 Cor. 2:14).

We may have people in our lives that lack the ability to accept spiritual wisdom. What seems clear to us is not at all clear to them. Often, these people think that their beliefs line up with the Christian faith, but they are "ignorant of the righteousness of God" and seek to "establish their own," (v3). They may think there are other paths to God and heaven other than Christ, but any other path requires complete and perfect adherence to the Law (which is impossible for anyone to obtain).

What to do in this situation? There is only one option, and it is exactly what Paul did for the Jewish people: pray. Pray for a movement of the Holy Spirit, for without that man does not accept the things that come from the Spirit of God. Pray for open eyes and open ears, that they might finally see and understand the gospel of Christ.

Jenny

Prayer: Lord, we are burdened in our hearts to see zeal without knowledge and spirituality without Christ surrounding us. We submit these friends and loved ones to you, Lord, and ask that you would move in their hearts, that your Spirit would give them the spiritual understanding that they need to become your children.

Psalm of the Day: 23.1-6

Holy - Root and Branch

Daily Reading: Romans 11

> *If the root is holy, so are the branches.* (Romans 11.16b)

Devotional Thought: A few weeks ago I took my chainsaw out to cut down a couple dead ash trees in my yard. I tried and tried to start it. My son-in-law tried. My daughter's friend tried. None of us could make the thing go. We could get it to fire - even run for a few seconds - but it just wouldn't stay running. We guessed that the problem was probably 'bad' fuel. We knew that if the gas had spoiled, there was no way we could get the thing to run, so we gave up.

When something is wrong on the inside, then eventually it will show up on the outside, won't it? Our walk with Christ is like that. Like that gas in my chainsaw, a bad spirit within us will cause us to misfire and sputter out. But the good news is that the inside can be replaced! That's right. Jesus can make us new, make us holy. And when that happens the fruit that appears on the branches is also holy! What's on the inside shows up on the outside!

In the Bible God has said, "And I will give you a new heart, and a new spirit I will put within you. And I will remove the heart of stone from your flesh and give you a heart of flesh. And I will put my Spirit within you, and cause you to walk in my statutes and be careful to obey my rules" (Ezekiel 36.26-27). God starts his work on the inside and then it shows up - it always shows up - on the outside!

Prayer: Father, thank you for making me holy on the inside through the blood of Jesus and the transforming power of the Holy Spirit. Grant me power to live out what you have put in. Amen.

Psalm of the Day: 24.1-6

Genuine Love
Daily Reading: Romans 12-13

Let love be genuine. (Romans 12.9a)

Devotional Thought: Last week I got a call from 'Emily'. She was so excited to talk to me! As a matter of fact, she was so happy that she couldn't stop talking. She was thrilled that I had stayed in one of their resorts in the past and that - can you believe it? - I qualified to receive 75% off at a stay in one of their beautiful resorts in Orlando! I tried to get her to stop so I could politely say, "I'm not interested," but she was like the Energizer Bunny. I think you can guess how the conversation ended.

Later, I thought about that call, about how Emily genuinely sounded excited for me. But, she didn't even know me. Her excitement wasn't genuine. I don't fault her, she was just trying to earn a living, but I wondered to myself, "Do I come across that way to people? Am I genuine?"

The Apostle Paul told the Christians in Rome to "let love be genuine" (Romans 12.9). I wonder what they thought that meant.

What do you think it means? What's genuine love look like? Is it gushy and sentimental? Is it tough and demanding? We don't have to wonder about what Paul thought genuine love looked like. In the remainder of the chapter and on into chapter 13, Paul lays it on the line: abhor evil, show honor, be patient, be constant, contribute to needs, bless those who curse you...

As you read the rest of Romans 12 and 13 ask yourself, "Is my love like this?" I think you will find along with me that we could spend the rest of our lives honing our genuine love skills. As a matter of fact, why don't we do just that!

Prayer: Lord Jesus, if I ever wonder what genuine love looks like, all I need to do is look at you. Thank you for your love! Help me to love others as you have loved me - with a genuine love. Amen.

Psalm of the Day: 24.7-10

You Can Feel Good about Yourself!

Daily Reading: Romans 14

Blessed is the one who has no reason to pass judgment on himself for what he approves. (Romans 14.22b)

Devotional Thought: Do you know what I love? Besides Lana and ice cream that is? I love when I can feel good about what I am doing. I love when I feel no guilt for harboring ill motives or for doing something I'm not sure I should. The Apostle Paul agreed with me, too. I feel blessed!

Have you ever been doing something and felt a pang of judgment? That is the conviction of the Holy Spirit. Jesus said that the Spirit would come to convict us of sin (John 16.8). We should thank God for that because there are some people "whose consciences are seared" (1 Timothy 4.2). Or, in the case of Romans 1: "They did not honor him as God or give thanks to him, but they became futile in their thinking, and their foolish hearts were darkened. Claiming to be wise, they became fools, and exchanged the glory of the immortal God for images resembling mortal man and birds and animals and creeping things. Therefore God gave them up in the lusts of their hearts to impurity" (Romans 1.21-24).

Strive to live this day so that when you pillow your head tonight you will have peace with God. And, if for some reason you do feel the sting of conviction, do not deny it and do not despair. Rather, confess your sin to God for he is "faithful and just to forgive us our sins and to cleanse us from all unrighteousness" (1 John 1.9). Then by faith live at "peace with God through our Lord Jesus Christ" (Romans 5.1).

Prayer: Father, thank you for giving me the Holy Spirit to keep me and to give me victory over the power of sin. Help me, O Lord, to so live that I might have peace with you. And should I fail, O Lord, convict me of my sin and grant me faith to confess my sin and receive your forgiveness. Through Jesus Christ my Lord. Amen.

Psalm of the Day: 25.1-7

Just Three Prayer Requests

Daily Reading: Romans 15

> *I appeal to you, brothers, by our Lord Jesus Christ and by the love of the Spirit, to strive together with me in your prayers to God on my behalf, that I may be delivered from the unbelievers in Judea, and that my service for Jerusalem may be acceptable to the saints, so that by God's will I may come to you with joy and be refreshed in your company.* (Romans 15.30-32)

Devotional Thought: The Apostle Paul was a man of prayer. And not only did he pray, he often sought the prayer support of friends and constituents. He even asked those he did not know personally - such as the Roman Christians - to pray for him. "Strive together with me in your prayers..." And for what specifically did this man of God ask that they pray?

Deliverance. Paul's ministry of proclaiming Christ often got him into trouble. He asked for his brothers and sisters in Christ to pray that he would be delivered from those who would stifle his message. He wanted to be free to proclaim Christ!

Acceptance. Paul didn't care if people liked him, but what he wanted was for the message of Jesus to be accepted by those to whom he ministered - at that time the saints in Jerusalem.

Acquaintance. Paul had not personally been to visit the church in Rome. He asked that they pray for him to be able to come there to share in their joy and be refreshed in the Lord.

As you pray for your pastor or spiritual leader, pray that he or she would be free to proclaim the gospel, that their message would be accepted by those who hear, and that they would continually meet new people and families to bring to Christ! Oh, and pray the same for yourself for we are all called to make disciples!

Prayer: Lord, I thank you for my pastor. I pray that you would enable him/her to preach with all power and boldness. Deliver him/her from detractors. May his/her ministry be acceptable to the saints. Grant that he/she would encounter new people to bring to Christ. Amen.

Psalm of the Day: 25.8-13

God's Holy Word or Man's Fancy Words?

Daily Reading: Romans 16

> *I appeal to you, brothers, to watch out for those who cause divisions and create obstacles contrary to the doctrine that you have been taught; avoid them. For such persons do not serve our Lord Christ, but their own appetites, and by smooth talk and flattery they deceive the hearts of the naive.* (Romans 16:17-18)

Devotional Thought: We live in a world where we find it easy to be persuaded in many different areas. I think of the late-night commercials that try to sell you something you probably don't need. The way they pitch the item and use all their fancy sales tactics we sometimes find ourselves calling the number on the screen or visiting a website to make a purchase. "But wait! If you call now, we'll double your order! That's right! Call now and you'll get two widgets for $19.95!"

This world tries to convince you that God is not the only way to get to Heaven and be saved. The Bible calls these people "False Prophets." However, we as Christians and followers of God can sometimes get caught up in the "smooth talk and glowing words" used by the enemy. That is why the Bible tells us to do research on our own: "That very night the believers sent Paul and Silas to Berea. When they arrived there, they went to the Jewish synagogue. And the people of Berea were more open-minded than those in Thessalonica, and they listened eagerly to Paul's message. They searched the Scriptures day after day to see if Paul and Silas were teaching the truth." (Acts 17:10-11, *NLT*).

When we read books, or listen to sermons we should check the content of what is written or said and not be fooled by smooth style. Christians who study God's Word will not be fooled, even though superficial listeners may easily be taken in.

I encourage you to do your own research. Make sure that what you are learning and being taught comes from the Holy Word and not just fancy words!

Pastor Chris Shallenberger

Prayer: Lord, we are your children living in a world that wants to grab and keep our attention on everything except you. Help us to stay focused on what is most important in our lives...YOU! I pray that when I read books and listen to sermons my heart would be challenged to dive into your Word deeper and make sure what I am hearing is supported by you and your Word. Develop me to be a true student of the Word of God!

Psalm of the Day: 25.14-22

Who Cares About a Silly Birthright?

Daily Reading: Genesis 25

Thus Esau despised his birthright. (Genesis 25.34)

Devotional Thought: There are times in life when we forget the big picture and instead focus on immediate satisfaction. Those are the times that get us into trouble. A few years ago, I took advantage of an offer to stay in a resort on Myrtle Beach. All I had to do was agree to sit through a two hour presentation... My wife, Lana, and I went to the presentation with no thought of buying into the resort's timeshare. But on the 12th floor, looking out over the Atlantic Ocean, it all seemed like such a good idea! I can't believe how close we came to buying. Not that it would have been bad, but it just didn't fit our long-range plans - nor our finances for that matter! We needed to consider the whole picture.

In Genesis 25, Esau failed to do just that. When he came in from the fields, he found his brother Jacob cooking away. Esau was famished, and his senses overcame his sense. He agreed to give his birthright to the conniving Jacob in exchange for some soup and bread. What a deal! Right? Wrong! Yesterday's inheritance customs are not like todays. The firstborn son was to receive a "double portion" of the inheritance. That meant that if there were 9 sons, then each received a tenth, except for the firstborn, who received two tenths - double what everybody else received. Esau gave away a lot for a cup of soup!

Are we any different? We have birthrights as children of God. Do we forfeit them for trinkets and pleasures that pass away? Do we fail to see the big picture? Child of God, do not give away what lasts forever for something that satisfies for only a season!

Prayer: Father, thank you for making us your sons and daughters. Help us, O Lord, not to despise our birthrights as your children. Instead, grant that we may remain faithful to you in the midst of temptation. Amen.

Psalm of the Day: 26.1-8

The Object not the Quality of Our Faith

Daily Reading: Genesis 26

> *When the men of the place asked him about his wife, he said, "She is my sister," for he feared to say, "My wife," thinking, "lest the men of the place should kill me because of Rebekah," because she was attractive in appearance.* (Genesis 26:7)

Devotional Thought: In Genesis 26, God promises Isaac that He would establish through him the oath that he swore to Abraham, Isaac's father. He would multiply Isaac's offspring as the stars of heaven and would give the land to his offspring. He also promised that through Isaac's descendants all the nations of the earth would be blessed.

What amazing promises given to Isaac! And, the Lord delivered these promises to him *personally*. How is it then that when Isaac settled in the land, one of the first things he did was lie about his relationship to Rebekah? Fear! Because Rebekah was beautiful, he feared that the men in the land would kill him to take her. Sound familiar? Flip back six chapters and you will find Abraham, Isaac's father, doing the exact same thing!

Why would God choose such fearful men to be the patriarchs?

The Lord chooses the weak and the humble so that when he reveals his glory, there is no doubt that the praise belongs to him. Moses was a great example of this. The entire nation of Israel was weak, fearful, full of doubt and lacking in faith.

Through these examples the Lord has shown us that it is not the quality of our faith that saves us, but rather the object of our faith. During the first Passover, the Israelite firstborn was saved in every household that was obedient to the Lord's instructions... the families that went to sleep confident in the Lord's protection, and also the families who couldn't even sit much less sleep because of their fear. Isn't that a reassuring thought for us when we struggle with fear and doubt? Trust the One in whom your faith rests, not in your own superior faith. He alone saves!

Jenny

Prayer: Lord, thank you that our salvation is not dependent on how strong our faith is at any point, for we are weak and prone to fearfulness and worry. But you Lord, in your mercy, paid the price once and for all, with the blood covering of the Lamb who was slain!

Psalm of the Day: 26.9-12

Don't Be Deceived and Deprived

Daily Reading: Genesis 27

Your brother came deceitfully, and he has taken away your blessing.
(Genesis 27.35)

Devotional Thought: Many years ago, my mom taught me that old proverb: "Fool me once, shame on you. Fool me twice, shame on me." I have had a hard time learning it, however. I'm like the eternally optimistic Charlie Brown who said, "This time I'm going to kick that football clear to the moon!" right before Lucy pulled the football away!

I think that Esau must have felt a little bit like Charlie Brown when he was told that his brother Jacob "came deceitfully, and he has taken away your blessing." Esau had, after all, already been swindled by Jacob over his birthright. Some folks never learn.

Satan is a deceiver. He deceived Adam and Eve in the book of Genesis and has been doing the same to their progeny ever since. He is called "Satan, the deceiver of the whole world" in the book of Revelation (12.9). We need to be aware of his schemes. He falsely accuses Christians. He may roar like a lion to intimidate or prowl silently to infiltrate. But whatever else may be said about him, He lies. Jesus called him "the father of lies" (John 8.44).

The world is especially susceptible to Satan's lies. But sadly, sometimes we in the church swallow his deceit. When we do that, we find that he steals our blessings: the unity of the fellowship is disrupted, the joy of the Lord fades away; the peace that passes understanding is replaced with confusion and fear; we pull away when we need to draw near...

But thanks be to God! We are not unaware of his schemes. He need not take us off guard. Be aware and be blessed!

Prayer: Father, help me to recognize the deceiver when he comes to me with his lies. Help me to turn always to the truth and live in the blessing of Jesus! Amen.

Psalm of the Day: 27.1-6

Note: If this is not a leap year, read tomorrow's scripture, devotion, prayer and Psalm along with today's...

Speak with Heaven's Accent
Daily Reading: Genesis 28

You must not take a wife from the Canaanite women. (Genesis 28.1)

Devotional Thought: When we first moved to North Carolina in 1983, I found the accent pleasing and charming. Living there 20 years, I picked up on it myself. When I moved to Illinois, I naturally switched back to a Midwestern accent. I noticed something, though. When I was around my southern friends, I found it easy to revert back to the southern accent.

We tend to adopt the manner of our environment, don't we? Rebekah - the wife of Isaac and mother of Jacob - knew that. She told Isaac, "I loathe my life because of the Hittite women. If Jacob marries one of the Hittite women like these, one of the women of the land, what good will my life be to me?" (Genesis 27.46) Isaac took immediate action to insulate his son from the ungodly influence of Hittite culture as he told Jacob, "You must not take a wife from the Canaanite women." (Genesis 28.1)

I was speaking with a friend last week - a former addict - who told me that an addict must break away from all those people and settings that trigger their addiction. The same principle applies to Christians in general - especially young Christians. It is so important for us as Christians to surround ourselves with godly influences and culture. Jesus taught us that though we are in the world, we need not be of the world. In other words, we don't have to embrace the culture; we don't have to "marry the Canaanites."

Let us heed the words of the Apostle Paul: "The appointed time has grown very short. From now on, let those who... deal with the world [live] as though they had no dealings with it" (1 Corinthians 7.29, 31). In other words, speak with Heaven's accent!

Prayer: Father, help me to discern the difference between engaging the world versus embracing the world. Help me to surround myself with Christian influence and values, and from that foundation to be salt and light. Amen.

Psalm of the Day: 27.7-10

*Note: If this is not a leap year, read today's entry
along with yesterday's or tomorrow's*

A Church for the One Who Loves the Church

Daily Reading: Genesis 29

So Jacob served seven years for Rachel, and they seemed to him but a few days because of the love he had for her. (Genesis 29.20)

Devotional Thought: In 1976, I met my future father-in-law, Nick Moore. He was a great father-in-law. He didn't make me work 7 years for my wife. (Nor did he switch her out for her homely sister on our wedding day! Lana didn't have a homely sister, anyway...)

Jacob didn't have as good a father-in-law as I had. When Jacob didn't have a dowry to give for Rachel, he offered to work for Laban in order to gain his bride. Laban took him up on it. Jacob didn't mind. Those seven years passed quickly because he loved her so much.

The Church is the bride of Christ. Like Jacob, Christ spent his life trying to win us. But more than that, he loved us so much that he *gave* his life for us!

Do we love The Church?

In one of his last encounters with the disciples, Jesus asked Peter, "Do you love me?" Peter said, "Yes, I love you!" Three times Jesus asked. Three times Peter answered. And what was Peter to do if he loved Jesus? How was he to show that love? Jesus didn't ask him to do great and mighty deeds. Jesus didn't ask him to spend his days writing and singing love songs for him. Jesus didn't ask him to buy him expensive and thoughtful gifts. Jesus simply told him, "Feed my sheep. Take care of my sheep." Jesus' concern was for his bride. He loves The Church!

How is it that The Church has become optional with some Christians? May God give us grace that we, like Jacob, would be willing to serve seven years for The Church, and then serve another seven, and another...

Prayer: Jesus, I know that you love The Church. You died for The Church. You are building The Church. Help me to love what you love, to live for what you died for, to build what you are building Amen.

Psalm of the Day: 27.11-14

Desperate for Children
Daily Reading: Genesis 30

> *Give me children, or I shall die!* (Genesis 30.1)

Devotional Thought: Having children is big-business. According to *Money* magazine, the fertility market in America is about $4 billion annually. Many couples are desperate for children.

Jacob's wife Rachel was barren and felt tremendous pressure, socially and biologically, to have children. When she saw her sister bearing sons to Jacob, that pressure increased exponentially. (Remember the social and moral codes were different concerning marriage in that day and culture. What we would consider shocking was commonplace.) I can almost picture this desperate wife, grabbing her husband's shirtsleeves: "Give me children, or I shall die!"

Yesterday we considered the marriage of Christ to The Church and how we ought to love and serve The Church as Christ did. Today, we will think about the outgrowth of marriage: having children. Are we desperate for children in the Kingdom of God?

The scripture says that "as soon as Zion travailed, she brought forth children" (Isaiah 66.8). If we want to have children in the Kingdom of God, we must travail! Childbirth will come about when we labor. That labor begins with soul-agonizing prayer: "God, give us children or we shall die!" It continues with the resetting of our priorities and attitudes toward the lost. The labor grows intense when we begin changing things - buildings, budgets, ministries - so that our churches are welcome places for new children. But it all must begin with prayer.

Are we desperate for children? Then let us pray until God comes and brings us souls. Are we indifferent when it comes to children in the Kingdom of God? Then let us pray until God stirs our cold hearts and makes us cry out for the lost to be saved.

Prayer: Father, give us children in the Kingdom of God! We are desperate for the salvation of souls. Move in the hearts of your people until we enter into travailing, prevailing prayer for the lost. Amen

Psalm of the Day: 28.1-5

To the End of the Age

Daily Reading: Genesis 31

> And Jacob saw that Laban did not regard him with favor as before. Then the Lord said to Jacob... "I will be with you." (Genesis 31.2-3)

Devotional Thought: Jacob was confused. He had worked hard for Laban even when Laban had taken advantage of him. Jacob had lived up to his part of the relationship only to have his father-in-law turn against him. In that time, far from home and family, Jacob needed encouraged. That's when God showed up and said to him in essence: I'm here, Jacob. I haven't forgotten you. And I will be with you in days to come.

Have you ever lost a friendship before? It is hard, isn't it? The one that you thought you could count on through thick or thin turns her back on you. The person you just knew would be by your side is suddenly nowhere to be found. The one to whom you have remained loyal has forgotten your faithfulness to him. Those times hurt deeply.

In Psalm 44, the Psalmist despaired, thinking that God had deserted his people: "Why do you hide your face? Why do you forget our affliction and oppression?" (v. 24). His mistake was a common one, a mistake we often make. He looked at his circumstances rather than looking at the character of God. In his discouragement, he failed to believe God's promise to never leave them or forsake them (Deuteronomy 31.6). We can be encouraged to know that even the Psalmist struggled with these kinds of feelings!

If you are going through a time of severed friendship, remember, "There is a friend who sticks closer than a brother" (Proverbs 18.24b). That friend is Jesus. Through misunderstanding, relocation, and even death - when others leave, Jesus stays; when others disappoint, Jesus defends. He says, "I am with you always, to the end of the age" (Matthew 28.20b)

Prayer: Thank you, Jesus for your faithfulness. Others may fail us, but you remain committed to us. Help us to trust in you when we are hurt and alone. Amen.

Psalm of the Day: 28.6-9

Two Camps

Daily Reading: Genesis 32

Jacob went on his way, and the angels of God met him. And when Jacob saw them he said, "This is God's camp!" So he called the name of that place Mahanaim. (Genesis 32.1-2)

Devotional Thought: It was a hot summer morning. We were on a trip to Columbus in the church van. On the way, the van broke down. We were able to pull over on a quiet country road. As we waited for someone from the church to pick us up, a pickup truck passed by. The driver wheeled around to see if we needed help. We told him our ride was on the way, but thanks. He went on his way, but in a few minutes he was back with a cooler full of ice and bottled water. "I thought you might need this," he said. As he was leaving he told us, "Just keep the cooler!" He was an angel from God!

Jacob needed some encouragement on his journey back home. His father-in-law, Laban, had cheated him. But many years before, his brother, Esau, had threatened to kill him because Jacob had cheated him! Now, Jacob was going home and was scared to death. He couldn't go back and he didn't relish the thought of going forward. So what did God do? He sent an entourage to meet him on the way to encourage him! Jacob was thrilled and exclaimed, "This is God's camp!" Then he named the place where he had met them Mahanaim, which means two camps.

What a thought! As we journey through life, we encounter difficulties and fears - some of our own making! We cannot see it, but in the midst of our trials, God is there. You see, there are two camps along the route home, our physical and earthly camp, and God's spiritual and heavenly camp. Though we cannot see him, he is there! Don't be surprised when he shows up with living water!

Prayer: Father, help us to see that you encamp about us, that we are never alone. When we're stuck between a rock and a hard place, it is so reassuring to know that you are there with us. Thank you! Amen.

Psalm of the Day: 29.1-6

65

Run!

Daily Reading: Genesis 33

> *But Esau ran to meet him and embraced him and fell on his neck and kissed him, and they wept.* (Genesis 33:4)

Devotional Thought: Some reunions we run *to*, and others we run *from*. In the reunion between Jacob and Esau, Jacob wanted to run away from his brother, but Esau ran to his brother. Jacob was afraid of Esau whom he had cheated out of his birthright and blessing. Then, Esau had threatened to kill Jacob who quickly fled. Now, a reunion was required.

Jacob was prepared for a fight. He had strategically divided up his household, expecting his brother to attack. He did, however, approach Esau in humility, bowing to the ground seven times until he came near to his brother. Imagine his surprise as Esau ran to him not with murderous intentions, but to embrace him, weeping. Esau, who had every right to withhold forgiveness from his brother, does not walk but RUNS to him in his eagerness to forgive! This is one of only a few times in the Old Testament where a man of this culture is said to run.

Esau's response to Jacob was one of wonderful grace and mercy. When we are called to forgive those who have wronged us, do we begrudgingly forgive because we know we should? Do we fail to have that forgiveness touch our hearts? Or, do we forgive as Esau forgave Jacob? Do we set aside our pride and our self-righteousness and forgive freely, knowing that we have also been forgiven much?

As amazing as Esau's example was, there was a more perfect example of this forgiveness given centuries later. Jesus "ran" to earth to take on the sins of the whole world - to offer us forgiveness through his blood, when we deserved it least. Let us offer forgiveness as freely as it has been offered to us!

Jenny

Prayer: Lord, thank you for offering forgiveness before our hearts were even turned towards you in repentance. It is through your grace and mercy that our hearts can turn to you in love, mourning our sin but then comforted by our Father. Please help us to forgive others as we were forgiven by you.

Psalm of the Day: 29.7-11

On the Third Day
Daily Reading: Genesis 34

On the third day, when they were sore, two of the sons of Jacob, Simeon and Levi, Dinah's brothers, took their swords and came against the city. (Genesis 34.25)

Devotional Thought: There are a lot of "third days" in scripture. On the third day of creation, land emerged from beneath the ocean depths and life sprung forth on the earth. On the third day of his journey, Abraham looked up and saw Mount Moriah where "God will provide." On the third day, the Lord appeared to the Israelites at Mount Sinai. On the third day, Hezekiah rose from his death bed and went to worship at the house of the Lord. On the third day, Esther appeared before the king to plead for the lives of her people. On the third day, Jesus performed his first miracle at a wedding.

Our scripture today speaks of another third day. A son of Shechem had seduced and violated Dinah, Jacob's daughter. They hoped to make the people of God a part of their culture of sin and immorality. They offered to intermarry with Jacob's family. The sons of Jacob, however, tricked the sons of Shechem and "on the third day," they redeemed their sister's dignity and honor.

This is a picture of what Jesus, the Son of God, has done for us! Satan has seduced and violated the sons and daughters of man. He offers us the 'opportunity' to become a part of his immoral and evil culture. He has stolen our dignity and honor. He has robbed us of hope. But just as the sons of Jacob came against the city of Shechem, the Son of God has strapped on his sword and come against the city of Satan. He has redeemed us! And on the third day he defeated the grave itself. Victory is secured! Victory is final! Victory is ours in Jesus, the Son of God!

Prayer: Jesus, on the third day you came forth from the grave, victorious over sin and death and hell. Hallelujah! And with you, we too are victorious! Amen.

Psalm of the Day: 30.1-5

Bethel

Daily Reading: Genesis 35

God said to Jacob, "Arise, go up to Bethel and dwell there. Make an altar there to the God who appeared to you." (Genesis 35.1)

Devotional Thought: Arise. That's a good, biblical word, isn't it? Lazarus heard it when Jesus visited his tomb (John 11). Jairus' daughter heard it on her death bed (Mark 5). The young man heard it when Jesus passed by his funeral (Luke 7). And, of course, Jesus heard it on resurrection morning! Arise!

Jacob heard it, too. Though not dead and buried, he was in serious trouble due to his hot-headed sons who attacked and killed the townsmen of Shechem. Jacob had recently escaped his father-in-law Laban and had faced his brother's anger. Now he had a whole community up in arms against him. He was in dire straits!

God knew what Jacob needed. He needed to go to Bethel! Bethel means literally "the house of God." Jacob was to dwell there. When we are in trouble we need to spend time with God! Find shelter in his tabernacle. Jacob was to make an altar there. When life is closing in on us, we need to worship. Jacob was to remember the way God had appeared to him and helped him in the past. When we lose sight of all other helpers, we need to remember that "God is our refuge and strength, a very present help in trouble" (Psalm 46.1).

What was Jacob's response? He took God up on his offer! "Let us arise and go up to Bethel, so that I may make there an altar to the God who answers me in the day of my distress and has been with me wherever I have gone" (Genesis 35.3). He did arise. He did go to the house of God. Knowing God is faithful, he took him at his word!

Wherever you are, whatever you face, arise and go to the house of God!

Prayer: Lord, I come to Bethel, into your house, to be in your presence - to worship you, and to remember all that you have done for me. In you I trust, O my God. Amen.

Psalm of the Day: 30.6-12

Not Forgotten

Daily Reading: Genesis 36

These are the generations of Esau (Genesis 36.1)

Devotional Thought: I have a friend who has two daughters. The older one has 'stayed faithful' to her upbringing and values while the younger has 'strayed far' from them. The younger feels she has grown up in the shadow of the older. We all have known people who have grown up in the shadow of others. It often causes resentment and problems.

Esau lived his life like that. Jacob was the one chosen for God's purpose of raising up a people to bring the message of redemption to the world. Esau felt resentment most of his life. At the end, the brothers patched things up, but Esau was always in the shadow of Jacob. That legacy even lasted to the New Testament. Yet, God did not forget Esau. He loved him just the same as Jacob. (The comment in Malachi 1 and Romans 9 - "Jacob I loved, but Esau I hated" - employed hyperbole and was never intended to be taken literally.) Even though Esau forsook his birthright and lost his blessing, God still cared about him. God still blessed him with a family and with a future: "These are the generations of Esau." The shadow of his younger brother did not veil Esau from God.

Today perhaps you feel hidden from God's sight. Maybe you feel that God has forgotten you. You may even feel that you deserve it, that you are very forgettable, having blown opportunity after opportunity to make your Father proud. Be encouraged my friend! God has plans for you, big plans, "plans to prosper you and not to harm you, plans to give you hope and a future" (Jeremiah 29.11).

Prayer: Thank you, Father, that no matter how far I have strayed, you have kept your eyes on me. I believe in your love, O Lord. I walk in assurance through Jesus Christ. Amen.

Psalm of the Day: 31.1-7

What Hinders You?

Daily Reading: 1 Thessalonians 1-2

Hindering us from speaking to the Gentiles that they might be saved
(1 Thessalonians 2.16a)

Devotional Thought: In many places of the world there are "proselytizing laws" that prohibit Christians from gaining converts from Muslims. In some instances conversion is punishable by death - to both the convert and the witness.

Things were the same in the first century in Judea and Greece. Both Jewish and Gentile authorities did all that they could to hinder Christians from speaking to the Gentiles so that they might be saved. Paul wrote to the Thessalonians to encourage them in their persecution, reminding them that even the Lord Jesus had been killed and his prophets driven out of Jerusalem. It is amazing that in such a climate, Christians prayed, "And now, Lord, look upon their threats and grant to your servants to continue to speak your word with all boldness" (Acts 4.29).

In light of the courageous witness of those early Christians, I think a legitimate question for us today might be, "What hinders me from speaking out for the Lord Jesus?" We might find the excuses to be rather trivial under examination:
I don't want to offend my neighbor... People will laugh at me... Religion is a very personal subject... Everyone should be able to make up their own mind... They don't want to hear...
The list is endless...

But what is at stake? Our excuses lose their appeal when we consider the alternative. Satan wishes to silence Christians from speaking so that others *will not be saved!* If they are not saved, they will be lost, they will die in their sins, and they will 'perish' (suffer eternal punishment away from God).

What hinders you from speaking?

Prayer: And now, Lord, look upon their threats and upon my fears and excuses, and grant that I may continue to speak your word with all boldness. Amen.

Psalm of the Day: 31.8-13

Established, Blameless, Holy
Daily Reading: 1 Thessalonians 3-4

So that he may establish your hearts blameless in holiness before our God and Father. (1 Thessalonians 3.13)

Devotional Thought: Jesus wants to establish your heart. He wants you to be blameless and holy. He wants you to stand without fear before our God and Father. Those are lofty goals!

Having an established heart means loving God with a pure and steadfast love. Jesus said we cannot serve two gods. There is so much to draw our love away from God, but God is able to give us grace to say no to sin and to love him with a pure heart. Do you love God in that way - with all your heart and soul and mind and strength?

Being blameless is a little trickier. It does not mean perfect performance, rather it means that you do not intend to sin. You may slip into sin, you may be surprised by sin, you may ignorantly or mistakenly sin, but you would never think of purposefully sinning. And, if anyone does sin, we immediately confess and are forgiven because we have an advocate with the Father. The blood of Jesus atones for sins of ignorance and we are held blameless. Are you blameless, or do you try to 'get away with' sin, presuming upon the grace of Jesus?

Holiness is the highest order of Christian experience. The call to holiness is a call to being completely set apart for God's use and to be purified from all sin - even the deepest inbred sin. There is an experience of heart holiness in which the believer is sanctified wholly, the carnal nature is purged, and the entire being is devoted to God. Are you living in holiness?

Established. Blameless. Holy. Then, and only then, are we able to stand before our God and Father. And it's all by the grace of Jesus!

Prayer: Father, I long to walk with you in the highest order of Christian experience. Establish me blameless and holy. I consecrate myself to you completely. Amen.

Psalm of the Day: 31.14-18

Created in Love
Daily Reading: 1 Thessalonians 5

For God has not destined us for wrath, but to obtain salvation through our Lord Jesus Christ (1 Thessalonians 5.9)

Devotional Thought: I love to watch my grandson Grayson play with his stacking cups. He is very careful to place them just right, keeping them from tipping over. He situates them, steadies them, and moves them as he tries to get the tower as high as he can. Then - Wham! - he knocks the whole thing over with great gusto! After that he starts the process all over again. It's lots of fun!

Some people think that God is like that, that he created certain people simply to cast them into hell for eternity. A misreading of Romans 9 - completely disregarding the love of God for *all* the world - has prompted a whole theology to be developed that says God has decreed that certain people will be saved and that certain people will be damned.

Thanks be to God that we are destined for salvation, and not for wrath! There are some who refuse that salvation, but their destination is their own choice. God wants people everywhere to repent and come to salvation. That means the worst sinner is not beyond the reach of God's love. That means that you and I are invited to believe and receive.

As Grayson grows, I think that he will become more and more like his Pahpooh (that's me!) and will enjoy building things that are meant to endure, things that he will enjoy and love. I trust that means he will build his life upon the Rock which is Jesus Christ. Thanks be to God that my little fella - and all God's creatures - are destined for salvation if they believe and receive!

Prayer: Father, thank you that your plan for me is salvation through our Lord Jesus Christ. I believe that Jesus died for me and rose again from the dead. I receive him and new life in his name. Amen.

Psalm of the Day: 31.19-24

Always Praying

Daily Reading: 2 Thessalonians 1-2

> *To this end we always pray for you, that our God may make you worthy of his calling and may fulfill every resolve for good and every work of faith by his power, so that the name of our Lord Jesus may be glorified in you, and you in him, according to the grace of our God and the Lord Jesus Christ.* (2 Thessalonians 1:11-12)

Devotional Thought: The church at Thessalonica faced intense persecution because the church was growing - both in quantity and in quality of disciples. Paul wrote to affirm their faith and to reassure them that righteous judgment from God will come upon their persecutors.

Then, Paul expresses his heartfelt prayer for the church, "that our God may make you worthy of his calling and may fulfill every resolve for good and every work of faith by his power, so that the name of our Lord Jesus may be glorified in you, and you in him, according to the grace of our God and the Lord Jesus Christ" (1:11-12). What an amazing prayer! Even today - especially today! - this needs to be prayed over the church. Imagine if we were to all desire that the church would be worthy of the calling of Jesus. Not perfect in performance, as that is impossible before the return of Jesus, but in the purity of the gospel message, in the love that we extend to the lost, and in the way we treat fellow believers.

To what benefit will this lead? The name of Jesus will be glorified... and we in him! There is no outreach program, no mission trip, no small group connection that can compare to this simple prayer. These people were suffering for their faith, and still Paul prayed not for relief from suffering, but that Jesus would be glorified in them, and them in him. When our will is so intertwined with the will of God, we share not only in his sufferings but also in his glory. And as Paul reassures another group of believers, "I consider that our present sufferings are not worth comparing with the glory that will be revealed in us," (Romans 8:18).

Jenny

Prayer: Lord, help us to focus on the eternal rather than what seems more comfortable now. Create in us a heart of love for the lost - and for each other - that would glorify you in a manner worthy of your calling.

Psalm of the Day: 32.1-7

Parkinson's Law
Daily Reading: 2 Thessalonians 3

Not busy at work, but busybodies. (2 Thessalonians 3.11)

Devotional Thought: Do you know the maxim, "Work expands to fill the time available for its completion?" Do you know it has a name? It's called Parkinson's Law and was coined by the twentieth-century British scholar C. Northcote Parkinson. It points out that people usually take all the time allotted (and frequently more) to accomplish any task. (Dictionary.com)

In my first job after college, there was a man who worked in our lab at Cooper Tire. He used to busy himself filling up papers with 4, 5, or 6 digit numbers. Occasionally we would find his papers and try to figure out the pattern to the numbers. We never cracked the code. We decided he was filling his time with something that made him look busy.

It happens in The Church. People who are not busy at work, busy themselves with other people's business! Paul ran into it in Thessalonica. They expected Jesus to return at any time. Some of them used that as an excuse not to work. Living off the labor and generosity of others, they had plenty of time to run other people's lives. Paul said of such people that they should just go hungry!

We need to be busy in the church. We need to support ourselves financially, but we also need to busy ourselves with doing the work of Jesus! He has given us the Great Commission, telling us to make disciples. Are we too busy with Facebook, Twitter, and Instagram to do that? Are we so busy searching the web for the next interesting tidbit of information that we don't have time to study the Word of God and pray?

I find it too easy to distract myself and think that I'm busy. But, what am I busy doing?

Prayer: Lord, help me, like you, to be about my Father's business. Help me to be busy loving and winning and helping others. And, Lord, should I decide to insert myself into someone else's business, may it be first and foremost in prayer! Amen.

Psalm of the Day: 32.8-11

Who Are You?

Daily Reading: John 1

Who are you? ... What do you say about yourself? (John 1.22)

Devotional Thought: Many years ago, when I worked for Cooper Tire Company, I made a business trip to Texarkana, AR to visit one of our plants there. Flying from Findlay, OH to Texarkana, AR was not a real easy thing to accomplish. Connections were impossible and it could take an entire day to make the flight. Since I was such an important executive (Not!), I was able to ride the company jet! I was only about 24 or 25, but thought I was a big shot! There were a couple other passengers on board, and I remember asking one of them, "Who are you?" He was a wonderfully polite man and told me his name. Then he said something that gave me pause, "I'm president of the company..." Ah... I wasn't such a big shot after all!

John the Baptist wasn't such a big shot after all either. There were those who wanted to know, "Who are you? What do you say about yourself?" John replied simply and humbly that he was not important, but that he had been given an important job - to prepare the way for Jesus!

Who are *you*? What do you say about yourself? None of us are big shots when you come down to it. But, we all have an important job to do: let people know about Jesus! What do our words, our actions, our attitudes, our faithfulness say about us? What kind of Jesus are we pointing others to?

Who are you? What do you say about yourself? What do you say about Jesus?

Prayer: Father in heaven, thank you for loving us when we were nobodies - apart from you and your kingdom. Help us to live such lives that when people see us they will see Jesus. Amen.

Psalm of the Day: 33.1-7

Fill Me Now

Daily Reading: John 2

And they filled them up to the brim. (John 2.7)

Devotional Thought: I tease my wife, Lana, that she's always trying to put 10 minutes of activity into 5 minutes of time. When we have several visits to make - nursing homes, hospitals, etc. - she invariably thinks that we can do more than we can. But, I can't really point my finger at her. I always try to put an hour's worth of sermon into 30 minutes of time!

Whether we are trying to pack work into the day, fun into the weekend, zest into a relationship, or purchases into our budget, it seems that we are always filling life to the brim. This can be either good or bad, depending on what we are pouring in.

When Jesus attended the wedding in Cana of Galilee (John 2) and turned water into wine, he instructed the servants to fill the stone water jars with water. They did so, filling them "up to the brim." Not knowing what was up, I can imagine caution on my part: "Hey, we might have to move these things. We better hold back a little!" They figured, however, that whatever was going to happen was going to be good, so they maximized the benefit!

We can approach God that same way. Are we going to exercise caution or maximize the benefit? I think we should do the latter and fill our lives to the brim with God! Let us pray with the Apostle Paul: "I pray that you, being rooted and established in love, may have power, together with all the Lord's holy people, to grasp how wide and long and high and deep is the love of Christ, and to know this love that surpasses knowledge—that you may be filled to the measure of all the fullness of God" (Ephesians 3.17b-19).

Prayer: "Fill me now. Fill me now. Jesus come and fill me now. Fill me with thy hallowed presence. Come, O come, and fill me now."

Psalm of the Day: 33.8-15

Hope Born-Again

Daily Reading: John 3

How can a man be born when he is old? (John 3.4)

Devotional Thought: A birth is an exciting event! I remember that when my granddaughter, Annabelle, was born I didn't want to miss the excitement, so in the rush of all that was happening in the labor and delivery room, I just faded into the background. I simply 'forgot' to leave as was the plan. Hiding out in the corner and keeping my gaze discreetly averted, I was there for it all. A brand new baby! What excitement! I'm glad I didn't miss it.

Undoubtedly, Nicodemus had this excitement in mind when he heard Jesus speak of being born again. But there was a problem. Nicodemus was 'old.' The excitement and potential of new life, the energy and optimism of youth... all that is over when a person is old. Nicodemus, disillusioned and disappointed by his empty religion, asked, "How can a man be born when he is old?" Sounds like he didn't have much hope, doesn't it?

But Jesus was then, and is now, in the hope-restoring business! He told Nicodemus, in essence, "Don't worry about the hows. Just have faith that God is able to do this."

In whatever stage of life we find ourselves, there is the temptation to think that things are set in stone and change is impossible - "How can I be 'born again'? How can something new and exciting come about?" But God says, "Not so fast! I can make hope come to life again. Don't give up."

Is your life on a trajectory of hopelessness and emptiness? Do you feel that your best days are over? Not so fast! The Spirit of God can transform your life and you can be 'born again'!

Prayer: Jesus, thank you that you are in the hope-restoring business. Thank you that you bring new life to old, worn out dreams. I receive this new life in your name. Amen.

Psalm of the Day: 33.16-22

The Well Is Deep

Daily Reading: John 4

Jesus, wearied as he was from his journey, was sitting beside the well.
(John 4.6)

Devotional Thought: I am fascinated by the wireless charging stations made for smart phones. "How do they get electricity from one to the other without wires?" I've found out that it is by 'electromagnetic induction.' When the two devices are properly positioned an electromagnetic field in the charger induces the same in the phone, transferring the energy. Wow! Almost seems miraculous, doesn't it?

Jesus found out that the principle doesn't work for satisfying thirst. One day as he was going about his ministry, he found himself sitting next to a well in Samaria. But, the Bible says he had "nothing to draw with and the well is deep." No matter how long he sat there, he would not receive the life-refreshing water from the depths of the well. Proper positioning was not the answer. He had to ask for help. The Samaritan woman helped him draw the water out and he satisfied his thirst.

Actually, the same is true for us when it comes to drawing the life-giving water from the well of salvation. While 'proper positioning' is helpful - we can hold our Bibles in our laps all morning, or we can sit in church all day long, or we can even be lifelong members of the church - it's like sitting beside the well. Those things won't satisfy our spiritual thirst. We need ask God to give us a drink. And then, we need to drink deeply of the water of life.

How about you? Are you thirsty for more of God? Are you wearied from the journey? Come to the well. Humble yourself. Ask God to satisfy you, to restore your strength, to renew your hope. The well is deep and the supply is endless.

Prayer: Lord, just as you grew weary on your journey, I sometimes get tired, too. Help me to sit down with you at the well of salvation and to drink deeply of your truth. Refresh me, O Lord. Amen.

Psalm of the Day: 34.1-7

You Have Someone

Daily Reading: John 5

When Jesus saw him lying there and knew that he had already been there a long time, he said to him, "Do you want to be healed?" The sick man answered him, "Sir, I have no one..." (John 5.6-7)

Devotional Thought: Have you ever found yourself surrounded by people yet feeling all alone? It's not a good feeling, is it? That's what the sick man felt like as he laid on his mat near the pool of Bethesda. The place was packed, but his woeful testimony was, "I have no one."

That changed when Jesus arrived! Jesus took a particular interest in the man's situation. He...

- *Saw him*: In the midst of the crowd, Jesus picked him out. With all the other needs around, Jesus was able to see this man and his specific need.
- *Knew him*: Jesus cared enough about the man to take his past into account. Instead of applying a 'one-size-fits-all' solution, Jesus recognized the unique circumstances that brought him to his present condition.
- *Spoke to him*: In speaking to the man, Jesus not only recognized his need, but he also made the man a part of the solution. He asked the man a painful question, "Do you want to be healed?" Behind that question there is the sense that the man had to get to the place where he wanted healed more than he wanted pitied.
- *Healed him*: Jesus must have been satisfied with the man's answer - vague as it was - for he told the man to get up and walk. The smallest faith was rewarded with the biggest miracle!

How about you today? Are you feeling helpless and alone? You're not! You have someone. Jesus has arrived, and he has taken a particular interest in you. May you hear words of hope and healing today.

Prayer: Jesus, thank you that you take note of my situation. Thank you that my situation is not too difficult for you. While I may have no one else, I believe that I have you. Help me to want you more than I want pity. Amen.

Psalm of the Day: 34.8-14

No Help at All

Daily Reading: John 6

> *It is the Spirit who gives life; the flesh is no help at all. The words that I have spoken to you are spirit and life. But there are some of you who do not believe. ... And he said, "This is why I told you that no one can come to me unless it is granted him by the Father."* (John 6:63-65)

Devotional Thought: Many of Jesus' followers grew disgusted with his teachings and turned away from following him. Why? They had a "flesh perspective." The flesh, however, is no help at all.

The disciples who stayed believed him. They believed that he had the words of eternal life, and they knew that he was the Holy One of God. The reason they stayed? Because the Spirit was already at work in their hearts, revealing the spiritual things that they could not dream of comprehending in their own power. Later in John 14, Jesus tells his followers of his plan for them: "I will ask the Father, and He will give you another Advocate to be with you forever – the Spirit of truth. The world cannot receive Him, because it neither sees Him nor knows Him."

The gospel is foolishness to those who have not experienced a movement of the Holy Spirit in their hearts. When we witness to those around us, we must always start with prayer – prayer that the Spirit would provide that person with a spiritual understanding that is impossible to achieve in the flesh. "The natural man does not accept the things that come from the Spirit of God. For they are foolishness to him, and he cannot understand them, because they are spiritually discerned," (1 Cor. 2:14).

We will never convince unbelievers of the truth of the gospel in our own power, but we can combat spiritual deafness by pleading with the Spirit to work in the hearts of the lost. And be encouraged, for as Jesus said in verse 40 of this chapter, "It is my Father's will that everyone who looks to the Son and believes in Him shall have eternal life..." The flesh is no help, but the Spirit gives life!

Jenny

Prayer: Lord, we know that without you, we cannot accomplish the Great Commission – to spread the gospel message and make disciples of all nations. We pray for an outpouring of your Spirit in the lives of those who need to hear the Good News, and we ask that you give us opportunities to speak the truth with boldness.

Psalm of the Day: 34.15-22

Jesus Would Not

Daily Reading: John 7

After this Jesus went about in Galilee. He would not go about in Judea, because the Jews were seeking to kill him. (John 7.1)

Devotional Thought: Jesus was courageous, but not careless. He lived by faith, but he did not tempt fate. He recognized that God's kingdom advanced reliably but not randomly. So, when he was faced with danger in Judea, he moved his ministry to Galilee.

As I thought about this, I couldn't help but wonder about the innocent people in Judea. The leaders rejected Jesus, but the populace paid the price. How many sick people died? How many lame people continued to limp? How many sinners continued carrying a load of guilt? All because some people - threatened by the truth of Jesus - sought to eliminate him and his influence.

I wonder, too, about innocent people today. I believe that Jesus freely goes where he's wanted and welcomed, but in those places where his message is rejected, he does not "go about."

- In homes where Jesus' love is shunned in favor of anger, jealousy and control, Jesus cannot go about with freedom and hope. Family members are hurt by the selfishness of others in the home.
- In hearts where Jesus' fire is quenched by negativity, complaint, greed, and bitterness, Jesus cannot go about freely and effectively. Doubt and fear thrive in those hearts where faith and confidence are thrown off.
- In houses of worship where Jesus' holiness is replaced by selfishness, Jesus cannot go about with conviction and power. The church falls into apathy and antipathy. Lost people stay lost, the lukewarm fail to be warmed, and the sick are not healed.

Let us determine that we will be among those who welcome and magnify the presence of Jesus. Let's set him free in our minds and in our midst. Welcome him where you are today!

Prayer: Jesus, come into my heart and help me to be a locus of holy love, a flame of holy fire, a zenith of holy zeal - so that my presence will invite your presence, so that those around me may be loved, warmed, and energized in you. Amen.

Psalm of the Day: 35.1-8

Soften the Sentence

Daily Reading: John 8

> *Let him who is without sin among you be the first to throw a stone at her.* (John 8.7)

Devotional Thought: I'm not sure if I want to laugh or cry when I watch the hypocrisy of pundits, condemning or justifying others based on political party. Political theater is pretty entertaining sometimes, isn't it? One thing that you can count on is that you better be careful what you say for sooner or later you are going to have to eat those words! Sadly, however, I think politicians today have developed an immunity to the 'taste' of their own inconsistency.

Thankfully, the players in the drama of John 8 were able to grasp their own sin before they grasped rocks to throw at a sinful woman. In a rare fit of honesty, the angry mob had to admit that they weren't perfect either, that they really had no right to judge the poor woman before them.

Aren't you thankful that you don't have to be the judge of others? In this complex world, it's hard enough to judge actions let alone motives. The only one I can even get close to judging accurately is myself. And, then I have to be careful that I judge not by myself but by God's Word.

There is only one person who ever lived without sin. That, of course, is Jesus Christ. He is the only One who can judge adequately and accurately. And he will, for the Bible says that God, "has set a day when he will judge the world with justice by the man he has appointed. He has given proof of this to everyone by raising him from the dead" (Acts 17.31).

So, the next time you are tempted to judge another, turn the magnifying glass back on yourself. I think that will soften the sentence!

Prayer: Father, help me to heed the words of Jesus: "Do not judge, or you too will be judged. For in the same way you judge others, you will be judged, and with the measure you use, it will be measured to you." Please forgive me when I fail to live up to that ideal. Amen.

Psalm of the Day: 35.9-17

And Who Is He?

Daily Reading: John 9

> *Jesus heard that they had cast him out, and having found him he said, "Do you believe in the Son of Man?" He answered, "And who is he, sir, that I may believe in him?"* (John 9.35-36)

Devotional Thought: Open eyes lead to open hearts. Several years ago I watched with fascination as my friend, Fran, ministered to Bridgette. When Bridgette, a cast-away from society, first came to our church seeking help, she was wary of church people. She was uncertain about God. But Fran befriended her and remained faithful and patient with her. Seeing the love of Christ faithfully lived out, Bridgette opened her heart to Jesus. She was baptized and joined the church. Bridgette was the perfect example of how people - when they see the love of God working through you - will open their hearts to Christ.

When Jesus healed the blind man in John 9, the man had left the presence of Jesus and gone to the pool of Siloam to wash his eyes. It was there that his sight was restored. Consequently, he had not seen Jesus. That is why he did not recognize Jesus when Jesus returned to him. He was, however, anxious to meet him and believe in him: "Who is he, sir, that I may believe in him?"

Even before people meet Jesus, they have been influenced and touched by the prevenient grace of God. This is God's grace that leads people to the knowledge of him. They are still unaware, however, that it is Jesus who has given them life and its blessings. So they ask, "Who is he that I may believe in him?" Like Fran did with Bridgette, it is up to us to bear witness to the One in whom they can put their faith. May our lives cause people to say, "And who is he, that I may believe?"

Prayer: Lord Jesus, thank you for giving me life in you, for forgiving my sins, for taking me into your family. Help me, O Lord, to love others and faithfully serve them so that they ask, "Who is he that I may believe in him?"

Psalm of the Day: 35.18-21

You Can Beat Winter

Daily Reading: John 10

It was winter, and Jesus was walking in the temple, in the colonnade of Solomon. (John 10.22b-23)

Devotional Thought: At this time of year, I am ready for spring. But, spring is not always ready for me. Spring may tease us with a few warm days in March, but often winter holds on tenaciously!

There are times that winter takes up residence in our souls, too. We feel cold and buffeted by the winds of life. We wonder if spring will ever come. We really need Jesus to show up. In John 10, that is just what happened. It was winter both in the season and in the history of the people of God. They needed hope. They needed Jesus to show up. And he did, "walking in the temple, in the colonnade of Solomon."

Do you feel cold in your soul? Are you ready for your spiritual winter to be over? Consider where Jesus appeared. Perhaps you will find a way back to a springtime of hope.

Jesus was "walking in the temple." I have often wondered why spiritually discouraged people tend to drop out of church. Being in church is just what they need! In times of spiritual coldness, we need to find our way to where Jesus is. We need the warmth and love and care of the temple - the people of God.

Jesus was "in the colonnade of Solomon." It was there where the people would gather and discuss the Law (the Word of God) with their teachers. When our soul temperature is in need of a boost, we need the wisdom of the Bible to warm our spirits. We will find Jesus in his Word!

You can beat winter. Find Jesus in the church and in the Word!

Prayer: Thank you, Lord Jesus, for walking in my life through the church and the Word. When I am cold in my soul, help me to find you there and to find hope for my soul. Amen.

Psalm of the Day: 35.22-28

Our Spiritual Journey
Daily Reading: John 11

Lazarus was ill... Lazarus has fallen asleep... Lazarus has died... Lazarus, come out. (John 11.2, 11, 14, 43)

Devotional Thought: As I read the account of Lazarus getting sick, dying, and then rising from the dead, I thought about how that represents our spiritual journey.

Sin makes us sick. All of us have inherited what theologians call 'original sin.' That is our bent toward evil, the thing that causes us to rebel against God. We are born with the seeds of this disease in us. Before we reach 'the age of accountability,' sin lies dormant as far as our culpability. But when we begin to understand "The Law", sin comes alive in us. Paul talks about that in Romans 7.

Sin causes us to 'fall asleep' spiritually. Jesus described Lazarus' condition as falling asleep. It was a 'sleep' that led to death. Sin makes us drowsy and unresponsive to the Spirit's voice. Unable to hear the Spirit, we become spiritually comatose.

Sin brings death to us. Just as Lazarus' illness stole his life from him, so sin takes away life. From the very beginning, God said it would be so: "For in the day that you eat of it you shall surely die" (Genesis 2.17). Sin slowly separates the sinner from God, the Source of life.

Jesus calls us out of death and into new life! Lazarus' death was not the end of the story. Even before leaving for Lazarus' hometown, Jesus reassured his disciples that "This sickness will not lead to death!" And the disease of sin does not have to lead us to death. Jesus has the final word and it is the Word of Life. Come out! Sin no longer has any dominion over the child of God. Thanks be to God!

Prayer: Lord Jesus, thank you that you have conquered sin. Through your death and resurrection, sin no longer has dominion over me. Help me to live in holiness and victory all of my days. Amen.

Psalm of the Day: 36.1-6

Worship, Learn, Serve

Daily Reading: John 12

> *Martha served, and Lazarus was one of those reclining with him at table. Mary therefore took a pound of expensive ointment made from pure nard, and anointed the feet of Jesus and wiped his feet with her hair. The house was filled with the fragrance of the perfume.* (John 12.2b-3)

Devotional Thought: I have seen the local church defined as "a group of believers who join together regularly for worship, learning and mission." In today's story of Martha, Lazarus and Mary, we find the three roles of the church.

Martha served. She made sure that Jesus received what he needed to nourish his body and enjoy the meal in comfort. Sometimes Martha gets a 'bad rap' based on the story in Luke 10, where she complains about her sister not helping her. But, just as Christ served his disciples by washing their feet, so we in the church are called to serve. The church needs servants, those who busy themselves seeing to the needs of the body of Christ.

Lazarus reclined with Jesus at the table. He was there listening and learning. This practice was established early on in the first church in Jerusalem, where the disciples "devoted themselves to the apostles' teaching." We also see it in Paul's ministry where he gathered the disciples together daily for 2 years in the lecture hall of Tyrannus in order to teach them in a group setting. Priscilla and Aquila took Apollos - a skilled preacher - and explained to him the way of God in individual discipling sessions. The church is always a place of learning.

Mary anointed Jesus. Her show of love filled the house with a beautiful fragrance. She didn't care what anyone else thought or said. She simply wanted to show Jesus how much she loved him. And, through that fragrance of worship, everyone there received benefit. I love to see people lavish their love and adoration on Jesus. What an encouragement!

Worship... Learning... Serving... How is your church doing? How are you doing?

Prayer: Lord Jesus, You are worthy of my love, my learning, and my labors. Help me to be a faithful member of your Church as I worship, grow and serve. Amen.

Psalm of the Day: 36.7-12

Saved to Serve
Daily Reading: John 13

> Peter said to him, "You shall never wash my feet." Jesus answered him, "If I do not wash you, you have no share with me." Simon Peter said to him, "Lord, not my feet only but also my hands and my head!" (John 13:8-9)

Devotional Thought: The disciples were shocked that Jesus would wash their feet - a task reserved for the lowest servant. At first Peter refused, but when Jesus told him, "If I do not wash you, you have no share with me," Peter changed his tune and wanted a thorough washing!

It takes complete surrender, and a washing from head to toe by Jesus, to be saved and have a share in his inheritance. But we have a hard time with being this needy. It takes a different type of humility to let another serve you, to admit that you need help. In some ways, it is much easier to pour yourself out serving others than it is to let others serve you. I struggle with this myself. I find it much easier to take a meal to someone in crisis than to admit I have my own crisis!

When we have been "served" by Jesus, we are to serve others. Jesus tells his apostles, "If I then, your Lord and Teacher, have washed your feet, you also ought to wash one another's feet," (v14). The Son of Man came not to be served but to serve and give his life as a ransom (Mark 10.45). How much more should we consider ourselves servants to others?

We are saved to serve. Some ways of serving are harder than others – it may be easy to spend a few hours on a mission project, or make a meal for a friend. What about those in our lives who are in need of consistent prayer, or in need of on-going emotional and spiritual support? This requires a true servant's heart, and it is through this type of love and sacrifice that we make known the love of Jesus to the world.

Jenny

Prayer: Lord, help us to feel compassion and humility when we look at the needy around us. Let us not strive for the best for ourselves, but rather look for opportunities to bless others. Thank you for sending your son, not to be served but to serve us by giving his life as a ransom for many.

Psalm of the Day: 37.1-6

Yeah, Right!

Daily Reading: John 14

> *Whoever believes in me will also do the works that I do; and greater works than these will he do, because I am going to the Father.*
> (John 14.12)

Devotional Thought: One of the traits that has made America great is the fact that each generation has been able to 'do better' than the prior generation. I know that my children have 'done better' than me - they gave me amazing grandchildren! I am proud when they outshine me, because I live for their joy. My daughter Jenny certainly has made me proud by becoming such a wise contributor on our daily devotionals! The others do well on those occasions when they write for me, too. They outshine their dad!

Just as we are pleased when our children 'do better' than us, Jesus is also pleased when we do 'greater works' than he did while on earth. Jesus wasn't nervous when he returned to the Father. He was excited as his disciples took the reins of the Church. But, what do you think crossed the minds of those twelve men when Jesus told them that they would do even greater things than him? Having seen the miracles of Jesus, they probably thought, "Yeah, right!"

And what do you think? Greater works than Jesus? "Yeah, right!"

Consider: All the people saved in all the churches around the world... all the people delivered from addiction through Christian recovery ministries... all the people healed in Christian clinics, hospitals, and mission trips... Do you see what Jesus was talking about? Added onto that, consider the Christian parents, doctors, teachers, lawyers, businessmen, etc. who are bringing the blessing of God through their daily lives. Truly greater works!

I encourage you to take your place in the 'greater works' that The Church - empowered and led by the Holy Spirit - is doing today!

Prayer: Jesus, as you build your Church, help us to do 'greater works.' And Lord, help me to do my part in these 'greater works.'

Psalm of the Day: 37.7-15

Pruning Time
Daily Reading: John 15

> *Every branch in me that does not bear fruit he takes away, and every branch that does bear fruit he prunes, that it may bear more fruit.* (John 15.2)

Devotional Thought: I've got a couple 5 year old apple trees that are 8-10 feet tall. Since I didn't get one apple last year, does that mean I should cut all the branches back to the trunk? Probably not, but I know I need to prune them in order to get some fruit this year. I've never had much luck with the fruit trees I've planted. I have learned something recently - it's time to prune the trees - now.

Jesus wants us to produce fruit, too: fruit of the Spirit, of righteousness, of soul-harvest. But, if we have too much growth, growth in the wrong direction, or diseased growth, we will struggle to produce any of these types of fruit. How do we prune our lives to produce more fruit?

Pruning follows the 3-D's:
- Prune the *dead* branches. Is there an area of your life that is controlled by sinful thoughts, desires, or attitudes? Sin brings death. Prune away anything that is sinful in your life. As the Bible says, we are to "lay aside every weight, and sin which clings so closely" (Hebrews 12.1).
- Prune the *diseased* branches. Disease spreads and leads to death. There may be some branches of our lives that are not yet 'dead' but they are certainly diseased. Spiritual diseases are things such as slacking in our church attendance, in prayer, and in Bible reading. It is allowing things to creep in between us and Jesus.
- Prune the *damaged* branches. Untended damage leads to decay and death as well. Have you been hurt? Have you hurt a sister or brother in the church? Those damaged relationships should be reconciled, pruning away hard feelings and unforgiveness.

Get your pruning shears out. It's time to prune - *now*.

Prayer: Lord, I know you want me to produce fruit. I also know that a healthy tree will produce fruit. So, help me to recognize those areas in my life that are in need of pruning and to be brave enough to do it! Amen.

Psalm of the Day: 37.16-24

More to the Story

Daily Reading: John 16

> *But because I have said these things to you, sorrow has filled your heart.*
> (John 16.6)

Devotional Thought: Have you ever heard words that filled your heart with sadness? I'm sure you have. Everybody has: Honey, I'm sorry, but you're father... We found a mass... We need to adjust our workforce... We're moving... I need my space... Words have the potential to bring joy, but they also can hurt us deeply.

Jesus said some things that upset his disciples. We wouldn't think that Jesus would do that, would we? What did he say that made them so sad?

Several things come to mind:
- "You also ought to wash one another's feet" (John 13.14). It's hard to hear that we need to serve others. We like being served!
- "One of you will betray me" (John 13.21). Have you ever hurt someone you love? Not fun!
- "Where I am going you cannot come" (John 13.33). When you're left out, you feel it!
- "Every branch in me that does not bear fruit he takes away" (John 15.2). Ouch, if we haven't been doing what we're supposed to!
- "If anyone does not abide in me he is thrown away" (John 15.6). Have you been keeping close to Jesus?

Yes, Jesus can say some things that cause us pain. But he does it for our good, for our healing and growth. And, Jesus had something else to say that would help his friends get through their time of darkness and despair: The Helper will come to you. I will come to you.

So, if you are hearing some difficult things from the Lord, take heart. There's more to the story!

Prayer: Lord Jesus, thank you for being honest with me - even when it hurts. I know that your words bring life, so help me to trust you even then. Amen.

Psalm of the Day: 37.25-33

Stay in Touch!

Daily Reading: John 17

I am no longer in the world, but they are in the world. (John 17.11a)

Devotional Thought: One by one, as my girls left home, I understood what Jesus felt when he had to say goodbye to his friends. I could no longer be with them and oversee their decisions and actions. I had to trust them. I could not be a present protector. I had to trust God. I didn't stop loving them, of course, but I had to transfer their care to One greater than me. And besides, I was able to be in touch with them anytime I wanted through the wonder of cell phones. I received pictures and videos of them - and more importantly my grandchildren! - many, many times. I still do!

In John 17, as Jesus was preparing his disciples for their separation, he prayed for them. I'm sure it was hard to say good-bye, but he found comfort knowing that he could entrust them into the hands of his heavenly Father. He knew that even after he was gone, God would answer his prayers on their behalf.

Jesus loves us just as much as he loved his disciples in the first century. He has given us a mission. He is leaving us in the world to fulfill that mission. So, even now he prays for us and entrusts us to the care of our heavenly Father. And we have the privilege of being in touch with him at any time through prayer, through worship, and through the Bible. Though Jesus is in heaven, we can still be in touch with him! He loves it! He loves you!

Prayer: Thank you, Father, for the modern wonder of communication that keeps us in contact with those we love. Thank you for the even greater privilege of being in contact with you! Help us to keep close to you! Amen.

Psalm of the Day: 37.34-40

Full Court Press

Daily Reading: John 18

> *Judas, having procured a band of soldiers and some officers from the chief priests and the Pharisees, went there with lanterns and torches and weapons.* (John 18.3)

Devotional Thought: When I married my wife, I didn't get a dowry. I got a legacy! Part of that legacy is that I am now a West Virginia University fan. In the spring, it's WVU basketball! I remember the seasons, under Coach Huggins, that they were known as "Press Virginia" because of their stifling defense - particularly their full court press. I loved to watch those Mountaineers press! But, to be honest, I sometimes feel sorry for the opposing team! One player would dog the guard all the way up the backcourt and then all of a sudden two - and sometimes three! - defensive players would be surrounding the guard, trying to steal the ball. Many times, panic ensued and the guard threw the ball away.

That's what Judas did when he betrayed Jesus. He did a full court press. He didn't go alone. He went with "a band of soldiers and some officers," overwhelming the small group of disciples. But not Jesus! Jesus remained calm, protected his disciples, and did not give in to panic.

Satan often tries the full court press on us. He may start his dirty work alone, but soon he gathers others to surround us, trying to steal victory from us. He is hoping that panic will ensue and that we will throw the ball away, give up and walk away. He wants to destroy us.

But remember - Jesus is with us. And, he doesn't panic. He will protect the ball and preserve the victory. Trust in him!

Prayer: Lord, when Satan comes against me, help me to keep my eyes on you - to look beyond the sometimes overwhelming circumstances, and see your face. Help me to taste victory with the Victor!

Psalm of the Day: 38.1-8

No King but Jesus!

Daily Reading: John 19

We have no king but Caesar. (John 19.15b)

Devotional Thought: What informs your politics? It is different for different groups, isn't it? I watch with amusement as senators squirm in the nomination process for Supreme Court Justices. Those in favor of their perceived political views say, "She can't tell you how she would rule on an issue ahead of time." But, what happens with those same senators when the nominee's judicial philosophy doesn't match their political views? They want clear answers on how the judge would rule! On the other side of the aisle, of course, we have learned to expect just the opposite. "Litmus tests" are applied by which the nominee is evaluated and rejected or accepted. Single-issue interest groups say, in essence, "We have no king but... abortion! gay rights! women's health! religious liberty! immigration! the 2nd Amendment!" If a politician does not agree with them, they are automatically rejected. In anger, they will crucify any opponent that threatens their tight grip on power.

Those leaders who condemned Jesus to die were no different from the politicians and interest groups of today. When they said, "We have no king but Caesar," they were throwing away centuries of deeply held religious convictions, sacrificed on the altar of power. Those men did not want to lose their advantage. Because of that, they teamed up with the party in control and lost their chance to know the true Messiah.

As followers of Jesus, we must be careful not to substitute political power for spiritual purity, not to sacrifice our Christian ideals on the altars of today's hot button issues. Who is your king?

Prayer: Jesus, you are Lord! Help us to remember that and to resist the urge to replace spiritual power with political power. We have no king but you, Jesus!

Psalm of the Day: 38.9-16

Believing Is Seeing!

Daily Reading: John 20

> *Blessed are those who have not seen and yet have believed.*
> (John 20:29b)

Devotional Thought: John 20 records the turning point in human history – the resurrection of Jesus Christ. It is the most crucial and game-changing moment of time, as creation is reconciled to the Father once again. Mary Magdalene was the first to see the empty grave, and the news quickly spread from there to the disciples and other followers of Jesus. The resurrection was met with joy, disbelief, doubt, and even fear.

So it is today also. Those who are spiritually deaf react to the gospel with skepticism, anger, and hostility, much like the Jewish religious leaders of Jesus' time. There are also people who do not believe, but are seeking spiritual things. The false doctrine that runs rampant in our anything-goes, tolerate-all, if-it-feels-right-do-it culture is perfect for these doubters. The gospel message of sin, repentance, blood, and suffering is offensive, and so they are easy prey to a watered-down theology. Then there are others who receive the gospel with joy, and a supernatural belief like that of Peter and John when they discovered the empty grave. Many needed time and physical proof before they believed, Thomas being the best-known example.

All who believe in Jesus receive salvation. Thomas needed to actually touch Jesus' crucifixion wounds before he would believe. Jesus said to him, "Have you believed because you have seen me? Blessed are those who have not seen and yet have believed," (v29). Most of us have not seen Jesus with our own eyes, but we can experience his presence plainly through the gift of the Holy Spirit. We can also read the Word to know him intimately, and even talk to him through prayer. These are gifts that we should never take for granted!

Jenny

Prayer: Father, thank you for the gift of your Son, sent to redeem the world and reconcile us to you. May we never lose the sense of joy and wonder over the resurrection and the gospel message.

Psalm of the Day: 38.17-22

Let's Go Fishing!

Daily Reading: John 21

> *Cast the net on the right side of the boat, and you will find some.*
> (John 21.6)

Devotional Thought: I read somewhere that one of John Wesley's (the great British evangelist of the 1700's and founder of the Methodist movement) secrets of success was to find where the Spirit was working and go there. He saw thousands of souls saved during his lifetime, and not just saved but discipled and organized into bands. He had learned the truth of what Jesus told the disciples in John 21: "Cast the net on the right side of the boat and you will find some."

Those disciples had planned just right and fished all night, but their nets were empty. They were expert fishermen, but their nets were empty. They had worked as hard as they could as long as they could, but their nets were empty.

Have you ever worked and worked and worked and yet gotten nowhere?

Jesus has told us to be fishers of men. He wants our nets to be full. Why aren't they?
- It could be that they're not in the water. We've forgotten what our job is. We need to get our nets wet!
- It could be that they're in the wrong place. We need to cast them on the right side. Some waters are 'fished out.'
- It could be that we're trying to find fish that are already found! We aren't in the member-transferring business, but the fish-catching business!
- It could be that the timing is not right. We must labor - even if it takes all night - and wait for Jesus to show up on the shore to lead us.

Do not grow discouraged, child of God. Keep on fishing!

Prayer: Father, help us to see the lost souls all around us and to tirelessly fish. Guide us to the 'right side' that our nets might be full. Amen.

Psalm of the Day: 39.1-6

With Friends Like This...

Daily Reading: Genesis 37

> *Meanwhile the Midianites had sold him in Egypt to Potiphar, an officer of Pharaoh, the captain of the guard.* (Genesis 37.36)

Devotional Thought: "With friends like that who needs enemies?" We've all felt that way at one time or another, haven't we? The one we thought we could count on let us down. The one we thought had our back, stabbed it!

Joseph's family was like that to him. First, his father let him down. It's not that Jacob didn't love Joseph; he did! As a matter of fact, we read that "Israel [Jacob] loved Joseph more than any other of his sons, because he was the son of his old age. And he made him a robe of many colors" (v. 3). The trouble wasn't Jacob's love, it was the fact that he spoiled Joseph. Jacob didn't do Joseph any favors by doting on him.

Because of Jacob's spoiling and favoritism, Joseph's brothers "hated him and could not speak peacefully to him" (v. 4). Eventually, they found a way to get even, selling him as a slave! With friends (brothers) like that, who needs enemies?

All of this, however, didn't happen in a vacuum. God was looking on. He was a friend that sticks closer than a brother. God directed the Midianites to sell Joseph to Potiphar. From there, God caused Joseph to rise in opportunity and responsibility. Through subsequent twists and turns, he became known to Pharaoh and was used by God to work a great salvation.

Perhaps you are feeling, "With friends like this, I don't need enemies!" Take heart. Look for God's hand at work. Allow God to use you where you are. He is working salvation for you and through you!

Prayer: Father, thank you that no matter what others may do, you always "have my back." Help me to wait patiently upon the Lord and see your great salvation worked out for me and through me. Amen.

Psalm of the Day: 39.7-13

Mercy or Judgment?

Daily Reading: Genesis 38

> Then Judah identified them and said, "She is more righteous than I, since I did not give her to my son Shelah." (Genesis 38.26)

Devotional Thought: After you get past the Old Testament principle of Levirate marriage (a form of social and family security that included "marrying" your brother's widow so she could have children...), Genesis 38 is a commentary on not being judgmental.

Have you ever wondered why some people seem to get harder treatment for moral lapses than do others? Why are some students applauded for threats of violence on college campuses while others are vehemently accused of shutting down discourse? I don't think it's a double standard that drives this. I think it is because of higher standards. Those who testify to higher standards are expected to comport themselves in a decent, ethical and moral way. Those who do not claim the need for ethical consistency are not held to those stricter standards.

Judah was one of those righteously indignant people in the Old Testament. He testified to the need for moral standards that he himself did not keep. When his son's widow tricked him into sleeping with her (Judah thought she was a prostitute) and she became pregnant, Judah was the first to call for her death! There was a problem, however. Judah was the father of the child! At least Judah had the good sense to repent and desist. I wish today's politicians would do the same, but they just double down when caught in moral inconsistencies. In the words of a former senator, "We won, didn't we?"

When a sinful lady was brought before him for judgment, Jesus said, "Let him who is without sin among you be the first to throw a stone at her." (John 8.7) May God give us grace to recognize our own faults before we pronounce judgment on another. Remember, "Mercy triumphs over judgment!" (James 2.13)

Prayer: Father, thank you for your mercy shown to me. When I am tempted to judge and condemn, may I look within and see how the wonderful grace of Jesus reaches me! Amen.

Psalm of the Day: 40.1-8

Are You Up to Your Neck in Alligators?
Daily Reading: Genesis 39

> *So Joseph found favor in his sight and attended him.* (Genesis 39.4)

Devotional Thought: "When you're up to your neck in alligators, it's hard to remember that your original objective was to drain the swamp." I suppose there were, if not alligators, then crocodiles in the area of Egypt where Joseph found himself after being sold as a slave by his brothers. It would have been perfectly understandable if Joseph had just given up. After all, he didn't even know what his objective was in Egypt. He couldn't see how God was using the 'alligators' to bring about a great deliverance for his family.

Some people would just try to skate by and stay low. Not Joseph. Instead of grousing, Joseph set about making the best of his circumstances. When he found himself in Potiphar's service, Joseph distinguished himself by working hard and making good decisions. He was quickly promoted.

The Bible says that "the Lord was with him and that the Lord caused all that he did to succeed in his hands" (v. 3). Note that God caused all that Joseph *did* to succeed. He had to *do* something! God will only bless the work of our hands (minds, etc.), if we actually work! If I want tomatoes from my garden in the summer, I have to plant tomatoes in the spring!

Through the twists and turns of life - false accusations, prison, and being forgotten - Joseph's life was by no means a straight line to success. Yet, Joseph kept his mind focused through it all. He worked hard and trusted in God.

Life is not always fair, but God is. When alligators are all you can see, remember Joseph and keep working hard and trusting in God.

Prayer: God, thank you for your promise to bless the work of my hands. Help me to keep my eyes on you and to keep right on working through the vagaries of life. Amen.

Psalm of the Day: 40.9-17

Aware Enough to Care
Daily Reading: Genesis 40

When Joseph came to them in the morning, he saw that they were troubled. So he asked Pharaoh's officers who were with him in custody in his master's house, "Why are your faces downcast today?"
(Genesis 40.6-7)

Devotional Thought: When it comes to people's feelings, I am one of the least observant males on the planet. My wife can tell what people are thinking and how they are feeling just by walking into a room. Me? I'm clueless. "Typical male" right? Well, not according to what I read in Genesis 40. A couple of Joseph's prison mates - the cupbearer and the baker to Pharaoh - were troubled one morning. Joseph picked up on their mood right away. "Why are your faces downcast today?"

Joseph listened intently to their responses and was able - with the help of the Holy Spirit - to give them answers to their questions. One wasn't a particularly happy response, but it proved to be accurate none-the-less. Because of his sensitivity, Joseph was able to help them understand life, and in the process he gave glory to his God.

Sadly, Joseph's sensitivity is not often duplicated. How often are we guilty of hurrying through life, bustling from one task to the next, without taking time to notice the people around us? They're troubled. It's written all over them if we would only take time to see. And then if we have courage and concern enough to inquire, we may find that - like Joseph - we can provide encouragement to those who are hurting. And in the process, we will give glory to God.

This is not to say that we should always be sharing our superior wisdom. The Bible says we should be quick to listen and slow to speak (James 1.19). As we have all heard, God gave us two ears and one mouth for a reason! Today, just remember to - like Joseph - be aware enough to care.

Prayer: Father, I know that today I will encounter people who are discouraged and downcast. Help me to spread the love, the hope, the peace of Jesus wherever I go. In the process, may you be praised! Amen.

Psalm of the Day: 41.1-9

Not Forgotten
Daily Reading: Genesis 41

> *After two whole years, Pharaoh dreamed that he was standing by the Nile.* (Genesis 41.1)

Devotional Thought: Forgotten. That's what Lana and I often felt in 2008 and 2009 when we were unemployed and unaware of any opportunities to change that status. That's a tough situation for a minister. It's difficult for anybody! Have you ever felt forgotten?

Joseph did. He had helped the cupbearer to Pharaoh interpret a dream and get out of prison. In response the cupbearer said he would remember him. The trouble is, the cupbearer forgot. But God had not forgotten Joseph. "After two whole years, Pharaoh dreamed..." It was not just an ordinary dream. God was the author of the dream. God used the dream to trouble the heart of Pharaoh, causing him eventually to call Joseph for an interpretation.

During those two years, Joseph was forgotten by man but remembered by God. The Lord not only brought Joseph to the attention of Pharaoh, but he also gave Joseph the interpretation of the dream, the wisdom to solve the problem, the courage (audacity!) to speak the truth, and the opportunity for advancement. Once again we hear a familiar refrain - God is working behind, going before, holding beneath, and standing beside Joseph.

Take heart, child of God! God is doing the same thing for you. In the silences of life, God writes the score to a memorable refrain. Be still and know that he is God!

Prayer: Father, thank you for your faithful love. When all seems silent, help me to rest in the knowledge that you are working behind, going before, holding beneath, and standing beside me just as you did Joseph. Amen.

Psalm of the Day: 41.10-13

Our Burden-Bearer

Daily Reading: Genesis 42

> And Jacob their father said to them, "You have bereaved me of my children: Joseph is no more, and Simeon is no more, and now you would take Benjamin. All this has come against me." (Genesis 42:36)

Devotional Thought: Joseph had had two dreams; in one, his harvested sheaf had risen above his brothers' sheaves. His second dream was like it: the sun, the moon, and eleven stars had bowed down to him. Both dreams symbolized his position of authority and power over his family. His brothers didn't like it! They sold him into slavery!

In fulfillment of these dreams, Joseph ended up in Egypt where he was in charge of the grain for all the land. Due to a severe famine, his brothers travelled to Egypt to ask for grain. Not recognizing their brother, they bowed in humility before him. Joseph withheld his identity from them and in so doing gives us opportunity to see the impact of their sin: guilt (v21), distress (v21), contention (v22), trembling (v28), fear (v35), and bereavement (v36).

Isn't this a perfect and fitting description of the consequences of sin in our own lives?

Though many years had gone by since Joseph's brothers had sinned against him, the consequences of that sin were still affecting the entire family. So it is with our own sin – the sin that we try to brush off or sweep under the rug will nevertheless affect us, our families, and those around us. It lays on us guilt, distress, contention, fear and bereavement. It is, indeed, a heavy burden. But, Jesus invites us in Matthew 11:28-30: "Come to me, all who labor and are heavy laden, and I will give you rest. Take my yoke upon you, and learn from me, for I am gentle and lowly in heart, and you will find rest for your souls. For my yoke is easy, and my burden is light."

Jenny

Prayer: Lord, cleanse us from the filthiness of our own sins. We know that the wages of sin is death, and the consequences of sin are far-reaching and long-lasting. Lead us in the way everlasting, we pray. Amen.

Psalm of the Day: 42.1-7

Be Careful What You Say *and* What You Hear!
Daily Reading: Genesis 43

> *Why did you treat me so badly as to tell the man that you had another brother?* (Genesis 43.6)

Devotional Thought: There have been times when I have said things without thinking that have caused pain for someone I loved. Though I was completely 'innocent,' their pain was just as real. Jacob's sons had done that to him. Without knowing what problems they would cause, they told 'the man' (they didn't know it was Joseph, their brother, who was the 'Secretary of Commerce' in Egypt) that they had another brother. This caused a situation that could have been avoided if they had kept their mouths shut!

Have you ever hurt someone unwittingly with your words? It makes you feel awful, doesn't it? There are (at least) two things we can learn from this incident in Jacob's family:

We need to be careful about what we say. Words have potential to hurt! The old saying "Sticks and stones may break my bones, but words will never hurt me" is just not true. Even words spoken without intent to harm can cause pain - some of it lifelong. In Jacob's opinion, what his sons had said was catastrophic. I've counseled many people with scars left over from words spoken years ago.

We need to be careful about what we 'hear.' Jacob unfairly blamed his sons for the predicament. His question only multiplied their pain. It was obvious that Jacob was speaking out of his frustration. His boys needed to hear it that way and not take offense. We will be happier and more congenial if we don't wear our feelings on our sleeves - if we give people the benefit of the doubt. There are enough real hurts in life. We don't need to make things up!

Be careful what you say. Be careful what you hear. You will be happier and those around you will too!

Prayer: Lord Jesus, you have shown us the power of words, to heal or to hurt. Help us to be careful with words, both hearing them and speaking them. May my words today bring others love, peace, and joy. Amen.

Psalm of the Day: 42.8-11

But I Wasn't at Fault!

Daily Reading: Genesis 44

Then they tore their clothes, and every man loaded his donkey, and they returned to the city. (Genesis 44.13)

Devotional Thought: Joseph's brothers were innocent, but had to pay the price. They had been framed and knew that they were in serious trouble. Have you ever been innocent and yet had to pay a penalty?

My daughter Amy found herself in that situation once. She was driving to school and someone backed out of a parking space into the street. Bang! I wasn't worried. The other student was at fault. He was even cited. But, there was a quirk in Illinois insurance law that required us to pay the deductable from our insurance policy! The other driver - at fault - didn't pay a dime out of pocket, but we were out $500! Unfair! But what could we do - the law was what it was. Unhappy, I paid the penalty.

Joseph's brothers were in big trouble for something they didn't do. At times we get caught up in things that are not of our own doing, but which cost us dearly. Often it is because we were in the wrong place at the wrong time. Sometimes it's because we are hanging out with others who get into trouble. Guilt by association. Sometimes we do something we didn't know was wrong. At any rate, the price has to be paid. We hate paying those costs, don't we?

But, that's exactly what Jesus did. He was completely innocent of sin, yet he went to the cross that he might bear our iniquities and pay the penalty for our sin! Fair? Hardly. But he was willing to do it because of his great love for us. What are we to do? As the old chorus goes: "I'll live for him who died for me!" Hallelujah!

Prayer: Jesus, though no fault was found in you, you suffered death that I might live. Thank you for dying on the cross for me. I commit this day to live for you. Amen.

Psalm of the Day: 43.1-5

Go, but Don't Stay

Daily Reading: Genesis 45

And now do not be distressed or angry with yourselves because you sold me here, for God sent me before you to preserve life. (Genesis 45.5)

Devotional Thought: There is a proper time for remorse, and there is a time to leave regret behind. Joseph's brothers were guilty to the core, and they knew it. For years their sin against Joseph remained hidden. They were living a lie, and I imagine that they often felt fear that they would be caught, that their father Jacob would find out the truth, and that they would pay for what they had done. Now, confronted by their brother, the full impact of their sin gave them great fear. More importantly, it was cause for great remorse. It was good for them.

Consider our need for remorse. Without proper remorse, we are unable to recognize our sins, much less repent from them. If we have no recognition that we are guilty before God, we will be haughty in our approach to him. It is the humble in heart who find the mercy of God. I believe that we have robbed a generation of young people in America today by alleviating their remorse before they even feel it. We don't want anybody to feel bad! But when we never face our error, we will continue in it.

We need to *go* there, but God does not want us to *stay* there. By faith, we are to leave our regrets behind and live in joyful freedom. We cannot go back and relive the past. Many things we have done cannot be undone. But, from this day forward, God gives new life. We need to accept that new life and go on. Remember, in everything, God is working for your good if you love him.

Joseph told his brothers as much. I believe that God is greater than Joseph, don't you? Leave your past behind!

Prayer: Thank you, Lord, that your mercy is everlasting. As you have forgiven me, help me to leave my past behind and live in the freedom and fullness of your love. Amen.

Psalm of the Day: 44.1-8

On Being an Abomination
Daily Reading: Genesis 46

> *For every shepherd is an abomination to the Egyptians.* (Genesis 46.34)

Devotional Thought: I receive *The Washington Post* editorial page in my inbox each morning and afternoon. *WaPo* has a very liberal bias, and most of the editorials have been - shall I say - unfriendly to President Trump in particular and to Republicans in general. Most struggle to say even something *neutral* about conservatives. I thought about that as I read Genesis 46. I had a good laugh, thinking, "Every Republican is an abomination to *The Washington Post!*" It is sad, really, that the political divisions and rancor are so deep that we can't even say nice things about each other - even when we agree!

Bias and prejudice are common among people, aren't they? For Jacob's family moving to Egypt, that turned out to be a blessing in disguise. The Israelites were given an area of land in which the Egyptians weren't interested - an area suitable for their flocks. Sheep and Shepherds were an abomination to Egyptians! I wonder if history would have turned out differently for a nation that knew not Jehovah if the Israelites had moved into their communities. Instead of enslaving them as foreigners, perhaps the Egyptians would have accepted them as neighbors. Instead of losing their firstborn to a plague of death, perhaps they would have consecrated them to the Lord's service!

It seems that we as Christians are increasingly like the shepherds of Israel. By preaching and standing on the Truth of God's Word, we have become an abomination. Sadly, America will suffer the consequences of rejecting God's ways. Let us do what we can to be exemplary citizens, but may we never compromise on the Truth!

Prayer: Father, help us to be salt and light in our world - even when we are ridiculed and rejected. Give us grace to love and pray for those who persecute us. Heal the divisions among us, O Lord, and grant that we may be found faithful. Amen.

Psalm of the Day: 44.9-16

Honest and Fair

Daily Reading: Genesis 47

> Then Pharaoh said to Joseph, "Your father and your brothers have come to you. The land of Egypt is before you. Settle your father and your brothers in the best of the land. Let them settle in the land of Goshen, and if you know any able men among them, put them in charge of my livestock." (Genesis 47:5-6)

Devotional Thought: Have you ever struggled in choosing *one* political candidate because of the dishonesty and corruption displayed by *all* of them? Often times when faced with such a situation, I look at those candidates with a sense of disgust and dismay over what our country has become. It is easy in those situations to feel as though anything you might say about them or actions you take towards them are justified.

We can learn something, however, in the way Joseph dealt with Pharaoh.

Pharaoh of Egypt worshiped pagan gods. Yet, Joseph and his family dealt honestly and fairly with him, displaying the character expected of a believer. Joseph prepared his brothers for what they should say to Pharaoh in order to ensure they were granted the land they desired. However, nothing they said was dishonest or deceitful. Jacob in his meeting with Pharaoh blessed him, not once, but twice! In return, God worked through Pharaoh to uphold his promise to Joseph's family (going back to Abraham) and they were granted the best of the land, where they could maintain their identities (rather than be absorbed into the Egyptian people), and grow and prosper into a great nation! How do you think God (and Pharaoh) would have responded if Joseph and his family had lied and used deceit in order to obtain those lands?

We must remember that in our dealings with nonbelievers, we are representatives of Christ and as such are expected to deal honestly and fairly with others, even when they themselves do not share our beliefs. While we might not always come out on the winning end of the deal, God can work through the nonbelievers we deal with and bring blessings on us and our families.

Eric

Prayer: Father, thank you for the blessings and opportunities of life, including the privilege of being your ambassadors in a sin-darkened world. Help us, O Lord, to live upright and charitable lives so that those who do not follow you may desire the one true God. Amen.

Psalm of the Day: 44.17-26

He Knows. He Always Knows.
Daily Reading: Genesis 48

> *But his father refused and said, "I know, my son, I know. He also shall become a people, and he also shall be great. Nevertheless, his younger brother shall be greater than he, and his offspring shall become a multitude of nations."* (Genesis 48.19)

Devotional Thought: Verse 19 is where we want to focus today, and not because we're the youngest and like where it's headed. Why was the primary blessing given to the younger of the two grandsons? Joseph had a clear idea of who should receive the greater blessing, demonstrated by where he placed them in relation to Jacob's hands (the right hand was "supposed" to go on the firstborn). And despite Jacob's failing eyesight, he knew exactly what he was doing when he switched his hands around.

God knows what he is doing, even when we don't understand, even when it might not even make sense. Joseph should have been the first person to understand this. This is the fifth time in Genesis that we see a reversal of birth order, with Joseph himself being the fourth!

We are all chosen by God - he wants to claim all of us and make us his sons and daughters, as Jacob adopted his grandsons (v. 5). But how do we react when others receive different blessings than we receive? How do we respond when God changes the order of something we had already decided on? If we are honest, we probably don't respond well. Like Joseph, we probably get upset and try to switch things back to the way we deem appropriate. But God reminds us that He knows.

I think we often do the same thing. God shows us over and over that He is in control... and when something doesn't go as planned, we immediately forget all those other things and say, "Not this way God, you have it wrong!" Spoiler alert? He doesn't have it wrong. He always knows.

Amy and Evan Berry

Prayer: Lord, thank you for the blessings you have specifically chosen for each one of us. Please help me to follow your path, because your way and will are always right. Thank you for your patience and guidance when I do not understand or even stubbornly still choose my own way. May I grow closer to you and follow your plan daily. Amen.

Psalm of the Day: 45.1-7

Like a Lion

Daily Reading: Genesis 49

> *The scepter shall not depart from Judah, nor the ruler's staff from between his feet...* (Genesis 49:10a)

Devotional Thought: Genesis 49 records the final blessings of Jacob on his sons, before he "breathed his last and was gathered to his people," (v33). The blessings were given to each son according to the "blessing suitable to him," (v28). (We should be grateful indeed that we will not be judged by our Father according to our past sins if we have placed our trust in Jesus!) But, notice the blessing of Judah.

Judah's blessing compares him to a lion's cub and as a lion and a lioness. Jesus is referred to as the Lion of Judah in Revelation 5:5, the only One worthy to open the book with its seven seals, initiating the final judgment of the world. Israel also prophesies that "the scepter shall not depart from Judah, nor the ruler's staff from between his feet, until tribute comes to him; and to him shall be the obedience of the peoples," (v10). We know that the kingdom and throne of Jesus will be established forever (1 Chr 22:10, 2 Sam 7:16). The final kingdom of the world will become the kingdom of Christ, and He will reign forever and ever (Rev. 11:15).

How beautiful that the Lord chose to bless not the firstborn son, as was customary in this time and culture, but rather chose to bless the entire world through One that would come from the line of Judah, his fourth son. So it has been all throughout history and continues now – we see God working through ordinary people, full of weaknesses but possessing hearts of humility and obedience through the grace of God. May we be not like Israel's firstborn, prideful and deceitful for his own gain, but like the Lion of Judah, the Lamb who was slain, sacrificing all for the kingdom of God.

Jenny

Prayer: Lord, give us eyes to see and ears to hear the story of redemption that you have been telling from the beginning of time. Thank you for the Lamb that was slain for our sins, the Savior of the world, the Lion of Judah that will return to establish his kingdom forever. Amen.

Psalm of the Day: 45.8-17

We Don't Live There Anymore
Daily Reading: Genesis 50

As for you, you meant evil against me, but God meant it for good, to bring it about that many people should be kept alive, as they are today. (Genesis 50:20)

Devotional Thought: Seventeen years had passed since Joseph invited Jacob and his brothers to live with him in Egypt. Jacob died, and Joseph's brothers feared that Joseph would now take vengeance on them. Joseph reassured them, "You intended to harm me, but God intended it for good". (Genesis 50:20, *NIV*)

Why was this necessary? Had the brothers not had enough time with Joseph to realize that he had no intention of harming them? He had openly forgiven them and made sure to provide for them. After seventeen years, they still felt the guilt for what they had done. This was unnecessary guilt. All had been forgiven a long time ago.

Do we ever carry around a backpack of guilt after Jesus has clearly forgiven us? I know it is tempting to dredge up our sins and feel bad about them all over again, that is a trick of the Devil. He wants us to remember everything that we have done wrong, but we don't live there anymore.

Corrie ten Boom, in her book *Tramp for the Lord* had these words to say regarding forgiveness: "It was 1947--. I had come from Holland to defeated Germany with the message that God forgives. It was the truth they needed most to hear in that bitter, bombed-out land, and I gave them my favorite mental picture. Maybe because the sea is never far from a Hollander's mind, I like to think that that's where forgiven sins are thrown. 'When we confess our sins,' I said, 'God casts them into the deepest ocean, gone forever--. Then God places a sign out there that says "'No Fishing Allowed."'"

We have been forgiven. The guilt is gone. We don't live there anymore. Thanks be to God.

Cheryl Young

Prayer: Dear Jesus, thank you that your love and grace is offered to us. Thank you that when we confess our sins, you are faithful and just to forgive our sins and to cleanse us from all unrighteousness. Help us to keep moving forward in the grace that you offer today. In Jesus name, Amen.

Psalm of the Day: 46.1-7

Steadfastness Doesn't Come Fast

Daily Reading: James 1

> *The testing of your faith produces steadfastness.* (James 1.3)

Devotional Thought: I began praying with Jim concerning a new job. He needed health benefits, better hours, and less stress. As we prayed together, opportunity after opportunity came up. Jim, however, was passed over each time. Both of us were getting discouraged. Then, almost out of the blue, an employer contacted Jim, "Are you still interested in a job?" It was a better job than he had been applying for, with better hours, and more responsibilities to match his skill set and significant experience. Praise the Lord! Both of us - and I'm sure his wife Debbie and many others! - were overwhelmed by God's goodness! Our faith certainly was boosted.

I know it doesn't always work that way, but isn't it wonderful when it does? What a boost to our faith!

Another 'Jim' - the author of the book of James in the New Testament - agreed with us. His faith, along with the faith of many other New Testament Christians, was tested over and over again. It began with the crucifixion of his Brother. When Jesus was crucified, James was not a believer, but after that grueling test and the victory of the resurrection, James' faith in his divine Brother, was molded into something strong and unwavering. His faith was to be tested through persecutions outside the church and through disappointments inside the church. In all of that James was steadfast. He became the leader of the Jerusalem church.

Ultimately, James' faith was tested through martyrdom. But, having remained faithful to the end, James received the crown of life from the hand of his Brother.

So, don't panic when your faith is stretched and the answer is delayed. Know that God is producing steadfastness in you!

Prayer: Father, it is hard to say, but thank you for the times when my faith is tested. Help me, O Lord, in my weakness and discouragement to remain true to you. By your grace may I be steadfast. And, Lord, help those whose faith is wavering. Deliver them through the trial to victory. Amen.

Psalm of the Day: 46.8-11

The Long View

Daily Reading: James 2

> *Listen, my beloved brothers, has not God chosen those who are poor in the world to be rich in faith and heirs of the kingdom, which he has promised to those who love him?* (James 2.5)

Devotional Thought: There was once a poor man who attended "First Church," a well-to-do church in a city. He loved the church, and wanted to become a member, but he just couldn't 'break through' and be accepted. After trying many years and being rebuffed each time, he finally cried out to God, "Lord, I've been trying to get accepted into First Church for years, and they just won't let me in!" The story goes that Jesus replied to him, "Son, don't fret over this. I've been trying to get into First Church for years. They won't let me in either!"

When Jesus came to the earth, he did not come to places of wealth or halls of power. He came to a lowly carpenter and his young wife, nobodies on the stages of earth. He did not seek to hang out with the rich or the rulers. He chose instead the poor and the outcast. And, he found fertile soil for faith in their hearts.

When I was 14 years old, there was nothing about me to commend me to the Nazarenes in Pioneer, OH. But, they didn't care. Like *The Nazarene*, they didn't want me for my money or my influence or my wisdom. In love, they simply wanted me to know Jesus. They accepted me where I was and as I was. Then, they joined me in a journey of transformation, beginning with my being born again right at an altar of prayer in the humble little church.

When we see youth and poverty what do we see? A drain on the church's resources? That's not what Jesus sees! He sees the potential for rich faith and for kingdom builders. Let's take the long view of things and see as Jesus does!

Prayer: Jesus, lowly Shepherd, thank you for coming to me where I was. Thank you for saving me in my poverty and powerlessness. Help me to see and love others as you see and love me. Amen.

Psalm of the Day: 47.1-9

Right!

Daily Reading: James 3-4

> :...but no human being can tame the tongue. It is a restless evil, full of deadly poison. With it we bless our Lord and Father, and with it we curse people who are made in the likeness of God. From the same mouth come blessing and cursing. (James 3:8-10a)

Devotional Thought: We all know that it is sometimes hard to keep quiet when we have an opinion. But you never have that problem, right? Right! In today's divisive climate, everyone is completely convinced of his or her own rightness and doesn't really want to hear the other side of the argument. But not you, right? Right! People don't want to hear about their faulty logic or their own moral deficiency. But not you, right? Right!

I have found that people usually are just as certain that they are right as I am certain that I am right! Arguments can become heated and unproductive, as both I and the other party get frustrated and defensive. It is in those moments of frustration and defensiveness that the debate is lost. When you lose control of your tongue, I would argue that you also lose that argument, and you do damage to the kingdom of God. God has called us to be a blessing, and not a curse. We are royal priests, sharing the light of the gospel with the world. Instead, we come across as prosecutors.

James knew that there is an answer. Though we are unable to control our tongues with our own power (v8), The Spirit will help us to know when to speak and when to remain silent. In today's culture, we should prayerfully consider the things that we "share" with our friends and acquaintances. Will speaking out result in encouragement, or in the building up of others? Will it bring glory to God and honor to the Church? Can the truth be spoken in love? If not, chances are we should hold our tongues. Right? Right!

Jenny

Prayer: Lord, we know that apart from you, our tongues are destructive, working against your kingdom purposes. Please fill us with wisdom and compassion as we engage with a world that is angry and lost. Give us words of love and encouragement that do not divide, but rather point others to you.

Psalm of the Day: 48.1-8

Right Now?

Daily Reading: James 5

> *Be patient, therefore, brothers, until the coming of the Lord.* (James 5.7)

Devotional Thought: Whump... whump... whump. "Oh, no! A flat tire!" I was enjoying a warm spring day, driving my little red convertible through some back country roads. I was miles from the nearest town and four hours from home. When I pulled over, I discovered that the spare was flat, too! It was getting late in the afternoon. Now what?

Then I remembered that I had roadside coverage with my insurance company. I called the 800 number, and they said they would locate somebody and send help. I hung up relieved, but soon the doubts came. Would they find help? Could they find me? I waited and waited. At one point a Good Samaritan stopped and offered to take me into town - wherever that was! I declined, "No thank you. Help is on the way!" That was hard to do.

After just a little more waiting, the flashing lights of a tow truck came around the bend. He pumped up my spare, put it on for me, waited to make sure it held pressure, and then we were both on our way. No charge! Thank you, State Farm!

If I had gone with the Good Samaritan, I would have missed him. My journey would have been delayed, and I would have had to pay for it myself. Patience was rewarded.

Have you ever wanted God to show up *right now*? It's hard to wait for him when you are in need. There are times when we feel God has lost track of where we are and can't find us. Those are the times when we are tempted to jump at *any* solution. But, if we will be patient, we will discover that "the coming of the Lord" is near, right around the bend.

Prayer: Thank you, Lord, that you never lose track of where we are. Even though I may feel that you are far away, you are just around the bend. Help me to wait patiently for you!

Psalm of the Day: 48.9-14

The Foundation

Daily Reading: Hebrews 1

> *You, Lord, laid the foundation of the earth in the beginning, and the heavens are the work of your hands; they will perish, but you remain.* (Hebrews 1.10-11a)

Devotional Thought: I fancy myself a builder. I have been a part of five building projects in churches where I have pastored and two as a layman. I also have been involved in the building of four houses. On the first two houses, the ones I served as the general contractor, I remember laying the foundation for each one - not an easy task. In order for a structure to stand, it has to have a good foundation. But, no matter how good the foundation, no building will last forever.

When the Lord "laid the foundation of the earth in the beginning," he knew that was true. Neither the earth nor the heavens - both with foundations laid by God himself - will last forever. It may be billions of years hence, but they are destined to perish.

What will last? When all of the created order dissolves, what will remain? "You, Lord," the writer of Hebrews said. And, the only way for me to live forever is to be in relationship with the Eternal One. Those fellowship halls, church buildings, and houses will not give me immortality. Only God will do that, for only he lives forever. Later in the book of Hebrews, we read that Abraham was looking forward to a city with eternal foundations. By faith he recognized that this world was not his final home. He built his life on God.

Each of my daughters caught the building bug from their dad and are living in homes in which they were involved in the building process. I'm pleased with their understanding of and involvement in their home-building projects. But I am even more pleased that they are building their lives on the Lord Jesus Christ. I urge you to do the same!

Prayer: Thank you, Lord Jesus, that you are the Rock upon which we can confidently build our lives. You are a foundation that will never perish. Help us, O Lord, to trust in you and commit to you completely. Amen.

Psalm of the Day: 49.1-9

Through Death to Destroy Death
Daily Reading: Hebrews 2

> *Through death he might destroy the one who has the power of death, that is, the devil.* (Hebrews 2.14b)

Devotional Thought: Lana and I were watching television the other night and a commercial for the shingles vaccine came on. We looked at each other and decided as soon as we turn 60 we're going to get the vaccine. We've had too many friends who have gotten the shingles, and we know how bad it can get. We don't want anything to do with that disease! That conversation got me to thinking about how the vaccine works: by putting a weakened form of the shingles virus into our bodies, we then produce antibodies that will fight the virus. Doesn't that seem strange? Fight the disease with the disease. But it works!

That is exactly what Jesus did when he went to the cross to die for the sins of the world. He fought the disease with the disease. Through his death and resurrection, Jesus took Satan's worst weapon - death itself - and turned it back on him. For millennia, Satan had used sin and death to destroy people, but on that epoch day, 2000 years ago, the tables were turned!

According to Revelation 20.14, death is "thrown into the lake of fire" at the final judgment. Having used this weapon to defeat the kingdom of darkness, Jesus will then destroy the weapon itself. Death will no longer exist to threaten, to frighten, or to destroy.

"Death where is your sting? Death where is your victory? ... Thanks be to God, who gives us the victory through our Lord Jesus Christ!"

Prayer: Worthy are you, Lord Jesus, to receive praise and honor and glory - for through your death you defeated death once and for all. You are the resurrection and the life, O Lord, and the one who believes in you will live forever! Amen!

Psalm of the Day: 49.10-15

Just When I Need Him

Daily Reading: Hebrews 3-4

For we do not have a high priest who is unable to sympathize with our weaknesses, but one who in every respect has been tempted as we are, yet without sin. Let us then with confidence draw near to the throne of grace, that we may receive mercy and find grace to help in time of need. (Hebrews 4.15-16)

Devotional Thought: I was recently talking with some friends of mine who told me about an experience they had when their son was in school. He had gotten into some minor trouble, and they had been called in to meet with the counselor. When they arrived for the appointment, they found that the counselor didn't have children of her own and was barely older than the students! She proceeded to tell them just what they needed to do to raise their son. Needless to say, her advice fell flat. She was unable to truly identify with them.

God knew that we needed not only a Savior, but we needed a Savior with whom we could identify. So, Jesus came into this world not as a superhero, but as a common, ordinary person. While he didn't experience every exact thing that we go through, he did experience representative temptations and trials. He got hungry just like us. His body grew weary. He got exasperated with thick-headed friends. He suffered rejection by his closest friends. He was subject even to temptation. And of course, he went through the greatest trial of all - death. A Savior such as that, is One whom we can approach, One whom we can trust.

What are you facing today? What trials and temptations threaten to undo you? Jesus has been through it already. And he understands your struggle. Draw near to him with confidence. You will receive mercy and find grace to help you in your time of need!

"Just when I need Him, Jesus is near; Just when I falter, just when I fear; Ready to help me, ready to cheer, Just when I need Him most."

Prayer: Lord Jesus, thank you that you are not a 'long-distance' Savior, but that you came close to rescue me. You have experienced trials and struggles like my own. I turn to you with confidence, and I thank you for your help. Amen.

Psalm of the Day: 49.16-20

Promises, Promises
Daily Reading: Hebrews 5-6

> *Abraham, having patiently waited, obtained the promise.*
> (Hebrews 6.15)

Devotional Thought: I love to go to my kids' houses. For one thing, they have to pay the light bill and buy the groceries for a change. But even better, a trip to the kids promises to be a visit with grandkids! Entering their homes, we immediately want that promise fulfilled! When I go in my middle daughter's house, I see something else that makes me smile, too. The kids have a framed photo from their wedding with the following words above and below the picture: "I might ask you something tomorrow..." and "I might say yes."

I've always liked that because it reminds me of the promise that they made to each other even before they were married. It was the promise to get married! And they waited patiently for it.

Abraham's walk with God was like that. God made a promise to him to give him a family that was greater than the stars in the sky. But, Abraham had to wait. And he did. All through his life he waited. Even after the son of promise - Isaac - came along, Abraham continued to wait. There was more to the promise! There was a city with foundations, whose builder and maker is God (Hebrews 11). Abraham never saw that part of the promise until he passed from this life to the next. But he kept his faith. He waited patiently. And now, he has obtained the promise.

Are you waiting on God? Wait patiently. You, too, will obtain the promise.

Prayer: Father, thank you that you are faithful to every promise that you make. In Christ you have said the Amen to all these promises. When you delay, O Lord, help me to wait patiently and so to obtain the promise. Amen.

Psalm of the Day: 50.1-6

Financial Partners
Daily Reading: Hebrews 7

> *In the one case tithes are received by mortal men, but in the other case, by one of whom it is testified that he lives.* (Hebrews 7.8)

Devotional Thought: Recently I spoke with a friend of mine who is struggling to get out from under student loan debts. At the same time, he has been developing his Christian stewardship. He told me that he and his wife weren't sure how they were going to be able to tithe (give 10% of their income to God), but that they did it anyway. His testimony: "We didn't miss it." They still had what they needed and did most of what they wanted.

In Hebrews 7, we read about how Abraham tithed to God through the priest Melchizedek. God had blessed Abraham, and Abraham honored God through his tithing. (You can read the background story in Genesis 14.) How many of us have discovered the miraculous truth of tithing? How many of us practice it?

I think that the reason most people don't tithe is that they misunderstand the nature of the tithe. It is not a gift to the church, it is a recognition of the sovereignty of God over all of life. We give 10% back to God because we know that he has given us everything that we have. In Abraham's case, tithes are described as being "received... by the one of whom it is testified that he lives." This is a reference to God. Though Abraham presented his tithe to Melchizedek, it was received by God.

I always find it amazing that God would receive anything from us, that he would allow us the privilege of partnering with him in the work of eternity. Are you financial partners with the Sovereign of the universe?

Prayer: Thank you, Lord God Almighty, for all the blessings you have given to me. All I have comes from your hand. Help me to honor you with the Christian discipline of tithing. As Jesus gave his all, help me to give my tithe as a token of my complete dependence upon you. Amen.

Psalm of the Day: 50.7-15

And Now You Know... the Rest of the Story
Daily Reading: Hebrews 8

> *Now the point in what we are saying is this: we have such a high priest, one who is seated at the right hand of the throne of the Majesty in heaven, a minister in the holy places, in the true tent that the Lord set up, not man.* (Hebrews 8:1-2)

Devotional Thought: Have you ever completed a Bible study of the Old Testament books of Exodus, Leviticus, and Numbers? This may not sound thrilling at first, but it is a very exciting and rewarding study. In these books we learn of God's people being delivered from slavery, receiving the Law, seeing the holy and glorious character of God, building the Tabernacle, and initiating the sacrifices. Some of these accounts make for good reading on their own, but most importantly, all of them point to Jesus.

Hebrews 8 gives us a glimpse of this, as the author tells us why the priesthood was originally created in the times of the exodus. The Tabernacle, the holy things in the Tabernacle, the priesthood and the sacrifices, were all a shadow of heavenly things. Jesus, as the ultimate High Priest, is the fulfillment of these symbols. There is no longer any condemnation for those who have put their faith in Christ, as Paul says in Romans 8:34. "Who is to condemn? Christ Jesus is the one who died – more than that, who was raised – who is at the right hand of God, who indeed is interceding for us."

For those of us who are tempted to focus only on the New Testament, maybe including some Psalms occasionally, we need to be reminded of the fact that God's Word tells a complete story from beginning to end. We cannot expect to fully understand the gospels without an understanding of God as he reveals himself through the Old Testament. Strive to understand the complete story – the story of God's love and his redemption of the world. The richness of the gospels will increase as you do so!

Jenny

Prayer: God, you are amazingly perfect, from beginning to end. Your story for us is richer than we can ever imagine, but we desire to see glimpses of the perfection, the completeness, and the beauty of your love. Please give us a desire for you and for your Word.

Psalm of the Day: 50.16-23

The Glory of a Growing Relationship
Daily Reading: Hebrews 9

> *Now even the first covenant had regulations for worship and an earthly place of holiness.* (Hebrews 9.1)

Devotional Thought: I remember when I met Al. He was 'guarded' in his conversation and openness. So was I. As we got to know each other, however, the guards came down and we became friends. We adopted nicknames for each other and enjoyed some humorous banter. Then I noticed something happening. Each of us began sharing very personal things that we were going through. We began praying for one another. It was as if a door to a whole new room had opened. The friendship changed qualitatively.

I think that most friendships go that way, don't they? There is a time of meeting, then a time of casual acquaintance, then a time of growing closer and more open. Then comes a time when you can share more personal joys and heartaches. Finally, you get to the place that you trust them implicitly and you know that they feel the same about you.

Our relationship with Christ is like that, too. Hebrews 9 talks about the earthly tabernacle and covenant in the Old Testament. There was a place outside the tabernacle and then places of increasing holiness as you entered into the tabernacle. The ultimate place was the Holy of Holies and the mercy seat on the Ark of the Covenant - where God met with the people through an intermediary - the high priest.

It is that place where Christ has gone and opened to us. It is that place where our most intimate friendship with Christ is possible.

Christ invites you. Have you entered in?

Prayer: Jesus, thank you for going to the Holy of Holies for me - the place where you shed your blood and redeemed me from sin and death. Help me, my Lord, to go there and have a deep and abiding friendship with you. Amen.

Psalm of the Day: 51.1-6

Fired Up!
Daily Reading: Hebrews 10

> *And let us consider how to stir up one another to love and good works, not neglecting to meet together, as is the habit of some, but encouraging one another, and all the more as you see the Day drawing near.* (Hebrews 10.24-25)

Devotional Thought: I have a wood-burning fireplace, and I have noticed that it is the nature of hot coals to cool and go out when they are isolated from other such coals. But, when coals of fire are compacted together in the fireplace, they burn completely and continue to give out heat. They maintain their heat by their proximity to one another. That is true also with Christians.

Church attendance has fallen on hard times recently. Is church attendance important? The Bible says it is. The evidence I have seen across nearly 30 years of ministry says it is. I cannot do any better than Richard Taylor (*Beacon Bible Commentary*, Hebrews, p. 129) did when he wrote:

> We should attend the means of grace regularly if for no other reason than out of 'consideration' for others. But such faithfulness is also one of the 'good works' to which we are to incite them - and surely we can do this in no better way than by example. The sad acknowledgment **as the manner of some is**, would imply that some of these Hebrew Christians no longer felt it necessary to attend the church services. This might be prompted by a mistaken piety, which supposed that solitary worship was better; or a religious conceit, which imagined that the need for corporate worship had been outgrown; or a decline in spiritual fervor, which resulted in sheer indifference. But regardless of the reason, carelessness in our attendance upon the means of grace is fatal, both to our influence and to our own souls... Only by meeting together can we fulfill the positive duty of **exhorting one another**.

Are you fired up about church?

Prayer: Jesus, you said you would build your church and that the gates of hell would not prevail against it. Help me to do my part through faithful attendance and participation that I may be strong against the enemy. Amen.

Psalm of the Day: 51.7-15

Laugh Your Head Off

Daily Reading: Hebrews 11

> *By faith Sarah herself received power to conceive, even when she was past the age.* (Hebrews 11.11)

Devotional Thought: Sarah and Abraham were given a promise by God. They waited for it many, many years. At first it was a fresh vision that kept them going and gave them hope. But, with the passing of years, the vision grew dim, and the promise faded from their thoughts. By the age of 89, Sarah had long given up the hope of bearing children. She was simply past the age. But then one day she and her husband were visited by messengers from God who told her she was going to do just that - have a son. At first she laughed. I guess I would have, too. Something clicked in her spirit, however, and she moved from disbelief to belief. In that movement of faith, the writer of Hebrews said, she "received power to conceive."

The ability to bear a child at the age of 89 was not within her. Actually, for whatever reason, she had never been able to. It was a frustration all her life. But at that unlikely moment, she "received power to conceive." God fulfilled the long-forgotten promise.

God gives us the "power to conceive" as well - even when we are "past the age."

What promises from God lie dormant in your heart? Have you given up on them? Lacking the resources and circumstances to see them fulfilled, have you simply said, "I'm past the age"? Hear the words of Jesus: "I came that they [you] may have life and have it abundantly" (John 10.10). Lay hold of the promise of God. Receive the power to conceive.

And then laugh your head off!

Prayer: Lord, speak a fresh word and a renewed vision into my heart today. Help me to believe, to receive, and to conceive. I lay hold of abundant life in Jesus today - even though I'm "past the age." Amen!

Psalm of the Day: 51.16-19

Come Out on the Victory Side!
Daily Reading: Hebrews 12

> *Consider him who endured ... so that you may not grow weary or fainthearted.* (Hebrews 12.3)

Devotional Thought: In the late 20th century, Nelson Mandela served 27 years in three different prisons - the reward he got for his efforts to eliminate apartheid in South Africa. Upon his release, he was elected president of South Africa. Those on the left and on the right have found cause to criticize Mandela, but it is impossible to deny that he brought opportunity and hope to a vast number of people. One of the things Mandela used to say was, "It always seems impossible until it's done." I suppose that he felt that way as he endured those years in prison.

Five years ago, my friend Vicky was treated for cancer. At the time, her oncologist told her that if she survived five years without the cancer recurring, she had a good chance of living out her normal lifespan. We recently celebrated that milestone. While no one is guaranteed even tomorrow, the journey that once seemed impossible is done. Throughout these last five years, Vicky has testified that she was leaning on God. In our conversations, we have often thought of the power of the present Savior. And even though we didn't know the outcome, we knew the faithfulness of God.

Others have endured even in the midst of loss. They have held onto the love of God even though they have gone through the valley of the shadow of death.

Are you in the midst of something that seems impossible? Consider Jesus. He endured so much for you. He came out on the victory side of death, the resurrection side. May you not grow weary or be fainthearted.

Prayer: Lord Jesus, thank you for enduring the cross for me. Thank you that you came forth from the grave as a Conqueror! Help me - in the light of your resurrection glory - to not grow weary or fainthearted. Amen.

Psalm of the Day: 52.1-9

A Lasting City

Daily Reading: Hebrews 13

> *For here we have no lasting city, but we seek the city that is to come.* (Hebrews 13.14)

Devotional Thought: Have you ever heard of Elk Lick, OH? Founded as a community for affluent citizens in Clermont County, it was at one time advanced as a possibility for the county seat. That never happened, and as a matter of fact, most of Elk Lick is now under water! East Fork Lake was constructed in 1972 and the little town of Elk Lick is no more. It was not a lasting city.

Across the millennia of human history, cities have come and gone, haven't they? Cities we read about in the Bible are buried under Middle Eastern sands and are of interest only to archaeologists and historians. Cities that flourished during the time of American westward migration are abandoned and have deteriorated. Even in our lifetime, Detroit - the once great American city - has lost hundreds of thousands of people. "Here we have no lasting city."

"We seek the city that is to come," not *a* city. We seek *the* city. There is only one city that will never be abandoned, that will never deteriorate, that will never collapse. That is the city of God, described in Revelation 21: "And I saw no temple in the city, for its temple is the Lord God the Almighty and the Lamb. And the city has no need of sun or moon to shine on it, for the glory of God gives it light, and its lamp is the Lamb. By its light will the nations walk, and the kings of the earth will bring their glory into it, and its gates will never be shut by day—and there will be no night there."

Take heart, my friend. The city we seek is a lasting city!

Prayer: Lord, when I grow discouraged or tired or weak, remind me that I have a lasting city - a city to come - where I will be with you forever. Thank you that you have gone to prepare that place for me. Amen.

Psalm of the Day: 53.1-6

The Child Was Beautiful

Daily Reading: Exodus 1-2

> *Pharaoh's daughter said to her, "Take this baby and nurse him for me, and I will pay you." So the woman took the baby and nursed him.* (Exodus 2:9 *NIV*)

Devotional Thought: Talk about Divine Providence! Fearing for her son's life, "when she could hide him no longer," Jochebed placed her sweet wiggly baby in a basket and walked away. We read in Hebrews, "By faith Moses, when he was born, was hidden for three months by his parents, because they saw that the child was beautiful, and they were not afraid of the king's edict" (Hebrews 11:23). Three months?! Moses' mother nursed, nurtured, and loved this baby for 3 months and then had to trust in God to deliver him - as He would later deliver the Israelites *through* Moses. To make it even more of a God-orchestrated-provision, Pharaoh's daughter chose Moses' own mother to be the one to nurse him and raise him as a child.

As a new mother myself, this passage causes so many new feelings for me! I simply can't imagine leaving my 3 month old. The faith that Moses' parents displayed is admirable and unbelievable. They saw that this child was something special and they chose to obey and trust in the Lord. The challenges of nursing and raising a child are great. The demands of parenting are intense. And the reward of seeing your child following the Lord must be incomparable. It has been my personal prayer, since the day I learned I was expecting, that my child would develop a heart for the Lord! May she choose to follow Jesus and have a longing for Him from a young age!

It took the faith of two parents to allow the Divine Providence of our Savior to work! May we have that faith and obey - even in the bleakest of days!

Emily Beasley

Prayer: God, instill in us an unwavering faith in you! May we press on, with our eyes on the cross, as we desire to live for you! Thank you for the promise of an eternal reward with you! Amen!

Psalm of the Day: 54.1-7

You Are Seen and Heard

Daily Reading: Exodus 3

> Then the Lord said, "I have surely seen the affliction of my people who are in Egypt and have heard their cry because of their taskmasters. I know their sufferings..." (Exodus 3.7)

Devotional Thought: When we share our feelings with other people or share about situations or circumstances happening in our life, we want to know they are listening. Even more so, we want to know that we are heard. We want to know that what we shared affects change or prompts action in the listener. Whether we cry out to the sky or share our troubles, heartaches, or concerns with a friend, we want to know that someone hears our cry for help and is ready to help.

This was certainly the hope of the Hebrew people. As the memory of Joseph faded in Egypt, the oppression and exploitation of the Hebrew people grew. What started out as an act of mercy (the invitation for the Hebrews to wait out the famine in Egypt) soon grew into a life of slavery and terror. The Hebrew people cried out for help, for someone to hear and to rescue them. And God did hear. But not just any god, the true God with a NAME who knew the Hebrew people intimately. This YAHWEH responded and sent a deliverer to rescue the Hebrew people, His children.

Sometimes we find ourselves in situations and circumstances as dismal as the Hebrews. Sometimes these troubles are of our own making, other times they just aren't. During these times, when you cry out for help, don't just call out to anyone, call out to God. If anyone truly can hear, respond, and deliver us, it is God. God is listening, and not in some passive, distant, or uninterested way. God cares and stands ready to deliver—and will! God cares about you; you are His child. Cry out to Jesus!

Joe Young

Prayer: Father God, help me to remember today that you care and hear my cry for help. Help me to cast my cares upon you and trust you for deliverance. Thank you that my prayers never go unheard, and that your plans for deliverance are complete.

Psalm of the Day: 55.1-8

Pliable Hearts

Daily Reading: Exodus 4

And the Lord said to Moses, "When you go back to Egypt, see that you do before Pharaoh all the miracles that I have put in your power. But I will harden his heart, so that he will not let the people go. (Exodus 4.21)

Devotional Thought: Some of us remember the Flip Wilson character, Geraldine: "The devil made me do it!" Geraldine didn't want to accept responsibility, so she just blamed it on the devil. Many people adopt this same excuse as their own. There are others, however, who look for another scapegoat: God!

I have friends who are foundering in drug addiction who are like that. They wait and wait for God to do something miraculous - for God to deliver them - without their having to do a thing! In essence they are saying, "I'm an addict because that's the way God made me. I'll stay an addict unless and until God changes me." Refusing to accept personal responsibility, they blame God.

I know of spouses who continually refuse to "love, honor and cherish." Instead, they withdraw their love, put down their spouses and refuse to treasure them. When the last straw has been added, the offended spouse separates. Inevitably, the offender blames the offended, but who is really responsible for the separation?

I wonder if Pharaoh blamed God: "Well, God, I would have let them go, but you hardened my heart." I somehow don't believe God would buy that argument. Pharaoh made the choice to hold the Israelites in slavery. God simply allowed Pharaoh's sin-calcified heart to harden in that condition. It's what the Apostle Paul described: "Since they did not see fit to acknowledge God, God gave them up to a debased mind" (Romans 1.28).

Let us keep our own hearts pliable to God. Let us also pray for the lost that their hearts would not harden in their rebellion and unbelief.

Prayer: Father, help me to remain tender to your touch and sensitive to your Spirit. May you never find cause in me to allow my heart to harden before you. Amen.

Psalm of the Day: 55.9-15

Are You Too Stressed to Be Blessed?
Daily Reading: Exodus 5

> *Let heavier work be laid on the men that they may labor at it and pay no regard to lying words.* (Exodus 5.9)

Devotional Thought: Have you ever been so busy that you didn't have time for good news? I know I have found myself in that situation. Many years ago, as we neared the end of constructing the first house we built, a deadline was looming, and I was under a lot of pressure. I had two pastor friends who would occasionally help me with some tasks. One morning, one of them showed up as I was frantically working to install some locksets. I thought, "Oh, great! Now I won't get anything done." After trying to make small talk for a while, I finally asked in exasperation, "What are you doing here?" My friend meekly said, "I've come to help you with those locksets, like we said." I felt about an inch tall! In my busyness, I had forgotten that we had arranged to do that!

When Moses showed up to help the Israelites, things didn't go smoothly. Instead of letting them go, Pharaoh put *more* work on the poor Hebrew slaves. Pharaoh's plan was to keep them so busy that they wouldn't have time to worry about going off to worship God. And it worked! The Israelites were not happy! They didn't have time to think about the good news of deliverance that Moses brought to them. I'm sure they felt like I did: "Oh, great! Now we won't get anything done!"

Satan wants us to be distracted and discouraged so that we do not have time to think about the good news of deliverance. Much of our busyness, however, is self-inflicted. We need to step back and remind ourselves that God is our Helper. In the midst of life's pressures, let his deliverance calm your stress and soothe your nerves. He really does love you!

Prayer: Father, thank you for the good news of the gospel. When the pressures of life mount, help me to remember that you are with me. May I keep my mind and soul free enough to receive your peace. Amen.

Psalm of the Day: 55.16-23

Broken Spirits and Stopped Ears
Daily Reading: Exodus 6

> *Moses spoke thus to the people of Israel, but they did not listen to Moses, because of their broken spirit and harsh slavery.* (Exodus 6:9)

Devotional Thought: In this chapter of Exodus, it appears that the mission of Moses to free God's people from Egyptian slavery isn't going well. Far from listening to Moses, Pharaoh has responded with anger to his demands, and is now oppressing the Israelites with an even heavier hand. But this is all part of God's plan, and he is now revealing himself to Moses as he makes promises regarding his people's salvation.

What did the Lord do and promise to do for his people? To name a few just from this chapter...
- I established my covenant (v4)
- I have remembered my covenant (v5)
- I will bring you out from your burdens (v6)
- I will deliver you (v6)
- I will redeem you with an outstretched arm and with great acts of judgment (v6)
- I will take you to be my people, and I will be your God (v7)
- I will bring you into the promised land and give it to you for a possession (v8)

Despite these amazing promises, the Israelites did not listen to Moses, "because of their broken spirit and harsh slavery," (v9). He extends these promises of salvation and redemption to us, as believers in Jesus Christ. What enslaves you, making you unable to hear the truth of God's promises? Is it pride? Addiction? Fear? Doubt? Greed? Their harsh slavery rendered the Israelites unable to hear the saving words of God. Don't let your burdens break your spirit and stop your ears to the promises of God.

Jenny

Prayer: Lord, free us from the bondage of slavery, the heavy and burdensome yokes that we put upon ourselves. May we fully grasp our freedom in your Son, and throw off the chains that bind us, becoming slaves to righteousness alone! Amen.

Psalm of the Day: 56.1-6

Weary of Warm Water
Daily Reading: Exodus 7-8

> *The Egyptians will grow weary of drinking water from the Nile.*
> (Exodus 7.18b)

Devotional Thought: I recently read an article about drugs and poverty in Portsmouth, OH. One of the statements that was so striking was that of a 19 year old addict: "I graduated with honors from high school. I want to join the army and get away. Far, far away. There are so many drugs here. I just don't want to be a part of it." Another one said, "I have no interest in [anything] anymore. I hate men. I just want to get clean and get out of this place." Addiction has become a burden that is unbearable. People trapped in it are weary.

It bear repeating that "sin will take you farther than you want to go, keep you longer than you want to stay, and cost you more than you want to pay."

The Egyptians found that out after they had cruelly enslaved the Israelites for generations. When Moses came to deliver them, God brought plagues upon the Egyptians. One of the plagues ruined their drinking water. They had to drink water from the Nile. It was dirty and tepid. The Egyptians grew weary of it. Their sin had caused a situation that made them miserable. And, as we read through these chapters of Exodus, we will see that this was only the beginning.

Sin ruins our wells. It forces us to drink tepid and dirty waters. We grow weary. But, there is good news! Jesus forgives our sins and gives us fresh, living water to drink: "If anyone thirsts, let him come to me and drink. Whoever believes in me, as the Scripture has said, 'Out of his heart will flow rivers of living water.'" (John 7.37b-38)

Prayer: Jesus, thank you that you are a spring of living water. Deliver us from the tepid and dirty waters of sin and grant that we may come to you and drink. Amen.

Psalm of the Day: 56.7-13

131

The People Paid the Price
Daily Reading: Exodus 9

> *This time I have sinned; the Lord is in the right, and I and my people are in the wrong.* (Exodus 9.28)

Devotional Thought: Our mistakes are not just our own, are they? What we do impacts others. I remember the time running cross country when one of the runners went the wrong way. Others followed. I was too far back to get caught in their mistake, but the ones near the front had some ground to recover!

Athletes make wrong turns and their teams suffer. Politicians say stupid things and their party suffers. Officials make bad decisions and their nation suffers. Parents lead in the wrong direction and their children suffer. You see, "None of us lives to himself, and none of us dies to himself" (Romans 14.7).

God sent sign after sign to Pharaoh. Pharaoh ignored them and went his own way. But, as Pharaoh continued to reject God, he came to a point when he realized that he was wrong. What is striking to me, however, is that Pharaoh confessed not only that he had sinned, but he said, "My people are in the wrong." Because Pharaoh had selfishly refused God's direction, the other Egyptians found themselves in the wrong, too. What a weight to be upon his shoulders! He led a whole nation to ruin!

When leaders go the wrong way, many others end up paying the consequences. How many people have been shipwrecked upon the shoals of their leader's sin! We need to pray for our leaders - both spiritual and national - that they will make wise decisions and go in the right direction. And, we need to determine in our own hearts that we will do what is right so that we don't lead others astray.

Prayer: Lord, we do pray for our leaders, that they would be wise and that they would be righteous. Bring our nation's leaders to you, O God, and make our spiritual leaders strong and holy. Amen.

Psalm of the Day: 57.1-5

Everyone and Everything
Daily Reading: Exodus 10-11

> *"Go, serve the Lord your God. But which ones are to go?" Moses said, "We will go with our young and our old. We will go with our sons and daughters and with our flocks and herds, for we must hold a feast to the Lord."* (Exodus 10.8b-9)

Devotional Thought: As Pharaoh felt the pressure of the plagues, his resistance to allowing the Israelites to go worship began to crack. He opened the door to Moses and asked, "Which ones are to go?" Pharaoh didn't want to allow the families to go with the men, but Moses didn't hesitate to answer the question: "Everyone!" And, not only was everyone to go, they were to take everything!

This is how we are to serve the Lord, with everyone and with everything.

Everyone. Are we doing all we can to ensure that both young and old are serving the Lord? A church is not 'complete' when a generation is missing. When planning our ministries we must include both. The old have something to teach the young, and the young have energy and excitement to share with the old. Too often we think it is an "either-or" situation, but it's not. Everyone must go and serve the Lord! Let's extend that kind of grace to the "other" generation!

Everything. Sometimes we try to compartmentalize our lives and say that certain things are "out-of-bounds" for God. Jesus did not paint that kind of picture for following him. God is not content to be pushed out of certain areas of our lives. As the old gospel song goes, "If He's not Lord of everything, then He's not Lord at all."

Satan will try to get you to question, "Which ones are to go?"- to convince you that you can draw limits around God. But remember, when it comes to serving the Lord, it is for "Everyone!" and demands our "Everything!"

Prayer: Father, forgive me when I try to hold things back from you. Help me to love you with all my heart and soul and mind and strength. Help me to love my neighbor as myself. Help me to serve you with everything and share you with everyone. Amen.

Psalm of the Day: 57.6-11

Fraidy Hole
Daily Reading: Exodus 12

None of you shall go out of the door of his house until the morning.
(Exodus 12.22b)

Devotional Thought: Several years ago, I was talking to my friends Don and Pat and she mentioned that they didn't have a basement, but they did have a "fraidy hole."

"A 'fraidy hole'? What's that?"

"Oh, you know... That's where we go if we're afraid of a tornado coming."

I had never heard a storm shelter called that. But, it made sense. I'm a "fraidy cat" when it comes to tornados!

The Israelites needed their own "fraidy holes" when the plague of death came upon the firstborn of Egypt. God had instructed them to sprinkle the blood of the Passover lamb on the doorposts and lentils of their homes. As long as they were in their homes, they were safe. If they ventured outside of their homes, however, death awaited them. They were secure as long as they stayed sheltered under the blood until the dawning of the morning.

There is coming the dawning of an eternal morning. When that day arrives, death will be forever past. We will be safe in our eternal home. Until then, we are not to go out the door. Outside, nothing awaits us but death. We are to remain inside, "covered by the blood." Thank God for the blood of our Passover Lamb, Jesus Christ! May we never stray outside!

Prayer: Thank you, Jesus, for shedding your blood on the cross. Thank you for forgiveness of sins and for life everlasting. Help me to always remain under the shelter of your blood. Amen.

Psalm of the Day: 58.1-8

Venusian Verity

Daily Reading: 1 Peter 1

> *The tested genuineness of your faith...* (1 Peter 1.7)

Devotional Thought: I am a fan of C. S. Lewis. One of his novels, *Perelandra*, is a work of fantasy in which Ransom, the protagonist, makes a trip to Venus, discovering the Venusian Adam and Eve. The plot revolves around the temptation of Tinidril (the mother of the planet) to spend the night on solid ground - something explicitly forbidden by God. When Tinidril was victorious over that temptation, then Venusian destiny was set. The people of Venus would be allowed to live on solid ground, but only because Tinidril's faith in God proved genuine.

There are some things that come into our lives that test our faith. We may not understand why we have to go through those things. We are often tempted to discount the importance of obedience in times of testing. But, our characters, our destinies are determined by decisions we make in times of testing.

The Apostle Peter recognized that fact. He knew that the faith of those early Christians was being tested. They were rejected by their communities and families. They were persecuted by their government and neighbors. They were confused about the delay of Christ's return. They suffered sickness, death, and economic setbacks. Peter told them, in essence, "Hold on! Your faith is being tested, and the faithfulness you show now will bring about the salvation of your souls. This is a joy beyond measure!"

Child of God, are you experiencing trials? Rejoice! You are not being punished. Rather your faith is being refined and the capacity of your soul is being enlarged. There is great reward for Venusian verity!

Prayer: Father, thank you for your faithfulness. Strengthen me, O Lord, that I may prove faithful to you - even when I experience trials and temptations. Refine me, O Lord, that my heart may be pure.

Psalm of the Day: 58.9-11

Pretty Rocks

Daily Reading: 1 Peter 2

A living stone rejected by men but in the sight of God chosen and precious... (1 Peter 2.4)

Devotional Thought: Not long ago when my grandchildren were visiting, we walked down to "the creek," and they enjoyed picking up some rocks and showing them to me. Do you remember picking up pretty rocks as a child? Some rocks are as common as gravel. Others are as rare as diamonds. Some are of little value. Others are of great value. But, none of them would be described as alive! What could be deader than a stone? To be stone-dead is to be "undeniably dead... lifeless..." (Webster's College Dictionary).

Stones are dead; yet Peter chooses that very metaphor to describe Jesus. But, Jesus isn't just any stone, he is a "living stone!"

As a stone, Jesus is the sure and solid foundation for our salvation. He is immovable, strong, and certain. We can come to him with confidence. But, Jesus is not rigid, unbending, and uncaring. Jesus is living. He is a stone with a heartbeat; he is strength with compassion.

This Stone was rejected by men. So great was the rejection of Jesus, he was tossed aside as worthless by the power players of Rome and Jerusalem. But our Jesus was not forgotten by God. On Easter morning, the Father rolled away the stone of death to release the Stone of Life!

When we come to Jesus, God takes the death out of our stony hearts and makes us alive in Christ. We ourselves become living stones! Then, we are placed side by side with others who have also been made alive in Christ. As Jesus walks with the Father, he stoops down and picks us up and marvels before God at how beautiful, how special, how precious we are.

Thanks be to God!

Prayer: Lord Jesus, you are the Living Stone. Breathe your life and your strength into me, I pray. Help me to live daily, victoriously, joyfully in you. Amen.

Psalm of the Day: 59.1-9

Clothes Make the Man

Daily Reading: 1 Peter 3

> *Let your adorning be the hidden person of the heart with the imperishable beauty of a gentle and quiet spirit, which in God's sight is very precious.* (1 Peter 3.4)

Devotional Thought: Mark Twain once wrote, "Clothes make the man. Naked people have little or no influence on society." That's a jarring thought, isn't it? Americans spend about $250 billion per year in clothing. We give a lot of thought to our outer adornment. What about inner adornment? What about the hidden person of the heart?

We've all known people who look good on the outside, but once we get "close" to them, we realize that inner beauty is lacking. Initially drawn to them, we discover that it is harder and harder to be around them. Of all people, Christians ought to have an inner beauty that draws people to them - and ultimately to Christ.

I wonder what this world would be like if we could go into our closets or open our dressers and pull out words and attitudes and behaviors that adorned the soul. Would there be a market for such a product? Would Americans spend $250 billion on that? Would Christians? We know, of course, the adornment of the soul is not a commodity we can purchase. It is when we clothe ourselves with Christ that we become beautiful on the inside.

What do we look like when adorned with Christ? Peter mentioned "a gentle and quiet spirit." The Apostle Paul said it considers others' needs above our own. I think we could add the fruit of the Spirit to that: love, joy, peace, patience, kindness, goodness, faithfulness, gentleness, and self-control.

It is true that clothes make the man or woman. But it's not the clothing on the outside. What are you wearing on the inside today?

Prayer: Jesus, you are beautiful to me. Help me to be clothed in you so that I may possess imperishable beauty. May my words, attitude, and behavior reflect your beauty in this world. Amen.

Psalm of the Day: 59.10-17

Suffering's Expiration Date

Daily Reading: 1 Peter 4-5

> *Yet if anyone suffers as a Christian, let him not be ashamed, but let him glorify God in that name.* (1 Peter 4:16)

Devotional Thought: Peter wrote his letters to encourage Christians in intense persecution. He did this by reminding them that they were blessed when they suffered and should rejoice to share in Christ's sufferings.

Most of us have never experienced intense persecution, fearing for our lives or the lives of our family members. In many areas of the world, however, sharing your faith is literally a matter of life or death. Thanks to the relative religious freedom we enjoy in the United States, most of us will never have to choose between our faith and life itself. And yet, in many ways we still suffer for holding on to the truth as it is given to us in God's Word. Increasingly, Christians are called on to soften their views of sin, to broaden their acceptance of sin within the church, and to simply tolerate their neighbors, rather than loving them (and exposing them to the gospel that some would consider highly offensive). Sadly, many have fallen victim to this "watered-down" form of Christianity, which isn't even remotely like what Jesus preached.

What are we to do as believers? Stand strong in love without shying away from the truth, because it is life-giving. Do not overlook your own sin, but acknowledge that we are all broken, sinful humans without the grace of Jesus. Rejoice in sharing our small part of suffering for Christ, letting it change our hearts and increase our gratitude. Rest assured that all suffering has an expiration date. "And after you have suffered a little while, the God of all grace, who has called you to his eternal glory in Christ, will himself restore, confirm, strengthen, and establish you," (1 Pet. 5:10).

Jenny

Prayer: Lord, in our lives we will face trials, persecution, and suffering. Use these experiences to draw us closer to you, to create in us hearts of compassion, and to glorify you.

Psalm of the Day: 60.1-5

With Him on the Holy Mountain
Daily Reading: 2 Peter 1

We ourselves heard this very voice borne from heaven, for we were with him on the holy mountain. (2 Peter 1.18)

Devotional Thought: Have you ever had an experience of God that you will never forget? The Apostle Peter did. One day Jesus asked Peter, James, and John to go with him up the mountain to pray. They saw a vision from heaven - Moses and Elijah talking with Jesus. They heard the voice of God himself saying, "This is my beloved Son; listen to him" (Mark 9.7). What a privilege! That experience never left Peter. Even here in 2nd Peter - his last preserved correspondence - Peter remembers it as if it had happened that very day.

I asked myself as I read this scripture - How long since I have heard "this very voice borne from heaven?" How long since I've spent time "with him on the holy mountain?"

Jesus had chosen just three of his disciples to go with him that day to the mountain. At that time, he was limited by geography and space. Now that he has ascended to heaven, he has no such limitations. He wants every one of us to ascend the holy mountain and hear the voice from heaven. The limit now is with each one of us. What am I willing to do? How far am I willing to go? What will I leave behind in order to have communion with him?

One morning I had a cancellation in my schedule which enabled me to attend a district meeting. Since they were not expecting me anyway, I decided not to go, opting instead to spend some extra time in my devotions. Lana told me, "I'm surprised you didn't go." I was somewhat surprised, too, but I knew that I needed to be with Jesus on the holy mountain.

How about you? Do you need to be with him on the holy mountain?

Prayer: Jesus, help us - in our self-imposed business and importance - to lay aside all hindrances and to go with you to the holy mountain. May we shut out all other voices that we may hear the voice from heaven. Amen.

Psalm of the Day: 60.6-12

The Age of Clarity
Daily Reading: 2 Peter 2

For, speaking loud boasts of folly, they entice by sensual passions of the flesh those who are barely escaping from those who live in error. They promise them freedom, but they themselves are slaves of corruption. (2 Peter 2.18-19a)

Devotional Thought: The Apostle Peter, writing to The Church, was incensed. False prophets blurred the lines between right and wrong, holiness and sin. Enticing through fleshly desires, they drew gullible Christians along a path to slavery and destruction.

Dean Koontz, in his novel *Innocence*, caught the essence of this problem in a politically correct culture: "In those times, life was simpler, and people had a clearer sense of right and wrong than they possessed later. I will call that long-ago period the Age of Clarity. No writer or reader would have imagined that an analysis of a villain's childhood traumas was needed to explain his wickedness, for it was well understood that a life of wickedness was a choice that anyone could make if he loved wickedness more than truth... I lived in the Modern Age, when it was said that human psychology was so complex, the chain of motivations so recondite and abstruse, that only experts could tell us why anyone did anything, and in the end even the experts were loath to render a definitive judgment of any particular person's specific actions..."

We are no longer in the Age of Clarity. "False prophets" tell us that all lifestyle choices are equally valid and that the only really bad thing is to judge certain behaviors as bad. The swing of culture has been dramatic in the last 20 years. What was once clearly wrong is now heralded as heroic. The voices are growing louder, and we have not yet seen the bottom of this moral abyss.

It is vitally important for Christians to spend time on the mountain and hear the voice of God. The Word of God is the true light that will help us navigate these days of darkness.

Prayer: Father, help me to know your Word and to listen to your voice. Help me to see through the lies of the enemy and to stand on the Rock of truth - Jesus Christ. Amen.

Psalm of the Day: 61.1-8

3G? Yes!

Daily Reading: 2 Peter 3

Take care that you are not carried away with the error of lawless people and lose your own stability. But grow in the grace and knowledge of our Lord and Savior Jesus Christ. To him be the glory both now and to the day of eternity. Amen. (2 Peter 3.17b-18)

Devotional Thought: As Peter closed his last preserved correspondence with The Church, his pastoral urge was clearly evident. Having warned against the dangers posed by false teachers, he gives Christians three preventative prescriptions:

Guard... I visit a lot of hospitals and nursing homes. I have read dozens of signs with a variety of wording that promote hand-washing as the single most effective way to prevent the spread of sickness. Even in places of treatment, it is recognized that prevention is better than medication. Just as important as guarding ourselves from the transmission of disease, is the taking care of ourselves spiritually. We guard ourselves by putting off sin and sinful attitudes and by putting on Christ.

Grow... When my grandchild, Ellis, was born in the height of flu season, the pediatrician recommended to my daughter and son-in-law that they avoid taking her places where she would be exposed to sickness. She needed to grow stronger. Growth is a wonderful preventative for the insidious creep of sin. The stronger we are in Christ, the less likely we are to be overcome by sin. We need to grow in *grace* - recognizing that God is the source of all our strength. We need to grow in *knowledge* - recognizing what the dangers are and what we can do to prevent them. This is especially true of new Christians. They should not be exposed to perilous relationships and places until they have had time to grow.

Glory... What will keep us vigilant? Worship! Giving God glory will bring our own souls encouragement and strength. "To him be the glory both now and to the day of eternity. Amen!"

So, try a little 3G today: Guard, Grow, and Glory!

Prayer: Lord Jesus, we want to go beyond surviving to thriving as a child of God. Help us, O Lord, to guard our hearts and to grow in grace and knowledge that you may receive glory! Amen.

Psalm of the Day: 62.1-4

Longcut

Daily Reading: Exodus 13

> *When Pharaoh let the people go, God did not lead them by way of the land of the Philistines, although that was near. For God said, "Lest the people change their minds when they see war and return to Egypt."* (Exodus 13:17)

Devotional Thought: When I moved from Ohio to South Carolina, my route took me through "The Gorge" - a tightly winding portion of I-40 on the Tennessee / North Carolina border. On my first trip, I was pulling a trailer behind the Budget moving truck. I did not relish the thought of going through "the Gorge" with that trailer following me! So, I chose an alternate route. Though I avoided the traffic of Cincinnati and the twists and turns of "The Gorge," it was a longer distance and added considerable time to my journey. It was not a shortcut, but rather a "longcut."

God did the same thing with the Israelites as they left Egypt for Canaan. Rather than taking the simplest, straightest path, God led them on another (longer) way. The Lord knew that his people, spiritually and emotionally weak after their enslavement and recent liberation, could not handle going through the land of the Philistines yet.

I wonder what they thought as God led them through the desert. Did they question him, asking why they had to take the hard way? They were tired, emotionally exhausted, and terrified. But still they followed his way. Because of their obedience, God showed the Israelites and the Egyptians His glory at the Red Sea crossing.

Do we sometimes wonder why God is leading us through a long, winding path that is fraught with difficulties? Take heart – our view of the situation is limited, but God can see exactly where he is leading us. Rest assured that his path for us is always the best way, for our good and for his glory - even if it is a "longcut"!

Jenny (and Pastor Scott)

Prayer: Lord, our way seems so difficult and winding at times. We are exhausted spiritually and emotionally by the journey. But in you we can renew our hope, and run with perseverance the race marked out for us. Give us the strength to do so, and may you be glorified in our journey.

Psalm of the Day: 62.5-12

The Red Sea of Decision
Daily Reading: Exodus 14

> *What is this we have done, that we have let Israel go from serving us?*
> (Exodus 14.5b)

Devotional Thought: Pharaoh and the Egyptians had what I call "EGS" - Engaged Girl Syndrome. That's what potential suitors get when the girl they were casually interested in gets engaged: "Oh, no! I let her get away!" So it was with Pharaoh and Egypt. Even though they practically pushed Israel out, they still panicked. And, as the story goes, they did not let Israel go without another fight at the Red Sea.

Pharaoh and Egypt symbolize Satan and his demons. When a child of the devil gets saved and begins following Jesus, the enemy panics: "I've got to get her back!" Do not be surprised when new Christians face battles and hardships after coming to Jesus. Satan will pursue us as far as the Red Sea of decision.

The Red Sea was the place where Israel first learned to put their complete trust in God. Their deliverance had been miraculous, requiring almost no faith. They were in a position to just walk through the door God had opened. At the Red Sea, however, they had to trust God in the face of the Enemy's onslaught. The good news was, that at that Sea of Decision, they left Egypt behind forever. Other trials would come, but Egypt was through.

I often see Red Sea experiences in people who come to faith. They experience an emotional high with the rush of life and peace that Jesus gives, but they are soon confronted with the ugly power and unrelenting pull of their former life. If they will trust God and pass through the Red Sea, they can defeat that enemy. Others will come, but they have learned that God is faithful.

Are you new to faith or know someone who is? Walk with them through the Red Sea of Decision!

Prayer: Father, thank you that you are faithful. Though the enemy prowls like a roaring lion, help me to trust you, to walk through the Red Sea of Decision. In the powerful name of Jesus, Amen.

Psalm of the Day: 63.1-5

Superhero
Daily Reading: Exodus 15

The Lord is my strength and my song, and he has become my salvation; this is my God, and I will praise him, my father's God, and I will exalt him. The Lord is a man of war; the Lord is his name. (Exodus 15.2-3)

Devotional Thought: After Israel passed through the Red Sea, Moses composed a psalm of praise to God their Deliverer. Moses gave God names that represented what he had done for Israel. It is good to 'name' God - giving him praise for his attributes and actions.

Praise God that he is your...
- *Strength*. Israel had no power with which to pass through the Sea. They were hopelessly trapped. But God had the strength to get them through. Whatever you face, it is not too difficult for God. Remember, "With God, all things are possible" (Matthew 19.26), God is "able to do far more abundantly than all that we ask or think, according to the power at work within us" (Ephesians 3.20), and "I can do all things through him who strengthens me" (Philippians 4.13).
- *Song*. Moses couldn't help but sing. God had put a new song in his heart and his mouth. I love to think of that scene in heaven when we will sing "a new song before the throne!" (Revelation 14.3) But don't wait. God is your song now!
- *Salvation*. Israel was in a mess. Between slavery and the sea, they needed God to save them. And he did! God looks upon us with compassion. Whether the mess is our own making or not, he saves us if we call upon him. Praise him for his abundant mercy!
- *Superhero*. That's basically what *Elohim* - the word for God used here - means. God was 'larger than life.' As he had been for their fathers, so now was God for them. Remember, God is your superhero!
- *Soldier*. The Lord is a man of war. He does not shrink back from the battle. Jesus went to the cross to utterly defeat Satan! He fights for us every day! Hallelujah!

Prayer: Oh Lord, you are my strength, my song, my salvation, my superhero and my soldier! I praise you, my God! Jesus has won the victory for me. I am today a winner, because of what Jesus has done and is doing for me now. Amen.

Psalm of the Day: 63.6-11

Between Certainties
Daily Reading: Exodus 16

> *All the congregation of the people of Israel came to the wilderness...*
> *And the whole congregation of the people of Israel grumbled...*
> (Exodus 16.1-2)

Devotional Thought: Have you ever been in a wilderness? Geographically, it is a wild place - uninhabited and untamed. I've never really been in a wilderness like that. There is, however, a spiritual wilderness, a frightening place - unknown and uncomfortable. I have been there. It is a place between certainties. Jesus went into the wilderness when he began his ministry. For him it was a place of triumph, but only after dark temptation.

The children of Israel had their own wilderness. They had told Pharaoh that's where they needed to go to worship God. But, when they "came to the wilderness... the whole congregation grumbled." This wilderness was between Elim - their first stop after deliverance - and Sinai - the place where they would learn how to live holy lives, pleasing to God. They grumbled because they were hungry and they didn't trust God or Moses to provide for them. In spite of their doubts, God fed them with manna and quail.

At times, we are between certainties. We face temptations. We've been delivered, but do not know exactly how to live to please God. In short, we are in the wilderness. The wilderness can be an overwhelming place. If we are not careful, we can begin to doubt God and even to regret his deliverance. "I was better off before I was saved!"

What advice would I give you if you are in the wilderness, when you are between certainties? First of all, resist that grumbling spirit. Second, follow God's instructions even when they don't make sense to you. And finally, keep moving. Don't camp there! Certainty awaits you. God is faithful.

Prayer: Lord, there are times when I struggle to see you, to understand your will. Help me, O Lord, to not give up. Help me to keep moving through the wilderness. Thank you, Jesus, that you have prayed for me that my faith would not fail. Amen.

Psalm of the Day: 64.1-10

Jehovah Nissi

Daily Reading: Exodus 17

> *Moses built an altar and called the name of it, The Lord Is My Banner.*
> (Exodus 17.15)

Devotional Thought: I love the story in Exodus 17 of how Israel defeated Amalek. The Amalekites had come out against God's people to destroy them. But, Moses sent Joshua - his general - out to lead the battle against them. Moses himself went up on the mountain to pray along with Aaron and Hur.

Moses' hands grew weary. His prayers grew faint. But there stood beside him his brother, Aaron, and a young man named Hur. They encouraged him - even to the point of holding up his weary hands. Israel prevailed that day because of a brave general, a godly leader, and two faithful intercessors who held up the hands of that leader. It was a team effort! But, the most important member of the team was God himself. Moses displayed that when he built an altar to the glory of God and called it "The Lord Is My Banner" - Jehovah Nissi.

The enemy has come against us, hasn't he? We are called upon to engage the battle against Satan. Our struggle is not against flesh and blood but against powers and principalities. Thank God for godly leaders and faithful intercessors who help us in the battle. These are key ingredients to our spiritual success. But above it all there is the banner of the Lord. He unfurls his banner over the battlefields of our lives and wins the victory.

What are your battles today? Do not be weary or discouraged. Lift up your eyes to the hills from whence comes your help. The Lord is your banner over you today. Jehovah Nissi!

Prayer: "The Lord is My Banner!" You have won the victory at the cross of Jesus Christ and at the empty tomb. Help me to look to you today - and to be victorious! Through Jesus Christ my Lord, Amen.

Psalm of the Day: 65.1-8

Why Do You Sit Alone?

Daily Reading: Exodus 18

Why do you sit alone? (Exodus 18.14)

Devotional Thought: Don't you just love in-laws? I know that I do! I thank God for giving me a wonderful mother and father-in-law who gave me love and counsel as a young man. Never pushy, they were instead wonderful examples of godliness, industry, and thrift. My life is better because of them. Moses could say the same thing about his father-in-law, Jethro. He came out to meet his son-in-law and found Moses hard at work, 'judging' the people.

When Jethro saw the long lines waiting on Moses, he said, "What you are doing is not good... You are not able to do it alone" (vv. 17-18).

Jethro reminded Moses some things that every Christian worker needs to remember:

- God will be with you (19)... If we get our eyes off the enormity of the task and onto the enormity of God, the task will seem so much smaller. Jesus has sent us a Helper - the Holy Spirit. Rely on him!
- Able men will be with you (21)... God has equipped servants and leaders in the church with abilities and strengths to complement our own. When we work without the help of others, we short-circuit God's plan.
- The people will be with you (23)... When God's people see their leaders including them, they will get behind the project and the leaders! Having the people with you is like having the wind at your back, filling your sails.

God has called us all into his service. When we try to do it alone, we grow weary. We burn out. We fail to see results. The question is, "Why do we sit alone?" There's no need to. For God is with us, other helpers are with us, and the people of God are with us.

Prayer: Thank you, Lord Jesus, that you are Emmanuel, God with us. Thank you for giving people skills and abilities to serve you. Thank you for the people that I serve. Help me to open my eyes to these wonderful facts and to never sit alone. Amen.

Psalm of the Day: 65.9-13

Moses Spoke

Daily Reading: Exodus 19

As the sound of the trumpet grew louder and louder, Moses spoke.
(Exodus 19.19a)

Devotional Thought: Lana and I have always looked at the ministry as a partnership. She actually works harder and is more effective than I'll ever be! She almost always knows what I've been up to, and when I get home from a long day, she greets me at the door ready to talk. Usually I don't have too many words left, but I'm thankful that she's interested in what I have to say! So I talk.

When God called Moses and the Israelites to the mountain to give them his Law, "the sound of the trumpet [God's voice] grew louder and louder." That is to be expected. What is unexpected, at least for me, is the next two words: "Moses spoke." In the midst of all the awesome displays of God's presence, Moses had the audacity to speak!

What Moses did must have pleased God, for the scripture says...
- *God answered him...* God was not offended by Moses' impertinence. He wanted him to talk! God desires to have a conversation with all of us!
- *The Lord came down...* God was so excited that he closed the distance between them. A shout across the valley wouldn't do! He wanted to be close to Moses. When we pray, God comes down to be with us. Hallelujah!
- *The Lord called Moses to the top of the mountain...* God invited Moses to grow in his experience with him. He didn't leave Moses at the foot of the mountain, but said, come on up here where you belong! Our place is not in the valley of defeat and doubt, but on the mountaintop of glory!

What did Moses do? He went up. What will you do?

Prayer: Thank you, Lord, for the sound of the trumpet that calls me to prayer. Help me to speak to you from my heart. Answer me. Come down to me. Call me higher up the mountain. I will follow you. Amen.

Psalm of the Day: 66.1-7

To Fear or Not To Fear...

Daily Reading: Exodus 20

> *Moses said to the people, "Do not fear, for God has come to test you, that the fear of him may be before you, that you may not sin."* (Exodus 20:20)

Devotional Thought: At Mount Sinai, God revealed his Law, his character, and his holiness to the people of Israel. Was Moses calmly standing at the base of that mountain, holding the two tablets containing the Ten Commandments? Hardly. The description we are given in Exodus 20 is a terrifying scene: Thunder, flashes of lightning, the sound of trumpets, a smoking mountain, and thick darkness. The people were literally trembling, as was the entire mountain!

Moses and Aaron were the only ones allowed to approach God on Mt. Sinai, and I can't imagine the courage it would have taken to climb up that mountain! Moses' words to the Israelites may seem contradictory at first: "Do not fear, for God has come to test you, that the fear of him may be before you, that you may not sin." The Lord does not want the Israelites to be terrified of him, but he does want them to have a "fear" – a reverence and respect – for him. He is their Father who loves them and has claimed them as his people, and yet they needed to realize his holiness, for their own good.

Do we fear the Lord? He is our good Father, and we are heirs to his kingdom. He loves us and has given everything to be reconciled to us. But he is also holy, majestic, and glorious beyond our imagination. As believers, we may "with confidence draw near to the throne of grace, that we may receive mercy and find grace to help in time of need," (Heb. 4:16). This does not mean that we casually or irreverently "saunter up" to our holy God, but that we humbly recognize our freedom that is only found in the righteousness of Jesus Christ.

Jenny

Prayer: Lord, thank you for providing a way to you through your Son, Jesus Christ. It is only by faith, through grace, that we can be saved, claim our identities in you, and approach your throne with confidence.

Psalm of the Day: 66.8-15

Most Vulnerable and Least Protected
Daily Reading: Exodus 21

> *When men strive together and hit a pregnant woman, so that her children come out... If there is harm, then you shall pay life for life.* (Exodus 21.22-23)

Devotional Thought: Protection and justice loom large in the chapters of Exodus following the Ten Commandments. Throughout these chapters of Exodus, we find an over-arching concern for the most vulnerable and least protected classes of society.

Some of the rules sound strange to us because we read them through the lens of 21st Century America. For instance we read the admonitions about slavery and wonder why the Bible seemingly justifies the practice. Through the eyes of an ancient slave, however, the protection afforded was significant. (Remember, too, that the term 'slave' connotes a wide variety of indentured servitude and employment contracts as well as what we would typically think of as a slave.)

We need to look for the principles as they are expressed within the framework of a nomadic 15th Century BC culture. It is exciting and enlightening to read these chapters asking the question, "What underlies this practice?"

One such principle is that the life of an unborn child is equally valuable as that of another person. The unborn needed to be singled out for protection because they were the most vulnerable. They had no voice in government, no powers of coercion, no means of protecting themselves. But in Exodus 21, God spoke out for them! A person who caused the death of a child *in utero*, was liable to the death penalty just as if they had murdered someone on the street. *You shall pay life for life.*

Are we protecting the most vulnerable in our midst?

Prayer: Father, open my eyes that I can see and open my mind that I can understand the principles underlying the rules found in Exodus. And help me to be a voice of protection for the most vulnerable of our society. Amen.

Psalm of the Day: 66.16-20

Impossible Power
Daily Reading: Acts 1

> *But you will receive power when the Holy Spirit has come upon you, and you will be my witnesses in Jerusalem and in all Judea and Samaria, and to the end of the earth.* (Acts 1:8)

Devotional Thought: Acts, authored by Luke, was written as an encouragement for the early church, and it serves that purpose for today's church as well. The stories in Acts reveal the Spirit at work bringing life and revival. Indeed, we can accomplish nothing eternal or significant without him!

Jesus' followers were still trying to grasp what had happened with his death and resurrection and asked him, "Lord, will you at this time restore the kingdom to Israel?" (v6). Then, as Jesus literally ascends into the clouds of heaven, the disciples are left standing in slack-jawed amazement. It is almost humorous to imagine! Jesus left them with this, "It is not for you to know times of seasons that the Father has fixed by his own authority. But you will receive power when the Holy Spirit has come upon you..." (v7-8).

He didn't leave them waiting and wondering for long. In just a few weeks, the day of Pentecost arrived; the day that the Holy Spirit came to the world to indwell all believers - giving them spiritual understanding, wisdom, supernatural love, unspeakable joy in unlikely circumstances, and the power to forgive and love their enemies, to name a few benefits! These believers (and all who have come after) were charged with taking the gospel message to the whole world, empowered by the Spirit.

Jesus knew that his disciples would face suffering, persecution and even death, so the spread of the gospel would have been humanly impossible without the indwelling power of the Spirit. We too need this power - the power to forgive the undeserving, to love the unlovable, to reach the unreachable. Just as we will see all throughout Acts, these things are possible with the gift of the Holy Spirit.

Jenny

Prayer: Lord, help us to realize and embrace the power of the Spirit that you gave us in our own lives. May he be evident on our very faces to all those who encounter us, and may the love that we have for others draw the unbelieving to you. Amen.

Psalm of the Day: 67.1-7

And Suddenly

Daily Reading: Acts 2

> *When the day of Pentecost arrived, they were all together in one place. And suddenly there came from heaven a sound like a mighty rushing wind, and it filled the entire house where they were sitting. And divided tongues as of fire appeared to them and rested on each one of them.* (Acts 2: 1-3)

Devotional Thought: What an action packed chapter in God's Word! It was a day of fulfillment of prophecies of the prophet Joel, Jesus and John the Baptist. These verses in Acts chapter 2, are the only biblical reference to the actual events of Pentecost.

It was not a sprinkling. It was a major outpouring of the Spirit, a significant event in the life of the church. It was here the disciples witnessed the birth of the New Testament church in the coming of the Holy Spirit to indwell all believers. The Day of Pentecost also saw the first converts to the Christian church. When Simon Peter delivered his sermon proclaiming that Christ had risen, some three thousand people became converted. (v. 41)

What does it all mean for us today – the coming of the Holy Spirit, the sounds of mighty rushing wind, the forked tongues of fire, the powerful preaching of Peter, speaking in other languages? It means the Spirit of God has come and is here with us today. That same Pentecostal power is ours. The Comforter has come and is here to guide us into all truth. The Holy Spirit continues the ministry of Jesus. It's a ministry of salvation, hope, renewal and refreshment. Jesus is in heaven, but his ministry empowered by the Spirit continues.

Pastor Dale Noel

Prayer: Father in heaven, thank you for sending your Spirit to dwell among us and for filling us with power to do your work. May our lives display the fruit of the Spirit as we follow you. Amen

Psalm of the Day: 68.1-10

Helping Others through Prayer
Daily Reading: Acts 3

> *"In the name of Jesus Christ of Nazareth, rise up and walk!" And he took him by the right hand and raised him up, and immediately his feet and ankles were made strong. And leaping up, he stood and began to walk, and entered the temple with them, walking and leaping and praising God.* (Acts 3.6b-8)

Devotional Thought: My friend, Barb, who was being treated for cancer, told me "When I am too weak to pray for myself, or even to think straight, it is such a comfort to know that there are people helping me with their prayers."

In Acts 3, as Peter and John went to the temple to pray, they encountered a man who was crippled from birth. He was carried there every day by family and friends so that he might beg. He was otherwise helpless. In this story we find that people of prayer can offer...

- *Hope*. Peter did not hesitate to speak hope in the name of Jesus. Too often we look for hope in earthly names. In hopeless situations, there is hope in the name of Jesus - the Psalmist said, "Do not put your trust in princes..." (Psalm 146.3) Are you - or is someone you know - facing a hopeless situation? Speak the name of Jesus!
- *Help*. Because Peter and John were faithful to pray, they were in the right place at the right time to offer help to the crippled man. Peter took him by the hand and lifted him up. Prayer compels us to get our hands dirty helping the helpless. If we are not willing to lift a hand to help another, we should not waste our time praying for them.
- *Healing*. The best help of all was restoring the man to health. It was complete healing - physically, emotionally, spiritually. As we pray in the name of Jesus, people will be healed. James said that we are to pray and anoint in the name of the Lord Jesus and that the prayer of faith will heal the sick!

Let us commit to help others through our prayers.

Prayer: Lord, thank you that there is power in the name of Jesus. Help me today to offer that hopeful, helpful, healing power to those who need you. Lord, I believe. Help my unbelief! Amen.

Psalm of the Day: 68.11-18

Can't Put a Lid on It!
Daily Reading: Acts 4

> *For we cannot but speak the things which we have seen and heard.*
> (Acts 4:20)

Devotional Thought: Oh, my goodness, Peter! Back in the Gospel of John we see you denying Jesus three times. We all have a tender place in our hearts for Peter because if we are honest, we would have to admit that we, too, have on occasion denied Jesus. Certainly not the same circumstances, but denial nonetheless. And, now in Acts we see a different Peter. Verse 13 says, "Now when they saw the boldness of Peter and John and perceived that they were unlearned and ignorant men, they marveled: and they took knowledge of them that they had been with Jesus."

From where did this boldness come? Well, the author tells us in an earlier verse, "Then Peter, filled with the Holy Ghost..." (4:8). There you have it. This Peter, who once cowered when faced with questions regarding his relationship with Jesus, is now not only speaking boldly, but refuses to keep quiet when ordered to do so! Yes, he boldly says, "I have to speak the things which we have seen and heard." Wow! No cowering now! He and John did not have a choice - they were compelled to speak!

We, like Peter, can speak boldly when we share the love of Jesus with others. We seek first to be filled with the Holy Ghost before we reach out. We, as believers, have all been with Jesus. Therefore, we should be unable to keep a lid on it! We should be telling and sharing!

Tutti Beasley

Prayer: Lord, fill me with the Holy Spirit that I might be a bold witness for your kingdom. I pray that your goodness and your Presence in my life would compel me to share my faith!

Psalm of the Day: 68.19-27

Lies' Destruction

Daily Reading: Acts 5

> *Ananias, why has Satan filled your heart to lie to the Holy Spirit?*
> (Act 5.3)

Devotional Thought: One does not have to be a scholar of world history to know that many great nations are destroyed by internal strife and not by the enemy from outside the nation; sadly, we are seeing that today in our own nation where honesty and civility have been cast aside. Telling the truth is just one option, and not telling the truth, if it helps your cause, is another option.

In Acts chapter 5, the church is being attacked both internally and externally. We conclude that Ananias and Sapphira were part of the believing church, but we learn they were more interested in looking good than telling the truth. How generous of them to give so much money, in fact all of it, from selling their land! Except they didn't. They kept back part. They lied about it. Doesn't it beg the question "how did they think they could lie to God and get away with it?" They didn't understand the true nature of a God that is sinless. The god they were listening to rather enjoyed lies. Ultimately, they were called into account.

Sometimes, as in this case, God's answer and judgment are immediate and severe. At other times, when it appears no one noticed our lie, we believe another lie: that we got away with it. Except we didn't. The lie is not erased, and we stand in judgment until confession is made to our loving, but Holy God. From the beginning, lies have been a powerful tool of Satan. We often prepare the ground for those lies with envy, greed and other deceptions of the heart. When God, in his wisdom, made a dramatic example of Ananias and Sapphira, he demonstrated how seriously he views lies, for the destroy both lives and congregations.

Joanne and Larry Powell

Prayer: Father, thank you that we have your word to live by and for the indwelling presence of your Holy Spirit to convict us when we turn our eyes away from your truth. Give us courage to confess our failures and faith to receive your forgiveness. Amen.

Psalm of the Day: 68.28-35

I'm Not Smirking Inside!

Daily Reading: Acts 6

> *And gazing at him, all who sat in the council saw that his face was like the face of an angel.* (Acts 6.15)

Devotional Thought: "You're smirking!" That's what my wife told me a few weeks ago when we were playing a table game and I was winning. I apologized and told her I didn't mean to be smirking, but I don't think she believed me. The sad thing was that my smirks just came right on through even when I tried to stop them.

Stephen, the first Christian martyr, had a similar experience, but instead of a smirk, he couldn't hide the angelic expression on his face. He was on trial before the council - on trial for loving Jesus! - and as those angry men gazed at him, heavenly glory shone on his face. I don't know about you, but I think I would have had a different expression on my face. I would have had a hard time concealing fear and anger.

What shines through you when the heat is on? When you are being unjustly accused, does your face shine like an angel? When you get blamed for someone else's mistake, does God's grace show through? When you are not getting the attention and service you think you deserve, do you display patience?

"I'm not smirking inside!" is sometimes the only answer we've got. For the fact is, we cannot always control what our faces are "saying." What we can do, however, is to control what is in our hearts. Like Stephen, may our hearts be filled with love - love for Jesus and love for those around us, even our accusers!

Prayer: Holy Spirit, pour your love into my heart right now. Fill me with heavenly glory so that those who see me will catch a glimpse of you. Amen.

Psalm of the Day: 69.1-5

The Real Hero

Daily Reading: Acts 7

And Stephen said: "Brothers and fathers, hear me..." (Acts 7.2)

Devotional Thought: Stephen, the first Christian Martyr, was a hero. He preached the longest sermon that Luke recorded in Acts. That makes him *my* hero!

There is so much contained in Stephen's heroic sermon, made under threat of death. Stephen argued his points for Christianity from Israel's history as recorded in the Old Testament:

- First, the activity of God is not confined to the geographical land of Israel. God spoke to Abraham in Mesopotamia and Haran. God blessed Joseph in Egypt. God spoke to Moses in the desert near Sinai during the incident with the burning bush. God performed wonders and signs in Egypt, the Red Sea, and the desert, and God gave His people the law at Mount Sinai.
- Second, worship that is acceptable to God is not confined to the Jerusalem Temple. The burning bush was holy ground, and Moses had to remove his sandals there. Moses encountered God on Mount Sinai and was given the living word. Stephen states that God was independent of any temple.
- Third, the Jews had constantly rejected God's representatives. Joseph was rejected by the patriarchs. Moses was rejected when he tried to intervene in a quarrel with two Jews. Yet God in his grace sent Moses to be Israel's deliverer.

All of this points to Jesus: 1) Jesus showed us that our God is not confined to one area or one person. He can reach us anywhere, and he can hear us from anywhere as well; 2) Jesus also taught that real worship that pleases God is from the heart. 3) Jesus is living (and dying and living again!) proof that our God never leaves us nor does He forsake us.

Jesus is the real hero!

Pastor Steve Sears

Prayer: Lord, help us to know you are always present in our lives even though sometimes we may not see what you are doing behind the scenes. Help us to know we can worship you anywhere at any time and that you will never leave us nor forsake us. Amen.

Psalm of the Day: 69.6-12

Miracles Still Happen
Daily Reading: Acts 8

> *But Saul was ravaging the church, and entering house after house, he dragged off men and women and committed them to prison.* (Acts 8:3)

Devotional Thought: Saul's savagery and hatred, revealed in the first three verses of Acts 8, is enough to take your breath away. It is hard to believe that this Saul would later become one of the strongest, most mature Christian men of his time, forfeiting his own life to preach the gospel!

While we marvel at the miraculous transformation of people in the early church, do we believe that God is still working these miracles? The church of today has developed a cynicism – a belief God cannot change people in today's culture. Miracles are rare and met with skepticism. People are blind to the work of the Lord. It is true that we face unique challenges in the church; addiction, busyness, half-hearted faith (which is to say a lack of faith) to name a few. But do these obstacles really compare to what the early church was facing? They were being martyred for their faith, and yet they were converting in droves!

Saul would later come to faith in Jesus, and would go from the persecutor to the persecuted. He knew well what he would face with his conversion to Christianity, and yet he still boldly proclaimed his faith. Why? As he tells the Philippians, "Indeed, I count everything as loss because of the surpassing worth of knowing Christ Jesus my Lord. For his sake I have suffered the loss of all things and count them as rubbish, in order that I may gain Christ," (Phil 3:8).

Church, do not become blind or cynical to the miracles of transformation that are happening all around us. Any time one comes to a saving faith in Christ, a miracle has occurred. Let us pray for those miracles daily!

Jenny

Prayer: Lord Jesus, help us to see the miracles you are performing daily around us... let us not be blind to your Spirit's work. Help us to boldly proclaim the name of Jesus, and move the hearts of those around us to believe and become part of your Kingdom.

Psalm of the Day: 69.13-21

Suddenly...

Daily Reading: Acts 9

> *Now as he went on his way, he approached Damascus, and suddenly a light from heaven shone around him. And falling to the ground, he heard a voice...* (Act 9.3-4a)

Devotional Thought: Have you ever tried to busy yourself so that you could put something out of your mind? We do that, don't we? Saul did it. Having witnessed the hateful and unjust execution of Stephen - along with Stephen's forgiving attitude - Saul furiously persecuted the church. Attempting to get Stephen out of his mind, Saul went to a foreign city to arrest Christians, to stomp out the church.

There was one thing, however, that Saul didn't consider. He may have seen the light of Stephen snuffed out, he may have silenced the voices of Christians he had imprisoned, but he could not extinguish the light of the Spirit or muffle the voice of God.

This happened as Saul...
- *Went on his way*. We've tried it. We've attempted to ignore the voice of God and just keep focused on life, on our plans, our agendas, our prejudices. We've seen people who are "too busy" for God or for church. They fill their lives with so many things that they don't have time to think about God.
- *Approached Damascus*. Saul's hatred was about to get exponentially worse. I've seen that happen so many times. People's spirals into sin and away from God come to crisis point.
- *Suddenly saw a light from heaven...* Saul had run as far as he could. He had ignored God as long as possible. Now Christ invaded his consciousness. He spoke. He stopped Saul. He saved him.

Do you know people like Saul, people whose hearts are set against God? Be encouraged and pray for them. Pray that the light of God will shine and the voice of God will speak. May the Spirit bring conviction!

Prayer: Jesus, you said the Holy Spirit would convict the world in regard to sin. I pray for _____, that he/she would see the light of God shining and hear the voice of God speaking. May they fall to their knees in surrender to you. Amen.

Psalm of the Day: 69.22-28

Up-and-Outers
Daily Reading: Acts 10

> *A devout man who feared God with all his household, gave alms generously to the people, and prayed continually to God.* (Acts 10.2)

Devotional Thought: Yesterday we read about Saul's conversion - a man who was hateful and violent toward the Church and Christ. Today, however, we read of a different kind of conversion - that of a generous and kind man: Cornelius, the Roman soldier.

Cornelius is described as devout. He was a moral man, a decent man. He feared God and led his family to do the same. He gave money to people who needed help. He prayed regularly. Cornelius even knew about Jesus (v. 37).

But, something was missing. Cornelius didn't know Jesus. He hadn't met Jesus. He didn't believe in Jesus as the Messiah of God and the Savoir of men. So, God sent Peter to this wonderful man to tell him and his family "that everyone who believes in him receives forgiveness of sins through his name" (v. 43). When Cornelius - this moral man, this upright citizen - heard that, he believed and received forgiveness of sins! Then, he was filled with the Holy Spirit!

This story reminds me of what Jesus said, "No one comes to the Father except through me" (John 14.6). No amount of goodness or generosity can save us. It is only by the blood and in the name of Jesus that we can be saved.

When we think of those who need Jesus, we tend to think of the "down-and-outers" - immoral, uneducated, socially rejected. But, the "up-and-outers" need Jesus, too! They might not have "as far to go," but their journey may be more intense - just as Cornelius had to be very intentional about responding to the vision God gave him.

So, when you pray for the lost, don't forget those who are "not far from the kingdom of God."

Prayer: Father, I pray that you would speak to the hearts of people who are morally good. Help them to see that they cannot count on their own goodness to get them into heaven. Show them that Jesus is the only true Way. Amen.

Psalm of the Day: 69.29-36

No Good Deed Goes...

Daily Reading: Acts 11

> *Now the apostles and the brothers who were throughout Judea heard that the Gentiles also had received the word of God. So when Peter went up to Jerusalem, the circumcision party criticized him, saying...* (Acts 11.1-2)

Devotional Thought: "No good deed... goes unpunished!" I once read a story about a University of Georgia Alumnus who found a wallet lost by a UGA student. It didn't turn out well for the Alumnus. He was accused of stealing the wallet and the $500 that was in it! The guy was just baffled. "You try to do something good, and then..."

I wonder if that phrase was in use when Peter was called on the carpet - by church people no less! - for winning people to Christ. He had gone in response to a vision from the Holy Spirit, and preached the gospel to Gentiles. The legalists of "the circumcision party" did not like that. "What business did you have of going into the home of a Gentile!?" Some Jews thought themselves too good to associate with ungodly Gentiles.

What did Peter do? Did he admit his error? Did he buckle under pressure? Did he just decide it wasn't worth it? Did he get angry with those hypocrites in the church? No! With grace and simplicity, he defended his position and patiently explained what happened.

Thankfully, the established Christians back in Jerusalem were open-minded and realized that it was they who were wrong. "When they heard these things they fell silent. And they glorified God" (Acts 11.18). They not only changed their mind, they publicly acknowledged their mistake and allowed the church to go in a new - and for them uncomfortable - direction.

I'm so glad that somebody took a chance on me! I was one of those 'unsaveables', but the folks at Pioneer Church of the Nazarene didn't care. They loved me and won me to Christ. Aren't you glad someone did that for you?

Prayer: Jesus, thank you that you died for my sins and that you have invited me into your family. Help me to be gracious and courageous enough to extend that invitation to those who may seem "unsaveable" to me and others. Amen.

Psalm of the Day: 70.1-5

Let's Get Going!

Daily Reading: Acts 12

> *And behold, an angel of the Lord stood next to him, and a light shone in the cell. He struck Peter on the side and woke him, saying, "Get up quickly." And the chains fell off his hands.* (Acts 12.7)

Devotional Thought: Today, my friend is released from rehab. I'm so excited to see her! I have been writing her and talking to her on the phone, but have not been able to see her in person for 4 months! Many times I have wished that I could bust her out and go get a burger and fries - her favorite meal! But, we just had to wait until the right time – God's time - for her to get out.

In the book of Acts, we read about how Peter was arrested and put in jail. I like what it says in Acts 12.5: "The church was earnestly praying to God for him." Suddenly it was the right time. God answered their prayers, and Peter was busted out by an angel of the Lord. Consider the symbolism of this "break-out."

The angel was...
- *Standing*. Have you ever felt that you were all alone? That all your friends had deserted you? Remember that Jesus is still with you. He will stand with you when no one else will. And, in that final judgment, he will stand up for you before the throne of God!
- *Shining*. When you don't know the way out, look for the light of God! He will show you the way so you can follow.
- *Striking*. There are times when we are trapped in the slumber of despair and doubt. God sometimes has to shake us to wake us. No matter how much we want to sleep through that wake up call, we need to respond when God is moving.
- *Speaking*. Yes, God is saying something. Listen to that still small voice. Read his Word. Search out the meaning. What is God saying to you right now?

Let's get going!

Prayer: Lord, I confess there are times when I get bogged down in my discouragement and depression. Forgive me, O Lord, and help me to see that you stand beside me. Shine your light to guide me. Awaken me and speak your will. I will follow you out of my prison of darkness and despair. Amen.

Psalm of the Day: 71.1-8

Keep Your Eyes Open
Daily Reading: Acts 13

They did not recognize him nor understand the utterances of the prophets, which are read every Sabbath. (Acts 13.27)

Devotional Thought: Have you ever had that experience of seeing someone but not recognizing them? It often happens when you encounter them outside "their setting." It's happened to me before. People from church run into me outside the church, and they look right past me. If I "get in their face," they usually start and say, "Oh, Pastor! I didn't see you." They actually saw me, but they didn't recognize me.

When Paul was preaching in Acts 13, he described how that very thing happened to Jesus. Although people saw Jesus, they did not recognize Jesus. I think that we can learn from their experience.

Jesus was preached "in the synagogue" which would be parallel to our "church" today. Over the course of centuries, faithful expositors of God's Word had preached about the coming Messiah. The Jews of Jesus' generation were in a perfect place to encounter him. Yet, they missed him. We must be careful of missing Jesus right in our own churches.

They "did not recognize Jesus." They had an idea of where and how they would see the Messiah. Jesus did not fit their expectations. He was not in the right context. Do we confine Jesus to the church and block him from the rest of our lives? He has something to say to us every day in every situation!

They did "not understand the prophets." Through his Word, God has given plenty of signs of what the coming Messiah would be like. But, people tend to read the scripture through the lens of their own prejudices and preferences. To truly encounter Jesus, let the Bible speak in your context. Do not force your context onto the Bible.

Jesus is near. Keep your eyes open!

Prayer: Lord, help me not just to see you, but to recognize you. Free me from my prejudices and preferences, and help me to receive your message from the most unlikely of sources. Amen.

Psalm of the Day: 71.9-16

Who Is Sitting Near You?

Daily Reading: Acts 14

> *Now at Lystra there was a man sitting who could not use his feet. He was crippled from birth and had never walked.* (Acts 14.8)

Devotional Thought: Staying at a hotel in a strange city, I made sure the door was closed – which automatically locked it. Then, I slid the security chain in place. After that, I turned the thumb lock, engaging the dead bolt. Safe... No wait... I undid the dead bolt, slid the chain off, opened the door and hung out the "Do not Disturb" sign! Nothing like a piece of cardboard to keep you safe from those dangerous housekeepers! My motto? When it comes to safety, redundancy pays off!

When it comes to communicating a spiritual truth, redundancy often pays off as well. Luke used it when he wrote that the lame man in Lystra... was sitting... could not use his feet... was crippled from birth... had never walked... All this redundancy has a spiritual message for us:

- *Sitting.* The lame man was sitting for real and practical reasons. He could not stand! We need to remember that the spiritually sick can do little more than sit. God, in his grace, sends us to see them, to minister to them, to invite them.
- *Cannot use feet.* Oftentimes we say that "The Lord helps those who help themselves." The fact of the matter is, the chains of sin cannot be broken except by the blood of Jesus! It's all grace!
- *Crippled from birth.* Wow. We need to remember that people are born with this debilitating condition we call sin. It's all they know until the light of Jesus penetrates their darkness.
- *Never walked.* When attempting to do something for the first time, we are all unsteady. We must patiently help those who would get up and walk. They will succeed, but they need our help!

Are there people "sitting" near you?

Prayer: Father, help me to see that those who are crippled by sin need your grace, just as I do. Help me also to see that they need my help, not my judgment. Amen.

Psalm of the Day: 71.17-24

On What Are We Standing?

Daily Reading: Acts 15

> *So when they were sent off, they went down to Antioch, and having gathered the congregation together, they delivered the letter. And when they had read it, they rejoiced because of its encouragement.* (Acts 15:30-31)

Devotional Thought: As the early church found its legs, they needed to determine on what they would stand. While they did believe in Jesus, some Jews were finding it difficult to grasp that Jesus came to fulfill the requirements of the Law, and that Christians were no longer bound by it.

Such was the case in the passage we read today, as some of the Jewish converts insisted on circumcising the Gentile converts. Centuries of tradition and religious requirements were hard to let go of. Peter made clear that this needed to happen: "God, who knows the heart, bore witness to them, by giving them the Holy Spirit just as he did to us, and he made no distinction between us and them, having cleansed their hearts by faith," (v8-9). The council's letter that was sent to Gentile believers was met with great joy and relief!

Do we meet the news of the gospel with the same joy? Or are we trying to live out our faith bound by legalism, just in case some of our deeds and works will be judged before the Throne at the end of our lives? It is true that we should strive for holiness – that is what the Lord calls his followers to do! But if we are *relying* on our own righteous deeds to save us, we are in trouble. As Paul would say in Romans 3, "None is righteous, no, not one... no one does good, not even one."

We can and should live holy lives to please the Lord. It is when we start relying on our own holiness to save us that we need to let the Lord change our hearts.

On what are we standing?

Jenny

Prayer: Lord, we know that our good and selfless deeds please you and further your Kingdom. Please keep us from the pride that can ensnare us. You are the only Savior we can trust – nothing we can do will be sufficient to cover our transgressions, so let us clothe ourselves with your righteousness, trusting only in you.

Psalm of the Day: 72.1-7

What to Do in a Dark Place
Daily Reading: Acts 16

> *About midnight Paul and Silas were praying and singing hymns to God.*
> (Acts 16.25a)

Devotional Thought: Have you ever been in a dark place? Paul and Silas found themselves in a very dark place in Philippi. They had been falsely accused, unjustly arrested, viciously beaten, and thrown into jail. As a matter of fact, the jailer "put them into the inner prison and fastened their feet in the stocks." I don't think that we can really appreciate what that was like. The jails of Paul's day were dark and cruel places. No light was provided. It was always dark.

And, Paul and Silas were in the *inner* prison - where no light would ever penetrate. Their feet were in stocks - where no comfort could be found. To top it off, it was midnight! Where no hope could be found. But they found hope. They felt comfort. There flared an inner light. And they sang. Yes, they sang!

I've been in dark places before. It was hard to sing. It was hard to pray. I've been with my people - those I love and serve for the sake of Christ - in very dark places. Prayers and songs are sometimes hard to come by.

What did Paul and Silas do? In the darkness of the inner cell - unable to see their hands in front of their faces, with their feet in stocks - unable to find any comfort, in the depths of the night - uncertain if morning would ever come for them, they prayed! "When they prayed, they felt a joy rising within their hearts. This caused them to break forth into singing. Sincere prayer always leads ultimately to praise. And praise dispels the gloom." (Earle, *BBC*, Acts, 450)

When you're in a dark place, remember to pray. Let your heart sing. God will dispel the gloom.

Prayer: Father, thank you for your faithfulness. In the dark places of my life, help me to pray. And when I do, put a song in my heart. May your light fill my gloomy nights. Amen

Psalm of the Day: 72.8-16

Is Your Spirit Provoked?

Daily Reading: Acts 17

His spirit was provoked within him. (Acts 17.16)

Devotional Thought: If you watch the news on television or read it online, you probably have times when you feel like screaming. "These people are nuts!" The world sometimes doesn't make any sense. We see obvious solutions that the world runs *away* from! Our spirits are provoked within us by the absurdity of it all. What should we do?

What did the Apostle Paul do when facing that situation in Athens in Acts 17?

Paul reasoned with them (v. 17). Paul did not ridicule; he reasoned. Ridicule slams the door. Most people I know - including myself - don't like to be called stupid. Reasoned and calm dialogue works a lot better. People shouting over each other may garner TV ratings, but it doesn't lead to communication. It just leads to noise!

Paul conversed with them (v. 18). Since he wanted them to listen, Paul listened to them. As the saying goes, God gave us two ears and one mouth for a reason! Having two ears actually helps us locate where a sound originates. When we listen intently, we understand where someone is. When we talk, we don't have a clue as to another's position. How can we hope to respond effectively? The Bible says, we are to be quick to hear and slow to speak (James 1.19). That's hard to do when we are "provoked," but that is just what we need.

Paul preached the gospel (v. 18). Having reasoned and conversed, Paul was in a better position to preach. There is a time and place for speaking! Too often we rush into the "preaching" (testifying, witnessing, etc.) mode when people are not ready to hear. But, when the time is right we need to speak up! After all, Jesus said the rocks would cry out if we didn't!

Prayer: Lord, may my spirit within me be provoked by the errors of the world. And when I am provoked, grant me wisdom and patience to communicate your Truth. Amen.

Psalm of the Day: 72.17-20

Though He Knew Only...
Daily Reading: Acts 18

> *[Apollos] had been instructed in the way of the Lord, and being fervent in spirit, he spoke and taught accurately the things concerning Jesus, though he knew only the baptism of John.* (Acts 18.25b)

Devotional Thought: Is it time for a little more fervency and accuracy in the house of the Lord? Then, we need more people like Apollos.

Apollos was instructed in the way of the Lord. We need to know the Bible, but beyond that we must "rightly handle the word of truth." Great error comes when people know just enough of the Bible "to be dangerous." Apollos had apparently undergone the discipline of careful study and training. When I was an aspiring minister, an older pastor told me, "The call to preach is a call to prepare." Theology does matter!

Apollos was fervent in spirit. He believed what he preached. He had experienced it firsthand. He knew Jesus. That changed his life! Can people tell that you know Jesus? A little excitement is called for among the people of God.

Apollos spoke and taught accurately. Is it enough to know the Truth and be animated by the Truth? Do we not need to speak the Truth? Apollos fed the flock of God and fostered a feeling of excitement by what he said. Keeping it to himself would have been unacceptable.

Apollos seemed to be the perfect pastor. But, something was missing. Human wisdom (instruction) and enthusiasm (fervency) and dynamic preaching could only take him so far. What was missing? Apollos knew only the baptism of John. That was the baptism of repentance. John had said there was another baptism, a baptism administered by Jesus himself. It was the baptism with the Holy Spirit!

I am convinced that is what we need in our churches and in our lives today. It changed Apollos. It changed the church he served (Ephesus in Acts 19). "Have you received the Holy Spirit since you believed?"

Prayer: Lord Jesus, you have saved me. Thank you! Now, I pray that you would baptize me with the Holy Spirit and fire! Purge the dross from my life that I may shine with your glory. Fill me with your Spirit that I may have power to serve you. Amen.

Psalm of the Day: 73.1-11

Though He Knew Only...
Daily Reading: Acts 19

There were about twelve men in all. (Acts 19.7)

Devotional Thought: In Acts 19, the Apostle Paul met the church that Apollos had pastored in Ephesus. It was a small group, about 12 men. Something was about to change, however.

God has a way of opening and closing doors at just the right time, doesn't he? As we read in Acts 18, Apollos had led them accurately and fervently, but then God called him off to Corinth. The congregation in Ephesus needed to 'release' Apollos in order to embrace Paul. It was a natural step in their spiritual growth. God's plan is always unfolding for his people who must step from one place to the next.

I like what Ralph Earle wrote about the Ephesian church in *The Beacon Bible Commentary*. The people in Ephesus were "Walking in the Light":
- They repented according to the preaching of John the Baptist. When confronted with sin and its devastating effects, the only right response is repentance - a complete turning away.
- They were baptized as Christians under the ministry of Paul. Having had repented, but not fully understanding the gospel message, they still needed to follow Christ in baptism. This they did at the hands of the Apostle.
- They were filled with the Holy Spirit. Repentant and obedient, the Ephesians were ready to be filled with the Spirit. Nothing stood between them and this glorious spiritual baptism.

Something amazing happened. This tiny congregation, now filled with the Spirit, turned their community upside down. Thousands came to know the Lord. The church in Ephesus became the leading Gentile church of that day, second in influence only to the church in Jerusalem. It is still a pattern for churches and Christians today. To be effective, we must be repentant, obedient, and filled with the Spirit.

Prayer: Father, thank you for your grace freely given through Jesus Christ your Son. I turn away from all sin and consecrate myself completely to you. Fill me with your Holy Spirit. Amen.

Psalm of the Day: 73.12-20

Wake Up!

Daily Reading: Acts 20

> *And a young man named Eutychus, sitting at the window, sank into a deep sleep as Paul talked still longer. And being overcome by sleep, he fell down from the third story and was taken up dead.* (Acts 20.9)

Devotional Thought: I love reading the story of Eutychus in Acts 20. If the Apostle Paul had trouble keeping his listeners awake, then I don't have to feel bad! As is typical for preachers, Paul "talked still longer," and as often happens to church members, Eutychus "sank into a deep sleep."

Eutychus' slumber and near-tragic ending paint a spiritual picture:

- Eutychus sank into sleep. It was a gradual process. It was not something that happened quickly and obviously. Spiritual slumber is like that. Sitting at the "windows", we become spiritually distracted. Unaware of what is happening, we lose track of where we are, and little by little, we fall asleep.
- Then, however, "overcome by sleep," Eutychus fell. From his lofty position, he toppled all the way to the ground and was "taken up dead." When we are spiritually asleep, it is not long until the gravity of sin takes over, and pulls us downward. No matter how high we are, spiritual sleep has only one result: a spiritual crash. And, the higher we are the harder the fall.
- But that was not the end of Eutychus' story. "Paul went down and bent over him, and taking him in his arms, said, 'Do not be alarmed, for his life is in him'" (v. 10). Though Eutychus was dead, there was a spark of life that could be revived. There is a point of no return when death becomes permanent, but Eutychus had not yet reached it. With Paul's quick response and ardent faith, Eutychus was revived. We in the church - who are awake! - must respond in the same way. We are not called to reject the spiritually sleepy, but to revive them.

To ourselves and those we love, we cry, "Wake up!"

Prayer: Lord, help me to stay spiritually awake. And help me, also, to prayerfully and courageously revive the spiritually sleepy. Through Jesus who lives forevermore. Amen.

Psalm of the Day: 73.21-28

Four Daughters

Daily Reading: Acts 21

He had four unmarried daughters, who prophesied. (Acts 21.9)

Devotional Thought: There are some churches today who prohibit women from preaching. Apparently the church in Caesarea, home of the evangelist Philip, had no such scruples. Philip's daughters 'prophesied' or preached. I admire them. Let's have a little fun and give them names today.

Let's call the first one *Obedience*. To prophesy, one had to carefully listen to God and courageously proclaim his Word. Prophets were often ignored and scorned, or even persecuted. And those were the male prophets! I can imagine it would have been easy to write off the women preachers. But Obedience did not flinch from her calling.

Let's call the second *Confidence*. This prophetess had great faith. First of all, she believed in God. But, she also believed in God's ability to work in her and through her no matter what obstacles she faced. Confidence leaned into God and boldly fulfilled her calling.

Let's call the third *Persistence*. Sailing into the wind of church culture can be hard. It would have been easy for Persistence to give in and give up. But she didn't. She stuck with it. Persistence walked with Obedience and Confidence over the long haul.

Let's call the fourth *Forbearance*. When we face resistance, we often find ourselves getting angry. Forbearance looked at things differently. She didn't lash out at those who disagreed with her. She understood their fears and remembered that she was sister to them, serving the same Lord.

Are you facing headwinds in your life and calling? Remember Philip's daughters! Oh, and let's not leave the Caesarean church out. Let's call it *Acceptance*. It realized that in Christ, "There is neither Jew nor Greek, there is neither slave nor free, there is no male and female, for you are all one in Christ Jesus."

Prayer: Lord, I thank you for giving me a purpose in life. When I face difficulties and resistance to my calling, help me to be obedient, confident, persistent, and forbearing. Amen.

Psalm of the Day: 74.1-8

Why Me?

Daily Reading: Acts 22

And I fell to the ground and heard a voice saying to me, 'Saul, Saul, why are you persecuting me?' And I answered, 'Who are you, Lord?' And he said to me, 'I am Jesus of Nazareth, whom you are persecuting.' (Acts 22:7-8)

Devotional Thought: This chapter of Acts provides us with a summary of Paul's conversion from Saul, the man who had persecuted Christians. He stands before a Roman tribune and tells of his experience and interaction with the Living God. He admits his involvement with the imprisonment and beating of innocent Christians, specifically his approval of the killing of Stephen. He speaks as a man who knows that he has been offered unconditional forgiveness, even though he himself acknowledges that he is "the chief of sinners."

When Jesus appeared to Paul (then Saul) on the road to Damascus, he identifies and describes himself in a somewhat surprising way. He says to Saul, "I am Jesus of Nazareth, whom you are persecuting." Jesus speaks in the present tense – Saul had not persecuted him during his life on earth, but was currently persecuting him through the way he was treating Jesus' followers.

What a comforting thought to us – when we are persecuted for our beliefs, or suffer as Christians, Jesus takes that suffering onto himself. We can rejoice as we share Christ's sufferings, that we may also rejoice and be glad when his glory is revealed (1 Pet 4:13). As our Savior, and as our heavenly Father, He claims our sorrows and trades our yokes for his own, for His yoke is easy and His burden is light (Matt 11:30). "For just as the sufferings of Christ overflow to us, so also through Christ our comfort overflows," (2 Cor. 1:5).

Jenny

Prayer: Lord, help us to remember that we share in your sufferings to be glorified with you in the future. Help us to remember that you share in our sufferings, surrounding us with songs of deliverance as we trust in you.

Psalm of the Day: 74.9-17

Car Thief

Daily Reading: Acts 23

> *And Paul said, "I did not know, brothers, that he was the high priest..."*
> (Acts 23.5a)

Devotional Thought: You've heard the one about the policeman who pulled a woman over. When he approached the window, she was not happy. She said, a bit peevishly, "Officer, what's wrong? I know I wasn't speeding."

"No, ma'am, but I saw you shaking your fist and screaming at the guy who cut you off. Then I noticed your 'What Would Jesus Do?' bumper sticker, and I assumed the car was stolen..."

That's what happened to the Apostle Paul in his trial before the Sanhedrin. The high priest had ordered that Paul be struck. Since, the high priest's actions were unjust and impious, Paul reacted rather harshly himself. Paul told the high priest that God would strike him! That caused quite a stir in court: "Would you revile God's high priest?" So, Paul explained that he had not realized it was the high priest.

Didn't know he was the high priest? How could Paul say that? The high priest was sitting in the right place, wearing the right clothes, and receiving the respect and adulation of those around him. How could Paul be confused about his identity? The only thing that it could have been were the high priest's actions. He was not acting like a high priest, so he must not be the high priest.

We can say all the right words, dress in the right way, be respected by the right people, but if our actions say otherwise, people will not know that we are followers of Jesus Christ. As a matter of fact, they will assume that we are not. I want people to know I am a Christian not just by my words, but by my actions - especially the way I treat others!

Prayer: Lord Jesus, live in me with such power that all my actions and words will be a reflection on your holy character and forgiving love. May people always see you in me! Amen.

Psalm of the Day: 74.18-23

Limited Time Offer

Daily Reading: Acts 24

> And as he [Paul] reasoned about righteousness and self-control and the coming judgment, Felix was alarmed and said, "Go away for the present. When I get an opportunity I will summon you." (Acts 24.25)

Devotional Thought: This is a "Limited Time Offer!" I really don't like that phrase. I feel if the sales price is good today, it ought to be good tomorrow. At the same time, there are things that are, by their very nature, "Limited Time Offers." Raising children is one. We have to take advantage of opportunities while they are young to train them up in the way they should go. Taking care of our health is too. We need to eat right, exercise and rest properly before our health declines. Studying for a test has a time limit, does it not? On test day the time for preparation is past! Preparing for retirement by saving, investing, and foregoing spending is a "Limited Time Offer."

The Apostle Paul reasoned with Felix about his spiritual state and the coming judgment. Consider the offer...

- Felix was *warned*. And not only was he warned by Paul, he was warned by the Holy Spirit, for he was 'alarmed,' indicating spiritual conviction. The Bible says that we are accountable for the good that we know yet fail to do.
- Felix *wrestled*. Time and again, Felix called for Paul to discuss spiritual matters with him. But he could not get past his greed to seriously consider surrendering his life to Christ. Felix had a comfortable life and he knew that following Christ would jeopardize his contentment.
- Felix *waited*. Over the course of two years, Felix kept putting off his decision for Christ. There is no record of Felix ever having believed in Jesus. When he was succeeded by Festus, it would seem that his best opportunity for salvation was past. He missed his "Limited Time Offer."

What about you? Are there things you need to do concerning God? Do not miss your "Limited Time Offer"!

Prayer: Father, thank you for giving me this day. I know it will never come again. Help me seize this day with you. I give myself to you. Live in me today. Amen.

Psalm of the Day: 75.1-5

I Appeal to Jesus!

Daily Reading: Acts 25

> *But if there is nothing to their charges against me, no one can give me up to them. I appeal to Caesar.* (Acts 25.11b)

Devotional Thought: In chapter 1 of the Old Testament book of Job, we read how Satan accused Job of serving God only because of the blessings. The rest of the book relates the story of Job's struggles and appeal to God's faithfulness. As it turned out, there was nothing to Satan's charges against Job. No evidence could be found to convict Job. In the New Testament, Paul faces a similar situation before a human court. He appeals, "If there is nothing to their charges against me, no one can give me up to them. I appeal to Caesar." No evidence could be found to convict Paul.

What a great picture of our salvation in Jesus! Satan charges us before God. He "throws the book" at us. Every sinful thought, word or action is presented as evidence. But, it turns out that there is nothing to these charges against us. Jesus, our Advocate, presents evidence to the contrary. All the charges have been taken away. The verdict is officially entered into the court record: "not guilty."

When we are declared "not guilty" by Jesus, there is no further court of authority. The verdict stands. No one can give us up to our enemy. Death and judgment stand condemned and we are innocent.

In the Great Judgment, Jesus will represent us. When we stand before God, we can say, "I appeal to Jesus!" Amen!

Prayer: Jesus, thank you that you are my Advocate with the Father. I thank you that you have taken all my sins and all my guilt away. And with them, you have removed all punishment. I have only one appeal, and it is to you! Help me to trust in you and live for you every day. Amen.

Psalm of the Day: 75.6-10

Seize the Day!

Daily Reading: Acts 26

But rise and stand upon your feet, for I have appeared to you for this purpose. (Acts 26.16)

Devotional Thought: When you read the book of Acts, you get the sense that Paul was a man with a mission. He was driven by the love of Christ. In his testimony before King Agrippa, we get a glimpse of "God's purpose for Paul" (*Beacon Bible Commentary*). It was...

- *Active.* Although Paul was a deep thinker, God did not call Paul to a life of quiet contemplation. At the outset he made this clear with action words: "Rise... Stand on your feet... I appoint you as a servant..." Even when he was in situations of forced inactivity, he was busy fulfilling God's purpose, writing letters to individuals and churches, letters that captured much of the New Testament's theology and Christian practice.

- *Progressive*: Like Abraham before him, God's purpose for Paul was constantly unfolding. God told him he would be "witness to the things... in which I will appear to you." There was always something more for Paul to learn. He did not have a final picture when he set out, but instead he had a faithful Partner.

- *Effective*: God did not call Paul simply to go through the motions. His was not a ceremonial function, but a practical function. God worked through Paul to get results: people with opened eyes, turning from darkness to light, turning from Satan's power to God's power, receiving forgiveness of sins and sanctifying grace. And, the record is clear. Paul's work resulted in people saved, churches planted, pastors trained, and lives changed.

As you think about God's purpose for you, remember it is active, progressive, and effective. Then go, seize the day!

Prayer: Lord, I consecrate myself to your purpose. Reveal your will to me and enable me to follow it. Fill me with your Spirit and with power to the glory of your name and the completion of your will. Amen.

Psalm of the Day: 76.1-7

South Winds Blow Softly

Daily Reading: Acts 27

Now when the south wind blew softly... (Acts 27.13a)

Devotional Thought: "The calm before the storm." You've experienced it. The Apostle Paul did, too, as he was on his voyage to Rome. They had already had some difficulty on the voyage, and they were running way behind schedule. So, "when the south wind blew softly," the ship's captain was lured into setting off. It proved a disastrous decision, with loss of ship and cargo. Thankfully, all of the passengers were saved.

I came across the following in the *Beacon Bible Commentary* (p. 573):
"The clause when the south wind blew softly has significant ... application. When young people are lured out of the safe harbor of home, the church, and the standards of the New Testament by the softly blowing winds of seductive worldly pleasure, they are apt to be caught by howling hurricanes and find their frail barks driven furiously across life's sea to be wrecked somewhere on the shores of time. On the basis of this passage one could well say: 'Watch out for those south winds that blow softly.'"

Are there soft winds blowing in your life? We must be careful about what wind fills our sails. The Bible says that "there is a way that seems right to a man, but its end is the way to death" (Proverbs 14.12). The soft winds that bring pleasure and repose today may result in pain and regret tomorrow. Know from whence the winds blow and to where they will take you.

Prayer: Lord, help me to recognize the south winds that blow softly. Help me to avoid them and to allow your Spirit to fill the sails of my life, taking me into the future you have prepared for me. Amen.

Psalm of the Day: 76.8-12

Convinced
Daily Reading: Acts 28

Some were convinced by what he said, but others disbelieved.
(Acts 28.24)

Devotional Thought: In 2016, some were convinced that President Trump obstructed justice. Others said, "No way!" No matter what the evidence, the membership in either camp did not seem to change. The same was true about Hillary Clinton. If you liked Hillary, she didn't do anything wrong with the private server. If you didn't like her, she deserved to be in jail. The lines in our political world are drawn sharply, aren't they? People make up their minds about a person depending on whether there is an (R) or a (D) after their name. People are in one camp or the other.

When Paul preached Jesus in Rome, "Some were convinced... but others disbelieved." Paul preached the same thing to both the believers and the unbelievers. Seeing the same evidence, they reached vastly different conclusions. They remained sharply divided.

The same is true today. Some will be convinced while others will not believe. Ralph Earle wrote this: "To one or the other of these two classes we each belong. The same fire melts wax and hardens clay; the same light is a joy to sound eyes and agony to diseased ones; the same word is a savor of life unto life and a savor of death unto death; the same Christ is set for the fall and for the rising of men, and is to some the sure foundation on which they build secure, and to some the stone on which, stumbling they are broken, and which, falling on them, grinds them to powder." (*BBC*, 591)

Are you convinced by Jesus?

Prayer: Lord, open my eyes and show me your truth. Help me to see Jesus and to believe on him for eternal life. Amen.

Psalm of the Day: 77.1-9

We Are All Sojourners

Daily Reading: Exodus 22

You shall not wrong a sojourner or oppress him, for you were sojourners in the land of Egypt. You shall not mistreat any widow or fatherless child. If you do mistreat them, and they cry out to me, I will surely hear their cry. (Exodus 22.21-23)

Devotional Thought: Was your heart moved by pictures of Central American immigrants atop trains? Were you somewhat conflicted? I was. Today's immigrant and refugee crises are complicated. We are torn between national security and compassion.

That is not a new dilemma. Even in the Bible, there were distinctions made (sometimes not successfully! See Joshua 9...) between 'sojourners' and those who would threaten the godly heritage of the faith community. Those ungodly influences were a national security threat to Israel. We see that played out vividly in the books of 1 and 2 Kings.

The undisputable fact, however, is that God is for the disenfranchised and the vulnerable of society. Further, he wants his people to champion the cause of these defenseless victims of powers and principalities. We saw that yesterday in God's concern for the unborn. Today, we see it in his concern for the sojourners.

Sojourners are literally 'strangers.' These are the different, the new, the unknown among us. Human nature, when motivated by fear, will naturally react against that which is 'strange,' oftentimes in oppressive ways meant to afford protection. God says, however, that we are not to mistreat them for he will hear their cry.

Back to refugees and immigrants. There is not an easy solution, but vetting out dangerous elements certainly is not illegitimate. Read the New Testament in regards to protecting the flock. But it is a principle that God is for the true sojourner. All of us are in reality sojourners, passing through this world on temporary visas. Let us react in love and compassion to the unknown among us.

Prayer: Father, thank you that you loved me while I was a stranger to your grace. Help me to love the sojourner and to be a voice for the neglected quarters of society. Amen.

Psalm of the Day: 77.10-15

A Snare to You

Daily Reading: Exodus 23

> *You shall make no covenant with them and their gods. They shall not dwell in your land, lest they make you sin against me; for if you serve their gods, it will surely be a snare to you.* (Exodus 23.32-33)

Devotional Thought: Yesterday we read about sojourners and God's concern for them. Today, we see the other side of that concern. Just as God was concerned with the safety and dignity of the most vulnerable of society, he was also concerned with the health and vitality of the people. God knew that if his people 'made covenants' with the inhabitants of the land, that they would follow them into sinful practices, including the oppression of the vulnerable! So, God established protections for Israel, the flock of his care.

I happen to live in a sleepy little village that is 99% Anglo. At first glance there is little about multi-culturalism to be concerned with. There are socio-economic differences, however. And there is the whole sub-culture of addiction. What is the principle that guides us? Are there threats about which God is concerned?

Let's look at it through a spiritual and moral frame. What 'covenants' should I avoid in that regard? Are there activities and people that I should avoid in order to protect my life of love, generosity, holiness, and grace? I have a lot of friends who are addicts who tell me that they simply have to leave behind their former friends because those relationships will cause them to relapse. I also know that unguarded viewing of the internet has led many people astray when it comes to pornography. For others, there are living arrangements that threaten to undermine their testimony and godliness.

What things will you face today - relationships, activities, mindsets, etc. - that pose a threat to your spiritual health? God says we are not to make a covenant with those things! Don't even let them in the door!

Prayer: Father, help me to hold dear those things that are dear to you. Help me to avoid those things that are at odds with your kingdom values. Give me strength to resist temptation and wisdom to avoid it. Amen!

Psalm of the Day: 77.16-20

The Sanctuary
Daily Reading: Exodus 24-25

Let them make me a sanctuary, that I may dwell in their midst.
(Exodus 25.8)

Devotional Thought: When Lana and I moved to Bethel in 2009, we built a home with lots of rooms, including a basement. We then worked hard over the course of several years to finish the basement. Why do that for two people? I think you suspect the answer. We did it so that our children and grandchildren could come and be with us! We wanted a space where we could all get together.

In the Old Testament, God wanted a space where he could get together with his family - the people of Israel. So, he instructed them to build him a sanctuary. They did so and called it the Tabernacle, or tent of meeting. It was a very sacred place. God met them there.

In the New Testament, however, that changed. God now 'tabernacled' among men and women in Christ. Christ identified himself as the temple and brought God close.

But now that Christ has ascended to the Father, the sanctuary has changed yet again. God still desires to have a sanctuary that he may dwell in the midst of his people, but that sanctuary is now the Church, the body of Christ. The Apostle Paul wrote, "Do you not know that you are God's temple and that God's Spirit dwells in you?" (1 Corinthians 3.16). When we neglect the church, we neglect the sanctuary and we miss a significant opportunity to be in the presence of God.

So, let us 'make God a sanctuary.' Let us be faithful to meet God in the Church.

Prayer: Jesus, thank you for building me into your Church. Help me to fully enter and support the sanctuary where you dwell, not a temple made with human hands, but the Church of the living Christ. Amen.

Psalm of the Day: 78.1-8

The Curtains and the Clasp
Daily Reading: Exodus 26

Couple the curtains one to the other with the clasps, so that the tabernacle may be a single whole. (Exodus 26.6b)

Devotional Thought: Though it may not be the inspired meaning of the ancient text, still I love to see symbolism in the Old Testament. When I read that the tabernacle - an aid for worship and a reminder of God's presence in the wilderness - was made of "ten curtains of fine twined linen," my mind went to the church, the New Testament tabernacle.

We are curtains coupled together...
- *Denominations.* God could have instructed that the tabernacle be made of one huge curtain. Instead, for the sake of portability, he had the Israelites make it of 10 smaller curtains. Ten individual curtains could navigate the wilderness much easier than one huge curtain. But, when it ultimately mattered - they were joined. Denominations serve as a way to make The Church portable in the wilderness of humanity. Denominations make it possible for The Church to go to all cultures and world areas.
- *Differences.* The 10 different curtains were designed to be united into a single place of worship. The ones on the left were as valuable as the ones on the right. The ones in the rear as valuable as the ones in the front. God puts liberals and conservatives, leaders and followers, rich and poor, Americans and Asians together in one Church.
- *Disciples.* I love the many different people in my church. Just like there would have been a gap in the tabernacle without all the curtains, so there would be a gap in our churches without all the individuals. One disciple couples to another to make the whole!

And, of course, thank God for the Clasp of Jesus Christ that ties us all together!

Prayer: Thank you, Lord, for the Church of Jesus Christ! Though we are many and varied, we are one in Jesus! Help us to value and appreciate each 'curtain' of the whole! Amen.

Psalm of the Day: 78.9-16

183

Give That the Light May Shine

Daily Reading: Exodus 27

> You shall command the people of Israel that they bring to you pure beaten olive oil for the light, that a lamp may regularly be set up to burn. (Exodus 27:20)

Devotional Thought: Through Moses, God instructed the Israelites to bring pure beaten olive oil for the light that was positioned in front of the veil and that was to be tended by Aaron and his sons 24/7 – the light that never went out.

This would have taken much oil! Notice the Lord's command is addressed to the Israelite people as a whole. This seems to be a risky command, almost certain to fall to "everyone else." Oil was very costly and not easily obtained in these days. Relating this to our own experience, pretend you have a friend in need of a large sum of money. Would you not be more likely to respond to the friend's plea for help if the request came directly and specifically to you, rather than a mass email to everyone on their contact list? And yet the Lord chose to place this burden on the people as a whole, rather than on specific tribes or clans.

The Israelites miraculously responded with incredible generosity! We see in Exodus 36, how generous they were feeling at this point in time: the men who were collecting the necessary items for the Tabernacle came to Moses and said, "The people are bringing much more than enough for doing the work that the Lord has commanded us to do," (Ex. 36:5). They had to be restrained from bringing any more (v6)! Do we give that joyfully or sacrificially? Or do we count on others to pull the weight and give what is needed? Believers, let us give cheerfully and generously, and watch as the glory of the Lord fills His temple!

Jenny

Prayer: Lord, open our eyes to the needs that exist around us. Help us to give from a cheerful heart, knowing that the sacrifice is eternal, because it was done with a heart of love towards you.

Psalm of the Day: 78.17-31

Judge from the Heart
Daily Reading: Exodus 28

> *So Aaron shall bear the names of the sons of Israel in the breastpiece of judgment on his heart, when he goes into the Holy Place, to bring them to regular remembrance before the Lord.* (Exodus 28.29)

Devotional Thought: "What? Don't you care about missions?" As soon as the words were out of my mouth I regretted saying them. I had reacted in a moment of frustration, but there was no way to explain away my words. And I paid for them. Dearly. Judgment was rendered according to the evidence, and I was found wanting. How I wished that I could take back my words. But, short of that, how I desired that judgment could have come from the heart rather than the mind.

God directed Moses to prepare the priestly garments for Aaron, the High Priest. Part of those garments was a breastpiece inscribed with the names of the twelve tribes of Israel. It was a *breast*piece of judgment. Not a turban - indicating the mind - of judgment. Not a visor - indicating the eyes - of judgment. It was a breastpiece of judgment, indicating the heart.

What wonder that our God who sees and knows all, judges us from the heart! By the grace of God, he sees our hearts and passes judgment based on the work of Christ on our behalf. Love is the guiding principle in his judgments.

We would be well-served to judge from our hearts and not our minds nor eyes. Let love be your guide as you consider the actions and words of your brothers and sisters in Christ. If we go strictly by the evidence, we will all be found wanting. Seen in the light of the mercy of Christ, however, our judgments will be more tolerant and forgiving.

Prayer: Father, thank you for seeing me through the eyes of love. Help me to extend that same grace to others so that I'm not critical and condemning. In Jesus' name, amen.

Psalm of the Day: 78.32-39

Fore!

Daily Reading: Exodus 29

> *There I will meet with the people of Israel, and it shall be sanctified by my glory.* (Exodus 29.43)

Devotional Thought: I enjoy watching golf on TV. Yeah, I can almost hear you say, "Boring!" - but it does help me catch up on my sleep! At times, the camera shows the golfers going to the next hole. They generally proceed within a roped-off area with fans on either side. These fans, of course, have their hands extended to receive a 'high five' from the passing star. I am amused by this desire to be acknowledged by the golfers. I get a little sad when I see the fans that are bypassed.

Our culture longs to be in the presence of greatness. In Exodus 29, God gave Moses instructions about the altar and the Tent of Meeting. Day by day, God said they were to offer their sacrifices and meet with him. Then he says that this place of meeting "shall be sanctified by my glory" (v. 43). This innate longing to be in the presence of Greatness is answered by the glory of the Lord. How often I pray for God to shower us with his glory when we come together in worship. To be in the presence of Greatness!

Do you long for the glory of God in your life and church? Better yet, do you pray for it? I think our prayers are like those golf fans who line up along the ropes - hands extended - in hopes of brushing up against greatness. Prayer puts us in the right place, with the right attitude.

May God sanctify our lives and our churches with his glory! Get ready and get those hands out!

Prayer: Lord, I am excited to go to church today to worship you. Come in your glory, O God! I reach my hands out to you in prayer and faith. Meet with all of us today. Amen.

Psalm of the Day: 78.40-49

Remembering Before God

Daily Reading: Exodus 30-31

> *And Aaron shall burn fragrant incense on it. Every morning when he dresses the lamps he shall burn it, and when Aaron sets up the lamps at twilight, he shall burn it, a regular incense offering before the Lord throughout your generations.* (Exodus 30.7-8)

Devotional Thought: I often bemoan the distractions of smart phones, but whenever I open my phone, the latest picture of one of my kids or grandkids pops up on the screen. Inevitably a smile comes to my face, and I get distracted from my original intent. I'm so glad that my children have sent me those distractions to brighten my days!

Do you think that God enjoys distractions? I think so, but he doesn't need a cell phone to remind him. Perhaps he is distracted - or shall I say attracted - by the intercessory prayers of his children. God is waiting to hear the prayers of his children: "I love the Lord, because he has heard my voice and my pleas for mercy... He inclined his ear to me." (Psalm 116).

The fragrant incense of Old Testament worship was symbolic of the prayers of God's people. (Rev. 5.8 describes it like this: "golden bowls full of incense, which are the prayers of the saints.") This incense was to be offered morning and evening. Intercessory prayer is a continual reminder before the throne of God. How comforting to know that when I pray for the people I love, it's like sending God a picture for his smart phone.

Do the people you love need the grace and help of God? Keep sending their 'pictures' to God. He will answer those prayers with his loving attention. Paul did it for the Thessalonians: "constantly mentioning you in our prayers, remembering before our God and Father your work of faith and labor of love and steadfastness of hope in our Lord Jesus Christ" (1 Thessalonians 1.2-3).

Prayer: Father, I know that you love your children. Help me to be faithful to pray for them, sending you reminders of their needs all through the day. In Jesus' name.

Psalm of the Day: 78.50-55

Genealogy

Daily Reading: Matthew 1

The book of the genealogy of Jesus Christ. (Matthew 1.1a)

Devotional Thought: How far back do you know your genealogy? I can't go back very far. My son-in-law has traced a little bit of our ancestry, but I think he ran into a dead end, too. The good news, however, is that my future genealogy history is not complete. There have been two generations added to my genealogy since I came on the scene. And more entries are coming!

Genealogies were important in the Old Testament. The New Testament opens with a genealogy: Jesus' genealogy! In Matthew, the family history of Jesus is traced back to Abraham. In Luke it goes back through Adam to God himself. As I read it, I thought about Jesus' genealogy *forward*. That's right. The family history of Jesus was not done when he was born. Though he did not have any children in the physical sense, he has billions of people in his spiritual genealogy. In Jesus the promise is fulfilled that God would give Abraham children as numerous as the stars in the sky and as plentiful as the grains of sand on the seashore.

Jesus' genealogy is still being written. With every passing day, people are being born again - born from above - into the Kingdom of God. How exciting! The question I have today is, "What am I doing to add to the genealogy of Jesus?" Jesus saved me, am I working to see salvation come to others?

The book of Revelation talks about "The Lamb's Book of Life." In it there are recorded all the names of the children of Jesus. I'm in that family! Let's do our best to see more and more entries in that genealogy!

Prayer: Jesus, thank you that I have been born again into the family of God. I am in your genealogy! Use me, O Lord, to bring others into your forever family. Amen.

Psalm of the Day: 78.56-64

Where Is He?

Daily Reading: Matthew 2

Where is he who has been born king of the Jews? For we saw his star when it rose [or in the east] and have come to worship him. (Matthew 2.2)

Devotional Thought: Smart phones are no big deal to my children, but I remember when phones were isolated to buildings - and they had cords! Now I can take my phone anywhere - in the car, in a meeting, at lunch with friends. I can call people, text people and email people from anywhere. I can get on the internet and look up anything at any time. I can check my appointments, check the weather and get directions to my next destination. I do have one complaint about my cell phone, however. When I open my phone to do something, there is usually something else waiting for me - a text, an email, or a voice mail. So I get distracted. Then, I forget what I was doing!

The wise men who were seeking Jesus did not have cell phones to lead them to their destination, but they did have a star - a star placed by God himself. They followed that star successfully for nearly 1000 miles. When they arrived at Jerusalem, however, something happened. They lost sight of the star. I wonder if it was all the distraction of the city. Or perhaps, when they consulted with Herod and the Jewish leaders, their vision was blurred. Once they got back on the road, the star reappeared and led them right to where they wanted to go.

How is your vision of Jesus? Can you see him clearly? Or, are you distracted by all the messages and images bombarding you? We try many ways to find our way back to him, but what we need to do is just go back to what is a timeless way to find him: The Word of God. That star is still shining! Are you looking in the right place?

Prayer: Lord, there are so many things that distract me, so many things that promise fulfillment, but the meaning of life is found only in you. Help me to keep my eyes on you at all times. Amen.

Psalm of the Day: 78.65-72

Repent

Daily Reading: Matthew 3

> *In those days John the Baptist came preaching in the wilderness of Judea, "Repent, for the kingdom of heaven is at hand." ... And they were baptized by him in the river Jordan, confessing their sins.* (Matthew 3.1-2, 6)

Devotional Thought: Have we lost something in our modern quest for tolerance and inclusion? I sometimes wonder where The Great Social Experiment of the 21st century will lead us. Instead of evaluating our lives based on the combined wisdom of our heritage and history, we now expect society to accept and accommodate our lifestyle choices - no matter what they may be. In the modern mind, there certainly is no room for an outmoded concept such as repentance.

John the Baptist was not a modern mind. He didn't have time for political correctness and safe spaces. He certainly didn't feel obliged to give any trigger warnings. His message was abrupt. It was simple. Repent!

John - along with Jesus after him - recognized that what ails humanity is the one thing we don't want to confront: Sin. The truth is, not all choices are equal. Not all decisions are right. Not all roads lead to heaven. The solution for sin is not accommodation. It is repentance.

John did not attack the sinner (except the religious hypocrites); he attacked the sin. And though his message was harsh, his arms were open wide. God will accept any person who repents. But there is no grace available for the person who will not acknowledge and turn from their sin.

When the people heard John's message, they confessed their sins and were baptized. In other words, they repented. It was not easy to do, but they knew it was the only real solution to their brokenness. People are not really that much different today, are they? We are still broken, and we still try every other solution to our sin problem. But there is only one that really works. It is simple, yet not easy: Repent.

Prayer: Lord, help me not to hide from the truth. If my actions or my attitudes are sinful, then help me to see it and to repent. Give me life and freedom in Jesus' name. Amen.

Psalm of the Day: 79.1-7

We Can Pray...

Daily Reading: Matthew 4

> *And he went throughout all Galilee, teaching in their synagogues and proclaiming the gospel of the kingdom and healing every disease and every affliction among the people.* (Matthew 4.23)

Devotional Thought: Something happened this past Sunday that gives me cause for great optimism. In Sunday School, I was talking to the children about being stubborn and wanting our own way. I asked, "What can we do to help ourselves be less stubborn?" Anna, one of the older students, said, "We can pray and ask Jesus to help us." She quickly went on to share two other things we can do to help our attitudes: read our Bibles and go to church. If those sound like "Sunday school answers," it is because they are. And, that's why I was encouraged! Anna, along with our other children, are learning to expect the help of Jesus.

Today's culture doesn't leave much room for Jesus, relegating him to a minor position on Sundays. We don't want his presence, his Word, or his values intruding into public life - even when we celebrate his birth or his death! As we have pushed Christ aside, we have seen the moral health of our nation decline. We don't need *less* of Jesus on the scene. We need *more* of him!

Today's scripture says, Jesus "went throughout all Galilee." Wherever he went there was truth (teaching), peace (the gospel), and wholeness (healing). That sounds like something we could use more of today!

How about you? Do you need more of his presence in your life? Take the advice of Anna: Pray!

Prayer: Lord, come to me today and teach me your truth. Grant me peace in your presence, and make me whole. Amen.

Psalm of the Day: 79.8-13

More Mountains, Please
Daily Reading: Matthew 5

> *Seeing the crowds, he went up on the mountain, and when he sat down, his disciples came to him. And he opened his mouth and taught them.* (Matthew 5.1-2)

Devotional Thought: Ah... The Sermon on the Mount. The next three days are going to be chock-full of challenges as we read this Kingdom message from Jesus. What strikes me right away is the reference to a mountain. As one writer said, it "is probably significant, just as Moses received the old Law on Mount Sinai, so Jesus, the new Leader, enunciated the law of the Kingdom on a mountainside." (BBC, 66)

And that is my challenge to you. Have you found your mountainside? That Jesus thought a mountainside experience was important is obvious by the fact that it came early in the development of his disciples. Those who would follow Jesus need to start with him on the mountainside of challenge. Our perspectives need to be challenged just as those first disciples' worldview was changed by spending time with Jesus.

A mountaintop experience is not necessarily an emotional experience, though it can be one. What is important is that we get closer to God and farther from the pressures and distractions of life. Jesus saw the crowds and then called his disciples up to him - away from the crowds. He sat down - this was not to be a hurried experience.

We need to be able to hear what he has to say. On another mountain with Jesus, the disciples heard, "This is my beloved Son, with whom I am well pleased; listen to him" (Matthew 17.5).

Are you spending time with Jesus on the mountain top of quiet listening? Do you do so daily? I would also suggest regular times of solitude and silence when you can spend a day - or even a half day with Jesus alone. We need more, not fewer, mountains!

Prayer: Jesus, thank you for the invitation to go up the mountain with you. Help us all to make time to spend with you. Teach us about your kingdom, O Lord. Change our perspective so that we think as you do. Amen.

Psalm of the Day: 80.1-3

Investments, not Favors

Daily Reading: Matthew 6

> *Where your treasure is, there your heart will be also.* (Matthew 6.21)

Devotional Thought: As a pastor, it often falls to me to raise money and recruit workers for the Kingdom. In doing so, too many times I have approached people with the attitude - if not the literal words - "Will you do me a favor?" I've got that wrong!

First of all, when people invest in the church, they are not doing it for me. I'm just the pastor. Christ is the Lord of the Church. So, when there is a need for teachers, leaders, greeters, singers or nursery workers, it is for Christ. I certainly am not a large enough figure to garner the kind of sacrifice and service needed.

Also, those investing in the Kingdom are not *doing* the favor. They are *receiving* the favor! That's right. When someone invests in God's cause, Christ himself said they would be paid back thirty-, sixty-, even a hundred-fold! What an amazing opportunity for the savvy investor!

Jesus told us that where our treasures are, there our hearts will go. If we invest in the Kingdom, we will find joy in the kingdom. If we invest in heaven, we will follow our hearts to heaven. One author said it this way: "If you encourage a man to give to the Lord's work, you are helping to tie him to heaven. Even soliciting a sinner to contribute to a special project of the church may lead to his salvation. Thus we do people a definite service when we give them a chance to make their offerings to the Lord. Where their money goes, there also their hearts will go." (BBC, 85)

I don't like to ask for money or volunteers. But, I do love to give people the opportunity to invest in ways that pay eternal dividends!

Prayer: Lord, I consecrate the treasures of my time, talents, and money to your Kingdom. Help me not to be so tied to earthly things that I neglect heavenly investments. Amen.

Psalm of the Day: 80.4-7

See Clearly

Daily Reading: Matthew 7

> *You hypocrite, first take the log out of your own eye, and then you will see clearly to take the speck out of your brother's eye.* (Matthew 7.5)

Devotional Thought: Matthew 7 contains so much wisdom: advice on judging others, the desire of the Father to give good gifts to his children, the "golden rule," knowing a tree by its fruit, building your house on the Rock, and the revelation from Jesus that not all who claim to know the Lord truly do (perhaps the most sobering scripture in the New Testament). This chapter is so full of wisdom from Jesus' teachings that it is hard to focus in on one particular section.

This is a continuation of Jesus' teachings to the crowd, the infamous Sermon on the Mount. Jesus knew he was addressing a diverse group of his followers – Jew and Gentile, religious superiors and self-proclaimed sinners. The command on judging others applies to all of his followers: "Judge not, that you not be judged... Why do you see the speck that is in your brother's eye, but do not notice the log that is in your own eye?" (v1,3). As human beings, I believe we are guilty of constantly judging others, good and bad. We see something, we analyze it, and we judge its goodness or its badness.

Jesus is not calling for blindness to sin among believers. To the contrary, what he is saying is that we should turn the eye of judgment onto ourselves first and foremost. We tend to give ourselves a lot more grace and patience than we do anyone else! Only after we have asked the Lord to inspect our own hearts for sin, and repented of that sin, can we "see clearly" to gently and lovingly help our fellow believers with the sin in their own lives.

Jenny

Prayer: Lord, give us a right heart – a heart full of grace and compassion and understanding towards others. Help us to repent of the sin in our own hearts first when we see the sin of others. Then give us the love and courage to help others.

Psalm of the Day: 80.8-19

What Sort of Person Am I?

Daily Reading: Matthew 8

The men marveled, saying, "What sort of man is this?" (Matthew 8.27)

Devotional Thought: "What kind of person are you?" That question can be asked from two perspectives. One perspective is negative: "How could you do this *to* me? Just what kind of person are you?" The other perspective is positive: "Why would you do this *for* me? What kind of person are you?"

When Jesus calmed the storm, saving the lives of his disciples, they asked, "What sort of man is this?" They marveled at him. I believe that they had a little fear and amazement mixed in together - a little of both the positive and the negative.

What sort of person are you? Today we will cause people to ask that question - perhaps not consciously, but they will ask. And, our lives will answer!

Which perspective do you want to leave? Do you want them muttering to themselves, "How could s/he do that to me?" Cross words, careless actions, and caustic attitudes leave behind an atmosphere of anger, mistrust, and pain. The world will be a little darker, a little less hopeful if we are mean-spirited or high-minded.

Would you rather want to leave people marveling to themselves, "Why would s/he do that for me?" A kind word, a helpful deed, and a forgiving spirit will leave behind the aroma of Christ. The world will be a little brighter, a little more joyful, a little easier to take.

"What sort of man/woman is this?" Try to remember this question today. It will change not only your day, but also the day of everyone you meet!

Prayer: Lord, go with me today. Be in me that divine Light that will make people marvel and not mutter. I want to spread your kingdom and your kindness everywhere I go today. Amen.

Psalm of the Day: 81.1-7

No Servant Is to Be Idle

Daily Reading: Matthew 9

The harvest is plentiful but the workers are few. Ask the Lord of the harvest, therefore, to send out workers into his harvest field.
(Matthew 9:37-38)

Devotional Thought: What are you doing? We have all been asked this question more times than we can count... The answer given most often is, "nothing." That does not mean there's nothing to do. We simply are not doing what needs to be done. Usually, we are avoiding a task we don't want to do.

Today I came across a sticky note in my Bible with this sentence written on it, "No servant is to be idle."

A crop does not harvest itself. The farmer must leave the comfort of his home and go to his field. Jesus says that there is plenty to harvest, but there's a problem: "The workers are few." Very few people are willing to roll up their sleeves, move out into the field and work. We find all kinds of excuses as to why we are not part of the harvest. Meanwhile, a few workers struggle to get the job done. The solution? "Ask the Lord of the harvest, therefore, to send out workers into his harvest field." There are workers available, they just haven't reported for work! Jesus wasn't talking about a physical harvest in an earthly field. He was referring to the lost people we see around us every day. Far too many Christians are oblivious to these desperate, needy people. They simply don't see the harvest.

As we pray for him to send workers into the harvest field, do we understand that we are the workers? The work may not be easy. We will face opposition. But we must never forget that our harvest is not only for time, but also for eternity. The crop is by far too valuable to be left in the field un-harvested.

What are you doing? "No servant is to be idle!"

Pastor Steve Bierly

Prayer: Father, you are the Lord of the harvest. We offer ourselves to be workers in your harvest field. Thank you for allowing us to be a part of the greatest harvest of all time and eternity. Amen.

Psalm of the Day: 81.8-16

From Disciple to Apostle

Daily Reading: Matthew 10

And he called to him his twelve disciples and gave them authority over unclean spirits, to cast them out, and to heal every disease and every affliction. The names of the twelve apostles are... (Matthew 10.1-2a)

Devotional Thought: Relationships change. There comes a point when a person moves from being an acquaintance to being a friend or from being a fiancé to being a spouse. Our relationship with Jesus is like that. We move deeper and deeper into intimacy with him. We see that happening in Matthew 10 when Jesus called his twelve *disciples* to him, but sent them out as twelve *apostles*.

What's the big deal?

Well, a disciple is a student, a learner, or a follower. We become disciples immediately when we decide to follow Jesus. But, what is an apostle? Strong's Concordance defines apostle as "a messenger, envoy, delegate, one commissioned by another to represent him in some way." How did the disciples become apostles? That's easy to answer when we look at what happened between those two designations: Jesus "gave them authority..."

The real question for each of us is this: "Will I be content to be a disciple, or will I press on to become an apostle?" I am not talking about taking some special place of power and prestige. That is contrary to the values of the Kingdom. What I mean is this - will I make myself available to Jesus to do his work under his authority? The answer to that depends upon our surrender. In order to receive the Lord's work we must rest from our own. In order to represent the Lord's purpose, we must lay down our own purpose. Then he gives us authority. The relationship changes.

God is constantly calling us, as he called Moses: "Come up here." What is your response to him?

Prayer: Jesus, thank you that you have called me to be a follower, a disciple of yours. Help me to follow you - to the place of complete surrender. May your purposes become mine. Fill me with your Holy Spirit and power. Amen.

Psalm of the Day: 82.1-8

And the Poor...
Daily Reading: Matthew 11

... and the poor have good news preached to them. (Matthew 11.5)

Devotional Thought: Have you ever had doubts? I would venture to say that everybody has. At least everybody who is human! John the Baptist had doubts. Though he was a man used of God to prepare the way for Jesus, and though he had spent his entire life in doing just that, and though he had seen great multitudes repent and come into the kingdom - still John felt doubts. In the darkness of prison, he sent word to Jesus asking, "Are you the one who is to come, or shall we look for another?"

Jesus did not leave his friend and cousin in darkness. He told John's messengers, "Go and tell John what you hear and see: the blind receive their sight and the lame walk, lepers are cleansed and the deaf hear, and the dead are raised up, and the poor have good news preached to them." Those were signs of the Messiah. All great signs, but the climactic sign was this: preaching the good news to the poor.

Do we place such a high importance on reaching the poor?

My particular "tribe" is Nazarene. The Church of the Nazarene was founded as a mission to the poor of Los Angeles. The name 'Nazarene' itself was taken by the founders as representative of the humble origins of Christ in the despised town of Nazareth. Like Jesus the Nazarene, the Church of the Nazarene has focused as Jesus did on the neglected quarters of society. As we grow and become 'successful', however, it is easy to get away from such a mission.

Whether Baptist or Presbyterian, Methodist or Lutheran, Catholic or Nazarene, let us never neglect preaching the good news of Jesus to the poor!

Prayer: Father, thank you that you sent your Son to be born in a humble stable and to be raised in a spurned community. You have shown that you will accept even me! Help me to always take on the qualities of The Nazarene and reach the humblest members of society with the love of God. Amen.

Psalm of the Day: 83.1-8

Greater Than the Temple?

Daily Reading: Matthew 12

> *I tell you, something greater than the temple is here. And if you had known what this means, 'I desire mercy, and not sacrifice,' you would not have condemned the guiltless.* (Matthew 12.6-7)

Devotional Thought: Back in the day I used to watch the TV sitcom "Everybody Loves Raymond." I still remember the scene when Marie took the plastic cover off the couch. That couch had been enshrouded for years. It was in 'mint condition,' but, it had never provided the family rest and comfort. Some folks treat religion that way: stiff, formal, to be preserved and protected. We need to always be aware of what true religion is all about.

Jesus brought true religion to the dead legalists of his day. But they did not recognize it. He made the claim that he himself - or at least the Kingdom he embodied - was 'greater than the temple'! That was sacrilege to those earnest religionists!

Jesus internalized and personalized religion. Because he is Emmanuel, he made a way for God to be with man: "For we are the temple of the living God; as God said, 'I will make my dwelling among them and walk among them, and I will be their God, and they shall be my people'" (2 Corinthians 6.16).

As Christians and churches age, care must be taken to keep buildings and rituals from becoming the focus. It is easier to take care of the outer temple than to care for the temple within. It's not as painful, not as intrusive, not as demanding to give attention to the outer trappings. But, what is more important? Paint and carpet or patience and care? Methods and style or mercy and sacrifice?

Prayer: Lord, help me to always keep my spirit alive by giving my attention to the inner rather than the outer temple. As I have received your mercy, help me to show mercy.

Psalm of the Day: 83.9-18

Everybody Loves a Good Story
Daily Reading: Matthew 13

And he told them many things in parables. (Matthew 13.3a)

Devotional Thought: When my grandchildren are home, they insist that *Pahpooh* - for that is what Avery, my oldest grandchild, named me when she was just a baby! - tell The Monkey Story. They've heard it so many times that they know it by heart. They often remember what's next before I do! Sometimes they even like to tell their own versions. It's always fun to hear what they come up with.

Everybody loves a good story - to hear and to tell. Jesus recognized this, so "he told them many things in parables." A story communicates a message much more powerfully than a recitation of facts and formulas. That's why presidents use stories in their state of the union addresses. People identify with sooner and remember longer a story that touches their hearts.

How do you tell the story of Jesus? Do you try to communicate it through truths and tenets? Is there a better way? Every Christ-follower has a story to tell. It is the story of their lives. People are reading your story every day. The Apostle Peter - himself an eyewitness to the story of Jesus - said, "In your hearts honor Christ the Lord as holy, always being prepared to make a defense to anyone who asks you for a reason for the hope that is in you; yet do it with gentleness and respect" (1 Peter 3:15).

Live the story, then when those around you ask - and they will - tell them the story of how Jesus has changed you.

Prayer: Lord, my story may not seem exciting to others, but I thank you for allowing me to live it. Help me to share the story of your love with others. Help me to do that with gentleness and respect. Amen.

Psalm of the Day: 84.1-7

Faith - Fear - Rescue - Worship

Daily Reading: Matthew 14

> *He said, "Come." So Peter got out of the boat and walked on the water and came to Jesus. But when he saw the wind, he was afraid, and beginning to sink he cried out, "Lord, save me."* (Matthew 14:29-30)

Devotional Thought: One of the most incredible, fantastic miracles of Jesus is recorded in Matthew 14, when Jesus walked on the water. The disciples reacted appropriately... they were terrified! Even his closest followers had difficulty understanding who exactly Jesus was, and when he revealed himself in ways like this, they always reacted with great fear: "What kind of man is this? Even the winds and the sea obey Him!" (Matthew 8:27).

This encounter between Jesus and Peter is personal. Peter, determined to walk out in faith when it made absolutely no sense at all to him, takes his first steps to Jesus on the water. Because of Jesus' great power and Peter's own faith in that power, he is able to do this. Then we see reality sinking in, as Peter looks around and his fear starts to overcome his faith. This was an impossibility after all, and Peter becomes afraid as the wind starts to blow, and then starts to sink. He calls out to the Lord to save him, and Jesus *immediately* reaches out his hand to take hold of him.

I love this passage for so many reasons. First, we too are called to walk out in faith in seemingly impossible situations. And then, like Peter, we tend to shrink back in fear as the storms of life start to blow around us. As our fear overwhelms our faith, we must cry out to Jesus for help. And, just as he did for Peter, he will *immediately* reach out his hand to take hold of us. How are we to respond to this display of love and absolute power? Just like Peter and the rest of the disciples, we worship our Savior, the all-powerful Son of God.

Jenny

Prayer: Lord Jesus, help us to keep our eyes on you at all times. It is when we lose sight of you and who you are that we start to sink in life's storms. Give us the strength to walk the path that you have laid out for us.

Psalm of the Day: 84.8-12

Great Faith

Daily Reading: Matthew 15

O woman, great is your faith! (Matthew 15.28)

Devotional Thought: One of the most intriguing conversations in the New Testament is between Jesus and the Gentile woman in Matthew 15. This woman came to Jesus to beg healing for her demon-possessed daughter. Jesus did not respond the way I would have wanted him to. In commenting on this passage, G. Campbell Morgan wrote: "Against prejudice she came, against silence she persevered, against exclusion she proceeded, against rebuff she won." (*BBC*)

This woman was confronted with...*Her race* - against prejudice she came. She was a Gentile and a woman. Not a good combination to get a hearing from a Jewish rabbi! Not only so, but she was a needy person with a needy family. I can almost hear people saying, "Oh great! What does she want?" *His face* - against silence she persevered. At first it seemed that Jesus ignored her. But I believe he was testing her faith and his disciples' hearts. The disciples just wanted her to go away, but Jesus not-so-subtly reminded them that they were "the lost sheep of Israel." We need to remember that, too, lest we get big-headed. *Her place* - against exclusion she proceeded. The disciples were certain she didn't belong there. She had to get past them. Then Jesus reminded her that the children were his first concern. It helps us to know that Jesus' word translated "dogs" is actually "pups," meaning the household pets that play with the children. She would not be denied, saying, "I will take crumbs from the table." *His grace* - against rebuff she won. Jesus answered her: "Great is your faith! Be it done for you as you desire." With those words, her daughter was healed instantly.

Through it all, she persevered, and great faith was rewarded.

Prayer: Lord, thank you that though I am needy, I am like a pup under the table. When life tests the limits of my faith, help me to persevere. Show me your grace, I pray. Amen.

Psalm of the Day: 85.1-7

God Confirmed

Daily Reading: Matthew 16

Blessed are you, Simon Bar-Jonah! For flesh and blood has not revealed this to you, but my Father who is in heaven. (Matthew 16.17)

Devotional Thought: "I want to hear it from the horse's mouth!" Have you ever said that? When someone tells me, "So and so said thus and thus..." a red flag goes up. It's not that I doubt their honesty, I just don't know if their memory and perspective would match that of the other person. Until I can get it verified, second-hand information is tentative.

When Simon Peter testified that Jesus was "the Christ, the Son of the living God," Jesus said that Simon was blessed because he had 'heard' that straight from God. God had revealed to him that Jesus was the long-awaited Messiah. There was no higher source. No verification was needed.

I once read that "only a divine revelation from the Holy Spirit can make us really know that Jesus is the Son of God. Such a revelation gives an inner certainty that cannot be shaken." (*BBC*) That's what I want for myself, and I know that's what it will take for another person to really believe in Jesus. So, when I pray for someone to be saved, and when I witness to them about Jesus, then I must leave it in God's hands to reveal who Jesus is. When God does that, they are blessed indeed. Then they can make a decision based upon their deeply held convictions and not upon my own. God will certainly use my words and my life, but he himself will confirm who Jesus is.

Are there people for whom you are praying for salvation? Pray that God would open their eyes so that they can see and believe that Jesus is the Son of God!

Prayer: Father, help me to be a faithful witness in my words and my deeds. But more than anything else, may you reveal who Jesus is to those who are lost in darkness. Amen.

Psalm of the Day: 85.8-13

See Jesus, Jesus Only

Daily Reading: Matthew 17

And when they lifted up their eyes, they saw no one but Jesus only.
(Matthew 17.8)

Devotional Thought: What an experience! High up on a mountain with Jesus (that in itself was a privilege not to be taken lightly...), Peter, James and John saw Jesus 'transfigured' and saw Moses and Elijah talking with Jesus. Wow! That will give your faith a boost. But, Moses and Elijah were only temporary phenomena. The glowing face and clothing of Jesus faded away. The trio of men with Jesus had to come down off the mountain top. I like what Matthew recorded: "When they lifted up their eyes, they saw no one but Jesus only."

Think about a couple things we can learn from this account: 'Spiritual transfiguration' takes place in times of prayer (*BBC*, 161). Time spent with Jesus on the mountaintop is so important to our spiritual formation. We must make time and space for these encounters with Jesus. Peter and James and John went with Jesus. Had they not made the effort, they would have missed this life-changing experience. Private prayer or public prayer, guided prayer or spontaneous prayer, at home or at church or in my small group - I should avail myself of these opportunities to be changed. No spiritual experience is of worth unless it leaves one with an increased consciousness of Christ's presence (*BBC* 162). An exhilarating experience of the presence of God is not an end in itself. When the experience is past, Jesus must still be present. I must avoid seeking an experience and instead seek Jesus. I must fix my eyes on Jesus!

So go high up the mountain in prayer and worship. Experience Jesus and his glory. But then, when the moment passes, lift up your eyes and see Jesus, Jesus only!

Prayer: Lord Jesus, thank you for those special times of communion when your glory is present. Change me in your presence, O Lord. Then, help me, I pray, to see you in regular moments of regular days. Amen.

Psalm of the Day: 86.1-10

The Key to Greatness
Daily Reading: Matthew 18

> *Whoever humbles himself like this child is the greatest in the kingdom of heaven.* (Matthew 18.4)

Devotional Thought: My friend Gerry has recently 'caught up' with me in having 5 grandchildren. He loves to have his grandchildren come to his house and play in Grandpa's pool. He says it's a grandchild magnet! I need one of those. Those kids just take it for granted that they are going to have fun Grandpa's. Grandpa has everything they need. They don't have to bring a thing but themselves. That's a good thing.

Jesus said we are to be like 'Gerry's kids.' We come to our Heavenly Father as a child comes to their earthly father. We just bring ourselves and trust God to take care of the rest. One person said, "The humility of a child consists mainly of a mood of trust and dependence. That is the attitude which God desires His children to take toward him. The prevalent modern mood of self-sufficient, worldly-wise sophistication is inimical to genuine spirituality" (*BBC*).

Isaiah 55.8 says, "For my thoughts are not your thoughts, neither are your ways my ways, declares the Lord." Christ's way runs directly counter to the way of the world. We want to accomplish great things so that we can be proud of our achievements and be important to God. But, if we want to be great in the Kingdom, the main characteristic we must have is humility. "Not ability, but humility. Not achievement, but humility. Not impressive performance, but humility." Trusting in our heavenly Father is the key to success.

Prayer: Father, thank you for your amazing love! Before I ever did anything to deserve your love, you welcomed me 'home.' Help me to always maintain the innocence and humility of a child in your presence. Through Jesus my Lord, Amen.

Psalm of the Day: 86.11-17

What Do I Still Lack?

Daily Reading: Matthew 19

"All these I have kept. What do I still lack?" Jesus said to him, "If you would be perfect, go, sell what you possess and give to the poor, and you will have treasure in heaven; and come, follow me."
(Matthew 19.20-21)

Devotional Thought: Often when I'm preparing for a meeting, I will get a sense that I'm forgetting something. Usually that niggling is accurate, and I remember an important detail that I had overlooked before.

The rich young ruler in Matthew 19 was like that. He was preparing for a 'meeting' with God - the judgment. He had done all he knew to do, yet he came asking Jesus, "Teacher, what good deed must I do to have eternal life?" (Matthew 19.16) Clearly, this man was not satisfied with his religion (*BBC*). He felt a lack inside. We must not ignore those spiritual nigglings! They are the voice of God preparing us for a meeting with him.

This young man was troubled and impotent, lacking spiritual peace and spiritual power. Jesus immediately saw through his charade of spiritual self-sufficiency and put his finger on the problem. "You love your money too much. You need to divest yourself of all that comes between God and you. Leave it behind and follow me..."

Dietrich Bonhoeffer wrote: "Is there some part of your life which you are refusing to surrender at his behest, some sinful passion, maybe, or some animosity, some hope, perhaps your ambition or your reason? If so, you must not be surprised that you have not received the Holy Spirit, that prayer is difficult, or that your request for faith remains unanswered."

Is the Lord niggling you? If you feel a spiritual lack, ask God to reveal what is holding you back. Then surrender that thing and follow Jesus.

Prayer: Search me, O God, and know my heart. Try me and know my anxious thoughts. See if there be any wicked way in me and lead me in the way everlasting. Amen.

Psalm of the Day: 87.1-7

Get Busy!

Daily Reading: Matthew 20

> *Why do you stand here idle all day?* (Matthew 20.6b)

Devotional Thought: Last week I read how the economy showed signs of strengthening because 222,000 jobs were added and the unemployment rate was steady at 4.4%. Fewer people are out of work, and that's good, but for the 4.4%, life could be better. Many are probably wondering when the strengthening economy will reach them. They are idle. Idleness is a bane on society and on individuals. How does that proverb go? "Idle hands are the devil's workshop."

Why do you stand here idle all day? Some possible answers...

Some - like the workers in this parable - will say, *"No one has hired us."* The master of the house quickly put an end to that excuse. He hired them! In the kingdom, there is more to do than we have workers to do it. There is no excuse for idleness. Jesus stands ready to give each one a job with eternal significance and rewards.

Others may say, *"I don't know what to do."* That's legitimate. I have found myself waiting for instructions because it was unclear exactly what my next step should be. But, I have found that - in kingdom work as well as most other endeavors - the best way to find out what to do is to start doing something. Clarity comes with activity, not apathy.

Still others say, *"I don't want to do it."* They reason it's somebody else's job, they've done their part, or they don't have the necessary skills. I've recently read how the roll of able-bodied people receiving food stamps went down drastically in those states and counties that began again to enforce the federal government's work requirement. What are the able-bodied of the *kingdom* doing? Are we waiting on God to force our hands?

Why do you stand here idle all day? Get Busy!

Prayer: Father forgive your church for being idle. The harvest indeed is plentiful but the workers are few. Help me to be among those few who are busy at your work, and send forth more workers into your fields. Amen.

Psalm of the Day: 88.1-5

I Have a Question for *You*

Daily Reading: Matthew 21

> And when he entered the temple, the chief priests and the elders of the people came up to him as he was teaching, and said, "By what authority are you doing these things, and who gave you this authority?" (Matthew 21:23)

Devotional Thought: Jesus' very entry into the city on a colt clearly signaled his identity as the king, the son of David. The Jews would have recognized this as a fulfillment of the prophecy in Zechariah 9:9. And yet, the religious leaders continued to challenge the authority of Jesus.

They were understandably stirred up after Jesus cleansed the temple, overturning the tables of the money-changers. How blinded we are by our own self-righteousness at times! The chief priests and scribes saw the wonderful things Jesus did, how he was healing the blind and the lame, and heard the praise he was receiving, and they were indignant. Their priorities had shifted from worship of the Lord to profiting from the spiritual needs of others. What misplaced indignation!

They challenged him, asking him who gave him the authority to do these things. Jesus answered their question by asking them a question, designed to guide them to think through the answer for themselves. This is such a wise response, and one that Jesus uses often. When we are trying to persuade others of the truth of the gospel, would this also be more effective for us? Rather than engage in heated arguments that get us nowhere and leave everyone feeling defensive and furious (I'm thinking mostly of the arguing that happens on social media and elsewhere online), why not respond to the challengers of our faith by getting to the root of their own beliefs? This gives us a much better starting point. It helps us gain the trust of others as they see that we are interested in their perspective and not just in forcing our own beliefs on them. This was a technique used by Jesus himself, so let's adopt it ourselves as we spread the good news!

Jenny

Prayer: Lord, please give us wisdom as we witness to the lost around us. Give us a heart of humility, full of confidence in you and you alone. And let us speak only the words that your Spirit would have us to say.

Psalm of the Day: 88.6-12

Whose Image Do You Bear?

Daily Reading: Matthew 22

> Therefore render to Caesar the things that are Caesar's, and to God the things that are God's. (Matthew 22.21)

Devotional Thought: I received a text from my middle daughter with a picture of my youngest grandchild - Ellis. The comment was simply: "Alright, so maybe she does look like Pahpooh!" (Pahpooh is what the grandkids call me...) I really don't see it, but some have said that Ellis has my likeness. I wouldn't wish that on anybody, but secretly I'm thrilled!

Jesus, in a discussion about paying taxes, said, "Show me the coin for the tax... Whose likeness and inscription is this?" (Matthew 22.19-20). The obvious answer was "Caesar's." The equally obvious response was "Render to Caesar the things that are Caesar's and to God the things that are God's."

The question remains, however, "What are God's things?" The answer? That which has the image of God inscribed upon it. You and I have been made in the image of God. Though marred by sin, we have his likeness and inscription. Erasmus, a Christian theologian from the 15th Century, wrote this: "Give back to God that which has the image and superscription of God - the soul."

Have you given God your soul - the very essence of your life? We try to substitute many things for this, trying to appease God with trinkets and treasures. God will settle, however, for nothing less than our very selves. Today, let us do what the Apostle Paul wrote in Romans 12.1: "I appeal to you therefore, brothers and sisters, by the mercies of God, to present your bodies [your very selves] as a living sacrifice, holy and acceptable to God, which is your spiritual worship [or reasonable service]."

Whose image do you bear?

Prayer: Father, thank you for making me in your image. I give myself to you completely and without reservation today. May I reflect your love and light in this world of hate and darkness. Amen.

Psalm of the Day: 88.13-18

Fan into Flame

Daily Reading: Matthew 23

> *Woe to you, scribes and Pharisees, hypocrites! For you build the tombs of the prophets and decorate the monuments of the righteous...'* (Matthew 23.29)

Devotional Thought: Biblical scholar Ralph Earle wrote this: "There are three stages in the life of every religious organization. First it is a movement, vibrant and vigorous, active and aggressive. Then it becomes an institution with 'more harness that horse.' Finally its vitality disappears and it becomes a museum, where the bones of the ancient leaders are put on display." (*BBC*)

For many in Jesus' day, their religion had become a museum: 'You build the tombs of the prophets...' That can happen in churches today as well. It can also happen in the lives of individual Christians.

How would you describe your Christian life today? Is it a museum, silent and stuffy, impersonal and obsolete? Is everything important from someone else's experience or from your experiences in the past?

Is your Christian life 'more harness than horse'? Are you more concerned with the outer trappings of religion than with the inner power and strength of the Spirit? Are you making sure that the appearance is right - how you dress, church attendance, etc. - while neglecting mercy, justice or humility?

Or, is your Christian life 'vibrant and vigorous, active and aggressive'? Is the life of Christ pulsing through your veins? Does it make a difference in the way you live, how you treat others, your attitude? Are you sharing your faith by loving your neighbor as yourself and giving people the reason for the hope that you have within you? Are your prayers fervent, your Bible worn, and your love hot?

I urge you - in the words of the Apostle Paul - "to fan into flame the gift of God, which is in you" (2 Timothy 1.6).

Prayer: Lord, today I pray for new life to course through my spirit. In the words of the Psalmist, I ask, 'Will you not revive us again, that your people may rejoice in you?' I present myself to you. Fill me with life and the Spirit. Amen.

Psalm of the Day: 89.1-4

Don't Be Led Astray

Daily Reading: Matthew 24

See that no one leads you astray. (Matthew 24.4)

Devotional Thought: Stan, a friend of mine, asked me if I knew about his recent accident. I did not, and I was prepared to hear about a minor 'fender bender.' Stan told me that he had had to replace his car (only a few months old) with a brand new car. I suddenly sat up: "What happened?!" Stan had been driving along a four lane highway when a car pulled through the intersection ahead of him - close, but not alarming. However, another car followed the first one, and Stan T-boned it! Miraculously nobody was hurt (which explains why I hadn't heard about it.) The cause? They concluded that the other driver had simply followed the first car into the intersection. She had been led astray.

In Matthew 24, Jesus warned us that we must be careful that no one lead us astray. Satan, using 'false prophets', will tell us lies and try to convince us that there is another, a better, way. We are responsible to recognize the dangers and "turn away from evil and do good" (1 Peter 3.11). Sometimes we follow others into the intersections of life - good people, family and friends. Forgetting to fix our eyes on Jesus, we find ourselves off course and we may even crash, putting ourselves and others in grave danger.

How are we to prevent being led astray? First and foremost, we must know the Word of God. It is "a lamp unto our feet and light unto our path" (Psalm 119.105). Then, we must be aware of our surroundings. It is easy to fall in line with our culture and begin to adopt the ways of this world. Finally, do everything in love.

See to it that no one leads you astray!

Prayer: Lord, today I will encounter things that lead me astray. Help me to make my decisions and set my course based on your Word and your love. Amen.

Psalm of the Day: 89.5-13

Well Done, Good and Faithful Servant
Daily Reading: Matthew 25

> *Well done, good and faithful servant. You have been faithful over a little; I will set you over much. Enter into the joy of your master.*
> (Matthew 25.21)

Devotional Thought: "Well done, good and faithful servant." I want to hear those words some day, to hear them from my Master, Jesus Christ. How can I live my life in such a way that I will hear them? Do I have to double my talents? I like how Ralph Earle answered that question in *The Beacon Bible Commentary* (pp. 226-227)...

"The first two men reported that they had doubled the talents given them. In reply the master said exactly the same words of commendation to both servants. The reward he promised was based on faithfulness, not ability. It is extremely significant that both servants were commended for being good and faithful, not for being capable and clever. These are two honest, solid virtues everyone can have - the poor as well as the rich, the uneducated as well as the brilliant intellectual. These are the only two things God requires of everyone - that he be good in character and faithful in service."

When we are saved by the blood of Jesus, the story is not over. It is just beginning. Having done the work of salvation for us, God still has work to do in us and through us. The saved person must become a good person, living according to the will of God, leaving his sin and entering into God's holiness. The good person, then, must become a faithful servant. He or she must doe the work of God, loving - in tangible ways - the lost and the saved, the haves and the have-nots.

Today, allow the Holy Spirit to fill you, to form you, and to guide you into works of service.

Prayer: Thank you Lord, that it is by grace I am saved, through faith not through works lest I should boast. But help me, Lord, to do the works which you have prepared in advance for me to do. Amen.

Psalm of the Day: 89.14-18

Do a Beautiful Thing

Daily Reading: Matthew 26

She has done a beautiful thing to me. (Matthew 26.10)

Devotional Thought: It is the nature of love to give, and sometimes love just needs to be extravagant. That is what happened to the woman in Matthew 26 - the woman who anointed Jesus with "very expensive ointment" (v. 7). Some scholars believe the alabaster flask of oil cost a year's wages. It quite possibly could have represented her life's savings.

When we are in love with Christ, there are times when our 'reason' is thrown out the window. It was not reasonable for this woman to make such a statement of love. Why, if nothing else, the ointment could have been sold and the money given to the poor! Your love for Christ - including sacrificial giving and service, including passionate worship and prayer - will be misunderstood and denigrated by those who know nothing of what Christ's sacrifice has done for you. The life he has bought you... The peace he has given you... The joy he pours out on you... The love that fills your heart...

Another thing this story teaches me is that there are certain things that must be done when the opportunity avails itself. As in Robert Frost's 'The Road Not Taken', we come to diverging paths in the woods. What we choose will determine our course of life. The woman who anointed Jesus "took the one less traveled by, and that has made all the difference." What choices are you pondering?

One more thing. A beautiful deed leaves a lasting fragrance. Not only was the house filled with the fragrance of her deed, but history itself has preserved the pleasing scent of love. Love has a ripple effect that expands and expands.

Do beautiful things for Jesus' sake today!

Prayer: Jesus, thank you for your extravagant love for me. I want to be extravagant in my response. I give you my heart and life today. Amen.

Psalm of the Day: 89.19-26

One Was Me. The Other Was You.

Daily Reading: Matthew 27

> *Then two robbers were crucified with him, one on the right and one on the left.* (Matthew 27.38)

Devotional Thought: Who were those two thieves hanging on the crosses next to Jesus? Ralph Earle writes, "It is altogether possible that they were fellow insurrectionists with Barabbas. If so, it is probable that Barabbas was the one slated to die on the middle cross. But Jesus took his place - a parable of His taking every sinner's place on the Cross." (*BBC*)

One of the robbers hung on Jesus' left, the other on his right. Left and right... They represent people from both sides of the political spectrum. Democrats, Republicans, Independents, Disillusioned - all have need of the saving grace of Jesus. Rich, Poor, Middle Class - these all, too, stand condemned. Educated, Uneducated - need Jesus. Whatever polar opposites you can think of - and all those in between - hang condemned on either side of Jesus. But Jesus died on that cross so that sin and death may no longer be our masters. And, all are able to turn to Jesus for salvation. One thief did. The other didn't.

Those robbers were convicted law-breakers. They deserved to die, as did Barabbas. The Bible says that we all have sinned and fall short of the glory of God. It also says the wages of our sin is death, but the gift of God is eternal life through Jesus Christ our Lord! Thank God that he gave his one and only Son, that whoever would believe in him should not perish but have eternal life!

Who were those two thieves hanging on the crosses next to Jesus? One was me. The other, you.

Prayer: Thank you, Jesus, for taking my place on the cross. Help me this day to deny myself, take up my cross and follow you. Amen.

Psalm of the Day: 89.27-39

All Authority

Daily Reading: Matthew 28

And Jesus came and said to them, "All authority in heaven and on earth has been given to me. Go therefore and make disciples of all nations, baptizing them in the name of the Father and of the Son and of the Holy Spirit, teaching them to observe all that I have commanded you. And behold, I am with you always, to the end of the age."
(Matthew 28:18-20)

Devotional Thought: In just a few sentences known as "The Great Commission" Jesus gives his final instructions. He first addresses any doubts that they may have had by telling them that "All authority in heaven and on earth has been given to me." That pretty much covers everything right there, doesn't it?

At times it may not feel or seem like Jesus is in control of everything on heaven and on earth. But we are living in the end times, the age between when Jesus came and when he will make his final return. We know that the Lord is patient and desires all to know him, and so in the waiting we see his great mercy towards those who do not yet know him. As we progress to the end, however, we can expect things in this world to go from bad to worse.

What are we to do in the meantime? Jesus gave his followers very clear instructions, thankfully! They are not easy, but they are clear. We are to go out, tell others about Jesus, and teach them his ways. To do this we must engage in and invest in relationships. We must enter into the brokenness and the pain and the mess of others' lives. None of us would choose that over the comfort of staying in our own world, but it is our calling. However, Jesus does not leave us to do this in our own strength. The last thing he tells his disciples is, "behold, I am with you always, to the end of the age," (v.20). He was true to his promise then, and he is faithful to that same promise even now, as the Spirit guides us in His will.

Jenny

Prayer: Lord we know that everything in heaven and earth is under your control and command. Please help us to lead others to you while there is still time to do so. Give us the strength to leave our comfort zone and enter into the pain of others, to your glory.

Psalm of the Day: 89.40-45

Rise Up, Oh Church of God

Daily Reading: Exodus 32

> *And the people sat down to eat and drink and rose up to play.*
> (Exodus 32.6b)

Devotional Thought: The teacher has left the room! I'm not sure what it's like in school today, but I remember when I was in school, if the teacher left the room pandemonium broke out! And the longer the teacher was gone, the greater the chaos!

That's what happened when Moses 'left the room' in Exodus 32. He had been called up the mountain to receive the Law of God. He had been up there almost 40 days - a long time, certainly longer than a classroom full of children could behave! The children of Israel certainly didn't behave. They made for themselves an idol and then "sat down to eat and drink and rose up to play."

As we look around at American culture today, it seems as if the teacher has left the room. In politics, in ethics, in sexuality, in manners, in respect, in family, in law enforcement - you name the social arena - the guidelines for life have been disregarded, and pandemonium has broken out. I wonder sometimes, "How long can God remain patient?"

There is good news, however! God looks down from the mountain of his holiness and sees the situation and stands ready to forgive, to mend, to put in order. But, he is waiting for a Moses to stand in the gap - to intercede on behalf of a wayward people. He is waiting on the church...

Two things prevent this. Either the church would rather stay on the mountain and ignore the problem below, or the church has joined in the pandemonium. So, let us stir ourselves into action, and let us forsake the sins of our culture. Then may we stand in the gap for lost souls.

Prayer: Father, thank you for your patience. Thank you that you are not willing for any to perish. Help your church to be set ablaze with a holy zeal for God and for souls. Help me to be a Moses to stand in the gap. Amen.

Psalm of the Day: 89.46-52

Ornaments

Daily Reading: Exodus 33

> *Therefore the people of Israel stripped themselves of their ornaments, from Mount Horeb onward.* (Exodus 33.6)

Devotional Thought: Roger, my friend, was recently in a head-on collision. He escaped serious injury - thanks be to God! - but he did have quite a scare. After impact, the cab of his pickup was filled with the 'smoke' of the airbags, and he smelled gas. Remembering that he had a can of gasoline in the back, he immediately thought, "My truck is on fire!" He struggled to get out, but the door was jammed. His seatbelt was holding him back. He freed himself as quickly as possible. Thankfully, it wasn't a fire, but he didn't want to hang around inside the truck to figure it out!

After the people of Israel crashed - and almost burned - making an idol at Mount Horeb, they were grieved that God would no longer travel with them. So they "stripped themselves of their ornaments." It was with ornaments that they had made the idol in the first place. So they wanted to rid themselves of the reminder of their sin and the temptation to repeat it. Like my friend Roger, they wanted out of that mess!

The writer of Hebrews encourages us to "lay aside every weight, and sin which clings so closely" (12.1). When God delivers us from sin, we are not to continue to dabble in it, but we must separate ourselves as far as possible - as far as the east is from the west! - in order that we can run the race with perseverance, in order that we won't be lured back into danger.

What are the 'ornaments' of sin in your life? Strip yourself of them from this point onward!

Prayer: Father, thank you for forgiving my sins. Lord, I don't want to be drawn back into sin, so help me to lay aside all those 'ornaments' that might drag me down. Help me to walk with you in holiness of heart and with honor in my conduct. Amen.

Psalm of the Day: 90.1-6

Remove the Veil

Daily Reading: Exodus 34

Moses did not know that the skin of his face shone because he had been talking with God. (Exodus 34:29b)

Devotional Thought: After smashing the first tablets with the Ten Commandments, Moses had to re-ascend the mountain where the Lord descended and stood with Moses. He revealed his glory to Moses there while the covenant was renewed. After spending another 40 days and nights with the Lord, the skin on Moses' face was shining. The Israelites were afraid to even come near him. Moses would eventually put a veil over his face every time he came out from speaking with the Lord. His encounters with the Lord were so powerful that they left a visible sign.

Jesus gave us another example. It is recorded in the gospels that as he prayed he was transfigured or transformed, his face shining with radiance. Even knowing the suffering that was in his future, Jesus glowed with the Holy Spirit when praying to his Father.

I wonder, do people notice such a change on our faces? Does prayer change us to the extent it did Moses and Jesus? We have that same capacity within us, if we are trusting in Jesus for our salvation. As Paul would say in his second letter to the church in Corinth: "But when one turns to the Lord, the veil is removed. Now the Lord is the Spirit, and where the Spirit of the Lord is, there is freedom. And we all, with unveiled face, beholding the glory of the Lord, are being transformed into the same image from one degree of glory to another. For this comes from the Lord who is the Spirit" (2 Cor. 3:16-18).

Remove the veil from your face and let the glory, the grace, and the love of the Lord be evident to all!

Jenny

Prayer: Lord, we pray for the honor of having your Spirit apparent in our very countenance. May our gentleness be evident to all, so that they long for the same peace and joy that they can see clearly in us.

Psalm of the Day: 90.7-12

219

The Indescribable Gift of Giving
Daily Reading: Exodus 35

Whoever is of a generous heart, let him bring the Lord's contribution...
Let every skillful craftsman among you come and make all that the Lord
has commanded. (Exodus 35.5, 10)

Devotional Thought: I was at Wendy's with some friends – Frosties and conversation - what could be better? How about *Free* Frosties and conversation? One of our friends had to leave early, but a minute after she left she hurried back in with a sly smile on her face and threw something on the table: "For our snacks tonight!" It was enough cash money to pay for the ice cream and drinks we had enjoyed. How generous! She didn't have to do that. She did it because she has a generous heart. She wanted to give.

A gift willingly and cheerfully given not only supplies a resource, it also lifts the spirit. But, a gift given begrudgingly is a drag on the receiver's heart. It may help with the need at hand, but it certainly doesn't help with the need of the heart. The Bible says that the Lord loves a cheerful giver (2 Corinthians 9.7). Do you give with a twinkle in your eye, or with a tear on your cheek? Does your giving bring you joy or angst?

When the Israelites were building the tabernacle in the wilderness, God instructed them that they should give their treasures with a generous heart toward its construction. Also, the skilled laborers were to give their talents to the Lord. In both instances, it was the Lord who had already given those things to the would-be givers!

A generous heart is a natural result of seeing that God has been generous to us. That's why Paul wrote, "Thanks be to God for this indescribable gift [of giving]!"

Prayer: Thank you, Lord, for all you have given me. You have supplied my needs and gone way beyond. I want to have a generous heart like yours, O Lord. I give you my talents and treasures. Use them today for your glory and the good of those around me. Amen.

Psalm of the Day: 90.13-17

In Accordance with *All*...
Daily Reading: Exodus 36

> *Work in accordance with all that the Lord has commanded.*
> (Exodus 36.1)

Devotional Thought: My daughter is planning a deck for her home in MI. She sent me a copy of the requirements for permits and inspections in her community. Wasn't that kind of her!? I got the message! Anyway, as I read the information, I first felt a twinge of, "I know what I'm doing!" But, as I considered it, I realized that if we just followed their directions life would be easier for us. We wouldn't need to be looking over our shoulders worried that the inspectors might show up. And, my daughter would undoubtedly get a better deck! We just need to "work in accordance with all that the *inspection department* requires."

As the Israelites were building the tabernacle in the wilderness, Moses instructed them to do their "work in accordance with all that the Lord has commanded." Life would be easier for them, and they would end up with a beautiful place of worship - if they simply followed the instructions given them by the Lord.

Life is like that, too. It is easier and much more beautiful when we live "in accordance with all that the Lord has commanded." And, if we just follow the instructions, we won't be looking over our shoulders, fearful of The Inspector showing up. And, where are those instructions? Thankfully, God has given us very clear instructions - even better than the building department in Wixom, MI - in his Word.

So, be 'hearers' of the Word, but also be 'doers.' Your life will be what God created it to be.

Prayer: Father, thank you for the Bible. Help me to read it, to understand it, and to live it. May my life be filled with the rewards of holy living. And, Father, may I bring glory to you as I live according to your will. Amen.

Psalm of the Day: 91.1-8

Better Than a Lampstand

Daily Reading: Exodus 37

> *The whole of it [the lampstand] was a single piece of hammered work of pure gold.* (Exodus 37.22b)

Devotional Thought: Pictures of grace! That's what I see when I read about the articles used in the service of the tabernacle. We no longer have a physical lampstand in a temple made with hands, but you and I - by grace! - are shining the light of Jesus in our world. We can do it better than a lampstand.

Consider the following traits of the lampstand and how they apply to us: *Entirety*. The instructions were for "the whole of it." There were not areas outside the requirements of God. So it is with us. We are to present ourselves completely - nothing held back - to God.

Integrity. It would have been tempting to construct the lampstand out of various and sundry pieces, separately fabricated and then joined together. But God wanted it to be "a single piece." Greater strength, beauty, and performance are possible when an instrument is one piece. Think about "seamless service."

Maturity. The lampstand was more than a hunk of gold. It was to be "of hammered work." The smith heated and hammered the gold into shape. In much the same way, we discipline ourselves to grow in the Lord. Maturity comes at a high and sometimes painful price!

Purity. Impurities in the gold would cause problems both in the shaping process and in the usage of the lampstand. When we try to hold on to sin, we become difficult to work with and sometimes even snap under pressure! It is so important that God purifies us!

Are you completely given over to God, in all parts of your life, growing in holiness? You can be. You should be. You're better than a lampstand!

Prayer: Lord, just as you gave Moses instructions for the articles of the tabernacle, so you have given me grace that I might serve you with my whole heart, pleasing in every way. Help me to grow into the grace you have given me! Amen.

Psalm of the Day: 91.9-16

God Works That Way

Daily Reading: Exodus 38

> Bezalel... of the tribe of Judah, made all that the Lord commanded Moses ... and with him was Oholiab, of the tribe of Dan.
> (Exodus 38.22-23)

Devotional Thought: God gave me and the church I pastored a vision to open a daycare. "A daycare? But God, I can't do that"! I still vividly remember the meeting when the board gathered around me, fervently praying for God to accomplish his purpose through us. I didn't do it alone. We hired a director. The director hired staff. The staff opened the daycare. God works that way.

God gave Moses a vision for the tabernacle. It was up to Moses to get the tabernacle built. But he didn't have to do it alone. God had a plan for that, too. I'm glad God works that way.

The vision began with the Lord. He knew what kind of worship facility the people needed - grandeur with portability, transcendence with immanence. He helped Moses flesh it out first in his mind, then in the offerings given by the people!

From the Lord, the work was passed on to Moses. Moses was the leader. Every cause needs a leader, someone to champion the cause and rally the people. Moses spoke with confidence and humility for he had been with the Lord.

From Moses, the vision went to Bezalel. He was of the tribe of Judah. (Moses was a Levite.) God gave Bezalel skills that he hadn't given Moses. Moses was wise enough to know he couldn't do what needed to be done. Bezalel was wise enough to follow the plan of his leader.

Even Bezalel was not alone. God gave him a helper, Oholiab, a Danite. (God likes to spread the responsibility around!) Oholiab was a quick study, adopting the wisdom of Bezalel in serving within his capacity and authority.

I'm glad God works that way!

Prayer: Lord, thank you for working the way you do. You not only give us vision, but you give us skills and helpers to get the job done. Help us to follow you where you lead us and depend on you to help us. Amen.

Psalm of the Day: 92.1-9

What's That On Your Hat?

Daily Reading: Exodus 39

> They made the plate of the holy crown of pure gold, and wrote on it an inscription, like the engraving of a signet, "Holy to the Lord."
> (Exodus 39.30)

Devotional Thought: Why should we care what the Old Testament priest wore? Think a moment. The Bible says that we are a kingdom of priests and that we have been clothed in the righteousness of Christ. Surely there is some insight to gain from what the priest wore!

Consider the plate that was attached to his turban.

Pure gold. It was made of the best material, without contamination. In our service to the Lord, do we offer less than our best? Do we willingly allow sin to contaminate our motives? We need to bring our best and ask God to sanctify it!

Inscription. This was the handwriting of God! This is reminiscent of the finger of God writing the Ten Commandments. God wants to write on the tablets of our hearts - his law and his way, the law and way of love.

Engraving. God's writing was carved into the priceless and pure gold. Jesus, our perfect Savior, was pierced for our transgressions... Are we willing to undergo pain and suffering, for the cause of Christ? Paul said," I fill up in my body what is lacking in the sufferings of Christ..." What is engraved on you, O Child of God?

Signet. The priest was an emissary of God himself. The signet ring gave the wearer all the privileges and authority and duties of the king. Christian service is done for Christ's purpose and glory!

Holy to the Lord. Sanctified... Set apart... The priest did not have his own life. He was God's at all times, in all places. As Paul would later write, "I am crucified with Christ. Nevertheless I live, yet not I, but Christ lives in me."

What's that on *your* hat?

Prayer: Lord, "purify my heart. Let me be as gold and precious silver... Refiner's fire, my heart's one desire is to be holy, set apart for you Lord, ready to do your will." Amen. (Brian Doerksen)

Psalm of the Day: 92.10-15

After the Wedding
Daily Reading: Exodus 40

Then you shall take the anointing oil and anoint the tabernacle and all that is in it, and consecrate it and all its furniture, so that it may become holy. (Exodus 40.9)

Devotional Thought: I love to meet with engaged couples as they prepare to get married. There is something fresh and exciting about their love. I also love to officiate at their weddings, two people becoming one. It is a holy thing. And, after the wedding, then the marriage begins, two people living as one. That is even holier! You see, without the marriage, the wedding would be mere pomp and circumstance.

In Exodus 40, Moses and the Israelites consecrated and began using the tabernacle. It was the 'wedding.'

Moses was instructed to anoint the tabernacle- and all of the things to be used in the worship of God - with a holy anointing oil. That anointing oil was so sacred, that it was not to be used for anything else. It was not even to be duplicated! When the oil was applied to the place and instruments of worship, they became holy - consecrated to God. Wouldn't it have been senseless for the Israelites not to use the finely constructed and wholly consecrated materials for their intended purpose? It would be silly to drag that stuff through the wilderness without using it!

You and I have been set apart - purchased by the sacrifice of Jesus and sealed with the anointing of the Holy Spirit. It would be silly to drag our holy selves through life without being used for our intended purpose - bringing glory to God and light to the world! It would be like going to the wedding but skipping the marriage. Where's the fun in that?

Prayer: Thank you, Father, for the holy anointing of Jesus and the infilling of the Spirit. Help me to live today in that fresh and exciting relationship with you. Amen.

Psalm of the Day: 93.1-5

Not Everything's a Nail!
Daily Reading: Jude 1

> *And have mercy on those who doubt; save others by snatching them out of the fire; to others show mercy with fear, hating even the garment stained by the flesh.* (Jude 22-23)

Devotional Thought: One thing that I have learned in my 28 years of pastoral ministry is that people are different and require different responses. Jude, the brother of Jesus, recognized that as well. As he closed his brief letter "To those who are called, beloved in God the Father and kept for Jesus Christ," he suggested at least three ways to respond to those who were wavering.

To one group, he said, *have mercy*. Some people have been "knocked around" by others' evil or sin. We should try to gently "convince them the whole truth as it is in Jesus" (*BBC*). Patient understanding is needed to those who are hurt, lest we add to their pain and push them away.

Some we are to *snatch out of the fire*. We need to react to some situations with a swift and strong hand to pull them back from the danger of sin and temptation. Just as we would grab a child ready to run out into the street, there are times when we need to take drastic measures to prevent a wavering soul from sliding into danger.

On others we are to *show mercy with fear* "in a milder and gentler way though still with a jealous fear, lest we become infected with the disease we intend to cure" (*BBC*). Especially when dealing with people who are engaged in something that tempts us, we need to be careful!

There's an old proverb, "When you're a hammer, everything's a nail." As Christians, however, we are called to be sensitive to where people are and what their situation requires.

Prayer: Lord, I pray first of all that you would help me not to be judgmental. But, when I do see my brother or sister struggling, help me to respond to them in helpful ways, appropriate to their situation. Give me insight and wisdom to help and not to hurt. Amen.

Psalm of the Day: 94.1-7

Not Exciting? Thank God!
Daily Reading: Galatians 1

And they glorified God because of me. (Galatians 1.24)

Devotional Thought: The Apostle Paul had one of those dramatic conversion stories. You know - the type that mesmerizes audiences with how far God can deliver someone. Paul had been a persecutor of Christians, but had met Jesus on the road to Damascus in a fiery vision that left him blind. He was miraculously healed when a fellow Christian came and laid hands on him. Then, he went out to preach the gospel. To top it off, he became the object of persecution himself. People stand in line to hear those stories retold! As Paul said, people "glorified God because of me."

I came from a difficult background, but my story is nothing like Paul's. People don't line up and pay money to hear my testimony. How about you? Is your story a little tame in comparison?

I know people whose stories are dramatic. And, the church glorifies God because of them. But I also know people like Brayden - the 6 year old boy that I baptized on Sunday, along with 3 other children and 3 adults. Is it any less of a miracle that God would save a boy like Brayden *before* he strayed deep into sin and rebellion? I think not. I think that God is glorified just as much by a child being saved as he is by a hardened sinner. And, the child, most likely, has done less damage and caused less pain than the adult.

So, the next time you feel like your story isn't too exciting, then thank God! Then, live your life to bring glory to him now.

Prayer: Lord Jesus, thank you that you have forgiven my sin. Help me, O Lord, to live my life to bring you more and more glory. Grant me courage to tell others that you save!

Psalm of the Day: 94.8-15

Permanent Framework of Love
Daily Reading: Galatians 2

For through the law I died to the law, so that I might live to God. I have been crucified with Christ. It is no longer I who live, but Christ who lives in me. And the life I now live in the flesh I live by faith in the Son of God, who loved me and gave himself for me. (Galatians 2.19-20)

Devotional Thought: "Jesus paid it all! All to him I owe. Sin had left a crimson stain. He washed it white as snow." Reading today's chapter of Galatians makes me think of that old hymn. There was no law that I could follow, no work that I could do, which would save me from my sin. Only Jesus could do that.

So what of the law? Why do we need it? For a couple reasons...

One, we need it to give us an understanding of what a godly life should look like. Even when we are saved, we do not automatically start living holy. That takes time and growth and discipline. The Bible gives us a goal. And, beyond helping us to live a holy life, the law helps us gauge a person's veracity to the faith. "By their fruits you will know them." If we don't know what the fruits look like, then we won't know if a person is genuinely following Christ. This is very important when it comes to those whose faith we emulate.

But, we also need the law to show us that conformity is impossible. We need the grace of Jesus. Through the law, we die to the hopes of ever being saved by the law. The law brings us in our frustration to Christ and his grace. I love what one author wrote: "In the edifice of the Christian life, the temporary scaffolding of duty should give way to the permanent framework of love" (R. E. Howard).

Prayer: Lord, I thank you for your law. Thank you that - as a schoolmaster - the law brings me to you. Help me, however, to build my life and faith not on the law, but on the love of God in Christ Jesus. Amen.

Psalm of the Day: 94.16-23

On What Do You Rely?

Daily Reading: Galatians 3

> *For all who rely on works of the law are under a curse; for it is written, "Cursed be everyone who does not abide by all things written in the Book of the Law, and do them." (Galatians 3:10)*

Devotional Thought: In Galatia, many Christians were attempting to combine Judaism with Christianity – legalism with grace. Paul would have none of it! As he says in verse 3, "Are you so foolish? Having begun by the Spirit, are you now being perfected by the flesh?" In other words, either the sacrifice of Jesus is enough to cover your sins, or you will be held accountable to every letter of the Law on the Day of Judgment.

The Law was given because of our sinful nature. It "imprisoned everything under sin, so that the promise by faith in Jesus Christ might be given to those who believe" (v.22). Before, we were slaves, but now through faith in Christ we are sons and daughters of God. Jesus came to live the perfect life that we could not live, died the death that we deserve, and then showed his lordship over death and sin – then and only then could the Law be perfectly satisfied and our salvation secured.

Do we live as the Galatians at times? Do we insist that everyone around us conform to our ideas of what it looks like to be a Christian? Do we only associate with people who look like us or act like us, afraid to embrace those new to the faith and needing discipleship? It is true - there is absolute right and wrong, and sin should be addressed. But there will also be times when we must lay aside our differences, as Paul encouraged the Galatians to do, to unite in the Spirit as the body of Christ – each one of us justified by grace through faith alone.

Jenny

Prayer: Lord, help us to understand that nothing we can do could ever be enough to save us. It is only through your Son's sacrifice that we have hope. Bring us together; unite us in your Son's holy name.

Psalm of the Day: 95.1-5

I'm Pahpooh, but Not to You

Daily Reading: Galatians 4

> And because you are sons, God has sent the Spirit of his Son into our hearts, crying, "Abba! Father!" So you are no longer a slave, but a son, and if a son, then an heir through God. (Galatians 4.6-7)

Devotional Thought: A few days ago I was in IHOP - witnessing, of course. I would never go there to eat pancakes with warm maple syrup! - and I overheard a gentleman say, "Stay with Pahpooh." I looked around quickly to see if I knew him. You see, I've met lots of Grandpas, some Gramps, and a few Papaws... But, I only know one Pahpooh. That's me! Pahpooh is what my first grandchild - Avery - christened me when she first realized who I was. She didn't / couldn't say Papaw. Instead, it came out Pahpooh, and it stuck! I didn't have time to ask the gentleman his story, but we had a good laugh at each of us being "Pahpooh." He, like me, loved to hear his granddaughter call him "Pahpooh."

Pahpooh. Nobody else calls me that, but because they "belong" to me, my grandchildren have that special name for me.

God has a special name that we can call him: Abba. It is the Hebrew equivalent of saying, Daddy. We get to call God Daddy! Why? Because we belong to him. Slaves don't get to do that. We are part of the family. As Paul wrote later in this chapter we, "like Isaac, are children of promise" (v.28).

All the promises of life are ours as children of God. We are *heirs* to the kingdom! Think about being an heir to a vast fortune and empire. It would change your outlook, would it not? Well, we are heirs to an everlasting inheritance. And that, my friends, changes everything!

I'm Pahpooh, but not to you, only to my grandchildren. And God is Abba only to *his* children. Are you a child of God? You can be!

Prayer: Daddy, thank you for your amazing love! I am so glad that you have made me a part of your family. Help me to live in confidence, victory and freedom because of the certainty of my inheritance in Christ. Amen.

Psalm of the Day: 95.6-11

What's the Difference?

Daily Reading: Galatians 5-6

> *Bear one another's burdens, and so fulfill the law of Christ.*
> (Galatians 5.2)

Devotional Thought: I heard the story once of a woman who was married to a very demanding and demeaning man. (No, it's not Lana's story!) When they first married he had given her a list of things she had to do for him every day, including cooking, cleaning and laundry. She kept that list in her dresser drawer to remind her to fulfill all his expectations. She did not wish to suffer his wrath if she failed. Every day she labored under those burdensome duties, resentful and sad. After many years, the overbearing husband died, and over the course of time she met another man. They married and he treated her like a queen. Their home was happy and her heart was full of joy and love. One day as she was going through some things in her dresser, she came across the old list, faded and torn. As she looked at it, she was surprised! She was doing every one of those things for her husband now without even thinking about it. What had been a burden had become a delight. What was the difference? The difference was love.

That difference, of course, explains the joy we find in serving God and one another. The old song goes, "He ain't heavy. He's my brother." It's true, of course. When we love somebody, bearing their burdens is not a heavy task but a joy and delight.

"Fulfill the law of Christ," Paul wrote. What is that law? It is the law of love. And that makes all the difference in the world!

Prayer: Thank you, Lord Jesus, that you love me with a perfect and unconditional love. Because of that love, you gave your life for me. Help me to love you and live for you and to love and serve others as well. Amen.

Psalm of the Day: 96.1-6

In Tribulation, Be In the Spirit

Daily Reading: Revelation 1

> *I, John, your brother and partner in the tribulation and the kingdom and the patient endurance that are in Jesus, was on the island called Patmos on account of the word of God and the testimony of Jesus. I was in the Spirit on the Lord's day, and I heard behind me a loud voice like a trumpet saying...* (Revelation 1.9-10)

Devotional Thought: Have you ever felt rejected because of your Christian testimony? It seems that it is more acceptable than ever to exclude people from public discourse and 'benefits' simply because they are men and women of faith. The writer of Revelation, John, was on an island of exile because of his faith. But that didn't stop him from worshiping on Sunday (the Lord's Day). He was 'in the Spirit' in spite of the persecution he endured. And while John was worshiping in the Spirit, Jesus showed up! John heard "a loud voice like a trumpet" reveal to him things to come.

Some of our most trying times, our times of rejection, our moments of despondency, are the occasions of God's revelation to us. When we feel forgotten and lost, God appears on the scene. "It was in exile that Jacob saw God at Bethel; in exile that Moses saw God at the burning bush; in exile that Elijah heard the 'still small voice;' in exile that Ezekiel saw 'the likeness of the glory of the Lord' by the river Chebar; in exile that Daniel saw 'the Ancient of days'" (Plummer, *BBC*)

Are you in exile now? Don't be dismayed. Look for Jesus. Like John, worship Jesus in Spirit and truth. Be brother and partner to those of like precious faith. In the midst of the clamor and confusion, listen for the still small voice. In tribulation and trials, endure with patience. You are a citizen of the Kingdom, and Jesus is your King. And he will come to you!

Prayer: Lord, when I am lonely, remind me that you are with me - Emmanuel. When I am discouraged, help me to worship you in Spirit and in truth. Speak to me, O Lord, and show me your ways. Amen.

Psalm of the Day: 96.7-13

Jesus Sees, Speaks, and Prevails
Daily Reading: Revelation 2

The words of the Son of God, who has eyes like a flame of fire, and whose feet are like burnished bronze. (Revelation 2.18)

Devotional Thought: In Revelation 2, we read the message of Jesus to several churches in Asia Minor. As he spoke to the church at Thyatira, he identified himself as having eyes like a flame of fire, feet like burnished bronze, and words to share with his church. As I read that I thought, "Jesus sees. Jesus prevails. Jesus speaks."

Jesus sees with eyes like a flame of fire. Yesterday was a full eclipse, and we were reminded that we need the sun to light our days, otherwise we are not able to see. Jesus is different, though. He supplies his own light. He is the light, and his eyes are a burning radiance that illuminates everything to him. When others don't know, when they don't understand, we can be confident that he sees through all our darkness and despair.

Jesus prevails over all of his enemies, treading over them with feet like burnished bronze. Jesus has been through the fire of death and grave and hell. He trampled those enemies with his feet of victory and strength. Having passed through those fires himself, he has shown himself to be the Victor over all our problems as well. His feet have gone where you struggle now. He has overcome. He comes to you now, so that you, too, may prevail with him.

Jesus speaks as the Son of God. He speaks to the Father for us, and he speaks to us from the Father. His words are trustworthy. They are power. They are life. He speaks with all the authority of heaven. Hear him and find strength for the day.

Jesus sees. Jesus speaks. Jesus prevails.

Prayer: Jesus, Son of God, in you I find direction, victory, and confidence. You see. You speak. You prevail. I trust in you. Amen.

Psalm of the Day: 97.1-7

Eclipsed by the Eclipse

Daily Reading: Revelation 3

Wake up, and strengthen what remains and is about to die, for I have not found your works complete in the sight of my God. (Revelation 3.2)

Devotional Thought: Lana and I were in Nashville to view the eclipse with our daughter and granddaughters. We took off for home in the late afternoon, shortly after the total eclipse was complete. We thought we had a five hour drive before us. That five hour drive turned into a ten hour marathon as two million people left Nashville together. There were times that I just wanted to pull out of traffic and find a place to stop, but I had a job to do - get Lana home safely and get me home, too! I just kept telling myself: "One more mile..." We made it. We were weary and bleary, but we completed the journey. And, oh, how good it felt to arrive at home!

As Jesus spoke to the church in Sardis, he realized that they, too, had become weary on the journey, so weary that they had fallen asleep! Life was still in them, but it was "about to die." They needed to take immediate action. He told them to wake up and complete the work that was theirs to do.

How about you? Are you growing weary on the journey? Are you tempted to give up your work for the Lord? Don't be eclipsed by the eclipse. Keep going. One more mile. Remember the words of the Apostle Paul: "Let us not grow weary of doing good, for in due season we will reap, if we do not give up" (Galatians 6.9).

Prayer: Father, thank you for giving me grace and strength for the journey. Help me, O Lord, to complete the work you have given me to do. In the name of Jesus - who did not stop short of the cross - I pray. Amen.

Psalm of the Day: 97.8-12

Sing a New Song!

Daily Reading: Revelation 4-5

And they sang a new song... (Revelation 5.9a)

Devotional Thought: Yesterday was an exciting day! Our choir started back up after taking some time off for the summer. Lana told us about some new songs and a new Christmas musical. We practiced some of the new songs as well as a few of the old favorites! I love them both - the new and the old.

Someone once observed that heaven is "the homeland of music." We see that in Revelation 5, where that great heavenly choir sings a new song! What is that song? It is a song to Jesus! "Worthy are you to take the scroll and to open its seals, for you were slain, and by your blood you ransomed people for God from every tribe and language and people and nation!"

Aren't you glad that he has ransomed you by his blood? Aren't you glad that he took you from the darkness of sin and brought you into the kingdom of his light? You and I at one time were foreigners and aliens to the kingdom of God, but we have been redeemed by Jesus!

We will be singing that new song forever and ever! One day Jesus will gather us to himself and the heavenly orchestra will strike the first chord. We will join our voices together and praise our Lord and Savior!

I can't wait to sing in *that* choir!

Prayer: Jesus, I praise you for redeeming me from sin and delivering me into your kingdom. Help me to sing every day from a heart overflowing with joy and freedom. You are worthy! Amen.

Psalm of the Day: 98.1-9

From *Every* Nation...

Daily Reading: Revelation 6-7

After this I looked, and behold, a great multitude that no one could number, from every nation, from all tribes and peoples and languages, standing before the throne and before the Lamb, clothed in white robes, with palm branches in their hands, and crying out with a loud voice, "Salvation belongs to our God who sits on the throne, and to the Lamb!" (Revelation 7.9-10)

Devotional Thought: Revelation is such a striking book of the Bible – unlike any of the others, containing symbolic imagery, prophecy, action, destruction and restoration. Many other books contain these elements, but none so full of the rich symbolism and strange images. It is difficult to understand at best! One section that stands out in the 6th and 7th chapters occurs in Rev. 7:9-10, as John is shown a great multitude from every nation, tribe, people and language, standing before the throne and before the Lamb, clothed in white robes and praising the Lord.

If this doesn't excite your heart towards missions, I'm not sure what will! The thought of worshiping alongside every type of person, with only our faith in common, is powerful and encouraging. There are none outside of the reach of Jesus – Muslim, Jew, Buddhist, atheist, agnostic; souls from Syria, Iraq, Guatemala, Nicaragua, Russia – even America! There is no commonality that could possibly link us all together other than faith in Jesus. It is this unlikely bond in the Spirit that attracts others to us. They are drawn to the love of Christ.

When we encounter those who don't look like us, act like us, or think like us in our churches, are we thrilled that they are there, or simply tolerant of it while keeping to our own smaller groups? That the body of Christ is made up of every nation, people, and tongue is no coincidence; we all have different and unique gifts to contribute to the body. And we will all eventually be worshiping around the throne, dancing and singing: "Blessing and glory and wisdom and thanksgiving and honor and power and might be to our God forever and ever! Amen!"

Jenny

Prayer: Our hearts long for that day of being home, of worshiping around the throne of our Father! Lord, give us hearts like yours, compassion for others and a desire that not one of the souls around us would be lost.

Psalm of the Day: 99.1-9

Shush Up!

Daily Reading: Revelation 8-9

> *And another angel came and stood at the altar with a golden censer, and he was given much incense to offer with the prayers of all the saints on the golden altar before the throne.* (Revelation 8.3)

Devotional Thought: "Shush up!" That euphemism is popular when we have taught our children not to use the words "shut up." I like it! As a matter of fact, I think maybe the Lord used it or something like it in Revelation 8. Chapter 7 concludes with a scene of highest praise. Then something unexpected happens. The Lamb opens the seventh seal, and "there was silence in heaven for about half an hour." In the midst of boisterous and excited praise, silence spreads across the heavenly landscape. It's as if the Lord said, "Shush up!"

Why? Why did the Lord shush up the heavenly praise rally?

The silence is explained in verse 3, when another angel came and offered up the prayers of all the saints. Heaven was shushed so that our prayers could be heard. Is that not amazing? At that moment at least, our needs were of greater concern than were the hymns of heaven. When you pray, remember that. Your prayers are being offered before the throne of God as an offering of incense.

The angel was standing "at the altar with a golden censer." There is only one altar in heaven. It is the altar of incense. No longer is the brazen altar of sacrifice needed. Christ has provided the perfect sacrifice for sins. Now it is our prayers that are offered in sacrifice - fulfilling the sufferings of Christ! (Colossians 1.24)

Prayer: Lord, with the Psalmist (Psalm 141.2) I pray, "Let my prayer be counted as incense before you, and the lifting up of my hands as the evening sacrifice!" Amen.

Psalm of the Day: 100.1-5

The Best Price of All

Daily Reading: Revelation 10-11

> *And I took the little scroll from the hand of the angel and ate it. It was sweet as honey in my mouth, but when I had eaten it my stomach was made bitter.* (Revelation 10.10)

Devotional Thought: "Your convertible's ready..." I was so excited to hear that message from Ronnie Price Upholstery & Top Shop. "Sweet! Just in time for spring!" But when I got there, I was reminded what the "Price" part meant in Ronnie Price Upholstery & Top Shop meant. I felt a little ill.

John the Revelator had an experience like that. He got a message from heaven that at first tasted sweet, but then it upset his stomach! It was such a little scroll... But it was bittersweet, revealing judgment as well as mercy.

The message of Christ to the church is bittersweet, isn't it? There is the wonderful news of redemption, but there is also the sad reality that there are those who will reject God's offer. Ralph Earle wrote: "To be close to Christ is to experience the exquisite sweetness of His presence. But there is also a price to pay, that of sharing His sorrows in the face of sin that destroys men for whom He died" (*BBC*, 561).

Actually, Ronnie Price gave me the best price of all the places I checked. It was in reality a bargain. We may think that God's way is demanding, but when we consider the price that Jesus paid, and the cost we would pay without him, then we see that we are getting a great deal. May God help us communicate that with others!

Prayer: Lord, help me to eat the Word of God, taking the bitter with the sweet. And help me to share the Truth with all those I meet. Amen.

Psalm of the Day: 101.1-8

A Great Sign Appeared in Heaven

Daily Reading: Revelation 12-13

And a great sign appeared in heaven. (Revelation 12.1a)

Devotional Thought: A solar eclipse prompted today's devotion. There was a lot of attention given to "The Great American Solar Eclipse" in 2017. Today's devotion is based - in part - upon an article by Doug Estes in *Christianity Today*, online edition.

Estes writes: "There are no clear-cut examples of eclipses recorded in the Bible. However, there is one clear use of eclipse in a book that was likely known to Jesus, Paul, James, and most of the first Christians. It occurs in the wisdom of Ben Sira, which many people today call Ecclesiasticus. In his book, popular among the Hebrew people in Jesus' day, Ben Sira reaches a point where he calls on the people of God to repent of their sins. People are nothing compared to God; we don't have the power to even change the course of our lives. 'What is brighter than the sun? Yet it can be eclipsed,' he wrote. We humans like to revel in our splendor, but we are so naturally eclipsed by our brokenness."

Usually there are dire warnings aplenty when natural events like an eclipse take place. Celestial phenomenon, meteorological anomalies, geological upheavals are all seen as harbingers of judgment and are occasions for predictions of doom and dismay. But, we need no occasion besides the great tragedy of sin and its effects. As Estes indicated, our own brokenness eclipses the imagined greatness to which we so desperately cling.

So, what can we learn from eclipses and earthquakes? Are they signs? If so what are they signs of? Yes they are signs. They are signs of the power and majesty of God. As the Psalmist said, "The heavens declare the glory of God." When we see these signs, may we remember we are a part of "God's grand creation" (Estes).

Prayer: Father, thank you for the wonder of creation all around me. Thank you that your love fills this vast universe you made. Thank you for the reminders of your love and power. Amen.

Psalm of the Day: 102.1-11

The End of Labors, Not of Deeds

Daily Reading: Revelation 14-15

And I heard a voice from heaven saying, "Write this: Blessed are the dead who die in the Lord from now on." "Blessed indeed," says the Spirit, "that they may rest from their labors, for their deeds follow them!" (Revelation 14.13)

Devotional Thought: A momentous milestone has come and gone in my life: my sixtieth birthday. Yikes! Having passed that marker, my mind seems to go more and more to my work and legacy. Am I making a difference? Will it last? The Bible says it will. While we will one day rest from our labors, our deeds will follow us.

The word for *labors* in this verse means, "trouble, toil, or labor that involves weariness and fatigue." One day we will rest from our labors. We will lay our burdens down. Our work on earth will be ended. At times that sounds like a great idea. At other times, I enjoy what I do so much that I can't fathom doing it no longer.

The word for *deeds* on the other hand has to do with accomplishment. What we have accomplished, what we have done, what we have completed - will not 'die' with our physical death. These things will continue their influence on earth until one day all accomplishments will be gathered up and placed before the Lord to his glory and praise.

Our works will bring honor to Jesus forever and ever! How will that be? It can only be because the lives we have influenced will live forever and ever. One day those you have helped on the journey will join you around the throne giving praise and honor and glory to Jesus!

Hallelujah!

Prayer: Help me, O Lord, to be faithful in all my trouble, toil and labor so that my deeds will follow me - in the form of ransomed souls! - all the way to heaven's throne. Amen.

Psalm of the Day: 102.12-17

The Speaking Altar

Daily Reading: Revelation 16

> And I heard the altar saying, "Yes, Lord God the Almighty, true and just are your judgments!" (Revelation 16.7)

Devotional Thought: In Revelation 16.6, John heard an angel speaking. Then something unusual happened. John heard the *altar* speak. What? How can an altar speak? It is an inanimate object, a piece of furniture, an aid to worship. How could John hear it say anything?

The answer to that question lies in the description of the altar in heaven. Three voices are heard from the altar in Revelation: the voice of those martyred for their testimony (6.9), the voice of the saints lifted in prayer (8.3) and the voice of angels announcing the judgment of God (9.13, 14.8). The altar, then, becomes the voice of the dying saints, the living (praying) saints, and the vindicated saints. When it speaks, it speaks as the combined voice of the saints.

What does this voice say?
From the martyrs we are made to understand that God sees our sufferings. One day we will see them in the full light of heaven.

From the praying saints, we are made to understand that God hears every word that we cry out to him. These prayers are being stored up in heaven to be poured out at the proper time.

From the vindicated saints we are made to understand that God keeps careful records and that we will receive our reward in due time.

"Yes, Lord God the Almighty, true and just are your judgments!"

Prayer: Father, may my voice to added to that of the saints across the ages. May my prayers and my sufferings, my faith and my fears, be vindicated by your Truth and Justice. Amen.

Psalm of the Day: 102.18-28

Tumult and Triumph

Daily Reading: Revelation 17

And he carried me away in the Spirit into a wilderness...
(Revelation 17.3a)

Devotional Thought: In Revelation 17, we are nearing the end. There is a great tumult to come (Chapter 18, the fall of Babylon, representing the collapse of this present age). There is also a great triumph to come (Chapters 19-22, the rise of the saints of God to everlasting life). Before John was to see the end, however, there was one more journey he had to make - the journey to the wilderness. It was from the wilderness that these things began to unfold.

That is often the case. The wilderness is the stage in our journey that prepares us for tumult and for triumph.

Moses went to the wilderness before the distress and deliverance of the Israelites. Paul went to the wilderness before his persecution for and preaching of the gospel. John the Baptist went to the wilderness to proclaim repentance and to prepare the way of the Lord. Jesus himself went to the wilderness to face his trials and to see the face of his Father.

Perhaps you are in a wilderness right now. You may not be sure how you got there. You definitely are not sure of what is next. Let your wildernesses be places of preparation - for further tumult perhaps (The darkest hour is just before dawn) - but definitely for ultimate triumph. Though silent, God is with you in the wilderness. As did Ezekiel, through the tumult may you hear his 'still small voice,' bringing you to triumph.

Prayer: Jesus, I feel that I'm in a wilderness right now. Help me to trust in you even when I can't see you. To keep the faith even when it seems I have lost my way. Amen.

Psalm of the Day: 103.1-5

Hard Truths

Daily Reading: Revelation 18

> *"Alas, alas, for the great city that was clothed in fine linen, in purple and scarlet, adorned with gold, with jewels, and with pearls! For in a single hour all this wealth has been laid waste."* (Revelation 18:16-17)

Devotional Thought: Contained in all the graphic imagery that we find in Revelation 18 are some hard truths, particularly the ultimate destruction of "Babylon" (representative of the world's economic and political power). We also find the responses from the nonbelievers and the believers.

The "kings of the earth" who participated in her debauchery stand "far off in fear of her torment" (v.10) and are selfishly mourning the impact of her destruction on their own wealth and well-being: "The merchants of the earth weep and mourn for her, since no one buys their cargo anymore" (v.11).

There is another perspective at the end of the chapter. In heaven, the saints and apostles and prophets rejoice, for "God has given judgment for you against her!" (v.20). From their point of view, God has vindicated those who were martyred by Babylon. We were given a vision of these souls earlier in Rev. 6:9-10, "those who had been slain for the word of God and for the witness they had borne."

We know as God's people we will be at odds with "Babylon"... no matter what people/nation that represents today. Without the righteous judgment of God coming upon this wicked people/nation, after much warning and many attempts at mercy, the goodness of heaven would fail. The new heaven and the new and perfected earth would not be realized, and God would not be good. But praise the Lord for his great love and his great justice! He will not let sin go unpunished, and because of that we have the wonderful hope of an eternity in the presence of God, with no tears, pain, death, or sorrow.

Jenny

Prayer: Lord, help us to see the Babylon influence in our own lives, hearts, and minds. Cleanse us from worldly desires and lead us in the way of righteousness, for your name's sake.

Psalm of the Day:103.6-14

Hallelujah!

Daily Reading: Revelation 19

> *Hallelujah! For the Lord our God the Almighty reigns. Let us rejoice and exult and give him the glory!* (Revelation 19.6b-7a)

Devotional Thought: Do you remember singing the children's chorus "Hallelu, Hallelu, Hallelu, Hallelujah! Praise ye the Lord!"? We still love to do that one in church don't we? Those of us who are a little older may not jump up like we used to, but our spirits leap within us when we sing those words! Do you know what hallelujah means? From Hebrew, Hallel means praise and jah is the suffix for Yahweh, or Jehovah. So Hallelujah means simply, "Praise the Lord!"

In Revelation 19, we see a picture of heavenly worshipers jumping up like kids and singing: "Hallelu, Hallelu, Hallelu, Hallelujah!" Like the children's chorus, there are four "Hallelujahs" in this chapter. Let's praise the Lord for...
His salvation and glory and power and judgments (vv. 1-2). God is worthy of praise just because he is God! His attributes are unspeakable!

Our vindication seen in the judgment of sin (v. 3). How can we ever praise God enough for Jesus, the Savior? We have been set free from sin's dominion!

Making us his servants, whether we are small or great in the eyes of man (v. 5). We do not need the praise of man who perishes, but that of God which lasts for eternity! I want to please him!

The marriage of the Lamb which is to come when we will reign with him in righteousness forever and ever! (vv. 6-8). Praise God from whom all blessings flow!

One day we will be transported from the veil of tears and we shall join the hosts of heaven singing his praises forever and ever. Hallelujah!

Prayer: O Lord, I want to be in that number when the saints go marching home, when they lift their voices in eternal praise to you. Hallelujah!

Psalm of the Day: 103.15-22

Living the Dream

Daily Reading: Revelation 20

Blessed and holy... (Revelation 20.6)

Devotional Thought: Often when I greet one of my friends and ask him how he is doing, he says, "I'm living the dream!" That's good! I want to live the dream, don't you?

In Revelation 20, we read about a group of people who are living the dream: "Blessed and holy is the one who shares in the first resurrection! Over such the second death has no power, but they will be priests of God and of Christ, and they will reign with him for a thousand years." Though I don't want to get bogged down with the various interpretations of the millennium, we can find some things in this verse that will help us all live the dream!

The word for blessed is *makarios*, and it means "blessed, happy." The word for holy is *hagios*, and it means "set apart for the Lord." From these two words in this verse, we can ask ourselves, "Why are God's people blessed? What makes holy people happy people? Like the resurrected saints in Revelation 20, we are happy and holy because...

We anticipate the resurrection of Christ. This present life is passing away, but we have our hope set on heaven. We live with happiness now - in spite of the trials and troubles of this world - because we know a brighter day awaits.

Speaking of power, we are happy because *death has no power over us*. Death has lost its sting. Whether our own death or that of one we love, Christ has defeated the last enemy!

We are priests of God and Christ. We serve God and his cause with joy!

We will reign with him. Forever. With Christ.

Happy, indeed, are we, for we are living the dream!

Prayer: Thank you, Father, for making me happy and holy. It is only by your grace that this is so. Help me to live the dream with confidence and overflowing joy, and with love for all those around me. Amen.

Psalm of the Day: 104.1-9

Will Call

Daily Reading: Revelation 21

> *Those who conquer will inherit these things, and I will be their God and they will be my children.* (Revelation 21.7, NRSV)

Devotional Thought: I've had people purchase tickets for me to pick up at the box office. The tickets were paid for and marked "will call." All I had to do was "call" - stop and get them. I like that!

In Revelation 21, heaven is described as our inheritance. It has been paid for. It is ours. We need only to call, conquering by the blood of Jesus.

What will we inherit when we conquer? Heaven will be a holy place, a healing place, a beautiful place. There will be no more tears there, no more sorrow there, no more sickness there. In heaven we will never die, we will never be lonely, and we will never walk in darkness. In heaven we will drink from the River of Life, eat from the Tree of Life, read from the Book of Life, and wear the Crown of Life. We will sing. We will worship. We will rejoice.

Those who conquer will inherit all these *things*. Wonderful! But wait! There is something more... God will be their God, and they will be God's children. I know how I love and care for my children and grandchildren. "Things" account for very little of the blessings of heaven. God himself is the true blessing. His love is the greatest of the gifts! I'm so glad I'm a part of the family of God!

What a glorious inheritance is ours in Jesus! The tickets are paid for by the blood of Jesus. Will you call?

Prayer: Lord, thank you for paying the price for me to inherit eternal life with you. I call upon your name right now to receive the gift and the assurance of eternal life. Amen.

Psalm of the Day: 104.10-15

What a Day That Will Be!

Daily Reading: Revelation 22

They will see his face, and his name will be on their foreheads.
(Revelation 22.4)

Devotional Thought: After a long day, I love coming home. There is a place on the road where I crest a hill, and the front of my house comes into view. It's a beautiful sight! But the best part of all is going through the door and seeing my bride! Sometimes I have to look for her - she's busy doing something somewhere else in the house - but I gladly take up the search! I never tire of seeing her face.

In Revelation 22, John wrote that those who enter heaven will see the face of Jesus, and his name will be on their foreheads. That is a picture of perfect fellowship and complete consecration.

Perfect fellowship. The Bible says now we see dimly, but one day we will see face-to-face. We will see him as he is and we will be like him. What we didn't understand before will become clear to us. The weaknesses of the flesh, the limitations of the mind, and the burdens of life will roll away and we will see Jesus.

Complete Consecration: The name of Jesus will be on our foreheads, indicating the fact that we belong to him. We have consecrated our lives to him, trusting him with every aspect of our being. For eternity, we will be in that condition of full surrender to and trust in him.

There is coming a day when we will crest the final hill and see the face of Jesus. What a day that will be!

Prayer: Jesus, thank you for loving me. Thank you for preparing a place for me. Thank you for the promise that one day you will welcome me there to be with you forever. Amen.

Psalm of the Day: 104.16-23

The Lord Spoke to Him

Daily Reading: Leviticus 1-2

> *The Lord called Moses and spoke to him from the tent of meeting, saying, "Speak to the people of Israel...* (Leviticus 1.1-2a)

Devotional Thought: Here we go! We are starting on a journey through Leviticus. You may wonder what in the world all these purification laws and ritualistic regulations have to do with the Christian. As we go through these chapters, I hope you will see the abiding truth behind these Old Testament practices.

Leviticus starts with God calling out to Moses from the tent of meeting. What a great image! There was a place where Moses could go and meet with God! And, God would take the initiative to speak to him from that sacred place. Do you have such a time and place in your life? Leave space for God and he will speak to you.

Lest Moses would get 'lost' in contemplation and spiritual ecstasies, God made it clear that this encounter with him was about more than God and Moses: "Speak to the people of Israel and say to them..." Too often we can get the idea that "Me and Jesus got this good thing going..." We feel that's what it's all about. I do want to have a good thing going with Jesus, and I want you to have the same. But, there is more to it than that. There should arise out of our conversations with God a concern for God's people. If our Christianity does not result in service and sacrifice in the church, it is something less than what God intends. Jesus knows of no "Churchless Christianity." That is an idea fabricated by folks who don't want to get messy with other peoples' stuff. It is a lie of Satan designed to diminish and cripple the Church.

Take time to go to church, to listen to the Lord, and to serve his people! God will bless you for it!

Prayer: Father, thank you that you were concerned for not just Moses, but for the people of Israel. Help me to take that principle and apply it to my relationship to your people. In the name of Jesus, who died to make the church holy. Amen.

Psalm of the Day: 104.24-35

Guaranteed Forgiveness

Daily Reading: Leviticus 3-4

> And the priest shall make atonement for him for the sin which he has committed, and he shall be forgiven. (Leviticus 4.35b)

Devotional Thought: I have spent time with various friends in court. It's not a fun place to be, but I have to admit, it is interesting! One thing that I find amazing is the failure of many defendants to take advantage of various offers by the judges. "If you will do this, then the court will..." Everything is provided for by the court except for the cooperation of the defendant. At that point, the judge's hands are tied. He or she has done all they can. If the defendant chooses not to cooperate, the sentence must be pronounced.

In the book of Leviticus, we read how God graciously provided atonement for the sins which people committed. When a person by faith fulfilled his end of the deal, then "he shall be forgiven." There was no question on God's part. God stood ready to forgive. "The priest shall make atonement for him..." The priest - on behalf of God - did the "work" of the sacrifice. The worshiper had only to put faith in the actions of the priest, who fulfilled God's side of the equation.

We have a Priest who has made atonement for our sins. It is Jesus Christ the Righteous. We only have to put our faith in the work of this Priest. When we do so, "We shall be forgiven." Hallelujah! If sins in the Old Testament were forgiven based on the sacrifice of lambs and rams, of birds and bundles of grain, think about how effective is the sacrifice of God's Son on the cross! There is no doubt as to the effectiveness of that sacrifice! Forgiveness is guaranteed!

Prayer: Thank you, Lord Jesus, for providing the perfect sacrifice for my sins. By faith I receive your perfect forgiveness and consecrate my life to you. Help me to live in ways that honor your sacrifice today. Amen.

Psalm of the Day: 105.1-6

Just Bring Yourself!

Daily Reading: Leviticus 5

> *But if he cannot afford a lamb, then he shall bring to the Lord as his compensation for the sin that he has committed...* (Leviticus 5.7a)

Devotional Thought: Often when my wife and I invite someone for dinner at our house, we are asked the question, "What can I bring?" When asked, we typically say, "Just bring yourselves!" People don't like that though. They want to bring something to contribute. We recognize that, for we do the same thing when we receive invitations.

God recognized that, too, for in Leviticus 5, he made provision for people to bring things for the sin offerings at the tabernacle. Worshipers of God, however, have varying abilities and resources. Some could bring lambs, but others could only afford turtledoves and pigeons. These could be purchased or caught in nets. There were some who did not have even that to bring. God said, "Just bring a bit of flour."

God bends over backwards to make a way for all of us. Lack of money is not to be a hindrance to our receiving forgiveness.

In the New Testament, we find Jesus looking at the temple treasury when a poor widow dropped in two pennies. Though her gift was not as big as those brought by well-to-do worshipers, she wanted to do something. Jesus surprised his disciples when he told them that her gift was actually bigger than what had been presented by those with great resources. Giving "all she had to live on," she basically gave herself.

And that is the key. No gift is big enough to buy God. What God wants is our complete trust. We just need to bring ourselves, to give ourselves completely. In his famous hymn, *Rock of Ages,* Augustus Toplady penned these words: "Nothing in my hands I bring. Simply to Thy cross I cling."

Do you need forgiveness of sins? Just bring yourself.

Prayer: Thank you, Lord Jesus that you paid the price for our sins. You have invited us to the table of life, to feast with you. We want to bring something, Lord, but all we have is ourselves. Here we are, Lord. We are yours. Amen.

Psalm of the Day: 105.7-15

Right With God and With You

Daily Reading: Leviticus 6

> *If he has sinned and has realized his guilt and will restore what he took by robbery... He shall restore it in full and shall add a fifth to it, and give it to him to whom it belongs on the day he realizes his guilt.*
> (Leviticus 6.4-5)

Devotional Thought: My Uncle Cedric was very generous to me. He 'graced' me with many things - most significantly his love. As I neared the end of college, I needed help to pay off a particular bill. I turned to Uncle Cedric for a loan of $134 (if my memory serves me correctly), not much by today's standards, but I needed it to finish school. It was important to me and it was a huge sum to a college kid.

After I graduated, Uncle Cedric continued to grace me with his love and gifts. I forgot the loan. For a time... But, in spite of all he had given me in the past and continued to give me, I knew that it wasn't right for me to ignore it. I did not want to presume upon his generosity, and I wouldn't have peace as long as I owed him that $134. So, I contacted him to pay it back.

In the reception of God's grace, it is tempting to neglect our obligations to others. But God doesn't want us to live that way. His mercy and forgiveness do not nullify what I owe someone else! Just because I'm right with God doesn't mean I'm right with you! So, packed into the chapter about atonement for sin, God makes it clear that I must right the wrongs of my past. We call it restitution. I've had to do it. It is a freeing experience.

Back to Uncle Cedric. When I contacted him, he laughed about it and said he had forgotten it and I could too. But, how grateful I am that I cleared that account! Do you have any accounts that need cleared?

Prayer: Father, thank you that my account with you is clear. I have received forgiveness of sins through Jesus Christ! But, Lord, help me to take care of any debt that I may owe others. In Jesus' name I pray. Amen.

Psalm of the Day: 105.16-22

It's Time for the Offering!

Daily Reading: Leviticus 7

His own hands shall bring the Lord's food offerings. (Leviticus 7.30a)

Devotional Thought: One evening at church, two of my little buddies, Griffin and Brennen, gave me a birthday card. I could tell they were excited, as they watched for me and ran up to me. After they gave me the card, they jumped into my arms for a big hug! What a great offering!

Do we feel that way when we bring our offerings to God? "It's time for the offering" are the most dreaded words in church! But should they be? God says: "His own hands shall bring the Lord's offerings..." There's a lot packed into that statement. We are to...

bring our offerings. I love to get gifts, don't you? Especially in person. The card would have been nice in the mail, but hand-delivered - with a hug! - it was wonderful! I think that God feels like this. He loves to see us coming with our offerings and hugs!

bring *our* offerings. The offering I bring in my hands should reflect the work that I've done with my hands. Griffin and Brennen both had signed the card - with their own unique writing. I loved it! They didn't bring me somebody else's card. They brought me theirs! So, it is with our offerings to God. We cannot bring something that is not ours.

bring our *offerings*. Griffin and Brennen were not forced to give me a card. They offered it. Willingly. Joyfully. Excitedly. We give to God that way. He doesn't force our gifts from our hands. He lets us freely give them. Our offerings then become expressions of trust and gratitude, of worship and joy. I don't have to, but I want to!

The next time you hear, "It's time for the offering," jump into God's arms for a big hug!

Prayer: Father, thank you for your love and generosity toward me. I am so excited to bring you offerings of my love and gratitude toward you. The next time the offering comes up, help me to jump into your arms for a big hug! Amen.

Psalm of the Day: 105.23-36

Get It Right

Daily Reading: Leviticus 8

And Moses said to the congregation, "This is the thing that the Lord has commanded to be done." (Leviticus 8.5)

Devotional Thought: Last week I sat in a "surgery consultation room" with an anxious family as the neurosurgeon explained what she had just done for their loved one. They listened intently as they received the good news! I listened purposefully, too, as I knew that I would have to repeat it for others who would want to know the condition of their friend. I wasn't the surgeon. I was the messenger, and I wanted to get the message right.

That was the role that Moses played as he wrote out the guidelines for Aaron and the priests in the book of Leviticus. Moses didn't make it up. He was reporting what God had said to him. As I thought about it, I realized that the people didn't really need to know what Moses said. They needed to know what God commanded them to do. Moses could have been wrong! God never is.

You and I stand in that place when it comes to speaking for God. People don't really need to know what we have to say. We could get it wrong. But, God never gets it wrong! Our role as spokespersons for God is to repeat what he says about a matter. In order to do that, of course, we need to know what he says! We need to listen intently and purposefully. We need to know the Word of God!

So, by all means speak up for God! But make sure you get the message right!

Prayer: Father, I thank you for your Word. Your Word is truth. Help me to convey your message in truth. Amen.

Psalm of the Day: 105.37-45

The Glory of the Lord

Daily Reading: Leviticus 9-10

> And Moses said, "This is the thing that the Lord commanded you to do, that the glory of the Lord may appear to you." (Leviticus 9:6)

Devotional Thought: The Lord instructed Moses and Aaron to institute the sacrificial system. It was a process with many different pieces, designed to help the Israelites understand the seriousness of their sins. Even their unintentional sins required blood sacrifice for atonement. As we read of these laws designed to show the holiness of the Lord, we also see the incredible mercy given to the Israelite people. The Lord always provided a way for his people to reconcile with him.

Aaron and his sons had successfully followed the Lord's requirements, as was evidenced by the end result: "And fire came out from before the Lord and consumed the burnt offering and the pieces of fat on the altar, and when all the people saw it, they shouted and fell on their faces" (v.24). I imagine that the Israelites would have felt a mixture of relief at the acceptance of their offering, and fear at the incredible display of the Lord's power.

We know that the need for this sacrificial system was abolished when the blood of the only perfect Lamb was spilled once and for all to atone for our sins and reconcile us to the Father. But, do we yearn for the glory of the Lord to appear to us still today? Moses' words can be taken into our own hearts: "This is the thing that the Lord commanded you to do, that the glory of the Lord may appear to you," (v.6). Do we strive to draw near to the Lord in prayer and meditation on his Word, and thus experience the same sense of wonder that the Israelites felt as they worshipped him? Let us yearn to encounter the presence and the glory of the Lord as we strive to know and love him more.

Jenny

Prayer: Lord, we long to feel your presence but acknowledge that we so often fail at making time to be with you. Please help us to desire you, and to make our time with you the highest priority in our lives.

Psalm of the Day: 106.1-5

When You Need Time to Get Better
Daily Reading: Leviticus 11-12

> I am the Lord your God. Consecrate yourselves therefore, and be holy, for I am holy. (Leviticus 12.5a)

Devotional Thought: Today's chapter talks about cleanliness after childbirth. One might think you had accidentally stumbled onto a medical book instead of the Bible. However, I see this chapter as another way God shows his love for his people, especially women.

I don't think we can fully understand that in Bible times, there were no hospitals, no doctors, and no one telling people how to stay clean in order to prevent disease. God gave these instructions to Moses because he was in charge of more than 600,000 people. God cared enough about women to address every detail of their lives, even this.

Women in this chapter are not being punished, they were given grace by God to have time to themselves in order to heal. I don't know about other ladies, but after I had my children, I needed time to rest and heal. It was a relief to me that I wasn't expected to be at church the next Sunday after having a baby on Friday night! But, in all seriousness, I see the loving hand of God, providing women a time to heal, to rest, to enjoy their new bundle of joy, without having to be a part of the community.

God cares about women, God cares about babies. He, just like any good parent, is showing his love by giving guidelines for people to follow that keep them safe and healthy. He didn't have to take care of the small details, he could have left that to Moses and Aaron to figure out on their own, but he didn't. God lovingly came down and spoke to Moses one on one to let him know the best way to do things. If that doesn't speak of Immanuel, I don't know what does.

Cheryl Young

Prayer: Lord, thank you for caring about the big and little details of our lives. Thank you that you care so much that you give us guidelines that we can follow that keep us safe. We praise you for loving us that much. Thank you for being Immanuel and always being with us and for us.

Psalm of the Day: 106.6-12

Quarantined!

Daily Reading: Leviticus 13

> *The priest shall shut up the diseased person for seven days...*
> (Leviticus 13.4b)

Devotional Thought: In two days I'm leaving for South Carolina for the arrival of my new grandson! I'm almost ready to go, but I need help loading something on my truck. My friend Matt has agreed to help me, but there is flu in his house! I really appreciate Matt, but I think I'll get someone else to help me...

At times we misread the instructions about leprous diseases, and we think that God is somehow malicious in his intent toward the unfortunate sufferer. Nothing could be further from the truth. God's heart is moved with pity for the one who is sick. His instructions are to help them on the road to recovery.

Part of that recovery included the instructions to "shut up the diseased person for seven days." In the process of diagnosing and treating the disease, the priests were to remove them from the normal interactions of life. What grace! These seven day sabbaticals served two purposes, both redemptive:

This period served as a time of rest. Shut up this way, the sick person was given time to recover. He or she was not bound to complete their regular duties. Others would step in and help. I know how thankful I am for the people who stand in the gap when I am sick.

This period served as a means of protection for the rest of the people. God didn't want people to be rejected in fear. Instead, he protected both the community and the afflicted by setting them aside for a week. In this way, their disease - if it was serious - would not spread. Also, there was a means of returning them into the culture.

Thanks be to God for his grace!

Prayer: Lord, thank you for your concern for the smallest details of our lives. When I am sick or others around me are sick, help us to rest in you and to regain our strength and place in the family and community. Amen.

Psalm of the Day: 106.13-18

He Came to Me

Daily Reading: Leviticus 14

> *And the priest shall go out of the camp, and the priest shall look...*
> (Leviticus 14.3a)

Devotional Thought: In Leviticus 14, we continue with some exciting stuff about the cleansing of infections and uncleanness – in lepers and in houses! Once again, if we are not aware of it, we can miss the grace of God in these instructions. I especially like what we read in Leviticus 14.3. God takes the initiative, instructing the priest to "go out of the camp and... look." The suffering saint is seen as one who - due to his illness - is shut out from the normal associations of life. He cannot even come to the place of atonement. That's OK. The atonement will go to him!

That reminds me of our Jesus! Jesus left the safety, glory and joy of heaven to deliver us from our danger, gloom, and despair. He left the health of heaven to take our sickness. He left the holiness of heaven to come and take our sin away. The Atonement came to us! Praise be to the name of the Lord!

Do you know the old gospel song, "He Came to Me" by Squire Parsons? Consider these words and praise our Savior:

"He came to me, O, He came to me.
When I could not come to where He was, He came to me.
That's why He died on Calvary,
When I could not come to where He was, He came to me.

He came to me when I was bound in chains of sin,
He came to me when I possessed no hope within,
He picked me up and He drew me gently to His side,
Where, today, in His sweet love I now abide."

Prayer: Thank you, Jesus, that as our great High Priest you came to me! I was bound in the disease of sin, but you came to me and set me free! Hallelujah!

Psalm of the Day: 106.19-23

Two Kinds of Uncleanness

Daily Reading: Leviticus 15

> *And this is the law of his uncleanness for a discharge: whether his body runs with his discharge, or his body is blocked up by his discharge, it is his uncleanness.* (Leviticus 15.3)

Devotional Thought: When I told my wife that I was going to write about the uncleanness of bodily discharges for today's devotion, she said, "Yuck! That's the worst!" It is not pleasant thinking about some of the topics in Leviticus. But as we have seen, God's grace is easy to see in these instructions and regulations - if we just look for it!

God is concerned for our cleanness. That concern takes shape in the form of our physical health in Leviticus 15. But, God's concern extends way beyond physical cleanness. He has provided atonement for our spiritual uncleanness. And, he points out the fact that not only is uncleanness in the discharge, but also in the disease that precedes the discharge!

Reading about unclean discharges reminded me of what Jesus said in the New Testament: "It is not what goes into the mouth that defiles a person, but what comes out of the mouth: this defiles a person" (Matthew 15.11). What comes out of our mouths (discharges) makes us unclean because of the heart. The festering envy, anger, hatred, and unforgiveness within us find expression in the harsh and cutting words we say. Both the discharge and the disease need cleansing.

Thanks be to God that Jesus has provided the remedy for all of our uncleanness. The actions and the heart of sin are
healed in Jesus. He forgives our sins (discharge) and gives us a new heart (disease).

Praise the Lord!

Prayer: Lord, by your grace, may the words of my mouth and the meditation of my heart be acceptable in your sight. Amen!

Psalm of the Day: 106.24-31

Who Is This?

Daily Reading: 1 Corinthians 1

Paul, called by the will of God to be an apostle of Christ Jesus, and our brother Sosthenes... (1 Corinthians 1.1)

Devotional Thought: In this day of instant messaging, we have lost much of the formal aspect of communication. Texting is the worst. One thing that is particularly missing in texting is the identification of the sender. I was reminded of that - again! - this week when I texted a teen in our church. I immediately received a text back: "Who is this?" "Kind of rude," I thought, but then I remembered that I have done it many times myself! We take for granted that people will know our number, and we feel slighted when they don't! Crazy, but true...

In writing to the Corinthians, the Apostle Paul was not going to take that chance. He identified himself right away. He was...

Personal. Paul had a name. Each of us are individuals before God. Today people are grouped into classes and races and types. Instead of being seen as individuals, they are seen as members of a particular group. God, however, values us personally.

Picked. On the road to Damascus, Paul heard the voice of Jesus calling him. We, too, have been called. Jesus interrupts the busyness of our lives to call us to follow him. He does not leave the wanderer to travel alone.

Purposed. Paul's particular commission was to be an apostle. What is yours? God has a purpose for your life. He created you to fulfill it perfectly.

Partnered. Paul recognized that he was not a lone ranger. Sosthenes was his brother in faith and in work. How about you? Have you recognized the importance of others in your journey? This life is not meant to be lived alone but in community with the church and fellow believers.

Who are you?

Prayer: Thank you, Lord, that you know my name, that you have called my name, that you have a purpose for me, and that I have sisters and brothers in this great adventure. Amen!

Psalm of the Day: 106.32-39

I'm Only Human!
Daily Reading: 1 Corinthians 2-3

While there is jealousy and strife among you, are you not of the flesh and behaving only in a human way? (1 Corinthians 3.3)

Devotional Thought: I overheard an interesting conversation the other day. An older teen was pontificating on position in the youth group: "I'm an adult, so I can..." His leader said, in effect, "You start acting like an adult, and we will give you some of the privileges you are talking about..."

Paul had to deal with the church in Corinth in the same way. They thought they were so grown up, so mature, so spiritual. Paul said, *not so fast. Spiritual people don't act the way you are acting. You are jealous and fighting like a bunch of adolescents!* The Corinthian believers were "behaving only in a human way." Paul did not say they were not Christians, but he did say that they were not living like Christians. They behaved like people who had never experienced the new birth in Jesus.

Jealousy and strive do not mark mature, spiritual believers. William Barclay writes of these kinds of people: "If man is at variance with his fellow men, if he is a quarrelsome, competitive, argumentative, trouble-making creature, he may be a diligent church attendee, he may even be a church office-bearer, but he is not a man of God." (BBC, 331).

It's so tempting - and so easy - to substitute church attendance and activity for a vital and humble relationship with Christ. Being in church is not enough. We need to be in Christ! If not, we are "only human." Are you behaving only in a human way? Allow the life of Christ to be lived out in you!

Prayer: Search me, O God, and know my heart. Try me and know my anxious thoughts. See if there be any grievous way in me, and lead me in the way everlasting. Amen.

Psalm of the Day: 106.40-43

Are You Recognizable?

Daily Reading: 1 Corinthians 4

> We are fools for Christ's sake... we hunger and thirst, we are poorly dressed and buffeted and homeless... When reviled, we bless; when persecuted, we endure; when slandered, we entreat. We have become, and are still, like the scum of the world, the refuse of all things.
> (1 Corinthians 4:10, 11-13)

Devotional Thought: Being a Christian is not easy. Paul's life demonstrated that for the Corinthians. His life makes our lives seem simple by comparison! If he was not completely confident in the Lordship of Jesus Christ, he would never have endured the lifestyle that went along with proclaiming the gospel – persecution, beatings, mocking, hunger, thirst, imprisonment, exile, and loneliness – to name a few. It is one of the many compelling evidences of the truth of the resurrection of Jesus. People were so utterly convinced of it that they were willing to lay down their lives to defend it.

Paul's message to the Corinthians was basically, "If you are comfortable as a Christian, you are probably not doing it right!" If we are doing it right, the world will think we are fools; we will be emotionally persecuted and maybe even physically persecuted for our faith. The world will see us as "scum... refuse" (v13). What marks us as believers? "When reviled, we bless; when persecuted, we endure; when slandered, we entreat." This runs counter to the way most people live their lives, and the world despises it even as they are drawn to it, as the conviction cuts to their very God-created core.

Do those around us recognize us for what we are? Do we have the faith to lay down our own pride, comfort, and rights -to trade them for humility, persecution, and deference to others? Paul entreated the Corinthians to imitate him. He was not perfect, but he was demonstrating to them what it looked like to "lose your life to gain it" (Matt. 16:25). Let this be our prayer for our own hearts, that we would be willing to lose everything for the sake of Jesus.

Jenny

Prayer: Lord, help us to desire you more than comfort, more than riches, more than pride. Give us the grace to be humble servants to others, reflecting the light of your love to the world around us.

Psalm of the Day: 106.44-48

C. Diff.

Daily Reading: 1 Corinthians 5-6

> *Do you not know that a little leaven leavens the whole lump? Cleanse out the old leaven that you may be a new lump* (1 Corinthians 5.6b-7a)

Devotional Thought: A few weeks ago I visited a friend in the hospital. There was a sign on the door instructing me to 'glove and gown' and to see the nurse before entering. I did, and I was told by the nurse that the patient had *C. Diff.*, a highly contagious infection. In addition to the gown and gloves, I needed to wash my hands with warm soapy water for 20 seconds when I left the room. Hand sanitizer was not enough. If I didn't want to get sick, I needed to physically wash the bacteria away.

In 1 Corinthians 5, Paul is dealing with a situation in the church at Corinth that was highly contagious: moral carelessness. He told the Corinthians that 'hand sanitizer' was not enough. They needed to physically cleanse out the old leaven. In that situation, the person involved was an unrepentant leader in the church. He needed to be dealt with decisively so that sin would not spread throughout the congregation.

The same thing is true in our own lives. "A little leaven leavens the whole lump." We need to deal with sin in a decisive manner. We cannot simply apply 'sanitizers' while leaving it in place. Sin in one area of our lives has a way of infecting all the other areas of our lives. It has to go!

Thank God for the blood of Jesus that washes us whiter than snow! "If we walk in the light, as he is in the light, we have fellowship with one another, and the blood of Jesus his Son cleanses us from all sin" (1 John 4.7).

Prayer: Thank you, Jesus, that you shed your blood for the forgiveness of my sin. Help me to cleanse out all the old leaven so that I may walk in newness of life. Amen.

Psalm of the Day: 107.1-3

A Bondservant and Freedman

Daily Reading: 1 Corinthians 7

> *For he who was called in the Lord as a bondservant is a freedman of the Lord.* (1 Corinthians 7.22a)

Devotional Thought: When we become part of a family, we are adopted into it, and we adapt to it. Adoption carries both blessings and duties.

1 Corinthians 7 is greatly needed in today's world of sexual promiscuity, marital abuse, divorce, and cohabitation. The Apostle Paul helps us sort out today's confusion. I recommend a careful reading of it periodically to help keep you grounded in Biblical morality. In the chapter, however, there is a brief interlude dealing with how we ought to comport ourselves in a more general way.

In view of the passing nature of this life, Paul says that a Christian is to live as "a freedman of the Lord." We are no longer bound by sin, but have been set free in Christ. Reading that from our Twentieth Century perspective is exciting enough, but when we get behind what Paul was saying, it becomes even more exciting!

"According to Roman law, a person freed from slavery by a generous benefactor was obligated to take his patron's name, live in his house, and consult him on business affairs. The Christian likewise owes a debt to Christ that he can never fully repay." (BBC, 382)

But, being "a freedman of the Lord" is so much more than procuring a debt we can never repay. Think about it. We get the authority of his name! We get to live in his house! And, we get to consult him on every aspect of our lives! Hallelujah!

Prayer: Thank you, Lord, for setting me free from sin and for making me your freedman. Thank you for giving me your name, taking me into your home, and granting me your wisdom. Amen.

Psalm of the Day: 107.4-9

In It To Win It

Daily Reading: 1 Corinthians 8-9

Do you not know that in a race all the runners run, but only one receives the prize? So run that you may obtain it. (1 Corinthians 9.24)

Devotional Thought: Last night ten-year-old Hailey came to quiz practice from a soccer game. She was a bit gloomy. "We lost..." she said. I told her to cheer up - she had been outside in the sun (and being in the sun is good for you), had gotten some exercise, and breathed in that good fresh air. "You're a winner!" I said. I don't think she bought it. Only one team could win, and she knew the score.

Paul knew the score, too. He told the Corinthians that they needed to run to win! He gave them some good winning techniques:

Determination. "So run that you may win" (v. 24). If we aren't fully invested in the outcome, we won't give it our best effort. We need to remember what the prize is - pleasing God and one day seeing Jesus!

Denial. "Exercise mastery" (v. 25). Those runners in Paul's day entered a 10-month period of intense training. They denied themselves anything that would weaken or fatten the body - even legitimate things that would otherwise hinder their success. As Christians, we too must master our appetites in all things in order to give attention to that which matters most.

Direction. "Do not run aimlessly" (v. 26). It does no good to be the fastest runner only to miss the finish line. I have known many well-meaning Christians who get sidetracked, endangering their own spiritual health and even that of their families.

Discipline. "Discipline my body" (v. 27). Paul literally said, he took his body captive! As Christians our bodies do not tell us what to do. Rather, we are masters over our bodies.

Are you in it to win it?

Prayer: Lord, I am in it to win it. Help me, to be determined, to deny myself, to get my direction right, and to discipline myself. I can't do this without you, Lord, so I ask for your help today. Amen.

Psalm of the Day: 107.10-16

Don't Be Ignorant

Daily Reading: 1 Corinthians 10

For I do not want you to be unaware... (1 Corinthians 10.1)

Devotional Thought: Recently Mark, a fellow minister and friend, told me how he had been raised without any meaningful awareness of Jesus. "I'm sure I used the Lord's name in vain a million times without even knowing it was wrong." He understood that people at times do sinful things without realizing their sinfulness. I responded that such people are ignorant. We didn't like that word because it has negative overtones to it, but we decided it captured the essence of what we were saying.

Paul used the word to warn the Corinthians. The word translated "unaware" in verse 10, actually means "ignorant." The Corinthians were mainly Gentile (non-Jewish) believers who did not have an Old Testament background. Paul didn't want them to be ignorant of what had happened to the Jews when they rebelled against God. The Corinthians - in Paul's mind - were in danger of the same attitude that had led to the downfall of the Hebrews in the wilderness. Paul uses several poignant examples of Israel's failure to warn against spiritual smugness. The Corinthians needed to know history in order to avoid repeating it.

Paul desired to educate the Corinthians in order to keep them from error and deliver them from judgment. So, too, we must live our lives in order that others may see the light of God's grace and live in the fullness of spiritual understanding.

I think it was Thomas Jefferson who said, "Ignorance of the law is no excuse in any country. If it were, the laws would lose their effect, because it can always be pretended." Pretending is a dangerous spiritual practice. May God give us knowledge and wisdom so that we are not ignorant.

Prayer: Lord, thank you for your Word, for your Spirit, and for faithful Christians that guide us into truth. Deliver us from ignorance so that we may live in the fullness of your blessing and favor. Amen.

Psalm of the Day: 107.17-22

Freedom and Confidence

Daily Reading: 1 Corinthians 11

> *Whoever, therefore, eats the bread or drinks the cup of the Lord in an unworthy manner will be guilty concerning the body and blood of the Lord. Let a person examine himself, then, and so eat of the bread and drink of the cup.* (1 Corinthians 11.27-28)

Devotional Thought: I serve communion monthly in the church I pastor. The Nazarene *Manual* stipulates that I serve it at least quarterly. I have friends who observe the sacrament weekly. Weekly, monthly, or quarterly, there is the danger that we will fall into habit as we partake of the Lord's Supper - that we will fail to realize and appreciate the significance of the act.

The Lord's Supper is an act of faith and grace. Faith on our part, grace on God's part. It brings to us spiritual life and strength. We should be conscious of that fact whenever we eat and drink it.

Paul told the Corinthians that they were not to eat and drink in "an unworthy manner." To do so would be to desecrate the body and blood of the Lord Jesus! But, what is "an unworthy manner"? *Beacon Bible Commentary* says this: "The adverb unworthily refers to a balancing of weights and so means 'of unequal weight' or 'improperly balanced.' The attitude of the person does not balance with the importance of the occasion. If a person partakes of the Lord's Supper in a light and frivolous manner, without reverence and gratitude, or while indulging in sin, or while manifesting bitterness against a fellow believer, he is partaking unworthily" (p. 420).

But, we are not turned away from the Table in despair. Paul says to examine ourselves and then to eat and drink. In other words, search our hearts, confess our sin, and receive the grace of God. I want that kind of freedom and confidence at the Table!

Prayer: Thank you, Jesus, for your body which was broken for me and your blood which was shed for me. Help me to live confidently in your grace. Amen.

Psalm of the Day: 107.23-32

The More Excellent Way

Daily Reading: 1 Corinthians 12-13

Love bears all things, believes all things, hopes all things, endures all things. (1 Corinthians 13.7)

Devotional Thought: 1 Corinthians 13, the chapter that celebrates love, is one of the most sublime chapters in the Bible. In verse 7, Paul exults in the superiority of love over all other virtues. This is not a sentimental, superfluous love. It is, instead, a love that makes a difference in the way we interact with others.

Love...

Bears all things. This week I attended the funeral of a friend. In her closing days, she had told her husband, "You have been a wonderful servant to me. Other husbands would not have served as you have in these past months." He told me that he was only doing what love would do. It was not a burden but a blessing to be with her and serve her in her need.

Believes all things. The Corinthians were a divided and suspicious congregation. Paul reminded them that they needed to have confidence in one another. True love - the greatest spiritual gift of all - does not denigrate others to one's own advancement. Instead, love believes in and promotes the best in others.

Hopes all things. While love is not blind to the faults of others, it does refuse to take failure as final. Love believes that a person who has disappointed in the past may take hold of the grace of God and truly change. Love also realizes that it does not always have all the facts in a matter, so patience must be shown.

Endures all things. Even when disappointed beyond hope, a Christian can continue to love. The root of love goes deeper than the sting of pain.

Love indeed, is "the more excellent way" (12.31)

Prayer: Jesus, thank you that you love me unconditionally. Fill me with that kind of love by the power of your Holy Spirit. Amen.

Psalm of the Day: 107.33-38

Building Program

Daily Reading: 1 Corinthians 14

> *So with yourselves, since you are eager for manifestations of the Spirit, strive to excel in building up the church.* (1 Corinthians 14:12)

Devotional Thought: To the Corinthians, Paul insisted on orderly worship "so that the church may be built up," (v5). It is beneficial to read this passage while considering that Paul was writing to this specific church to address their specific needs, but much of it can also be applied to our church and worship experience.

Though many churches today are not primarily focused on gifts of the Spirit, such as speaking in tongues or prophecy, throughout early church history these gifts were a major part of their worship. Paul could see some of the pitfalls to these methods, as it could lead to chaotic, disordered worship. It is clear that Paul considered these to be true gifts of the Spirit and does not discourage their use in worship, but rather warns of their abuse in corporate worship, in ways not contributing to the building up of the church as a whole.

In the same way, we should be thoughtful of our roles in our church families. Does your presence in your local church body build it up? Are you using your gifts to serve one another in love? Or are we church "consumers," expecting the church to serve us? This has become more of the attitude in some churches, as more and more of the congregants expect the "paid professionals" to handle the needs that the church was meant to meet: whether that be evangelism, discipleship, teaching, or helping the needy. It was never the intention that the few should serve the rest, but rather that we should all be essential parts of the body of Christ, serving one another in love. Let us all take Paul's advice to heart and "strive to excel in building up the church." (v12).

Jenny

Prayer: Father, equip us for service to you and to your body. Make clear our gifts, given to us with the acceptance of your Spirit, that we can use them to build one another up, and to glorify you.

Psalm of the Day: 107.39-43

Gratitude Quotient

Daily Reading: 1 Corinthians 15

> *But by the grace of God I am what I am, and his grace toward me was not in vain. On the contrary, I worked harder than any of them, though it was not I, but the grace of God that is with me.* (1 Corinthians 15.10)

Devotional Thought: Lana and I have a dear friend who got into a bit of a tight place. We love her and want to help her any way we can, giving her jobs to do to earn some money. One 90° day, she worked for 6 hours in the hot sun. I paid her a little, but that wasn't why she was doing this work. Afterwards, I received the following text from her: "Jus wanna say again, that am so thankful of y'all being such a huge part of my life, your support, and every bit of help that y'all give to me. Y'all are truly a blessing from our good Lord above!!! I love y'all."

Paul had gotten into a bit of a tight space spiritually. He had spent considerable time, energy and resources trying to stamp out the early church, threatening and arresting believers and even serving as a witness to the martyrdom of Stephen. Paul knew that he did not deserve the grace of God. But he also knew that he had received it anyway! And because of that, his heart was filled with gratitude, causing him to work hard for the Lord.

What do your efforts say about your gratitude quotient? You see, it wasn't the few dollars of reward that caused her to work out in the hot sun. (She would have done it for no pay as she has helped me in the past so many times.) It was love and gratitude that drove her.

That's how Paul felt about Jesus. That's how I feel about Jesus. Is that how you feel about Jesus? What's your gratitude quotient?

Prayer: Jesus, how blessed I am to be a worker in your vineyard. I willingly put my talents, my time, and my energy into your hands. Use me, O Lord, for your glory and the good of those around me! Amen.

Psalm of the Day: 108.1-6

So You Also Are to Do

Daily Reading: 1 Corinthians 16

Now concerning the collection for the saints: as I directed the churches of Galatia, so you also are to do. On the first day of every week, each of you is to put something aside and store it up, as he may prosper, so that there will be no collecting when I come. (1 Corinthians 16.1-2)

Devotional Thought: Do you ever want to give to help those impacted by natural disasters? There are many avenues and agencies for giving help to the victims of disasters. How do you know who you can trust? How do you know your gift is getting through to the need? That's a real concern, isn't it?

The same concern existed in the New Testament church. When Paul wrote to the Corinthians, in addition to the spiritual content of the letter, he also was helping raise money for famine relief in Jerusalem. He wanted to give the Corinthians assurance that their gifts would reach their intended goal.

Compassionate giving in the church is...

Expected... Paul directed the churches to give. Helping others is what Christians and churches are to do.

Regular... It helps if we have a regular system and advance notice of the need to give. Paul told the Corinthians that they were to lay their money aside throughout the week and then give their offerings on the first day of the week, presumably when they gathered to worship. Helping others is best accomplished when you have a plan.

Inclusive... "Each of you..." No one was left out. Giving is something that the entire church should practice. No gift is too small. Children learn to be generous through such times as disaster relief.
Proportional... We need to give according to our ability - 'as we may prosper' - not according to what someone else can give. But in times of disaster, we should be sacrificial for the needs of others.

Do you see a need? Respond through avenues you can trust.

Prayer: Father, help us to be generous as you were generous when you gave your one and only Son to rescue us from the disaster of sin. Help us to give wisely and effectively so that those suffering may find help and hope. Amen.

Psalm of the Day: 108.7-13

Why All These Rules?

Daily Reading: Leviticus 16

> And the Lord said to Moses, "Tell Aaron your brother not to come at any time into the Holy Place inside the veil, before the mercy seat that is on the ark, so that he may not die. For I will appear in the cloud over the mercy seat." (Leviticus 16:2)

Devotional Thought: Health professionals want you to visit patients in the hospital. They know that people who receive care and attention from family members heal more quickly and more completely. But, if you have ever visited in the ICU, you know that - though they want you to be there - you have to follow their rules to get in!

This chapter of Leviticus details the process for the Day of Atonement that was to occur once a year for the sins of the Israelite people. It was a very complex process that had to be done exactly right for the Lord to accept the offering from Aaron, the high priest. It was also a very dangerous process for Aaron. He was required to be completely ceremonially clean to appear in the Most Holy Place before the Lord, or risk his own death.

This may seem extreme to us now, and perhaps even unfair to Aaron. But, this more than anything can highlight for us the amazing privilege given to us through Christ to enter into God's presence without this cleansing process. When Jesus was crucified, the veil in the Temple was torn in half. This was no coincidence, but a clear indication of our freedom to stand before the throne of the Lord with complete confidence in the sufficiency of Christ's blood to cover and cleanse us.

We should not do so with a cavalier attitude. The Lord's standards for holiness have not changed. On our own, we would still be bound to follow every letter and intention of the Law to approach our Creator. Let us in humility, gratefully accept the sacrifice of Jesus on our behalf, and stand before our God with wonder and holy reverence.

Jenny

Prayer: Jesus, thank you for your amazing love for us, that you were willing to lay down your life - a life of innocence and perfection - to clothe us with your own righteousness.

Psalm of the Day: 109.1-5

Churchless Christianity?

Daily Reading: Leviticus 17-18

> ...*bring it to the entrance of the tent of meeting to offer it as a gift to the Lord...* (Leviticus 17.4)

Devotional Thought: The Bible knows nothing of a "Churchless Christianity." But, there are some who think that the church is not necessary in God's economy of grace. All they need is to have a personal relationship with Jesus. What an impoverished view of Christianity!

In the Old Testament there were people who had that same tendency. They thought it would be acceptable to worship God where and how they pleased. God corrected that in Leviticus 17 when he said, in essence, *No, you need to worship me at the place I have designated.*

What was the danger in offering their sacrifices at their homes or in the open fields? God makes that plain a few verses later when he says, "So shall they no more sacrifice their sacrifices to goat demons..." (v. 7). God knows from the beginning days of human history, that mankind's tendency would be to have a free-wheeling approach to him. Cain thought he could sacrifice as he pleased, but discovered that God was not pleased with his sacrifice. His self-justifying behavior ended up in the murder of his brother Abel!

We need the Church today for many reasons, not least of which is to serve as a corrective to our irreverent and nonchalant approach to God. May God renew in our day a faithfulness to the Church!

Prayer: Jesus, thank you for shedding your blood to make the Church holy and blameless. Help us to love the Church as you have loved the Church and to give our lives to see you build the Church. May the gates of hell never prevail against your Church!

Psalm of the Day: 109.6-15

The Stranger Who Sojourns Among You
Daily Reading: Leviticus 19

> *When a stranger sojourns with you in your land, you shall not do him wrong. You shall treat the stranger who sojourns with you as the native among you, and you shall love him as yourself, for you were strangers in the land of Egypt: I am the Lord your God.* (Leviticus 19.33-34)

Devotional Thought: Donald Trump was not the first American President who had to figure out what to do with refugees and foreign nationals. Nor is that problem new to our day and culture. It has been around for at least 3500 years – from the time God gave Moses the book of Leviticus. As we consider what God told Moses to do, I think we can learn about our approach to refugees and foreign nationals.

First, let me say that God did not countenance 'illegal immigration.' He was very strict that those who were coming into the culture would not do the culture more harm than good, leading the Israelite people away from the worship of the one true God. In other words, the spirituality, safety and sovereignty of the nation had top priority. That, however was not to be used as a justification to deny or mistreat foreign nationals.

Israel was to treat the "stranger who sojourns with you" in the following way:

Do him no wrong. We should not take advantage of or abuse the human rights and dignity of foreign nationals. I believe that we have a lot to learn from that fact.

Treat him as a native among you. On the flip side of #1, a foreign national should be expected to uphold the duties of citizens. If they are to have the rights of the native, they must have the responsibilities of them, too.

Love him as yourself. All people are created in God's image. While we must protect our safety and sovereignty, a secular government must ensure that all are treated equally within the parameters established by safety and sovereignty. (Israel also had a filter for spirituality, but we cannot.)

Prayer: Heavenly Father, thank you that you have adopted us into your family. We are strangers – foreign nationals and refugees – in the kingdom of God. Help us to love the stranger as you have loved us. May you keep America safe as we receive the stranger who sojourns among us. Amen.

Psalm of the Day: 109.16-20

A High Price

Daily Reading: Leviticus 20

> *I myself will set my face against that man and will cut him off from among his people, because he has given one of his children to Molech.* (Leviticus 20.3)

Devotional Thought: I was interested in seeing the response of the media to the passing of Hugh Heffner, founder of *Playboy*. He was an icon in the sexual revolution, heralded by progressives as good and right. But, what would they do with his treatment of women as sex objects? Feminists cannot accept that. As I expected, many outlets did not know exactly how to handle it. God, however, is not ambivalent about it. God sees the horror unleashed on the children of America and the world, and he sets his face against it.

In ancient days, children "given to Molech" were newborns thrown in the fire to be sacrificed to the pagan deity in hopes of prosperity and fertility.

Hugh Heffner has said that what he was most proud of in his life is the normalizing of promiscuity, the acceptance of sex outside of marriage. In saying that, I wonder if he gave any thought to the thousands of children who would become victims of sex trafficking and child pornography in this day of sexual immorality.

millions of children who would be born to unwed mothers and subsequently left in poverty so that he could have his free sex and personal prosperity.

millions more children whose lives would be taken before they would ever see the light of day.

A high price has been paid as America – in her thirst for unrestrained sex – has thrown her children to Molech.

Prayer: Father, on behalf of the millions of lives snuffed out through abortion and the millions of children raised in material and spiritual poverty, we do repent and beg your mercy on America. Amen.

Psalm of the Day: 109.21-25

Better than 'Good Enough'

Daily Reading: Leviticus 21

No man of the offspring of Aaron the priest who has a blemish shall come near to offer the Lord's food offerings; since he has a blemish, he shall not come near to offer the bread of his God. He may eat the bread of his God, both of the most holy and of the holy things, but he shall not go through the veil or approach the altar (Leviticus 21.21-23a)

Devotional Thought: "I'm not good enough to serve God!" Do you feel that way? Perhaps it is something from your past that causes guilt and shame. Maybe you think that your talents aren't quite up to par. Or maybe you don't come from the right family or have the right connections.

There's good news for you! By the grace of God you are good enough. As a matter of fact, you are better than good enough!

How can I say that? Especially in light of today's verses from Leviticus...

Yes, God did set strict parameters for those who could serve him in the food offerings. He selected some Levites - the sons of Aaron. Other Levites, however, were passed over. God did this to show that we serve him according to his rules, not our own. Of the sons of Aaron, there were some who could not serve the Lord's food offerings because they were blemished. Nobody was turned away from the Lord's Table...

You may argue, "But they weren't good enough to serve!" That was then, and it was for a season. How do I know that? Because Jesus Christ, our Great High Priest, was blemished beyond recognition, and his service was acceptable to God. The prophet Isaiah said of Jesus, "There were many who were appalled at him—his appearance was so disfigured beyond that of any human being, and his form marred beyond human likeness." Yet God chose him to "justify many and bear their iniquities."

Now, we are all, by the grace of Jesus Christ, better than good enough because he was the perfect sacrifice!

Prayer: Jesus, you "were pierced for our transgressions, crushed for our iniquities," and yet God chose you to serve him in the most Holy Place. Since I am connected to you, Lord, I too am better than good enough to serve! Thank you!

Psalm of the Day: 109.26-31

Perfectly Acceptable

Daily Reading: Leviticus 22

> *To be accepted it must be perfect; there shall be no blemish in it.*
> (Leviticus 22.21)

Devotional Thought: A good friend of mine has a tee-shirt that says, "I may not be perfect, but Jesus thinks I'm to die for"! I love that shirt! How I agree with that sentiment! And, the older I get, the more I find myself agreeing with it. Perfect seems like such an unattainable goal, doesn't it? My two-year old granddaughter, Ellis, sometimes says, "That's not perfect." For her, that simply means something is not quite right. Not quite right... Almost, but not quite.

In Leviticus, God instructed the Israelites to bring only perfect animals as sacrifices to him. Perfect? Animals do get wounded and bruised and scarred after all. I wonder if those Old Testament worshipers sometimes despaired at being able to find a perfect sacrifice from among their flocks and herds.

Then, in the New Testament, we are told to offer ourselves as living sacrifices (Romans 12.1). Surely a New Testament sacrifice cannot be any less perfect than an Old Testament sacrifice. Can it? How can I bring myself to God? I'm not perfect. I've been wounded and bruised and scarred.

Do not despair! The perfect sacrifice has been found! It is the man Jesus Christ. When John the Baptist first saw him, he said, "Behold the Lamb of God who takes away the sin of the world" (John 1.29). Jesus - as the perfect man - gave his life on the cross as our sacrifice. There is no blemish in him. It is when I enter into his death that my sacrifice is made perfect, acceptable to God. Thanks be to God!

Prayer: Thank you, Jesus, that you bore my sins on the cross of Calvary. You became the perfect sacrifice, acceptable for my sins and for the sins of the world. I enter into your death and thereby receive your life and power today. Amen.

Psalm of the Day: 110.1-4

It Doesn't Just Happen
Daily Reading: Leviticus 23

> You shall dwell in booths for seven days. All native Israelites shall dwell in booths, that your generations may know that I made the people of Israel dwell in booths when I brought them out of the land of Egypt: I am the Lord your God." (Leviticus 23.42-43)

Devotional Thought: My friend Allen has recently returned from a two week 'camping' trip through the north-west / north-central United States. What he saw of God's creation was life-changing! But, in order to experience that life change, Allen had to very specifically plan and sacrifice for that trip. He and his wife Jane had to adjust their schedules, prepare their motor home, set up their house, buy their groceries, fill their tank(s), and map their journey. It didn't just happen. But, as he shared with me, it was worth it!

God gave the Israelites the opportunity for a life-changing 'camping' trip every year. It was called the Feast of Booths. God instructed them to gather in Jerusalem and live in temporary shelters made from branches of trees. They did so in order that their "generations may know that ... I brought them out of the land of Egypt." This pilgrimage was a national reenactment of their deliverance from Egyptian slavery. It was a time of great worship and praise and celebration. It was life changing!

But, it didn't just happen. Just like my friend Allen, those ancient Israelites had to plan and prepare to be gone for two weeks. Someone had to care for their flocks and farms. They had to pack food and water and even the sacrifices they wished to offer God. Did they think, "Is it worth it? We can worship God right here." I'm sure they did - at least some of them - but then they went and found that it was life-changing!

How about you? Do you plan and prepare to experience God? Do you sacrifice in order to attend worship or to gather for prayer? It doesn't just happen, but it's worth it!

Prayer: Father, forgive me when I complain about the effort required to worship and to pray. Help me to remember that Jesus left heaven to come to me where I am. Give me strength and zeal to live for you, O Lord. Amen.

Psalm of the Day: 110.5-7

Kept Burning Regularly

Daily Reading: Leviticus 24-25

> *Command the people of Israel to bring you pure oil from beaten olives for the lamp, that a light may be kept burning regularly. Outside the veil of the testimony, in the tent of meeting, Aaron shall arrange it from evening to morning before the Lord regularly* (Leviticus 24.2-3a)

Devotional Thought: Recent hurricanes pressed many people into using home generators for power. I wonder, though, how many people went to fire up those generators only to discover that they were out of gas. What good is a generator without fuel? The church's programs and services and ministries are like those generators, and prayer is the fuel that keeps them running. Prayer connects us to the power source.

Refueling through prayer requires deliberate attention:

Prayer takes determination. Prayer doesn't just happen. The people of God must make a conscious decision to pray, to seek his face and power. The people of Israel had to raise those olives for the oil. They had to adjust their business plans in order to have enough oil to bring. Without determination, the lamps in the tabernacle would have gone out.

Prayer takes discipline. Prayer isn't easy. The Israelites had to beat the olives for the oil. The Apostle Paul said, "I beat my body and keep it under control" (1 Corinthians 9.27). If we let the flesh rule, we will never pray. And, it may be that if we fail to discipline ourselves, God will send us discipline to force us to our knees.

Prayer takes dedication. Prayer must be done according to the will of God. Our prayers are not to be self-centered wish lists. The people of Israel had to bring the olive oil to God for his purposes. "Not my will, but thine be done!"

Are you keeping the fire of prayer burning regularly in your life?

Prayer: Teach me, O Lord, to pray, and enable me to pray with determination, with discipline and with dedication. I consecrate myself to this holy calling. Amen.

Psalm of the Day: 111.1-5

Proper Conditioning

Daily Reading: Leviticus 26

If you walk in my statutes and observe my commandments and do them, then... You shall chase your enemies, and they shall fall before you by the sword. Five of you shall chase a hundred, and a hundred of you shall chase ten thousand, and your enemies shall fall before you by the sword. (Leviticus 26.3, 7-8)

Devotional Thought: Noah is a big boy. He plays football. Defensive line. In a recent game, he burst through the line and blocked a punt - with his chest! His dad told me that he would like to get him into the gym in the off season to build his arm and leg strength. He challenged Noah, "Can you imagine what you could do with that conditioning? Those other boys wouldn't stand a chance!"

As I thought about that, I wondered if God might be saying something similar to us. "Can you imagine what you could do with the proper conditioning?" He tells us in Leviticus 26: "You shall chase your enemies... They shall fall before you... Five of you shall chase a hundred... A hundred of you shall chase ten thousand." We need to put the enemy to flight! With the proper conditioning, our enemies don't stand a chance! Jesus said it like this: "I will build my church, and the gates of hell shall not prevail against it" (Matthew 16.18).

Why aren't we seeing that kind of overcoming power?

I believe it is because we lack the proper conditioning.

For the Church, for the believer within the Church, the conditioning and the weapon are one and the same: Prayer! Our prayers break through the enemy's defenses and scatter darkness, fear, doubt, and despair. Our prayers bring deliverance and hope and freedom.

Let's hit our knees, Church!

Prayer: Father, may my prayers be empowered and directed by the Holy Spirit so that I might to put a hundred to flight! May I this day burst through the enemy lines and see the hand of the Lord bring about a great victory! Amen.

Psalm of the Day: 111.6-10

Holy to the Lord

Daily Reading: Leviticus 27

> *Every tithe of the land, whether of the seed of the land or of the fruit of the trees, is the Lord's; it is holy to the Lord.* (Leviticus 27.30)

Devotional Thought: How I thank God for my pastor teaching me about tithing! When I was just a young teen, Rev. Nelson Perdue prayed with me to receive Christ. And, he cared enough about me to teach me about tithing. I have never regretted it, for God has blessed me and my family abundantly throughout the years. I haven't missed a penny of that money that I have given to the Lord!

When I was mowing yards, painting fences, and washing windows, I didn't make a lot of money. Maybe $10 or $20 per week. But I learned to faithfully set aside that money and bring it to the church on Sundays. That $1 or $2 a week didn't make much of a difference to the church's budget. That's not what it was about. But, what that money did make a difference in was my future. I learned to put God first, and he has multiplied it a hundred fold in blessings - materially and spiritually.

I am not boasting. I only was doing what was right. You see, "The tithe... is the Lord's." Had I held it back, I would have been robbing God (See Malachi 3.8). By giving it to the Lord, I placed my whole financial plan in God's hands. And when we do that, God is able to bless our whole financial picture!

The same principle applies to all of life. When we place it all under God's dominion, then he is able to bless it far beyond our wildest dreams. I urge you today, give all of yourself to God. You are, after all, "holy to the Lord."

Prayer: Father, thank you for giving your Son Jesus to be my Savior. I give you all of myself, Lord, my time, my talents, my treasure. I consecrate especially the tithe to you today. Amen.

Psalm of the Day: 112.1-5

Unshaken Hope

Daily Reading: 2 Corinthians 1

> *And it is God who establishes us with you in Christ, and has anointed us, and who has also put his seal on us and given us his Spirit in our hearts as a guarantee.* (2 Corinthians 1.21-22)

Devotional Thought: The Apostle Paul was a great preacher, evangelist, theologian, and pastor. He served some wonderful people and churches. But, those people and churches were not perfect. As I understand the New Testament, I feel that one of the most "imperfect churches" was in Corinth. They had trouble with morality, prejudice, pride, and division. At one point, they nearly rejected Paul and his leadership. Why in the world, then, could he write "Our hope for you is unshaken" (2 Corinthians 1.7a)?

Paul's hope was not *in* the Corinthians, it was *for* the Corinthians. His hope was in *God*! Why? For it is God who...

Established them in Christ. We are not established in our own resources and power, nor in our own works and merit. We are established in Christ. It is Jesus who died for our sins. It is Jesus who conquered death. It is Jesus who ever lives and intercedes for us. Amen!

Anointed them. Anointed signifies ownership by and use for God. When we are anointed, we are 'set apart' for sacred service. We are set aside not for temporal pursuits, but for eternal purposes. When we are God's treasure to do his pleasure, then we have confidence he will keep us!

Sealed them. The seal indicates that we convey an authentic and genuine message from the Sender. We have been given the ministry of reconciliation and our message is genuine. You and I are sealed with the love of Christ!

Filled them with his Spirit. Christ lives through us by the power of the Holy Spirit in us. Let us 'step aside' and 'step up' to abundant and powerful living!

Is your hope unshaken?

Prayer: Thank you, God, for establishing me in Christ, for anointing me for your service, for sealing me with the good news, and for filling me with your Spirit. I receive all this and more from your generous and strong hands. Amen.

Psalm of the Day: 112.6-10

Forgiveness Is a Must

Daily Reading: 2 Corinthians 2-3

So you should rather turn to forgive and comfort. (2 Corinthians 2.7a)

Devotional Thought: Have you ever had to forgive someone? Of course! Have you ever had to forgive someone whom you just didn't want to forgive? The pain and memories were just too ingrained to ignore. The resentment and bitterness were just too familiar to forget. The anger and self-righteousness were just too sweet to surrender... It really takes an effort to forgive in those circumstances.

The Apostle Paul knew that forgiveness in such instances would take effort. He told the Corinthians they should "turn to forgive." That speaks of intentional effort, focused resolve. Why bother? Why make the effort?

Frank Carver wrote, "Forgiveness Is a Must" (*Beacon Bible Commentary,* 516) for several reasons...

For the sake of the wrongdoer. Paul said that the offender in 2 Corinthians had been through enough. It was time, for his sake, for him to be forgiven and reestablished in the church. Those who do us wrong are deeply wounded themselves. Our forgiveness goes a long way toward their healing. Thank God that by the stripes of Jesus we are healed!

For the spiritual well-being of the wronged. If we do not forgive we are being disobedient to the Lord. Our spiritual vitality and reputation are strengthened when we are like Christ in showing mercy.

For the unity and integrity of the church. When the offending party is in the church, unforgiveness drives a wedge of division into the fellowship. We are weakened and our testimony is hampered when we allow this to happen. "By this all people will know that you are my disciples, if you have love for one another" (John 13.35).

Forgiveness is a must. Are you forgiving?

Prayer: Father, help me to forgive even as I have been forgiven, so that there may be peace in my heart and unity in your church. Amen.

Psalm of the Day: 113.1-3

Misquoted

Daily Reading: 2 Corinthians 4-5

We refuse to... tamper with God's word. (2 Corinthians 4.2)

Devotional Thought: Not long ago, I was misquoted by someone who wanted another person to adopt a particular stance toward an issue. When I was told about it, I quickly and passionately responded, "I never said that!" Have you ever been misquoted? Have you ever had somebody twist your words or take them out of context? It gets you fired up, doesn't it? Especially when their agenda is at odds with yours!

Paul knew that there was a temptation to do that very thing to God's words. He told the Corinthians that he had adopted a conscious and conscientious policy not to "tamper with God's word." How do we "tamper with God's word"?

Additions. When we can't find scriptures to justify ourselves, we might be tempted to come up with things that sound spiritual, but are not really in the Word of God. We can also attribute our opinions to coming from God: "God told me..." When we put words in God's mouth, claiming divine origin for our own thoughts and biases, I call that sanctifying our opinions.

Alterations. Satan is a master at this technique. He just barely changes what God's Word says, so little in fact, that it is hard to recognize as changed. We must stick closely to God's Word in order to preserve the Truth in this generation that wants to justify all manner of evil behavior.

Accommodations. Speaking of today's culture, there is tremendous pressure to accommodate sinful behavior and justify it by forgetting the plain teaching of the Bible. "Oh that doesn't mean what it says" or "That was for another time and place." Let us be vigilant for Truth!

If you have ever been misquoted, you know that it is very offensive. Let's not misquote God!

Prayer: Father, thank you for your Word. Help me to be faithful to your Word even when it does not fit with today's progressive views. May I never tamper with your Word! Amen.

Psalm of the Day: 113.4-9

Good Grief!

Daily Reading: 2 Corinthians 6-7

> *For godly grief produces a repentance that leads to salvation without regret, whereas worldly grief produces death.* (2 Corinthians 7:10)

Devotional Thought: How many of us have had that mentor or friend in our lives who "says it like it is?" The person who doesn't mince words, but instead hands out a hearty dose of truth with a steaming side of conviction? It is sure to cause us to bristle in defensiveness and grumble about the person, even when he or she is well-intentioned and correct! This is what Paul is addressing in this section of his letter to the Corinthians.

He had some hard things to say to these new believers, who needed instruction and correction. Knowing that he has offended some people, how does he address it in his letter? He tells them that not only does he not regret his words, but that he is rejoicing over their grief! But he clarifies, "I rejoice, not because you were grieved, but because you were grieved into repenting," (v9). "For godly grief produces a repentance that leads to salvation without regret, whereas worldly grief produces death," (v10).

If you are a believer you have most likely felt the difference between these two types of grief. Worldly grief over sin has been nailed to the cross, we need not bear the burden of the guilt once those sins have been forgiven. Scripture tells us that God removes our transgressions from us "as far as the east is from the west." On the other hand, we have also felt godly grief over sin that is found in our lives. Maybe it's an attitude, a grudge, ingratitude, or something else. When we feel this godly grief, may it lead us to repentance! Then, like Paul, we too can rejoice over the temporary grief that leads to our refining in the Spirit.

Jenny

Prayer: Lord, help us to discern the difference between worldly grief and godly grief. Search our hearts and by your Spirit lead us in the way everlasting.

Psalm of the Day: 114.1-8

But, They All Gathered!

Daily Reading: 2 Corinthians 8-9

Whoever gathered much had nothing left over, and whoever gathered little had no lack. (2 Corinthians 8.13-15)

Devotional Thought: But they all gathered!

As Paul encouraged the Corinthians to be generous in light of the great needs of their day, he reminded them of the story of manna in the wilderness. God had sent the Israelites manna to feed them on their journey to The Promised Land. It was always sufficient for their daily needs. It came, however, with specific instructions. One of those instructions was to gather just enough for the day, not to hoard it for tomorrow.

Even today, we are to follow God's instructions as we enjoy and share our material benefits, as God gives us our daily bread. Paul wrote: "For I do not mean that others should be eased and you burdened, but that as a matter of fairness your abundance at the present time should supply their need, so that their abundance may supply your need, that there may be fairness" (2 Corinthians 8.13-14).

I like how Frank Carver described it: "All wealth is as manna from the Lord, intended not for intemperance and luxury but for the relief of the necessities of the brethren. Wealth enjoyed at the expense of those in want soon corrupts like hoarded manna and leads to inequalities that are contrary to the nature of the Christian community" (*Beacon Bible Commentary*, 581).

Let us remember the words of Jesus: "Freely you have received; freely give" (Matthew 10.8). But also remember, "They all gathered!"

Prayer: Thank you, Lord Jesus, for giving so generously to me: life and love and my daily bread. Grant me opportunities to reflect your generosity today. Amen.

Psalm of the Day: 115.1-8

Boast! (In the Lord)

Daily Reading: 2 Corinthians 10

> *"Let the one who boasts, boast in the Lord." For it is not the one who commends himself who is approved, but the one whom the Lord commends.* (2 Corinthians 10.17-18)

Devotional Thought: Do you like being around boastful people? Hardly anybody does. Why? Because most boasting is done to lift up the boaster at the expense of others. Is there something we can boast about or some way we can boast about it that will lift up others? Yes! When our boasting is "in the Lord."

We cannot, after all, really judge our own actions. We are not wise enough nor do we have sufficient information to know all the details. So, let us brag on Jesus! On...

What he has done. Jesus created all things perfectly. When we (humanity) messed up his perfect creation, Jesus came to redeem our mess and our lives. Jesus died on the cross and rose again from the dead! Jesus showed us the way to the Father. Jesus set us free from the dominion of sin.

What he is doing. Even now, Jesus sits at the right hand of the Father making intercession for us. Jesus does not leave us nor forsake us; he is with us always - to the end of the age. Jesus is holding all things together by his powerful word. Jesus is watching over us; he guards our lives. Jesus is preparing a place for us.

What he will do. Jesus will return to rapture us. Jesus will receive us unto himself. Jesus will judge us in righteousness and equity. Jesus will present us before the Father's throne as his redeemed bride. Jesus will shine forever and ever and ever! Amen!

Look at that list of boasts... Doesn't that make you feel better? It does me! Friends, let us boast in the Lord!

Prayer: Thank you, Jesus, for what you have done, for what you are doing, and what you will do. I make my boast in you all day long. Hallelujah!

Psalm of the Day: 115.9-13

Another Jesus?

Daily Reading: 2 Corinthians 11

> *For if someone comes and proclaims another Jesus than the one we proclaimed, or if you receive a different spirit from the one you received, or if you accept a different gospel from the one you accepted...*
> (2 Corinthians 11.4)

Devotional Thought: Who could argue with the fact that our world is changing? Lines that were once clearly drawn - right and wrong, male and female, legal and illegal - have been blurred and even erased. New understandings and philosophies are presented as exciting and 'liberating.'

The early church faced the same things. The Corinthian congregation was duped into accepting something new - just because it was new. You can almost hear them smugly saying, "We are so enlightened!" What were they 'enlightened' about?

Another Jesus. The Jesus that Paul preached, the Jesus that the Corinthians had come to know, was crucified. That fact revealed two things: 1) Sin was real, requiring mercy and forgiveness. 2) The cross was a way of weakness not political strength and maneuvering. Today, we discount the idea of sin and we make demands that we not be offended in any way.

A Different Spirit. In Paul's life, the Holy Spirit was a spirit of powerful preaching and selfless service. The Corinthians had somehow gotten the idea that the Spirit could be used to advance their personal glory and gain. We need a fresh infusion of the Holy Spirit in the church today to show the world the power and love of the gospel.

A Different Gospel. The Corinthian's gospel (good news) had become a message centered on them. Paul's gospel was a gospel of Christ. When the center of our universe is ourselves, we end up with division and animosity because not everyone can be the center. Let's put the good news - as found in the Bible! - back in the center!

Prayer: Father, thank you for the certainty of your Word, the hope of the gospel, the power of the Holy Spirit, and the love of Christ. Grant me strength to hold on to those truths in the face of relentless rejection by this world. Amen.

Psalm of the Day: 115.14-18

288

Walled Garden

Daily Reading: 2 Corinthians 12-13

> *I know that this man was caught up into paradise.* (2 Corinthians 12.3)

Devotional Thought: One day last week I found myself done at the office by 4:30. I went on home and 'put my feet up' for the evening. I didn't even go to my study in the basement. Instead, I read a novel and relaxed. As the evening drew to an end, Lana and I reflected how wonderful it was to have a quiet night at home. It was paradise!

The Apostle Paul spent an 'evening in paradise.' He described it in 2 Corinthians 12. He didn't fully understand it: "whether in the body or out of the body I do not know, God knows" (v. 3). He couldn't fully convey it: "he heard things that cannot be told, which man may not utter" (v. 4). But he knew it was real. It changed his life.

The word for paradise comes from a Persian word meaning "walled garden." When a Persian king wanted to honor someone, he would invite the honoree into his private garden and spend time walking and talking in the beautiful setting. It was into the garden of God that Paul was invited. (*Beacon Bible Commentary,* 603)

Have you been to the garden of God recently? He invites you there. You may not (probably won't) have an ecstatic experience like Paul's, but you can have a refreshing, renewing, restful experience with God. Come to the garden...
I come to the garden alone - While the dew is still on the roses
And the voice I hear, falling on my ear - The Son of God discloses
And He walks with me - And He talks with me - And He tells me I am His own
And the joy we share as we tarry there - None other has ever known

Prayer: Lord Jesus, I come into your garden to spend time with you today. Thank you for inviting me in, for walking with me and talking with me. Thank you for the joy we share. It is paradise to know you. Amen.

Psalm of the Day: 116.1-4

Numbers!

Daily Reading: Numbers 1

> *All those listed were 603,550* (Numbers 1.46)

Devotional Thought: Aauugghh! It's Numbers! How can I read a book called *Numbers*? I know that's what some people think when they get to this book in the Old Testament. Patient, thoughtful reading, however, will give you much to think and much to rejoice about. Numbers are pretty exciting things!

But you may have to look at them a while in order to see any of those exciting things. When the Hubble telescope was pointed into an 'empty' area of space, it discovered 3000 new galaxies. 3000! In a width of one quarter the size of the moon. Some were as far as 12 billion light years away. By training the telescope for 100 hours in one area, and increasing the exposure times up to 45 minutes, astronomers saw things that no one - except God of course! - had ever seen before. How exciting! But Hubble time was valuable; it could have been looking at other things, known things, interesting things. It took a 'brave' and dedicated astronomer to insist that he use the telescope for 100 hours on 'empty' space.

When we look at Numbers we find things like "All those listed were 603,550" (1.46). That's a big number, too. And every one of those numbers represented something big - one of God's children. And, God has no trouble keeping track of 603,550 of his children. After all, he put billions of galaxies in space and keeps track of all of them. How exciting!

And, there is another listing of numbers and people. It is the Lamb's Book of Life. If you are a follower of Jesus, your name is there. That's exciting reading, too!

Prayer: Father, you are amazing, and you have created an amazing universe. Thank you that in all the numbers of the universe, you keep track of me. I love you, Lord! Amen!

Psalm of the Day: 116.5-9

Order!

Daily Reading: Numbers 2

The people of Israel shall camp each by his own standard, with the banners of their fathers' houses. They shall camp facing the tent of meeting on every side. (Numbers 2.2)

Devotional Thought: At the dawn of creation, the Spirit of God hovered over the chaos and brought forth order. The Apostle Paul urged the church to do everything in order "for God is not a God of confusion but of peace" (1 Corinthians 14.33). And, in the book of Numbers, God instructs the people of Israel to camp and move in order.

What a great picture of the church! The people shall...

Camp by their own standard. We are not all the same. God does not call us to uniformity, but to unity. Order in God's household means that all the rich variety of people will maintain their own distinctiveness while joining together in a beautiful mosaic.

Raise the banners of their fathers' houses. Within the unity of the camp, God expected that people would identify more readily with those of their own family. It has to be so. In order to care for all, there must be a sense of loyalty and duty on the part of each. Human nature being what it is, God instructs us to recognize and function within the natural loyalties of family and friends.

Face the tent of meeting. In order to avoid elitism of family loyalty, God instructs us that everyone should be focused on him. When he is at the center, we will not lift ourselves and our clans above the rest. While we organize around groups and families, nothing destroys order quicker than having cliques and snobbery.

Surround the house of God. In all things, the people of Israel were to defend the faith. Centuries later Jude wrote that we are to "earnestly contend for the faith." We must support and attend church faithfully!

That's the kind of order even the freest spirit can live with!

Prayer: Thank you, Father, that you have brought order to chaos - to my chaos! Help me to live in a God-ordered way so that I can do my part in the work of the kingdom. Amen.

Psalm of the Day: 116.10-14

Children: A Blessing from the Lord

Daily Reading: Numbers 3

Nadab and Abihu died before the Lord when they offered unauthorized fire before the Lord in the wilderness of Sinai, and they had no children. (Numbers 3.4)

Devotional Thought: I recently read an article about how to "make your pastor's day on clergy appreciation day." I had to chuckle when one of the things that would make your pastor happy was to make sure your children are in church - and to do your part in having children to bring to church! I thought that is a really great idea - for young people, of course!

In all truth, having children is a blessing from God. But, it is also a blessing to the kingdom of God. Children populate the kingdom and grow to do the work of the kingdom. Without children the future of any particular church is in jeopardy!

When Nadab and Abihu, Aaron's children, offered unauthorized fire before the Lord (worshiped in a self-serving way) they died. And sadly, "they had no children." There was no one in their families to carry on the work of the Lord. God did have others at the ready, but Nadab and Abihu's posterity and legacy died out.

Nadab and Abihu had no children to carry on their work because of their sinfulness and selfishness. Those same maladies can affect a church today, robbing it of its posterity and legacy. We in today's generation should take a hard look at our practices and attitudes. We need to ask ourselves if we are contributing to or taking from the future of the kingdom.

Prayer: Thank you, Father, for the gift of children. Help your Church to so live and love that we would have many spiritual children to carry on the work of Christ in the generations to come. Amen.

Psalm of the Day: 116.15-19

Go and Be the Church!

Daily Reading: Numbers 4

When the camp is to set out, Aaron and his sons shall go in and take down the veil of the screen and cover the ark of the testimony with it. (Numbers 4.5)

Devotional Thought: In recent years, we have been instructed, "Don't go to church. Be the church." While I understand the sentiment behind that statement, I can't help but think it may be a little self-defeating. It doesn't have to be an either/or proposition, does it? Can't I go to church to worship, to pray, and to serve? And when I've done that, can't I go out and be the church more effectively and powerfully?

In the travels of Israel, there were times when they camped, and there were times when they set out. It is a picture of what it means to 'go to church' and to 'be the church.'

We are to camp. Jesus called his disciples that they might be with him" (Mark 3.14). In one place, Jesus instructed them to come away with him and rest (Mark 6.31). It is important to spend time with Christ - alone but also in a group. A regular practice of worship will renew the tired soul and refresh the dry spirit.

We are to go out. Jesus called his disciples to himself that "he might send them out" (Mark 3:14). God forbid that we would stay confined in the church! That means we should get out from the physical building, but it also means that we need to expand our friendships and interactions with people who are "outside the church."

The presence of God is to go out with us. God gave careful instructions about how the Israelites were to carry the ark of the testimony. The ark represented the presence of God in their midst. God intended to get outside the sanctuary himself, and he did that as the people carried him out!

So, go to church this Sunday. Then be the Church on Monday!

Prayer: Thank you, Lord Jesus, for your promise to build the Church and to make us such a force that even the gates of hell cannot prevail against us. Help us to come together to worship and to go out to witness! Amen.

Psalm of the Day: 117.1-2

Protective Provisions

Daily Reading: Numbers 5

> *When the spirit of jealousy comes over a man and he is jealous of his wife. Then he shall set the woman before the Lord, and the priest shall carry out for her all this law.* (Numbers 5:30)

Devotional Thought: Numbers 5 give us a perplexing ritual for the Israelite man who suspects his wife of adultery, involving a priest, a sacrifice, water of bitterness, and a swollen womb and thigh. This lengthy description is sure to leave us scratching our heads in bewilderment!

The cultural context of some of the Old Testament is difficult for us to understand today. Our equality and freedoms are so engrained in us, we balk at the thought of oppression or unfairness, and rightly so. When these commands were given, however, they were revolutionary and provided an uncommon mercy towards the wife in question. In those ancient days, no proof or witness was required to stone the woman suspected of adultery... if the husband so much as suspected her of infidelity, she would be murdered without further question. The Lord gives the Israelites this law to ensure that the wife has a path to justice and is not susceptible to her husband's "spirit of jealousy."

In these cases, the woman was set *before the Lord*, rather than being subject to judgment by other people. The Lord alone would determine her guilt. So it also is for us – we are commanded to not judge the unbelieving around us, because justice belongs to the Lord. Our perspective is limited, but the Lord's is not. Our compassion and mercy is prone to failure, but the Lord's is everlasting. There will be a day of judgment, on which all of those who rejected the Son of God will be eternally condemned, but until then the days stretch on as the Lord continues to extend his love and mercy to the lost souls that he desires to come to him. Will you be a worker in his harvest?

Jenny

Prayer: Lord, please help us to remember that it is not our place to judge those around us. That when we do so, we hurt your name and fail to bring you the glory that you are due. Give us supernatural love for the lost around us, and lead us to those who you would claim as your own.

Psalm of the Day: 118.1-4

Take the Name of Jesus With You

Daily Reading: Numbers 6

> *The Lord bless you and keep you; the Lord make his face to shine upon you and be gracious to you; the Lord lift up his countenance upon you and give you peace.* (Numbers 6.24-26)

Devotional Thought: Have you ever wondered how to pronounce a blessing on someone? In Numbers 6, Moses was given instructions as to how Aaron and his sons (the priests) were to bless the people of Israel.

The Lord bless you... The word for bless actually means to kneel down and adore. It is used for our worship of God. That obviously doesn't work when we speak of God blessing us. But, the picture I get from it is God stooping down to show us his love - much like a grandparent would do for a small grandchild. God came down in Jesus to show us his love!

God has other blessings for us, too: standing guard over us, shining the light of his love and favor before us, coming to us when we are unworthy, granting peace in our turmoil!

We are the priests now, and we have been given the awesome privilege of blessing one another in the name of the Lord. When we do so, we "put [his] name upon the people of Israel, and [so he] will bless them" (v. 27).

Today, I bless you in the name of the Lord! In the words of that old hymn, take the name of Jesus with you:
Take the name of Jesus with you, Child of sorrow and of woe;
It will joy and comfort give you, Take it then where'er you go.
Precious name! Oh, how sweet! Hope of earth and joy of heav'n;
Precious name! Oh, how sweet! Hope of earth and joy of heav'n!

Prayer: Lord, bless my family and friends today. Come down and take their face in your tender hands, showing them love and giving them peace. Amen.

Psalm of the Day: 118.5-9

Holy Things Carried on the Shoulder
Daily Reading: Numbers 7-8

But to the sons of Kohath he gave none, because they were charged with the service of the holy things that had to be carried on the shoulder. (Numbers 7.9)

Devotional Thought: Are you familiar with the story of Nehemiah? He was given the task of rebuilding the walls of Jerusalem. Over and over again the enemy threatened him, distracted him, or flattered him, trying to get him to stop the work. Nehemiah stood firm in his conviction that his work was too precious, too holy to do anything else. So, Nehemiah "sent messengers to them, saying, 'I am doing a great work and I cannot come down'" (Nehemiah 6.3) Do you have any great works like that in your life?

The sons of Kohath did. In Numbers 7, God provided for carts to transport the tabernacle and other items of worship. There were some things so precious, however, that they were not to be placed on carts but were to be carried on the shoulders of the priests.

Do you have any holy things like that in your life? Are you laying them down to do lesser things? Don't fall prey to the lies of the enemy when he tells you that you don't have time to pray or that going to church isn't important or that your children can learn about God from others who are 'experts.' Those are holy tasks given to you.

Because the sons of Kohath bore the holy things on their shoulders, "when Moses went into the tent of meeting to speak with the Lord, he heard the voice speaking to him from above the mercy seat..." (7.89). Because we carry the burden of the Lord, God will speak in our day!

Prayer: Oh, Lord, thank you for the awesome privilege of carrying the holy things of the Lord. Help me to be strong, to be faithful, and to not come down to do something else. Amen.

Psalm of the Day: 118.10-13

Give Me That Glory!

Daily Reading: Numbers 9

> *On the day that the tabernacle was set up, the cloud covered the tabernacle, the tent of the testimony. And at evening it was over the tabernacle like the appearance of fire until morning.* (Numbers 9.15)

Devotional Thought: It had been a year since they left Egypt. The Israelites had received the Law - including the Ten Commandments. They had experienced some distressing events. And, they had gathered the needed materials and constructed the tabernacle with all its furnishings. Leaving Mt. Sinai - the scene of lightning and thunder, of smoke and fire - they embarked on their journey to The Promised Land.

Would they leave God behind at Sinai?

No! God had a plan to assure them of his presence, to guide them in their travels. It was the fire and cloud of his glory. He was there in the morning when they arose from their rest. He was there in the evening when they returned to their tents. Guiding, guarding... the glory of God was there. But they must keep in step with the God of glory. When the glory set out, they set out. When the glory camped, they camped.

Oh, give me that cloud and fire! I want the presence of God to accompany me as I make my way to The Promised Land. I need the guidance, the protection, the vision, and the assurance of God for my journey. Every day I need to know that he is there. Every night I long for his peace to cover my soul. So, I must keep in step with his Spirit (Galatians 5.25). Through obedience, through faith, through holy living, I must set out and camp with him.

Prayer: Thank you, Father, for the promise of your presence for this day. I pledge myself to follow you when you set out and to rest in you when you camp. In Jesus' name I make my prayer. Amen.

Psalm of the Day: 118.14-18

Leading, Lifting, Looking
Daily Reading: Numbers 10

> *Then the standard of the camp of the people of Dan, acting as the rear guard of all the camps, set out by their companies.* (Numbers 10.25a)

Devotional Thought: "I got your back..." That's something good to hear. There are times when we are required to get out front and take risks. The needs are great and there's nobody else able (or willing) to take ownership and leadership of a situation. When those times come, it's good to know that there is somebody who is running defense for you.

When the children of Israel travelled in the wilderness, God had a specific order in which they were to move out. Can you imagine trying to get 2 million people moving in the same direction at the same time? They had to be organized. They had to have leaders. But, they also needed to have a rear guard as well. That was the function of the last three tribes, under the banner of Dan, as the Israelites moved from place to place.

Organization is important in any task. It is no different in the work of the kingdom. There are people who do the

human leading - like Moses and Joshua who would tarry in the tent of meeting to know God and to communicate his will. Leaders are absolutely essential if we are to get anywhere.

heavy lifting - like the priests and Levites who would carry the tabernacle and furnishings. We cannot do without those willing to do the heavy spiritual lifting of prayer, study, correction...

holy looking - like the camp of Dan who would be wary of the dangers and stragglers. What good is it to get to our destination only to discover that we have lost our loved ones along the way?

Leading... Lifting... Looking... Are you doing your part in the work of Christ's kingdom?

Prayer: Father, thank you for giving to the Church your servants to lead, to lift, and to look. Help me to discover my place and to fulfill it faithfully. Amen.

Psalm of the Day: 118.19-24

They Shall Bear the Burden of the People
Daily Reading: Numbers 11-12

> *And I will take some of the Spirit that is on you and put it on them, and they shall bear the burden of the people with you, so that you may not bear it yourself alone.* (Numbers 11.17b)

Devotional Thought: Recently, I was asked to anoint someone for healing. When we were finished, I put the oil in a brother's hand and asked him - along with the others - to pray for me. I explained that I had had a tough week and was tired and discouraged. My brother prayed: "Help us church members to get behind him and support him and his work." That did more to encourage me than you can imagine.

There are times when a leader grows weary. Consider what Moses said in Numbers 11.14-15: "I am not able to carry all this people alone; the burden is too heavy for me. If you will treat me like this, kill me at once, if I find favor in your sight, that I may not see my wretchedness." That's discouraged!

How did God answer his prayer? Did he kill him? No. Did he give him super-human strength to bear more of the burden? No. God gave Moses Spirit-filled 'prophets' to help carry that spiritual burden: "Gather for me seventy men of the elders of Israel, whom you know to be the elders of the people and officers over them, and bring them to the tent of meeting, and let them take their stand there with you" (v. 16). The Israelites already had leaders (Jethro's plan) and laborers (Levites). What Moses needed was someone to carry the spiritual burden with him.

I have found it easier (though not easy!) to gain workers than it is to get people to bear the spiritual burden of the church. My prayer is that of Moses in v. 29: "Are you jealous for my sake? Would that all the Lord's people were prophets, that the Lord would put his Spirit on them!"

Prayer: Jesus, raise up for your church 'prophets' on whom the Spirit of God rests, and use these men and women to bear the spiritual burden of your church. Amen.

Psalm of the Day: 118.25-29

First Pray

Daily Reading: 1 Timothy 1-2

> *First of all, then, I urge that supplications, prayers, intercessions, and thanksgivings be made for all people.* (1 Timothy 2.1)

Devotional Thought: After the tragedy in Sutherland Springs, Texas, there were many reminders and much encouragement to pray for the victims and their families. It also was the occasion for much ridicule: "What can prayer do...", "The people were praying when it happened...", "You should do more than pray..." Some of the comments were quite derisive, some callous, some even hateful.

There are those who think that prayer is a cop-out, that it's meaningless to say, "I'll pray for you." But, the Apostle Paul would have disagreed with such sentiments. He said, prayer should be "first of all." Prayers "for all people." More importantly, God wonders at the lack of prayer: " Why, when I came, was there no man; why, when I called, was there no one to answer? Is my hand shortened, that it cannot redeem? Or have I no power to deliver?" (Isaiah 50.2)

I recently read something that I would like to share with you today. "No Christian duty toward our fellowmen compares in importance with one's duty to pray for them... No one can do anything to help another until first of all he has prayed for him. After he has prayed, there are many things he can do; but until he has prayed, there is nothing he can do except pray." (J. Glen Gould, *Beacon Bible Commentary*, 569).

Prayer is not a substitute for action, rather it is a precursor to action. By all means, we should stretch out our hands to help, but first let us lift up our hands in prayer.

Prayer: Jesus, we pray for our land. There is much hatred and violence. You - the Prince of Peace - will bring the only solution. Help us to be once again a people of prayer. Amen.

Psalm of the Day: 119.1-8

Promise for the Life to Come

Daily Reading: 1 Timothy 3-4

> *Rather train yourself for godliness; for while bodily training is of some value, godliness is of value in every way, as it holds promise for the present life and also for the life to come.* (1 Timothy 4:7-8)

Devotional Thought: Sadly, false teaching abounded in the early church (as it does still today), and we listen in as Paul warns Timothy to "have nothing to do with irreverent, silly myths," (v7); instead, train yourself for godliness... "for while bodily training is of some value, godliness is of value in every way, as it holds promise for the present life and also for the life to come," (v8).

In today's humanist culture, we are obsessed with our physical well-being. It shouldn't surprise us, and apparently it was an issue in Paul's time as well. There is nothing wrong with concerning ourselves with our physical health and condition. To the contrary, our bodies are the temple of God and we should treat them with respect and care. However, it should never be at the expense of our spiritual well-being and growth. The focus around us is almost exclusively on the outward appearance and the inward physiological health. It makes sense from a worldly perspective – if there is no God, no eternal life, then the best you can do is to try to outlive as many as you can.

We know better. Paul sees the folly on focusing on the outward at the expense of your spirit condition. After all, Paul argues, bodily training benefits you in this life, but training in godliness will not only benefit you in this life but in the life to come. I can tell you from personal experience that my greatest victories in life have not come from healthy eating habits or an exercise routine, but from my growth in the Lord through prayer and Scripture. Why do we toil and strive to this end? Because we have our hope set on the living God!

Jenny

Prayer: Lord, please remind us daily that growth in you is not optional. When we are tempted to ignore the eternal to pursue the temporary, give us your perspective and wisdom.

Psalm of the Day: 119.9-16

#YouToo

Daily Reading: 1 Timothy 5

> *The sins of some people are conspicuous, going before them to judgment, but the sins of others appear later. So also good works are conspicuous, and even those that are not cannot remain hidden.* (1 Timothy 5.24-25)

Devotional Thought: When the #MeToo movement got going, famous actors, movie producers, U. S. Senators, popular athletes, even septuagenarian and nonagenarian former presidents found themselves the topic of the evening news and various Twitter storms! The list went on and on... The number of people whose past indiscretions (or at least accusations!) have come into the public's eye exploded. I imagine that there are some very nervous people out there still!

In writing to Timothy, Paul said that the sins of some people are conspicuous. I'm sure you can recall some very dramatic and heart-breaking news coverage of the past few weeks to confirm that for yourself. But Paul also said that the sins of others would only appear later. "Be sure your sin will find you out" (Numbers 32.23).

But that's the negative side. Paul said that good works as well as bad would ultimately be known, too. The fact is that "Nothing in all creation is hidden from God's sight. Everything is uncovered and laid bare before the eyes of him to whom we must give account" (Hebrews 4.13). Since everything will eventually come out into the open, don't you think that the wise course would be to live a good life?

When that day comes in heaven when "the books will be open" (Revelation 20.12), I want my works to bring glory and honor to my Savior - in whose book my name will be written! You, too, can have your name written there!

Prayer: Father, thank you for your mercy! Thank you for giving your only Son to be the Savior of the world and to forgive my sins in particular. Help me to live my life so that Jesus is glorified on the day my works are revealed. Amen.

Psalm of the Day: 119.17-24

More *Than*

Daily Reading: 1 Timothy 6

> *But godliness with contentment is great gain, for we brought nothing into the world, and we cannot take anything out of the world. But if we have food and clothing, with these we will be content.* (1 Timothy 6.6-8)

Devotional Thought: This world is full of discontented people, isn't it? People want more and more, not for the sake of having more, but for the sake of having *more than* their neighbors. Whether it is wealth, or fame, or accomplishments, the human animal is driven to out-earn, out-shine, and out-perform. That is not the way of happiness, is it? You will always find a person with more money, more popularity, more opportunity, and more ability. What is the secret to being content? Paul said it is godliness!

Why does godliness bring contentment and a sense of gain?

First, because we were created to be like God. Sin has marred the image of God and obscured our created purpose. As the image of God is recreated in us, we feel like we are coming home. We are 'made right.'

Another reason is that godliness brings peace. Whenever a relationship is strained due to differences, there is a sense of unease. We avoid the person with whom we are at odds. But, when the relationship is restored, we are free and at peace in the presence of the other.

Finally, godliness holds the promise of plenty. Not plenty of this world's goods - we often sacrifice to be like God. But godliness holds promise for an eternal inheritance. When a person is in the process of building a house, they can put up with a lot of inconvenience because they know what is ahead. In the same way, we know what lies before us!

Purpose, peace, promise. Godliness brings contentment!

Prayer: Thank you, Father, for making me like you. Help me to be content and to keep my eyes on the prize. Amen.

Psalm of the Day: 119.25-32

Revive Us Again!

Daily Reading: 2 Timothy 1

Fan into flame the gift of God, which is in you. (2 Timothy 1.6)

Devotional Thought: "Revivals" are a thing of the past... I've heard that many, many times. And, I suppose if we think about "revivals" as special meetings with an evangelist, then there are certain aspects of "revivals" that are things of the past. But revival itself? Hardly!

Paul was a believer in personal revival. On a previous occasion, he had already written to Timothy, "Do not neglect the gift you have" (1 Timothy 4.14), to urge him to give proper attention to his soul: to introspection and correction. Apparently Paul thought his beloved son in the faith still needed a reminder, for he wrote again for Timothy to "fan into flame the gift of God, which is in you."

I like what J. Glenn Gould wrote in the *Beacon Bible Commentary*. There is "a perennial need in the hearts of all Christians and especially in those who are cast in the role of leaders of the church. Our constant danger is the lessening of our ardor and the slackening of our pace. Periodically we need to seek renewal of our commitment and to reaffirm our loyalty... This is the basic meaning of revival and it must come periodically to us all." (*BBC*, p. 628)

Let us sing from our hearts today: "Hallelujah! Thine the glory! Hallelujah! Amen! Hallelujah! Thine the glory! Revive us again!"

Prayer: O Father, help me to fan into flame the gift of God's grace that is in my heart. Revive me, O God! Amen.

Psalm of the Day: 119.33-40

Entanglements

Daily Reading: 2 Timothy 2

No soldier gets entangled in civilian pursuits, since his aim is to please the one who enlisted him. (2 Timothy 2.4)

Devotional Thought: When I was a child we learned a chorus that went something like this: "I may never march in the infantry, ride in the cavalry, shoot the artillery; I may never zoom o'er the enemy, but I'm in the Lord's army. I'm in the Lord's army. Yes, Sir!" We weren't very sensitive to offending others in those days!

While songs of soldiery are a bit frowned upon today, the Apostle Paul didn't have any problem using the analogy. Paul reminded Timothy that the austere life of a soldier was to be the expected lifestyle of the servant of God. Soldiers knowingly and willingly separate from their societies and their families and become part of a highly specialized community. Stripped of their own clothing, they are clothed in uniforms of another's choosing. A soldier comes and goes at their superior officers' bidding. "He sleeps where he is told to sleep and eats what is provided for him." His life is not his own any longer - even to the point of laying down his life for the good of his country.

Are you a soldier of Jesus Christ? Is it your aim to please him? Remember, we are not our own. We have been bought with a price. Let us do as the writer of Hebrews wrote: "Throw off everything that hinders and the sin that so easily entangles" (Hebrews 12.1).

Prayer: Lord Jesus, you are my commanding officer. I am reporting for duty today. Use me according to your plan. Amen.

Psalm of the Day: 119.41-48

What's in Your DVR?

Daily Reading: 2 Timothy 3

Avoid such people. For among them are those who creep into households... (2 Timothy 3.5b-6a)

Devotional Thought: I love the fall of the year when college football gets into high gear. My plans don't always work out, but I try to get everything done by Saturday afternoons so that I can get home, sit down, and take in a few games that I've DVRed. Until the recent craziness surrounding the national anthem, I got pretty excited to watch some NFL games, too.

But, I've noticed something. Sports programs are sometimes more than sports. Whether it's NFL players making a statement or ESPN play-callers becoming social commentators, many times there is a message accompanying the games. On top of that there are the commercials, trying to sell me things I don't want. Often these 'messages' surrounding football are totally contrary to my way of thinking and - even worse! - to the teachings of the Bible.

Many messages that come into our homes under the cloak of sports or entertainment or humor have a hidden agenda. According to what Paul wrote to Timothy, we should "avoid such people... who creep into households." We have to be very discerning about what we watch and about what we allow our children to watch. Many things appear 'godly' (pass as ultimate wisdom and truth) but do not have the power and authority of true godliness.

I recently read an article entitled "Inside America's Largest Religious Revival You Know Nothing About" by Heather Smith. I recommend it to all, especially those who are sports lovers. You can find it online. As you read it, remember I, too, am a sports fan. I just want us to keep things in perspective.

Prayer: Thank you, Lord, for your Word. Help me to gauge all things by that Word so that I can discern what has the appearance of godliness versus what is truly godly. Amen.

Psalm of the Day: 119.49-56

Are You Ready?

Daily Reading: 2 Timothy 4

> *Be ready in season and out of season.* (2 Timothy 4.2)

Devotional Thought: I have a friend who is waiting on me. I told her several months ago that I would be happy to get some help together and pressure wash her house. She has a small ranch home, and I could wash hers whenever I rent a washer to do my own. It will be a piece of cake compared to washing my 2-story home. The problem is that the season is rapidly passing and I still haven't gotten the job done - her house or my own! I just wasn't ready when the season was right! Too bad! The job still must get done. I have a feeling that I'm going to be very cold!

Paul told Timothy that he needed to "be ready in season and out of season." The job must get done! What job? For Timothy it was preaching, reproving, rebuking and exhorting. You see, Timothy was a pastor who had responsibility for the souls of his flock. I have those same responsibilities, and I, too, must be ready in season and out of season.

But being ready at all times is not limited to just pastors. All of us must be ready at all times. For what must we be ready? I can think of a few things:

- The onset of temptation
- The opportunity to witness
- Suffering reproach for the name of Christ
- The end of our lives
- The return of the Lord

Are you ready?

Prayer: Lord, help me to be ready in season and out of season so that I can bear witness to your Truth and Love. Amen.

Psalm of the Day: 119.57-64

They Deny Him

Daily Reading: Titus 1

They profess to know God, but they deny him by their works. They are detestable, disobedient, unfit for any good work. (Titus 1:16)

Devotional Thought: When Paul wrote to the churches - especially to pastors - he didn't mince words. The church in Crete, where Titus pastored, had some who were "insubordinate, empty talkers and deceivers," (v10). He says this especially of the circumcision party (Jewish believers) and is most likely referring to their determination to turn Christianity into an extension of the Jewish faith by requiring certain laws and rituals from Gentile believers. Paul warns about "not devoting themselves to Jewish myths," (v14) which is especially powerful considering that all of Paul's life up to his moment of conversion had been dedicated to this very thing!

These empty talkers and deceivers can be easily found in our own time. Though not teaching Jewish law and circumcision, they are certainly "teaching for shameful gain what they ought not to teach," (v11). Think of the popular church leaders who preach the "health and prosperity gospel." They "profess to know God, but they deny him by their works," (v16). Faith in Jesus does not come with a promise of health or wealth. In fact, believers are told to expect the opposite. "Take up your cross and follow me," (Matthew 16:24); "In this world you will have trouble..." (John 16:33); "If the world hates you, understand that it hated me first," (John 15:18).

For us to expect our lives to be easier as Christians is simply not Biblical. However, we have promises and a hope that is far superior to any "easier" life now. We know that we can take heart through any tribulation, for Jesus has overcome the world! Let us not tolerate teaching from the detestable and disobedient, but instead surround our hearts and minds with the true gospel that is proclaimed in Scripture.

Jenny

Prayer: Lord Jesus, guard our hearts and our minds from heresy, from false teaching, from anything that would lead us astray from the purity of the gospel that you have laid out in your Word. Thank you for the certainty of the Scriptures.

Psalm of the Day: 119.65-72

"Sound" Advice

Daily Reading: Titus 2-3

> *Remind them... to speak evil of no one, to avoid quarreling, to be gentle, and to show perfect courtesy toward all people.* (Titus 3.1-2)

Devotional Thought: I heard something refreshing this week in "What's on Your Mind?", a men's discussion group at our church. Craig reminded us that we need to know when to "quit listening - even to Fox News!" I immediately thought about how rancorous public discourse has become! It seems we no longer have conversations; we have shouting matches!

I have a feeling that public discourse was anything but friendly even in Paul and Titus' day: "Remind them [the people of the church!] to speak evil of no one, to avoid quarreling, to be gentle, and to show perfect courtesy toward all people" (Titus 3.1-2). *All* people? Are you sure, Paul? Can't I just be courteous to those I like? Or maybe I can be courteous only to Christians?

Nope.

Timothy Keller, in his book *The Reason for God*, gives three questions that are good to ask whenever we are speaking to or about another person:

Is it necessary? So much of what is said today is just not necessary, filling the room with sound that has no meaning. Wasn't it Will Rogers who said, "Never miss a good chance to shut up"?

Is it true? There's a thought! If we would limit what we say to just the truth, the world would be a quieter place! So much of what passes for truth is simply opinion and innuendo.

Is it kind? Is it designed for the benefit of others? Does it serve good purposes?

In another place, the Apostle Paul said basically the same thing: "Speak the truth in love!" (Ephesians 4.15). That is "sound advice"!

Prayer: Father, help me to "keep [my] tongue from evil and [my] lips from speaking deceit." By your grace may I speak the truth in love. Amen.

Psalm of the Day: 119.73-80

Timing

Daily Reading: Philemon 1

I am sending him back to you, sending my very heart. (Philemon 1.12)

Devotional Thought: Do you remember that Kenny Rogers song, *The Gambler*? I'm not one to bet, of course, but there is one particular line in the song that resonates with me: "You got to know when to hold 'em, know when to fold 'em,
know when to walk away and know when to run..." In "laymen's terms" what The Gambler was saying is that you need to know when to strike aggressively and when to wait for a better time.

The Apostle Paul had grasped that concept in the First Century as he dealt with the issue of slavery. Paul found it necessary to send Onesimus, a slave, back to Philemon, a slave-holder. Both Onesimus and Philemon were Christians, owing their salvation to God's work through the ministry of Paul. So when Onesimus was saved, Paul sent him back to Philemon. Sent him back?! To a Christian slave-holder?! We don't understand that in our culture today because we think of slavery in terms of the African slave trade. Slavery in the New Testament time, however, was quite different. At any rate, Paul knew it was a battle for another day. A strategic delay was what was needed.

So, Paul worked within the culture and "inject[ed] the Christian solution into the prevailing culture. The leaven of that concept continues to permeate society for its ultimate betterment and correction." (Neilson, *Beacon Bible Commentary*, 700) We may not always want to wait, nor should we always wait. But, we must also be aware of when is the best time to address social issues.

Prayer: Father, thank you that it is for freedom that Christ has set us free. Help us to live in such a way that others may know the freedom that comes in serving Jesus Christ. Amen.

Psalm of the Day: 119.81-88

Show Us Your Glory!

Daily Reading: Numbers 13-14

> *None of the men who have seen my glory and my signs that I did in Egypt and in the wilderness, and yet have put me to the test these ten times and have not obeyed my voice, shall see the land that I swore to give to their fathers. And none of those who despised me shall see it.* (Numbers 14.22-23)

Devotional Thought: In Exodus, Moses pled with God, "Let me see your glory." God was gracious and showed him his glory: "The Lord descended in the cloud and stood with him there, and proclaimed the name of the Lord. The Lord passed before him and proclaimed, 'The Lord, the Lord, a God merciful and gracious, slow to anger, and abounding in steadfast love and faithfulness'" (Exodus 34.5-6). God also showed the Israelites his *reflected* glory in the pillar of fire and cloud that accompanied them through the wilderness. The Israelites, however, rebelled against the Lord and chose safety and comfort over faith and obedience.

Their choice kept them out of The Promised Land. God's declaration, "They shall not see the land," was not a declaration of final judgment, but rather an indication that though they may be 'saved' they would not see days of victory and prosperity.

I wonder about the church today. Are we choosing safety and comfort over faith and obedience? And by so choosing, are we missing out on days of victory and prosperity? As we conform to the standards set by the world and ignore the Word of God, we are losing our authority and power. We also lose the glory of God in our midst. After the people rebelled, Moses told them, "The Lord is not among you" (v. 42).

I want the glory of the Lord among us! Let us choose obedience and faith!

Prayer: Father, I want to see your glory! Grant that I may choose your ways so that your presence will be with me. Amen.

Psalm of the Day: 119.89-96

Alike Before the Lord

Daily Reading: Numbers 15

> *You and the sojourner shall be alike before the Lord. One law and one rule shall be for you and for the stranger who sojourns with you.* (Numbers 15.15b-16)

Devotional Thought: Recently, I was a presenter for Career Day at one of our local schools. How exhausting to stand in front of 5 groups of 3rd-5th graders for 40 minutes at a time! Teachers are my heroes! I had planned an activity that required the students to stand. In the first group there was a child in a motorized wheelchair! "Oh no," I thought, "I didn't think about this possibility!" I certainly didn't want to leave this child out, but I had to do something or else those third graders would eat me alive! Thankfully, the child was able to stand up and move about, so he was able to participate in the activity. We all had a blast!

Later, I asked the principal about how his students interacted with the disabled students - "Most of the time they are very respectful and considerate." He added, "A lot depends on the attitude of the disabled student."

When God formed his people, he made provision that everyone would be treated the same. Even the foreigner who was among them was to be afforded the same consideration as the native-born Israelites. However, foreigners had to do their part by fulfilling the same laws that were demanded of the Israelites. It went both ways! Everybody was on equal footing before the Lord and in the eyes of the government.

Reflect upon this in light of refugees and immigrants (both legal and illegal) in the United States. How does this principle apply today? Remember, "It goes both ways..." and "A lot depends on the attitude of the sojourner..."

Prayer: Father, help us to see the sojourner as you see them. Grant wisdom for our government to know how to make sure we are safe while at the same time respecting the dignity and value of every person. Help all of us to remember, "It goes both ways." Amen.

Psalm of the Day: 119.97-104

Between the Living and the Dead

Daily Reading: Numbers 16

So Aaron took it as Moses said and ran into the midst of the assembly. And behold, the plague had already begun among the people. And he put on the incense and made atonement for the people. And he stood between the dead and the living, and the plague was stopped.
(Numbers 16.47-48)

Devotional Thought: Sometimes people blame God for what other people do. Sometimes people blame people for what God does! That happened in Numbers 16. A community leader named Korah had rebelled against Moses and Aaron, and God had intervened, visiting judgment upon Korah and his supporters. Moses and Aaron actually interceded for Korah and the others who had rebelled, but the people accused them, "You have killed the people of the Lord" (v. 41). Moses did not take it personally, however, and sent Aaron among the people to intercede for them.

When Aaron stood between the living and dead, "the plague was stopped." How wonderful to know that our prayers make a difference even when it comes to the judgment of God! Jesus told us to pray for our enemies. Have you ever thought that your prayers may be the only thing standing between your 'enemy' and ruination?

The Bible says, "If anyone sees his brother committing a sin not leading to death, he shall ask, and God will give him life" (1 John 5.16). The prayers that you pray have a mysterious power to give spiritual life to your brother or sister! The Apostle James wrote "The prayer of faith will save the one who is sick, and the Lord will raise him up. And if he has committed sins, he will be forgiven."

Whether it is Moses, Aaron, John or James - or you! - "The prayer of a righteous person has great power" (James 5.16). Be faithful to pray for people's salvation!

Prayer: Father, I am amazed and humbled that you should put such power in my hands. Help me to be faithful to pray so that others may find your forgiving grace. In Jesus' name, Amen.

Psalm of the Day: 119.105-112

Who Do You Think You Are?

Daily Reading: Numbers 17

> *The staff of Aaron for the house of Levi had sprouted and put forth buds and produced blossoms, and it bore ripe almonds* (Numbers 17.8)

Devotional Thought: In Numbers 16, we read about how Korah, Dathan, Abiram, and On "took men, and they rose up before Moses, with a number of the people of Israel, 250 chiefs of the congregation, chosen from the assembly, well-known men. They assembled themselves together against Moses and against Aaron" (Numbers 16.1-3). Rebellion was afoot! These four men said, in essence, "Everyone is holy! Who do you think you are?"

God knew who Moses and Aaron were - his chosen leaders. God also knew that - although everyone is holy, everyone is loved by God - progress demanded leaders and leadership. He didn't love Moses and Aaron more than the others. He simply chose them to accomplish his plans. As a matter of fact, it was God's love for everybody that caused him to choose a few to lead them.

Moses and Aaron - though not without fault - proved themselves worthy of the call of God when they selflessly intervened to stop the plague of judgment. God recognized the good hearts of these two men, and he wanted the children of Israel to know that they could trust them. Instead of them being jealous and suspicious, God wanted the Israelites to follow these leaders with joy and confidence. God affirmed his call when Aaron's staff "sprouted and put forth buds and produced blossoms, and ... bore ripe almonds."

God did the same thing when he chose to send his Son. Jesus did not come to be served, but to serve. He did not come to bring glory to himself, but to bring children to God. So, when he died on the cross, God caused his staff to sprout and put forth buds. When Jesus rose from the dead, new life was made possible for you and me.

Prayer: Thank you, Jesus, that you came to earth to show us the way to God and to *be* the way. Thank you that your resurrection empowers new life to come forth! Help me, O Lord, to follow your lead and share your love. Amen.

Psalm of the Day: 119.113-120

The Gift of Service

Daily Reading: Numbers 18

I give your priesthood as a gift. (Numbers 18.7)

Devotional Thought: We received a new member into our congregation Sunday morning. As we stood in the foyer following the service, our newest member, Rachael, was talking with Tara, another member of the church. As I commented on how Rachael was already finding ways to serve in the congregation, Tara just looked at her and said, "Oh, honey, it's just getting started!" I get blamed for a lot of things!

But, isn't it wonderful to be of service to God and his people? What an awesome privilege to be called servants of the Most High!

God told Aaron that the priesthood had been given to him as a *gift*. It came with great responsibility, but also with great reward. The priesthood came with burdens, but also with blessings. It came with heartache, but also with honor.

The same is true today. As followers of Jesus Christ, the priesthood has been given to us as a gift! "You are a chosen race, a royal priesthood, a holy nation, a people for his own possession, that you may proclaim the excellencies of him who called you out of darkness into his marvelous light" (1 Peter 2.9). Yes, it comes with burdens, but also with blessings!

Friend, as a child of God you have been given a place in the courts of the Lord. Serve him with distinction!

Prayer: Thank you, Lord, for making me a priest and servant of God. Help me to faithfully fulfill my duties so that others may know the glory and majesty of my King! Amen.

Psalm of the Day: 119.121-128

Stay-Clean
Daily Reading: Numbers 19

> *They shall be kept for the water for impurity for the congregation of the people of Israel; it is a sin offering... This shall be a perpetual statute for the people of Israel, and for the stranger who sojourns among them.* (Numbers 19.9b-10)

Devotional Thought: God is interested in more than forgiveness. He wants his people to be clean. He gave Moses instructions for various sacrifices for the remittance of sins, but in Numbers 19, he also gave a prescription for the cleansing of people from all manner of uncleanness. It was the "water of purification." God knew that his people would encounter things in everyday life that would render them 'unclean.' Those things did not require blood sacrifice, but simply a way of cleansing.

This is "a perpetual statute." God has made a way for us to be kept clean as well. Through the blood of Jesus we have forgiveness of sins. But, we encounter things in everyday life that would render us unclean. Jesus himself came in contact with sin and suffering and death. Jesus was not made unclean through those social contacts. Rather, he brought his holiness and purity to them. By the same token, his presence in our lives has a cleansing effect. He is the perpetual water of cleansing!

So, we can enter into life with confidence knowing that his holiness is greater than the contaminating aspect of sin. We don't have to hide away lest we somehow are rendered unclean. The Bible says, "If we walk in the light, as he is in the light, we have fellowship with one another, and the blood of Jesus his Son cleanses us from all sin" (1 John 1.7)

Prayer: Jesus, thank you for dying on the cross that I might be forgiven of my sins. Thank you also that you provide a perpetual cleansing for me. Help me to live with confidence in your amazing grace!

Psalm of the Day: 119.129-136

Super Hero

Daily Reading: Numbers 20

> *Tell the rock before their eyes to yield its water. So you shall bring water out of the rock for them and give drink to the congregation and their cattle.* (Numbers 20.8b)

Devotional Thought: Being a super-hero is risky business, isn't it? When you're up on a pedestal, people can see you. When they can see you, they see not only your strengths, but also your weaknesses! Just let me stay in the shadows, please!

I don't think I would want to be Moses. Moses didn't have that opportunity to stay in the shadows. God was all the time telling him to do crazy stuff - like turn his staff into a snake and grab it by the tail, or to raise his staff over the battle. In Numbers 20, Moses had to go out and get water out of a rock. And he couldn't do it on the side. No! God said, "Tell the rock before their eyes!"

God invites us to exhibit that same faith! We can stand before people and tell them that if they drink deeply of the Water of Life, that God will satisfy their thirst! Are we up to the task? It's so much easier to stay in the shadows. "I could never testify like that, preacher!"

I know what you mean, friend. Just writing these words makes my palms sweaty. I think about Peter saying, "In the name of Jesus walk!" Can I do that? Could you?

How about we start with what we *can* say? "Jesus has saved me and changed me." The miracle of a changed life is just as powerful as the miracle of water coming out of a rock. Let your light shine that people may glorify your Father who is in heaven! Then, you will be a "Super Hero!"

Prayer: Lord Jesus, give me faith and courage to testify for you. And help me to give all praise to you, for you alone are worthy. Not by might nor by power but by your Spirit and for your glory! Amen.

Psalm of the Day: 119.137-144

Look and Live

Daily Reading: Numbers 21

So Moses made a bronze serpent and set it on a pole. And if a serpent bit anyone, he would look at the bronze serpent and live.
(Numbers 21:9)

Devotional Thought: Numbers 21 records a foreshadowing of Christ through the bronze serpent. The Israelite people, as was their tendency, were complaining in the wilderness, speaking against God and against Moses, "Why have you brought us up out of Egypt to die in the wilderness? For there is no food and no water, and we loathe this worthless food," (v5). Oh, you mean the miracle food that rains down from heaven every single day, enough to feed millions of people in the desert? As easy as it is to criticize the Israelites, we can easily see the same attitudes at work in our own flesh.

God responded to the Israelites for their complaining, grumbling, ungrateful attitudes. He sent fiery serpents among the people, which bit them and killed many of them. However, in his characteristic show of mercy to even the most ungrateful among them, he provided a way for salvation; if they would simply look up to the likeness of a serpent on a pole (made by Moses at the Lord's instruction), they would live.

The Israelites were all deserving of death, and yet God continued to honor his covenant with these stubborn, undeserving people. Just as they received mercy they didn't deserve, so do we through the Son of God, lifted up not on a pole, but on a Roman cross. All we must do is look up to him for our salvation. He has paid the terrible debt that we owed. He has taken the wrath of the righteous Father upon himself. And, he has bridged the chasm to reconciliation that we could have never built ourselves. Praise the Lord!

Will you "look and live" today?

Jenny

Prayer: Lord, thank you for providing a way for us to be with you forever, for bridging the enormous chasm that lay between us with your great Mercy.

Psalm of the Day: 119.145-152

Road Block

Daily Reading: Numbers 22

> *I did not know that you stood in the road against me.* (Numbers 22.34)

Devotional Thought: In Numbers 22-24 we read the account of Balaam being called to curse Israel. A careful reading of these three chapters, along with knowledge from other places in scripture, reveals that Balaam had two sides to his personality. God spoke to him, and he was a prophet entrusted to repeat what he had heard. In one sense he was selfless in standing on the Truth. Yet we find him quite selfish as well. He spoke words of blessing on God's people while he worked behind the scenes to facilitate their downfall. His name is derived from two Hebrew words meaning, "Not of the people." In other words, though he (grudgingly?) blessed God's people, he was not with them heart and soul. He was a conflicted man.

As Balaam made his way to curse or bless the people of Israel, his inner conflict reared its ugly head, and God had to get his attention. God caused Balaam's donkey to resist him. When Balaam beat his donkey - after which God spoke to him through it! - God revealed himself to him. Balaam quickly confessed he had gotten his eyes off the Lord: "I did not know that you stood in the road..."

There are times that God stands in the road before us, to prevent us from going down the wrong path. Too often, we disregard the signs and keep plowing ahead. Instead, we ought to be paying attention to what God is trying to say.

When you run into difficulties, obstacles, or even uneasiness, stop and consider what God might be saying to you. If you do, you will save yourself much grief!

Prayer: Thank you, Lord, for standing in the road before me, to prevent me from going places I should not go. Help me to heed your warnings and surrender to your will. Amen.

Psalm of the Day: 119.153-160

Get Away With God

Daily Reading: Numbers 23

> *And he went to a bare height, and God met Balaam.*
> (Numbers 23.3b-4a)

Devotional Thought: In the New Testament, we often find Jesus going to a solitary place of prayer. In order to hear from God, Jesus knew that he had to get away from the press of the crowd and the burden of his daily responsibilities. We see that same pattern in Joshua, the great conquering general who led the people of Israel into The Promised Land. He would often tarry in the tent of meeting away from the distractions and duties of life. Moses also spent times alone with God when he would experience God in unique and powerful ways.

Even Balaam, the secular prophet, knew that it was important to find time and space to be with God alone. He "went to a bare height, and God met Balaam."

Isn't it wonderful that God invites us to meet with him! And when we make the effort to do so, we are not disappointed. Christ is faithful and responsive to us. As a matter of fact, Christ himself is proactive - calling our names, knocking at our doors, seeking entry into our consciousness, desiring fellowship with us. How blessed we are!

So, if you don't know what to do, find a place where you can get alone with God. If you are overwhelmed by the duties of life, take a moment to pray. If you are weary and heavily burdened, come to Christ. He is waiting for you!

Prayer: Father, thank you that you are faithful and will meet with me when I take the time and make the effort. Help me to do that, Lord, for so often I forget to slow down and listen. Amen.

Psalm of the Day: 119.161-168

Love Makes the Church Lovely

Daily Reading: Numbers 24

How lovely are your tents, O Jacob, your encampments, O Israel!
(Numbers 24.5)

Devotional Thought: When I first got saved, the Malones and Frieces would pick me up and take me to church. I grew and prospered in my soul because of their faithfulness to pick up a teenager who had no other way to get to church. At first it was just Sunday morning church. I remember one occasion, however, when there came a knock on my door on a Sunday evening. It was the Malones!
"What are you doing here?" I said.
"We came to take you to church."
"What? You mean there's church on Sunday night? I'm coming!"

Why was a fourteen year old kid so excited to go to church? There was not a gym where we had 'youth night' with games and refreshments. There was not a youth pastor who would entertain us and talk to us about important life issues. There was not loud, upbeat music that got us excited. As a matter of fact, according to today's 'experts' I should not have been in church at all. What was it that drew me to Pioneer Church of the Nazarene? What made that church a lovely place to me?

It was love that made the church lovely! I wanted to go there because I was loved - by God, of course, but also by people. I couldn't get enough love. I wonder if that is what is missing in today's strategies of reaching a new generation.

How lovely are your tents, O Church of Jesus Christ!

Prayer: Thank you, Jesus, for the love which fills your church. Help me to add to that love level by being on fire for God and in love with saints and sinners alike. Amen!

Psalm of the Day: 119.169-176

Strike First

Daily Reading: Numbers 25

Harass the Midianites and strike them down, for they have harassed you with their wiles. (Numbers 25.17-18)

Devotional Thought: Football is a tough sport! The players are all the time knocking each other down - even when their opponent is not directly in the line of action, a good offensive player will try to knock him to the ground. Why? Because if they don't strike first that very player might be the one to tackle the ball runner downfield.

Numbers 25 is not a 'pleasant' chapter to read. But, sin and its consequences are not pleasant, are they? While we do not deal with sinners in the same way that Moses had to - protecting and preserving the people - there is a principle in this chapter from which we can benefit. The entry of sin into the nation had caused a plague. Twenty-four thousand people died over the course of the plague. As the evil grew, Phinehas dealt decisively with it, and the plague of sin was stopped before it could destroy the entire people.

The problem was not solved yet, however. God instructed Moses to, "harass the Midianites and strike them down." These Midianites represented the presence of sin among the people. It had to go.

Jesus, of course, taught us to love the sinner and to treat others with dignity and compassion. Are we willing, however, to deal with sin in the same way Phinehas did? When sin starts to destroy us and the people around us, will we destroy sin in our lives? Or, do we sugar-coat sin and make allowances for it? It is so easy to do in today's culture of acceptance and tolerance for all manner of deviancy.

Let us strike down sin before it strikes us down!

Prayer: Jesus, thank you for your forgiveness and mercy. Our sins are forgiven by your sacrifice. Help us, O Lord, not to make allowances for it, but to strike it down in our lives wherever we find it. Amen.

Psalm of the Day: 120.1-7

Multifaceted

Daily Reading: 1 John 1-2

> *But the anointing that you received from him abides in you, and you have no need that anyone should teach you. But as his anointing teaches you about everything, and is true, and is no lie—just as it has taught you, abide in him. And now, little children, abide in him, so that when he appears we may have confidence and not shrink from him in shame at his coming. (1 John 2.27-28)*

Devotional Thought: As I have aged, something wonderful has happened between me and my daughters and sons-in-law. Instead of being just one-dimensional, my relationship with them is multifaceted. They are more than my children. They are my friends, helpers, and sometimes counselors.

The same is true as our relationship with God changes and grows. It is multifaceted. In him we have...

Anointing. Anointing refers to having been set apart for God and his work. In the Old Testament - prophets, priests, and kings were anointed to enter their sacred service; tabernacles, tables, and altars were anointed to consecrate them for holy purposes. In the New Testament, the anointing is done not by a special blend of oil but by the Spirit of God Himself.

Abiding. We also have a wonderful teacher - the indwelling Spirit. As the Spirit abides in us, and as we abide in Christ, we are taught more and more of the truth. We do not have to figure things out on our own, but with the Spirit abiding in us we are given the mind of Christ (1 Corinthians 2.16).

Appearing. There is more to come in our relationship with Christ. Now we see dimly, but the day is coming when we shall look upon his face! He is coming for us, to take us to be with him forever! In this world we have troubles, but we can take heart, he has overcome the world! "Even so, come Lord Jesus!"

Assurance. Christ says to us, "I've got this..." Our sins are forgiven, our future is set, and nothing can separate us from his love. We look forward to the Day of the Lord with confidence!

Prayer: Lord Jesus, abide in me! Help me to abide in you and live the dream- not my dream but God's dream for me. I love you, Lord! Amen.

Psalm of the Day: 121.1-4

Viewed from the Outside

Daily Reading: 1 John 3

> *The reason why the world does not know us is that it did not know him.*
> (1 John 3.1)

Devotional Thought: "What does she see in him?" Have you ever heard that or wondered it yourself? Love, viewed from the "outside", just doesn't make sense.

It's not just with human relationships, either. Often, people just don't understand why we love Jesus. John gives three reasons why the world cannot and will not accept our faith:

Christ's Humanity. People can accept Jesus as a great teacher, a wonderful prophet, a compassionate friend, and a social warrior. What they can't accept is that this Jesus is God himself come in flesh. To think that God became human in Christ is to be confronted with two things: our problem and God's solution. Sin is the problem and complete surrender is the solution. Self-justification, self-centeredness, and self-sufficiency must give way to the demands of a God who joined us in our misery that we might join him in his glory.

Their Vanity. To confess our sins and repent requires that we humble ourselves before God. I'm not able to save myself. I depend on Another. The human animal is steeped in pride. That can be good on the human sphere - taking responsibility for ourselves is a commendable behavior. But we simply do not have the capability to address eternal things on our own. We need the help of The Eternal.

Our Christianity. We are in a predicament. We are not perfect in our performance and we will disappoint people. The Apostle Paul said it like this: "We have this treasure in jars of clay." And, people will even look for reasons to reject our faith. I know that if people want to, they can find many things about me to criticize. So, we must let Jesus shine as brightly as possible in us.

Prayer: Lord Jesus, I want to bring you glory. Please help me to live a holy and God-honoring life so that others may see you in me. Amen.

Psalm of the Day: 121.5-8

Thanks Giving

Daily Reading: 1 John 4

> *This is how we know that we live in him and he in us: He has given us of his Spirit. And we have seen and testify that the Father has sent his Son to be the Savior of the world.* (1 John 4.13-14)

Devotional Thought: I love reading John's writings. He says so much that is worth heeding, and 1 John 4 is not an exception. In this Thanksgiving season, we can be thankful for every word breathed by God and infused to man through the Holy Spirit.

Thanksgiving can be restated as Giving Thanks. Why do people give thanks? Because something has been given to them! It may be a bountiful harvest, or a loving family, or any of the thousands of blessings that have been given us. But the biggest gift we can be thankful for is listed in 1 John 4.13-14, and in so many other verses throughout the Bible.

What have we been given? God's Spirit. What else? God's Son. Why? To save the world. Who is saved? All who believe and profess that Jesus is the Son of God. How can we be sure? Because he has given us his Spirit. I'm not trying to draw a circle here, but certainly one does exist. You might call it the Circle of Life, that is, the Circle of Eternal Life. God has given us Eternal Life. We have not earned it, but we can accept the gift just the same. In fact, we must accept it, or else we will lose the blessing.

Recently there has been an advertisement on television that I've not completely zeroed in on, but its catch phrase is "Thanks for Giving". We should give thanks every day for what has been given us. How much more so on a day we have traditionally set aside to give thanks. Be sure to thank God today for everything you have.

John Wade

Prayer: Thank you, Lord, for blessings so many that I can't even count them, and those are just the ones I know about. Give me a grateful heart every day for all your provisions. Especially thank you today for giving me your Son. Amen.

Psalm of the Day: 122.1-5

Hard to Grasp

Daily Reading: 1 John 5

> *Who is it that overcomes the world except the one who believes that Jesus is the Son of God?* (1 John 5:5)

Devotional Thought: 1 John 5 is a chapter of wonderful assurance for believers. To those feeling burdened or buffeted by the winds of life, we have this promise: "For everyone who has been born of God overcomes the world. And this is the victory that has overcome the world – our faith," (v4). We have overcome through Jesus, we have been given eternal life, and we know that God hears and answers our prayers.

To the agnostic or atheists around us, the concept of eternal life has no meaning. That fact is evidenced in the way people live their lives, greedily grabbing as much fleshly pleasure as possible while they live out their 80-some years. What a horrible thought, that this world could be the best we have to look towards! These unbelievers spend their lives attempting to "overcome the world" through their own methods of pleasure-seeking, comfort-seeking, and peace-seeking. We know that their efforts, even when they appear good and are well-intentioned, are in vain. "Who is it that overcomes the world except the one who believes that Jesus is the Son of God?" (v5).

Yet to these unbelievers, we must seem very odd. Those who love Jesus will "keep his commandments," (v3) and will find that they are not burdensome because the Spirit is their helper. But self-sacrifice and denial of the flesh seems like a bad investment to an unbeliever. As Paul says in 1 Corinthians 15:19, "If in Christ we have hope in this life only, we are of all people most to be pitied." But praise God, we have been born again to a living hope through the resurrection of Jesus Christ from the dead, to an inheritance that is imperishable, undefiled, and unfading, kept in heaven for us!

Jenny

Prayer: Father, we praise you for the living hope that you have provided in your Son, Jesus. Lord, help our actions and the way we live our lives be a testimony to your love and a light to draw those around us.

Psalm of the Day: 122.6-9

Reminder to Love

Daily Reading: 2 & 3 John

> *And now I ask you, dear lady – not as though I were writing you a new commandment, but the one we have had from the beginning – that we love one another.* (2 John 1.5)

Devotional Thought: In 2 John, John is writing a personal note intended to be read aloud to the congregation of the local church. In this letter, he reminds them that we should love one another. He says he is telling them this not as a new commandment, but as a reiteration of the commandment given by Jesus. I'm glad I'm not the only one who needs regular reminders of Jesus' commandments!

We are approaching "the holiday season" of Thanksgiving and Christmas. As odd as it may seem at first, love can be hard to remember during this time of year. Love for the lady who elbowed you out of the way to get to her Black Friday sale item, love for the people who demand public nativity scenes be torn down and love for those friends and family members who are best taken in small doses.

Even though the command to love one another is so well known among us, let us continually take the time to again remember to love as Jesus loved. We should pray for God to give us opportunities during this season to show love for others and then be careful listeners for the Spirit's urging when opportunities do arise. We need to be courageous to step out of our comfort zone and perhaps become a little uncomfortable as we show love to others. Acts of love, no matter how small they may seem to us, can mean so much more to the recipients. Be amazed at what God can do with a small act of love for both you and the person to whom it is shown.

Eric Powell

Prayer: Father, thank you that you loved me so much that you gave your one and only Son for me. Give me, I pray, opportunities to show that kind of self-giving love to others this season. In Jesus' name, Amen.

Psalm of the Day: 123.1-4

Left Standing

Daily Reading: Numbers 26

Not one of them was left, except Caleb the son of Jephunneh and Joshua the son of Nun. (Numbers 26.65b)

Devotional Thought: Today's chapter seems to be simply a list of tribes, names, and numbers. But, there is something important happening. God is fulfilling his promise to bring Israel into a new land. A generation had passed since God had delivered the Israelites from Egypt. The fledgling nation had gone through some significant tests, "passing" some, but sadly "failing" others. Moses himself was about to die short of the goal. A new census was taken. There were only two men left: Caleb and Joshua. They were the last men standing.

Why - of over 600,000 men - were only two of that original generation allowed to enter The Promised Land? What made Caleb and Joshua stand above even Moses in this regard?

A generation prior, the Lord had sent twelve spies into the land to discover how they would enter and possess the promise of God. Of the twelve, only two - you guessed it - Caleb and Joshua brought back a good report. Only two believed that God would indeed deliver them into Canaan.

If - when the end comes - we are to be left standing, then we must be men and women of faith. God has provided a way to life - to abundant life here and to eternal life in heaven. That way is Jesus Christ. Whoever believes in him will not perish, will not fall in the wilderness of this life, but will enter into eternal life. They will be left standing.

When that day comes, I want to be standing.

Prayer: Father, thank you for providing a way for me to enter into life. I believe in your Son Jesus, the Savior of the world. I stand by faith upon him. Not on my feelings. Not on my works. Not on my family. I stand on Jesus. Amen.

Psalm of the Day: 124.1-5

True Character

Daily Reading: Numbers 27

> *Moses spoke to the Lord, saying, "Let the Lord, the God of the spirits of all flesh, appoint a man over the congregation who shall go out before them and come in before them, who shall lead them out and bring them in, that the congregation of the Lord may not be as sheep that have no shepherd."* (Numbers 27:15-17)

Devotional Thought: Our true character is seen not when we get our way, but when we don't!

The Lord told Moses to commission Joshua in the sight of the entire congregation. He is to do this publicly so "that all the congregation of the people of Israel may obey," (v20). Moses was then to go up the mountain to see the land that would be given to Israel. There he would die and be gathered to his people. Moses would not be permitted to enter The Promised Land due to his rebellion recorded in Numbers 20:10-12. Moses accepted this as fair and kept his concern upon the congregation, commissioning Joshua so that "the congregation of the Lord may not be as sheep that have no shepherd," (v17).

Do we respond in the same way when disciplined by the Lord? Later, King David would pray and fast earnestly for the Lord to spare the life of the baby born to Bathsheba from their sinful union. But, when the baby died, David did not bitterly blame God. He went to the temple to worship the Lord who could have spared his baby's life but chose to take him instead.

Sometimes our own difficult circumstances are a result of sin's consequences, but other times suffering comes through no fault of our own. Either way, we are to respond with trust and obedience. Trust in a God who has proven himself over and over to be merciful and just, who gave his only Son to redeem us.

Jenny

Prayer: Father, we sometimes don't understand the purposes you have in our sufferings. Help us to seek you when we are in times of distress - to pray to find your will in the midst of it all.

Psalm of the Day: 124.6-8

Appointed Times

Daily Reading: Numbers 28

> The Lord spoke to Moses, saying, "Command the people of Israel and say to them, 'My offering, my food for my food offerings, my pleasing aroma, you shall be careful to offer to me at its appointed time.'" (Numbers 28.1-2)

Devotional Thought: Not long ago, I was setting some dates with a friend who sheepishly said, "Now, you're going to need to remind me about this. Since I retired, I know the day of the week, but not the date." I laughed and said I would. Thankfully, I remembered to remind him! But only because I put it on my Google calendar!

Before the advent of Google calendars, God devised a way to remind his people of their relationship to him. It was a cycle of worship that occurred daily, weekly, and on special occasions. He told Moses that the people needed to be careful to offer their worship to God at each "appointed time."

In Numbers 28, God specified morning offerings, Sabbath offerings, Passover offerings, and Feast of Weeks offerings. As the people of God observed these offerings, the habit of worship was engrained into the rhythm of life. There is value in habit and discipline in our spiritual endeavors!

Do you make a morning offering? It is good to have a daily time with God to set the direction of your day.

What about a Sabbath offering? Jesus said that God made the Sabbath for humanity. When we observe the Sabbath - one day out of every seven - we are enacting our faith in a God we can trust to provide for us without frantic worry on our part. Weekly worship helps us set and keep our focus on God!

How about special days? We can use Christian holidays and even the secular calendar to remember God's great actions on our behalf - Jesus' birth, sacrifice, and resurrection - as well as things like a new year, our freedom and God's provision at harvest time.

Keep your appointed times with God!

Prayer: Thank you, Lord, for daily, weekly, and annual times that help me draw near to you. Help me, through discipline and repetition, to establish a rhythm of worship in my soul. Amen.

Psalm of the Day: 125.1-5

Male and Female

Daily Reading: Numbers 29-30

> *If a man vows a vow to the Lord, or swears an oath to bind himself by a pledge, he shall not break his word. He shall do according to all that proceeds out of his mouth... If a woman vows a vow to the Lord...* (Numbers 30.2-3a)

Devotional Thought: When I read Numbers 30, I thought to myself: "I can hear it now: 'What's with these two different standards? This is patriarchy!' Yes, I must confess, it is. But, is all patriarchy bad? Is all matriarchy bad?

In ancient cultures the weakness and vulnerability of women was often unprotected. The instructions in Numbers 30 actually served as protection for women, a rarity in those times. (By the way, as our sexual mores have disintegrated, women have been left vulnerable. That is why we are seeing all the chaos and backlash in the #MeToo movement.)

Gender roles have almost become almost obsolete in our day. We believe, "What a man can do, a woman should be able to do as well. And they should receive equal pay for it!" I don't have an argument with that, but can we recognize that there are differences between the male and female of our species? That difference - and accompanying differences in roles - is seen in almost every species on the planet. It is not a bad thing. As a matter of fact, the only species which seems to have a 'problem' with it is the human species!

God was and is *for* the liberation of women, but he does not erase gender identities and roles. Instead, he recognizes the value of each. That's why "male and female he created them" (Genesis 1.27).

Prayer: Thank you, Lord God our Creator, for making us male and female. Help us to celebrate our differences and protect those vulnerable to abuse. Amen.

Psalm of the Day: 126.1-6

Bucket List

Daily Reading: Numbers 31

> *Avenge the people of Israel on the Midianites. Afterward you shall be gathered to your people.* (Numbers 31.2)

Devotional Thought: Do you have a 'bucket list'? What's in it? Mine contains the goal to travel around each of the Great Lakes. In Numbers 31, God gave Moses something to put on his 'bucket list'. "Avenge the people of Israel on the Midianites." Seems harsh, doesn't it?

Several days ago, as we read about the Midianites, we considered the fact that we cannot understand all the ways of the Lord, but we do know that we must deal resolutely with sin. Today's chapter isn't any more pleasant than what we read before, but there is still something for us to learn.

The Israelites were still living in the vicinity of the Midianites. And, once again, we need to consider the Midianites as a symbol of sin. God knew that Moses was soon to die (be gathered to his people) and that the people would miss his spiritual leadership. He knew that they would be easy prey for the temptations of sin. So God continued the campaign to cleanse sin from among his people.

Each one of us has an influence that will live on after we are "gathered to our people." Each of us also will give an accounting to God for our own lives at that time. We may have 'Midianites' from our past - sins that have been forgiven and we can do nothing more about. But, let us put on our bucket list that we will deal decisively with sin and leave a legacy of holiness for our children and their children after them.

Prayer: Thank you, Father, for giving us the way of life, which is a way of holiness, purity, and integrity. It is a way that honors you and helps others. Grant that we would so live - from this day forward - to your glory and others' good. Amen.

Psalm of the Day: 127.1-5

Which Side of Jordan?

Daily Reading: Numbers 32

> *Your servants will pass over, every man who is armed for war, before the Lord to battle, as my lord orders.* (Numbers 32.27)

Devotional Thought: Aren't you glad that we don't all have the same goals in life? Aren't you glad that there are a variety of ways we can fulfill God's will? Aren't you glad that we don't all have to live in the same place, following the same customs, in order to be the chosen, the children of God?

The people of Gad, Reuben, and Manasseh are a perfect example. They found desirable land outside the borders of Canaan that they thought would be best for them and their families. So they went to Moses to ask permission to settle there, wanting assurance of the blessings of God and unity of God's people. Moses (and God by way of extension) agreed - with one condition. These tribes must help their brothers and sisters possess their portion of the promise.

We have different churches, denominations, and theological perspectives in The Church of Jesus Christ. That's fine. As I said, we don't all have to agree in order to be children, the chosen of God. But, we must remain united! We must all fight the spiritual warfare that has been given to all God's people. That warfare, of course, is for the souls of men and women.

God desires that all people should be saved. And he wants to accomplish that through His Church. Which side of the "Jordan" are you on? It doesn't really matter. Whether on this side or that side, let us put our hands and hearts together to further God's Kingdom on this earth and for eternity.

Prayer: Lord, we thank you for our own churches and denominational backgrounds. These are our spiritual families, given to us to nurture and guide us. But, may we always remember, Lord, that we are part of your family, and may we always be about our Father's business - the saving of souls! Amen.

Psalm of the Day: 128.1-6

Stages

Daily Reading: Numbers 33

> *These are the stages of the people of Israel...* (Numbers 33.1a)

Devotional Thought: A few days ago, we came across "Moses' Bucket List." I mentioned that I want to travel around each of the Great Lakes. I have something else on my bucket list that I would someday like to do: Make a journey of all the stages of my life, seeing the places I've lived - and celebrating God's guiding grace in every stage of my life. In Numbers 33, today's chapter, Moses did just that... "These are the stages of the people of Israel."

The people of Israel had made it to the border of a new land. Their future stretched out before them. Their life as a nation was just beginning, but it was helpful to look back. The recounting of their history served not only as an occasion of praise and gratitude to God, but also as a reminder that they must drive out sin: "If you do not drive out the inhabitants of the land from before you, then those of them whom you let remain shall be as barbs in your eyes and thorns in your sides, and they shall trouble you in the land where you dwell" (v. 55).

Have you ever recounted the stages of your journey? I would encourage you to take some time to reflect on God's grace in bringing you to today. And, do so not only for nostalgia's sake, but also to spur you on to walk faithfully with your God in the days to come.

Prayer: O God of my past, thank you for accompanying me and guiding me in all the stages of my life. I consecrate myself to you, to walk with you in holiness and integrity, in love and faithfulness - for you have been faithful to me. Amen.

Psalm of the Day: 129.1-4

Inside the Box?

Daily Reading: Numbers 34

> *This is the land that shall fall to you for an inheritance, the land of Canaan as defined by its borders* (Numbers 34.2b)

Devotional Thought: Sometimes I think that we view our spiritual lives as Moses and the people of Israel viewed the boundaries of Israel and their tribes. We feel that there are definite borders that must be established and maintained, defined lines that we have to get inside of in order to be a Christian. We imagine the Christian life as being inside a box.

One side of the box may be certain experiences we have to have in order to be "in" - baptism, confirmation, joining the church. Another side of the box might be our emotions - we have to feel a certain way. Still another side of the box might be theology - we have to have a certain educational or intellectual level. And the final side of the box might be our ethics - we have to live right in order to be accepted by God and get inside the box.

Those boundaries may be helpful as far as they go, but they can also be harmful. We may look at those boundaries and say, "I'm so far from the borders, that I'll never enter the land."

I think a better way of seeing our 'citizenship' in the Kingdom of God is to consider - not how close or far we are, not if we're inside a certain set of boundaries - but rather to see if we are facing Jesus. I like to ask people, "Are your 'arrows' pointing toward the cross? What are you shooting at?" When we are facing Jesus, we will become more like him, for we can't help but get closer to what we are looking at.

So, don't worry if you're inside the box. Just turn your eyes upon Jesus and follow him. You'll get where you need to be!

Prayer: Thank you, Jesus, for calling me to follow you. Help me to turn my eyes upon you and start walking. Amen.

Psalm of the Day: 129.5-8

Sanctuary Cities

Daily Reading: Numbers 35

> *Speak to the people of Israel and say to them, "When you cross the Jordan into the land of Canaan, then you shall select cities to be cities of refuge for you, that the manslayer who kills any person without intent may flee there."* (Numbers 35:10-11)

Devotional Thought: Numbers 35 details the requirements and the intent of the 48 cities given to the Levites as their inheritance, six of which were designated as cities of refuge. Although that term may sound similar to today's so-called "sanctuary cities" in the U.S., the intentions behind the two terms could not be more different.

Cities of refuge were designed to be a refuge for the Israelites, along with the strangers and sojourners among them, who had unintentionally killed a person. They would flee to one of these six cities to prevent immediate death from the avenger. If a person intentionally murdered another person, the city of refuge would not protect the murderer, but he would be put to death immediately. Also important to note, the manslayer was judged by the congregation and if he was determined to be guilty of murder, he would be turned over to the avenger and be rightly killed for his crime. This could not be more different than today's warped version of what the Lord intended as a place of safety prior to judgment.

In his great mercy, the Lord established the cities of refuge to protect the manslayer from the punishment reserved for the murderer. He is making a distinction in a cultural justice system that demanded "an eye for an eye, a tooth for a tooth." What the Lord does not do is pardon the guilty or lesson the requirements for justice in these cities. Simply from reading this seemingly specific chapter of Numbers, outlining a small section of the Law for God's chosen people, we can see clearly both the Lord's great mercy and compassion, and also his unwavering justice. Let us view the world around us with the same measure of both.

Jenny

Prayer: Lord, we know that without your Spirit it is impossible to rightly discern true justice. It is also impossible to feel compassion and mercy towards those who do not deserve either. Through your Spirit, help us to see things as you see them, and respond as you would lead.

Psalm of the Day: 130.1-4

Look Before You Leap

Daily Reading: Numbers 36

> *Let them marry whom they think best, only they shall marry within the clan of the tribe of their father.* (Numbers 36.6b)

Devotional Thought: I don't remember the date, but how I remember the day! I was a nervous wreck and I had to arrange it so Mr. Moore and I were in the same room while his daughter and wife were otherwise occupied. "Mr. Moore, I would like to marry Lana." I was surprised by the first words out of his mouth: "She's spoiled, Scott." He did give his blessing, however, and a year later we were married.

It is good to marry with the blessing of your family, but even better to marry with the blessing of God. God, after all, sets the parameters for marriage. (That could open up a whole topic of discussion, couldn't it?!)

In Number 36, we find the Israelites on the banks of the Jordan, ready to enter into the Promised Land. There was a problem, however: the land assigned to the daughters of Zelophehad. Through marriage it could pass out of the clan to which God gave it. God solved that problem by allowing them to marry whom they thought best - as long as it was within the clan of their father. If they married outside the clan, they forfeited their inheritance rights.

What great insight for today. Legally, we are free to marry whom we choose, but we need to recognize the costs. If we marry someone outside of our culture and values, there will be 'adjustments' necessary. If we marry outside of God's will for us, there will be a price to be paid.

In all this, remember the admonition of the Apostle Paul: "Do not be unequally yoked with unbelievers. For what partnership has righteousness with lawlessness? Or what fellowship has light with darkness?" (2 Corinthians 6.14).

Prayer: Father, thank you for the wonderful gift of marriage, that most intimate and most enduring bond between two people. Help us to honor you by honoring marriage as you formed it. And, Lord, help our young people to marry within the faith. Amen.

Psalm of the Day: 130.5-8

Joyful Memories

Daily Reading: Philippians 1

> *I thank my God in all my remembrance of you, always in every prayer of mine for you all making my prayer with joy.* (Philippians 1.3-4)

Devotional Thought: Someone once said, "Memory is the fine art of forgetting."

Last week, Lana and I went to visit a couple at the hospital who had just experienced the birth of their healthy 8 1/2 pound boy. They were so happy. Already faded from their memories was the experience of labor and delivery. Their joy was overflowing because of the child that they held in their arms. I didn't have the heart to tell them that they would be forgetting many other things as well: long nights up with a fussy baby, changing messy diapers, frustration at not knowing what is wrong... But, the truth of the matter is that those things will pale in comparison with the joy of having and loving their child.

 The Apostle Paul experienced that in his ministry with the Philippians. Did he thank God for *every* remembrance of them? The beating he experienced in Philippi? The night spent in the city jail? The hardships of ministry in that place? I think that Paul - by God's grace - was able to forget those things when he remembered his ministry and friends in Philippi. He only thought about the joy he had because of their faith and their love.

Have you developed "the fine art of forgetting"? If some of your memories are painful, pray for God to remove the sting of those memories and give you in its place the joy of the Lord. I believe he will answer that prayer. Then, you can pray as did Paul, "I thank my God in all my remembrance of you."

Prayer: Father, thank you for my family and friends and for my brothers and sisters in Christ. Where there is pain in remembering them, replace it with heavenly joy. In Jesus' name I pray, Amen.

Psalm of the Day: 131.1-3

A Common Way, Work, and Warfare

Daily Reading: Philippians 2

> *Epaphroditus, my brother and fellow worker and fellow soldier...*
> (Philippians 2.25)

Devotional Thought: The Apostle Paul's friendships ran deep. He treasured his friends, mentioning them often in his letters, thankful for what they enjoyed in common. Epaphroditus was one such friend.

Paul and Epaphroditus shared...

A common way. Paul called Epaphroditus his **brother**. They both walked with the Lord. They had been born again into a living hope, into the family of God. What one valued the other valued as well. I'm sure that they had differences - no two people are exactly alike - but more important to Paul were the things they shared as brothers.

A common work. Epaphroditus was Paul's **fellow worker**. Working together on a project brings people together, doesn't it? I remember experiencing that on a mission trip to Guatemala. Dan and I knew one another when we left for the trip, but we weren't close. Spending 10 days together working on the same things- even sharing a room! - brought us closer together. I still treasure Dan to this day.

A common warfare. Paul called Epaphroditus his **fellow soldier**. They both reported to the same Commander: the Lord Jesus Christ. They were both engaged against a common enemy: the kingdom of darkness. They were together in the trenches, protecting one another, encouraging one another on the day of battle. Spreading the light of Jesus in a sin-darkened world, they depended on and supported each other.

Thank God for the Church, the beautiful family of God!

Prayer: Thank you, Lord, for my brothers and sisters in the Church. Thank you that we share a common way, a common work, and a common warfare. Help me to be a faithful and true sister/brother. I pray this in the name of my Elder Brother, Jesus Christ. Amen.

Psalm of the Day: 132.1-5

Explaining Why I'm Right
Daily Reading: Philippians 3

Let those of us who are mature think this way, and if in anything you think otherwise, God will reveal that also to you. (Philippians 3.15)

Devotional Thought: I recently saw a t-shirt that I liked: "I'm not arguing. I'm explaining why I'm right!" Paul could have worn a t-shirt like that, couldn't he? "If in anything you think otherwise, God will reveal that also to you." In other words, "You'll come around and see things my way."

Paul didn't wish to quibble with the Philippians about finer points of theology. Paul knew that they were solid at the core of their doctrine and any superficial differences were not worth arguing about. He recognized that they possessed the spirit and love of Christ. Given time, the Spirit would reveal to them - as he does to all of us - the truth as it is in Jesus. Paul didn't need to set everything straight. We've all dealt with people like that - people who have to "be right," people who continue to argue their point even after the need for arguing is over.

"Normally we judge others in relation to our own level of attainment; somewhat less often we judge with reference to Christ; very rarely indeed do we form our judgments with reference to the progress an individual has made since he became a Christian." (Ralph Gwinn, *The Biblical Expositor*)

Aren't you glad that the Lord is patient with you? Let's show that same patience as we wait for one another to "grow in wisdom and stature and in favor with God and man."

Prayer: Lord, help me not to have to always be right. Give me the grace to allow others to grow and mature in you. Help me to recognize that I have growing to do myself. Amen.

Psalm of the Day: 132.6-10

No Yellow Flags!

Daily Reading: Philippians 4

> *Let your reasonableness be known to everyone. The Lord is at hand.*
> (Philippians 4.5a)

Devotional Thought: "It's always the second guy that gets caught." I find myself repeating that maxim as I watch football. A guy takes a cheap shot out of bounds and retaliates by throwing a punch. The ref didn't see the cheap shot, but did see the punch and throws the yellow flag. "Unsportsmanlike conduct. 15 yard penalty!"

When we feel wronged, it is often difficult to hold back our passions. We want to respond and settle the score. That only makes things worse.

Paul found himself dealing with two influential people in Philippi who were embroiled in some sort of disagreement. The argument must have been a pretty public affair, for Paul wrote in his letter to the church, "I entreat Euodia and I entreat Syntyche to agree in the Lord" (v. 2). He reminded them and all of the Philippians that they needed to get past their differences and come together in the Lord. We are not told what the disagreement is about, but we do know that Paul did not consider it worth taking sides over! Paul - not so subtly - told them: Get over it! "Let your reasonableness be known to everyone."

The word translated reasonableness there can also be translated "moderation" or "gentleness." When we disagree with our brothers and sisters, we need to remember this. We should not escalate the fight, but we should respond with moderation and gentleness.

Let's make sure that no yellow flags are needed when we find ourselves disagreeing in the church. Instead, let our reasonableness be known to everyone.

Prayer: Lord, help me to be like you - for "when you were reviled you did not revile in return." May I respond with gentleness and reasonableness. Amen.

Psalm of the Day: 132.11-12

Hello, Mary. Hello, World!

Daily Reading: Luke 1

And Mary said, "My soul magnifies the Lord, and my spirit rejoices in God my Savior, for he has looked on the humble estate of his servant. For behold, from now on all generations will call me blessed; for he who is mighty has done great things for me, and holy is his name. (Luke 1:46-49)

Devotional Thought: The gospel of Luke picks up the story after generations of silence. God's people had been waiting for the Messiah. Faith wavered with no sign of the promise. An angel appears to a young virgin. God's timing is not our timing, nor are his ways our ways.

Mary was most likely in her early to mid-teenage years when the angel visited her. She must have been terrified, not only at the heavenly being speaking to her, but also because of his message! She, a virgin, would conceive a child who would be called "the Son of the Most High," (v32). In this culture, becoming pregnant outside of marriage would have cast her into the lowest possible category of humanity, and perhaps even endangered her life. Not to mention that she must now explain her condition to her fiancé! But the Lord in his mercy sends an angel to Joseph as well, and he accepts the situation.

Mary - rather than feeling entitled to her own right to live her life as a normal, God-fearing Israelite - gives up her rights to receive God's blessing. As shocked and fearful as she must have felt, she praises the Lord. "My soul magnifies the Lord, and my spirit rejoices in God my Savior... from now on all generations will call me blessed..." (v46-48). Though she knew she would face ridicule and judgment, she had faith that the Lord would do as he promised. She was an obedient vessel, willing to sacrifice her reputation to bring the Savior into the world. Do we recognize our role in our relationship with the Lord? He is the Potter, we are the clay, (Is. 64:8). Let us obey his will and reap the blessings he has in store for us.

Jenny

Prayer: Lord, help us to give up our desires that conflict with your desires for our lives. Open our hearts to opportunities to be your vessels and to love others sacrificially, just as your Son did for us.

Psalm of the Day: 132.13-18

Where's My Son?

Daily Reading: Luke 2

> *Did you not know that I must be in my Father's house?* (Luke 2.49b)

Devotional Thought: A few weeks ago, one of our 'choir kids' climbed up on the pew and let me pick her up. Those of us in the back row of the choir watched with interest and mischievousness. In a few moments her mother looked down where the child had been standing, and didn't see her! "Where's my daughter?"

When Jesus was just a lad of twelve, he went to Jerusalem with his parents to observe a religious festival. As was common in those days, extended families mingled and blended all through the week of religious activities. When it came time to leave, they all left together. Except for Jesus. He stayed behind.

Naturally, his mother panicked. "Where's my son?" She scolded Jesus (Now that's a thought, isn't it? We wonder how she could do that, but I wonder if we don't do it ourselves in more subtle ways...), thinking he had been disrespectful to his earthly parents. Jesus, however, had a higher perspective, a heavenly perspective. God had sent him to earth to accomplish a mission, and he always moved toward that end. "Mom, I had to be in my *heavenly* Father's house! How could you not know that?" Jesus respected his parents; that much is clear.

The scripture says that he "went down with them and came to Nazareth and was submissive to them" (v. 51). In this episode, however, Jesus teaches us a valuable lesson. Our allegiance to God supersedes all other loyalties. Jesus recognized, and wants us to recognize, that our heavenly Father must come first.

How about you? Is your allegiance to God higher and greater than any other loyalties?

Prayer: Thank you, Jesus, that you came to earth to be the Lamb that takes away the sin of the world. You left your Father's house to obey your Father's will. Help me to have that same level of allegiance and loyalty to the will of our heavenly Father. Amen.

Psalm of the Day: 133.1-3

Prepare the Way of the Lord

Daily Reading: Luke 3

> *Prepare the way of the Lord, make his paths straight. Every valley shall be filled, and every mountain and hill shall be made low, and the crooked shall become straight, and the rough places shall become level ways, and all flesh shall see the salvation of God.* (Luke 3.4b-6)

Devotional Thought: "Megan loves Christmas!" Earlier this week, Lana and I visited in the home of some friends. We were commenting on their beautiful decorations. And that was her husband's response. It was evident! And it was evident that she loved to prepare for Christmas.

Are you getting ready for Christmas? That's great if you are, but even more important are the preparations we make for his coming to earth again. Luke tells how we can "Prepare the way of the Lord":

The paths must be straightened. To be ready for the return of the Lord, we must be done with crooked living. When he returns, "what you have whispered in private rooms shall be proclaimed on the housetops" (Luke 12.3).

The valleys must be filled in. To be ready for the return of the Lord, we must be done with low living. I love that hymn that says, "I want to live above the world, though Satan's darts at me are hurled; for faith has caught the joyful sound, the song of saints on higher ground."

The hills and mountains must be made low. "God opposes the proud but gives grace to the humble" (James 4.6). The twin peaks of pride and hypocrisy must be brought down to the plane of true humility.

The rough places must be leveled. In order to excuse rough behavior and harsh words, some people tell me, "That's just the way I am!" That may be, but that's not the way God wants to leave you. The crooked and rough ways of our lives must be brought into conformity to the ways of the King.

Prepare the way of the Lord!

Prayer: Lord Jesus, just as John the Baptist prepared for your first advent, help me to prepare myself for your second advent. Amen.

Psalm of the Day: 134:1-3

Good News!

Daily Reading: Luke 4

> *The Spirit of the Lord is upon me, because he has anointed me to proclaim good news to the poor. He has sent me to proclaim liberty to the captives and recovering of sight to the blind, to set at liberty those who are oppressed, to proclaim the year of the Lord's favor."*
> (Luke 4.18-19)

Devotional Thought: We had been praying for a little pre-born named Levi who had some skeletal concerns. I received an email: "It's a miracle! Levi is OK!" Pastor Amber was so excited to share the good news! Her excitement was obvious even through cyberspace.

Don't you love to share good news? Jesus did. When he began his ministry, he was so excited that he exclaimed in the synagogue: "God has anointed me to proclaim good news!" What was that good news?

The poor are not forgotten. There is a whole class of people who live below our level of vision. As we drive to work and play, oblivious of their plight, they struggle every day. But God has not forgotten them. And he sends them help through his people.

The prisoners are no longer bound. I've worked with many, many people who are struggling to get *out* of the legal system. I marvel that anybody could ever successfully navigate all the twists and turns that are required to be finished with the courts and the charges. Jesus sets us free and we are to help others find their way to freedom.

The blind can see. Do not despair over the darkness that covers the eyes of those you love. The light shines in the darkness!

The oppressed are set free. God is **for** the downcast! Jesus came to the ones that nobody else cared about.

It is the year of Jubilee. It is a time to forgive debts. God is in the new-start business.

We have good news! We are part of the solution that Jesus brings. Let us faithfully do our part to proclaim "the year of the Lord's favor."

Prayer: Father, as I think about the good news, I am overwhelmed that it reached me! Help me, like Jesus, to proclaim good news to the poor, the prisoners, the blind, the oppressed, and the downhearted. Amen.

Psalm of the Day: 135:1-7

Put Out, Let Down, and Catch!

Daily Reading: Luke 5

Put out into the deep and let down your nets for a catch. (Luke 5.4b)

Devotional Thought: "You have to get out on a limb if you want to pick fruit. You don't get any off the trunk." I agree in principle, but in practice those limbs can be so scary!

Jesus told Peter basically the same thing in Luke 5. He told him to...

Put out into the deep. My son-in-law recently did some deep sea fishing off the Carolina coast. He sent pictures of a nice fish, one he wouldn't have caught off his dock in the tidal marsh. In order to get the big fish, we have to go where they swim. What 'big fish' does God want to help you catch? What 'big deal' does God want to help you close? What 'big idea' does God want to bring into reality in your life? Put out into the deep!

Let down your nets. That's work! Peter had just got in from fishing all night. He even explained it to Jesus. "I've already worked that area, and there's nothing out there." He was tired. He wanted to rest. But, because Jesus told him to do it, he went out and let down his nets. How about you? I can identify with you if you say you're tired. But, is Jesus whispering, "Don't give up. Try one more time"? May God give you faith and strength to let down your nets.

Catch! When Peter went against what his experience told him, when he went against his pride and wisdom as a fisherman, when he went against his "flesh," he caught so much he couldn't handle it alone! The blessing God intends for you will not only fill your nets, it will pour out and bless the lives of those around you. Catch!

Prayer: Jesus, help me to hear you as you stand beside me. And though I may be weary, help me to put out into the deep, to let down my nets, and to catch! All for your glory. Amen.

Psalm of the Day: 135:8-14

Stretch Out Your Hand

Daily Reading: Luke 6

Stretch out your hand. (Luke 6.10)

Devotional Thought: One day, the Lord went to "church" where he found a man who needed healing. Those in charge thought that healing was a work to be done on another day, in another place, by another person. Jesus was of a different opinion. He said healing can come any day, any place, by God's hand through any man.

In this story, we see the stark contrast between sin and grace. Sin depicted by both the withered hand and by the withered spirits of those leaders of the synagogue. Grace resides in the person of Jesus Christ.

Consider...

Sin disables ... Grace enables. We are not told what caused the right hand of the man to be withered. But, we do know that originally disablement was not in the created order. It was only with the entrance of sin that withered arms became a reality. Sin disables us in so many ways, but Christ says to us: "Stretch out your hand!" What is hidden in fear and shame can be brought out to the light and made whole. Thanks be to God!

Sin delays ... Grace demands. In this instance, "sin" is represented by the attitude of the synagogue rulers. "There's plenty of time for healing later. We are here for 'church'! We can't be distracted by this nonsense." They completely missed the opportunity for good. Sin would have us delay and delay and delay until the time of healing was past. Again, Jesus saw it differently. In grace he demanded: "Stretch out your hand." Grace says, "Behold, now is the favorable time; behold, now is the day of salvation" (2 Corinthians 6.2).

Prayer: Father, thank you for your grace. Help me to respond here and now to that grace in faith. Help me to 'stretch out my hand' and receive the healing of the Lord. Amen.

Psalm of the Day: 135:15-21

Do You See Them?

Daily Reading: Luke 7

Do you see this woman? (Luke 7.44)

Devotional Thought: Have you ever walked right past someone without seeing them? I don't care to admit to you how many times I've been guilty of that. Many of you have been the recipients of my distraction! Sorry!

Jesus asked Simon a telling question, "Do you see this woman?"

"Of course! She's in my house! She crashed my party!"

"But do you really see her? Do you understand anything about her?

"Yes, I do! And if you did you wouldn't have anything to do with her!"

"Do you see her pain? Do you even know her name?"

I'm afraid that Simon saw only a loose-living, useless woman. Perhaps she had one use. Perhaps Simon himself had 'used' her services at one time and that was why he ignored her instead of booting her out of the house right away.

Jesus is crying out to the Church today, "Do you see this woman? Do you see this man? Do you see this child? Do you see this teenager? Do you really see them?"

What is your answer?

Prayer: Lord, help me to see people as you see them, "harassed and helpless, like sheep without a shepherd." Amen.

Psalm of the Day: 136:1-9

PG-13

Daily Reading: Luke 8

> *Then the demons came out of the man and entered the pigs, and the herd rushed down the steep bank into the lake and drowned.*
> (Luke 8:33)

Devotional Thought: A few weeks ago my 11 year old daughter informed me that she had just read Song of Solomon. My dad (Pastor Scott) asked her, "What did you think?" She said, "Interesting!" There are some parts of the Scripture that require a "PG-13" rating!

One of those kinds of stories is found in Jesus' confrontation with a demon-possessed man. In today's standards, such a man would have been called insane, or mentally ill, or downright evil. Even then, people knew how unstable the man was and he was kept under guard with chains and shackles. The demons, recognizing immediately the authority and power of the Son of God, begged Jesus to not force them into the abyss. Jesus instead chose to send them into a herd of nearby pigs, all of whom stampede down a hillside into a lake and drown.

While this story may send a chill down our spines, I believe the Lord is showing us something. Could Jesus have sent the demons into the abyss of hell right then? Certainly. We know that Jesus was given "all authority in heaven and on earth," (Matt. 28:18). Even the demons know it well, and they "tremble in terror," (James 2:19). So, having the power to cast the demons into hell, why did Jesus choose this horrifying alternative? The text does not tell us, but given the context as we are reading about these beautiful healing miracles of Jesus, I wonder if we were meant to reflect on the stark contrast of such evil against such good. Sin is ugly. It enslaves God's creation. And it invariably results in death. Jesus, on the other hand, is the essence and the very embodiment of beauty, goodness, freedom, and eternal life.

Jenny

Prayer: Lord, we confess that the evil and sin around us is overwhelming at times. The attacks on your children are horrifying, but we will not despair. We trust in you and in your perfect plan for those who love you and are called according to your purpose.

Psalm of the Day: Psalms 136:10-16

Wake Up!

Daily Reading: Luke 9

As he was praying... those who were with him were heavy with sleep.
(Luke 9.29, 32)

Devotional Thought: This morning in church, I was fortunate enough to be holding Lyric. She was wide-awake when we went into the sanctuary, but about 10 minutes in she fell fast asleep!

Have you ever nodded off in church? There are times that our bodies and minds cannot hold off any longer and we succumb to the quietness and weariness. I've seen that happen to people even in exciting services where the Spirit and energy are running high.

Such was the case with Peter and James and John on the Mount of Transfiguration. One would think that praying with Jesus himself would be sufficient to keeping them awake. But, as Jesus prayed, these three were "heavy with sleep." So, don't feel too bad if it happens to you. Spiritual heavyweights such as these were guilty of it, too!

But there are lessons to be learned:

Jesus' prayers are powerful. Though Peter, James, and John slept, the prayers of the Savior were sufficient to bring the heavenly glory and visitors. I'm glad that he is interceding even now *for* me. Pray *in* me, Lord Jesus!

When we "fall asleep" in prayer, we are going to be out of touch with what God is doing. We can't help but being disconnected. The men with Jesus were quite taken aback by what was happening and offered a rather lame response. Jesus didn't scold them, but allowed them time to get back in sync. Don't give up if you have fallen asleep in prayer. Jesus will help you get back to where you need to be. Just listen to him!

"Awake, O sleeper, and arise from the dead, and Christ will shine on you" (Ephesians 5.14).

Prayer: Thank you, O Lord, that you never slumber nor sleep. Help me to be awake and to pray with fervor and focus. In the name of Jesus, our Great Intercessor, I pray. Amen.

Psalm of the Day: 136:17-26

No? Go Do So!

Daily Reading: Luke 10

You go, and do likewise (Luke 10.37)

Devotional Thought: Have you ever met anybody who puts more energy into making excuses than making progress, who tries harder to look good than to do good? In Luke 10, Jesus met a man who was like that. When Jesus told him to love God and love his neighbor, he tried to justify himself rather than doing the simple truth found in the Bible. Basically, he said, "No!"

No. When called to love and lend, to sacrifice and serve, our first response may be, "No" but Jesus says...

Go. I love being "at church", but I can't stay there. In order to serve God effectively, I must get beyond the four walls of the church building and out into world. Jesus doesn't take us out of the world, but keeps us from the evil of the world.

Do. I do not go out to be a spectator in life. I go out to be a participant. God has things for me to do. What are they? Look around. There are plenty of people by the side of the road. There are more than enough for all of us Samaritans if we would just be willing to roll up our sleeves and do the work.

So. Jesus said we are to do likewise. We are to love and serve like the Samaritan did. He wasn't loved and served by the Jewish man he helped, but still he helped him. Commentator William Barclay says, "We must help a man even when he has brought his trouble on himself (30); Any man of any nation who is in need is our neighbor (31-33); Our help must be practical, and must not consist merely in *feeling* sorry. (*Beacon Bible Commentary*, 505)

Prayer: Jesus, thank you that you came and rescued me from the side of the road. Help me to go and do likewise. Amen.

Psalm of the Day: Psalms 137:1-9

Teach Us To Pray

Daily Reading: Luke 11

> *Now Jesus was praying in a certain place, and when he finished, one of his disciples said to him, "Lord, teach us to pray, as John taught his disciples."* (Luke 11.1)

Devotional Thought: Sometimes we regard prayer as something mysterious, personal, ethereal. Jesus left a different impression on his disciples:

It was in a "certain place." Prayer is more than just a vague feeling throughout the day. It is rooted in a definite time and place. To "pray without ceasing" we must first of all pray without distraction. We must go to a place where we can be alone with God.

It was a specific task which he "finished." I believe that Jesus was in communion with the Father throughout the day as evidenced by those spontaneous bits of conversation we see in the gospels. But, there was a particular task of prayer that he finished so that he could then focus on his other duties. The old timers used to call that "praying through." Do we pray through?

It could be taught - "Teach us..." We sometimes think that prayer is so mysterious that some people have the gift of prayer while others do not. That is not true according to this passage. John taught his disciples to pray. Jesus taught his disciples to pray. Since prayer is a skill that can be taught, it obviously is a skill that can be learned. And, what better way to learn than by doing? Let's get started on our lessons!

You can take the mystery out of prayer by going to the place of prayer, completing the task of prayer, and learning the practice of prayer.

Prayer: Thank you, Jesus, that you have taught us to pray. Help us to faithfully learn and apply the prayer skills you give us. Help us to develop into strong men and women of prayer. Amen.

Psalm of the Day: 138:1-8

PG-13, II

Daily Reading: Luke 12

> But God said to him, 'Fool! This night your soul is required of you, and the things you have prepared, whose will they be?' (Luke 12.20)

Devotional Thought: Sometimes movies are rated PG-13 because of their "Language." This episode in the life of Jesus is another instance of PG-13, but this time it is due to "Language." Jesus used language that we wouldn't let our children use...

At one point in his ministry, Jesus had told his disciples that to call someone a fool (*moros*) was as bad as murder (Matthew 5.22). What in the world, then, would prompt God to call the man in this parable a fool (*aphrenos*)?

As indicated above, what seems to be the same word in our English translation is actually two different words in the original Greek. The word Jesus used in Matthew 5, was actually a derogatory term that conveyed the idea of being "completely senseless, not capable of thought." The word used in Luke 12, however, carries a different meaning: "failing to consider the larger picture." This is exactly why God called him "foolish":

God was nowhere in this man's plans. In considering his future, his only perspective was this world: "I have nowhere to store my crops... I will tear down my barns and build larger ones."

He did not think about the immortality of his soul. Eternity was the last thing on his mind: "Soul, you have ample goods laid up for many years."

His perspective was limited to himself. He cared not one whit for the needs of others: "I will store all my grain and my goods... Relax, eat, drink, be merry."

This Christmas season, let us enlarge our perspectives to include God, eternity, and others around us. Then PG-13 language won't be needed to describe us!

Prayer: Father, I do not wish to act in foolish ways. Help me to keep eternal things in mind as I consider how to use my temporal possessions. Help me to worship, to invest in heaven, and to share with others. Amen.

Psalm of the Day: 139:1-6

Possibilities of Grace

Daily Reading: Luke 13

> *A man had a fig tree planted in his vineyard, and he came seeking fruit on it and found none.* (Luke 13.6)

Devotional Thought: I know people who have given up on themselves. They need to hear this story of the fig tree. I have often been challenged by this parable of Jesus. I don't want to be an unfruitful fig tree! Consider this story...

This tree had every *opportunity* to bear fruit. It was "planted in his vineyard." There was better soil and conditions in the vineyard. The tree was protected and "pampered." As children of God, we are planted in his vineyard, fed and watered by the hand of God himself. May we take advantage of our opportunities to bear fruit for the Master!

Another thing I notice is that the owner of the vineyard had an *expectation* that a fig tree in his vineyard would produce fruit. He "came seeking fruit."

But there may be a fig tree which proves to be a *disappointment*: "found none." Having opportunity and expectation is not enough. Something within the fig tree must bring forth fruit.

But there is grace for even the unfruitful fig tree! It is given another opportunity to bear fruit. It is given extra *attention*. Failure need not be final. God provides a solution to fruitlessness. It may not always be pleasant - digging around it and putting on manure (v. 8) - but God's grace is just what we need. Give thanks to God that he doesn't give up on us!

I like the picture painted of the possibilities of grace: "It should bear fruit next year." And so the cycle of grace is renewed!

Prayer: Father, thank you for your infinite patience and grace. Help me to take advantage of my opportunities and fulfill your divine expectations for my life, bearing fruit to the praise of your glory. In Jesus' name, Amen.

Psalm of the Day: 139:7-16

Rules for Hosts

Daily Reading: Luke 14

> *"When you give a dinner or a banquet, do not invite your friends or your brothers or your relatives or rich neighbors, lest they also invite you in return and you be repaid. But when you give a feast, invite the poor, the crippled, the lame, the blind, and you will be blessed, because they cannot repay you. For you will be repaid at the resurrection of the just."* (Luke 14.12-14)

Devotional Thought: When time permits (all too seldom in our busy schedules!) Lana and I love to have guests over for Sunday lunch. Our favorite menu is homemade lasagna and fresh-baked bread. Do you enjoy entertaining around the dinner table?

The following outline in Beacon Bible Commentary (p 549) is shared as "Rules for Hosts" (BBC 549). I've added my own thoughts to these simple rules:

Shrink your guest list: "Do not invite..." It is so easy to get focused on a few people that we like and that are like us. Entertaining our family and friends is more comfortable and holds promise for more good times in the future. Jesus isn't saying that we should not do that, but that we should not do that exclusively. We need to make space in our lives for those who cannot repay us in kind. After all, Jesus left the familiar scenes of heaven to come to us!

Expand your guest list: "Invite the poor..." God has always been mindful of the poor, neglected segments of society. Poverty is defined by more than a lack of material goods. Some people may be poor in spirit - reach out to them. Some may be poor in friends - reach out to them. Some may be poor in social graces - reach out to them. I like the example of Jesus. He went to sinners, outcasts, despised, and lonely people.

Let God reward you: "You will be repaid at the resurrection..." Remember that we ourselves have been invited to an eternal banquet! We need not be repaid in earthly banquets. When we invite the poor, the stranger, the lonely to our tables, God invites us to his.

Prayer: Jesus, thank you for your example of grace when you reached out to us. Help us to be like you and reach out to others who are not like us - to give them space in our lives and hearts. Amen.

Psalm of the Day: 139:17-24

Kids These Days!

Daily Reading: Luke 15

> For this my son was dead, and is alive again; he was lost, and is found.
> (Luke 15:24)

Devotional Thought: "Kids these days!" Have you ever heard that? It's usually not spoken in a positive way. That's just what the people probably thought when they heard Jesus tell of the prodigal son.

There are many cultural implications in this story that are lost in our modern, Western understanding:

The son asking for his inheritance was akin to him telling his father that he wished him dead...

The loss of his inheritance in a "far country" meant that he had lost part of Israel's property and wealth to a pagan people...

His determination to return to his father and his scheming to escape from the terrible living conditions he had created for himself was quite possibly fraught with deceit. At least that is what the original audience would have understood.

But they would have been amazed at the next part of Jesus' story. The humiliated father does not simply welcome his son back home, we read that he is waiting and watching for his beloved child, longing for his return even after all this time. We read that he felt compassion and RAN (unheard of for men of this time, and considered undignified) to embrace his son and kiss him. Whatever the son had schemed or planned on the long journey home, his father showed selfless, sacrificial grace and love toward him.

This story does not celebrate the son who managed to turn his life around for the better as much as it celebrates a father (The Father) who never stopped loving and longing for his child. This is the glorious heartbeat of the gospel. God longs to celebrate over us: "For this my son was dead, and is alive again; he was lost, and is found."

Jenny

Prayer: Father, how we praise your great name for your unrelenting love! For even when we were dead in our trespasses, you made us alive together with Christ.

Psalm of the Day: 140:1-6

Steal, Beg, or Dig?

Daily Reading: Luke 16

'What shall I do? ... I am not strong enough to dig, and I am ashamed to beg. I have decided what to do... (Luke 16.3-4)

Devotional Thought: When I read the story of the dishonest manager, I feel like asking the manager, "What gives you the right to go into your master's accounts and take his possessions?" The dishonest manager gives his answer in vv. 3-4. I like how J. B. Chapman outlines this response: Shall I "Dig, Beg, or Steal?" (J. B. Chapman, quoted in *Beacon Bible Commentary*, 562)

What gives you the right?

"I can steal because I'm too lazy to dig." Too many people don't want to work for it. Today we would simply vote in politicians who would do the stealing for us!

"Well, I have my dignity! I can steal because I'm entitled to equality." Too many think that those who won't work have a right to the fruits of others' labors. After all they shouldn't be made to feel self-conscious or different. They shouldn't have to resort to begging.

"Because I can." Finally, exhausting his excuses and our patience, he would just say, "Because I can get away with it." That dishonest manager was in a position to take advantage of his employer. And so he did it. He had no scruples, no pride in himself, no sense of what was right.

When it comes to spiritual things, do we steal, expecting others to do the hard work of prayer and service? Do we beg, saying things like, "God, I know I should have done this, but I didn't. Can you take care of it?" That's a step better, for we can cloak it in piety and humility. Or, do we dig? Are we willing to roll up our sleeves and get our hands dirty?

Prayer: Lord, help me not to be a spiritual thief or beggar, but to be willing to exert myself in the seeking of your kingdom and righteousness. Amen.

Psalm of the Day: 140:7-13

Spiritual Inventory
Daily Reading: Luke 17

Pay attention to yourselves! (Luke 17.3)

Devotional Thought: Sometimes I meet people who take themselves too seriously. I just want to tell them, "Lighten up!" Other times I want to say to people, "Do you hear what you're saying?" In short, we need to pay attention to ourselves and live life in balance.

Jesus, in Luke 17, reminds us that we need to pay attention to ourselves. One author entitled this section *Spiritual Inventory* (Childers, *BBC*, 571). Pay attention to...

Your motives (vv. 1-2). We should be motivated by spiritual concerns, the condition of our souls and the souls of others. In another place Jesus asked, "What can a man give in exchange for his soul?" There is nothing more important than our spiritual condition. There is nothing longer in duration than eternity. Let us give first and best attention to things of the spirit.

Your spirit (vv. 3-4). Speaking of our spirits, we should, like Jesus, have a spirit of forgiveness. You may not have it in yourself right now. Don't despair. That's why we need to give it our attention! Ask Jesus to put his forgiving Spirit in you!

Your faith (vv. 5-6). We should do things to develop and express our faith. There is much we won't do if we don't do it in faith. But with faith there is even more we can do!

Your service (vv. 7-10). Are we consumers or servants? Do we seek ways for the church to serve us or for us to serve others in the church? Do we come to Jesus because he is worthy or for hopes of something in return? Let us serve him with an undivided spirit. All for Jesus!

Prayer: Search me, O God, and know my heart. Try me and know my thoughts. See if there be any grievous way in me and lead me in the way everlasting. Amen.

Psalm of the Day: 141:1-10

Don't Lose Heart

Daily Reading: Luke 18

> *He told them a parable to the effect that they ought always to pray and not lose heart.* (Luke 18.1)

Devotional Thought: The Bible says, "Let us not grow weary of doing good, for in due season we will reap, if we do not give up" (Galatians 6.9). One of those places we are most tempted to lose heart and give up is in the work of prayer. Jesus says we must always pray!

The story of the widow and the judge reminds us that in these days when Jesus has been taken from the earth, we are like the widow. Some of this world's judges "neither fear God nor respect man." Consequently, prayer may be our only means of support and redress. We must not lose heart!

For the widow in this story, there was only one course of action. She had to come back. Again and again. She must press her case for justice. Refusing to give up, she chose to take the way of prayer.

The good news is that God is *not* like the unjust judge of the story. Nor is he like the judges of today's legal system who have limited knowledge and leeway. God always answers our prayers when we come in the name of Jesus Christ. God will give us justice speedily. So may Christ find faith on the earth when he comes - faith in your heart and in mine! Amen!

Prayer: Thank you, Jesus, for teaching us that we ought to always pray. Help us to be faithful in this most sacred privilege and responsibility. Amen.

Psalm of the Day: 142:1-7

Salvation Comes Home
Daily Reading: Luke 19

> *Today salvation has come to this house.* (Luke 19.9)

Devotional Thought: Two millennia ago, in a tiny village outside Jerusalem, there was a humble home with an "inn" or guest room. However, on the night it was needed the most, it was occupied. Because of that, a young couple had to lodge for the night in the home's stable. There, in that place of welcome shelter and privacy, but lacking in comforts and cleanliness, the Baby Jesus was born. "Salvation" came to that humble home!

Over thirty years later, in the town of Jericho, another home was blessed when "Salvation" came to it. Zacchaeus' house welcomed the Man Jesus. Jericho was one of the chief cities of priests, but Jesus went to the home of a sinner. Jericho was a city rich in the nation's freedom heritage, but Jesus went to the home of a Roman agent.

"Salvation" came to this seeking sinner when the seeking Savior said, "Zacchaeus, hurry and come down, for I must stay at your house today!" You see, Jesus recognized in Zacchaeus what he failed to find in others - a seeking heart. Was Zacchaeus' understanding perfect? No! Was his morality impeccable? No! Were his motives pure? Probably not at first. But that's why "Salvation" needed to come. The very need of this man and his family compelled Jesus to come!

This Christmas season, may "Salvation" come to our hearts and homes. May we find comfort and assurance that it is our very need that compels the love of God to come to us. Let us receive him joyfully!

Prayer: Thank you, Jesus, for coming to my heart and home. I receive you joyfully. May I also share you with everyone around me, just as Zacchaeus did when you came to him. Amen.

Psalm of the Day: 143:1-6

They Cannot Die Anymore

Daily Reading: Luke 20

For they cannot die anymore... (Luke 20.36)

Devotional Thought: I once heard it said, "There is none freer than the one who has nothing to lose." Are you living your life like that? You can.

Jesus was confronted by a group of skeptics who wanted to debunk his belief in heaven. They were saying, in essence, "This life is all there is to live for." In other words, this life was all they had, so they had everything to lose. Jesus said, "Oh, but you are wrong. There is a life to come, and when you reach *that* life there will be no more death."

In heaven we have nothing we can lose. We cannot lose our lives, for the resurrection has banished death forever. We cannot lose our health, because there is not sickness there. We cannot lose our friends, for neither is there separation in that land. We cannot lose our joy, for sorrow cannot cast its shadow there. We cannot lose our way, for there is no darkness there.

We cannot die in any measure in that place that is called heaven.

Through Jesus Christ, we are promised eternal life. Nothing can steal it away from us, not even death. We are promised abundant life. Nothing can diminish its joy, not even sorrow.

Are you laying up treasures in heaven, "where neither moth nor rust destroys and where thieves do not break in and steal" (Matthew 6.20)? Or, are you living for this world only where everything you are living for will be lost?

I want to go to that city where "they cannot die anymore." Amen!

Prayer: Thank you, Jesus, for giving me eternal life, abundant life. Help me to live this life that I may enter the life where I will never die anymore. Amen.

Psalm of the Day: 143:7-12

All She Had

Daily Reading: Luke 21

> *"Truly, I tell you, this poor widow has put in more than all of them. For they all contributed out of their abundance, but she out of her poverty put in all she had to live on."* (Luke 21.3-4)

Devotional Thought: A few weeks ago, Lana and I received one of the best gifts ever. It was simply a card with a hand-written message inside. It represented the giver's heart and touched us deeply. It may not have impressed other people, but oh, how we rejoiced!

Jesus encountered a situation like that one day at the temple. A poor widow gave an offering that overwhelmed him. It represented her heart. It represented "all she had."

Christmas season is a good time to check our giving quotients. Using this story, we are reminded that we should give...

Out of our abundance. Jesus, commended those who were able to give from their abundance. God blesses us so that we might in turn be a blessing, giving away what he has so freely given us. It may not be wealth that we have an abundance of, but we can still give our abundance away. "Silver and gold I do not have, but what I have, I give you. In the name of Jesus..." We have an abundance of joy, peace, hope and love in Jesus Christ!

Out of our poverty. Even when we don't have much to give, giving to the Lord is still a joy. Giving to others is the same. Paul spoke of the Macedonians who were blessed and who themselves blessed others because they gave out of their poverty. When you lack, do you grouse, or do you give?

All we have to live on. We must, of course, give God our all. I think we also can open up our hearts to others as well, sharing with them all the love we have.

Jesus gave out of his abundance and out of his poverty. He gave all he had. Do you?

Prayer: Thank you, Jesus, that you gave all you had for our salvation. Help us to give in abundance and poverty alike. We give you our all today.

Psalm of the Day: 144:1-8

Consent and Conviction

Daily Reading: Luke 22

> *So he consented and sought an opportunity to betray him to them in the absence of a crowd.* (Luke 22:6)

Devotional Thought: Have you ever been betrayed by a close friend? If so, then you know how Jesus felt when Judas betrayed him.

We are told in this passage that the behavior of Judas was the result of Satan indwelling him. What a horrifying thought! "He went away and conferred with the chief priests and officers how he might betray him to them. And they were glad, and agreed to give him money" (v4-5). Money! He put a price on Jesus' friendship. When offered enough money, "he consented and sought an opportunity to betray him."

Judas recognized the evil intention of his heart. He knew that it stemmed from a place of sin and darkness, and therefore was determined to keep it hidden. The Jewish leaders paying Judas for his betrayal recognized this as well, knowing that putting Jesus to death would cause an uproar from "the people" (v2). So, they arrest Jesus as he is praying in the Garden of Gethsemane, in the middle of the night. The gospel of Matthew records the fate of Judas: guilty, he throws his payment into the temple and hangs himself.

When we become convicted of sin in our lives, there are two responses: we will either try to push it away, hiding it from others and even ourselves, or we will feel a godly sorrow that leads us to repentance (2 Cor. 7:10). Is there anything in our lives that we are trying to hide under cover of darkness, ashamed at its ugliness? God already knows. Pull it into the light of Christ, surrender it to him, and trust that he is "faithful and just to forgive us our sins and to cleanse us from all unrighteousness" (1 John 1:9).

Jenny

Prayer: Lord, we ask that you cleanse us from all sin. What a terrible price you paid for that sin! Help us to see the true ugliness of our rebellion against you, and lead us in the way everlasting.

Psalm of the Day: 144:9-15

Believable

Daily Reading: Luke 23

> Do you not fear God, since you are under the same sentence of condemnation? And we indeed justly, for we are receiving the due reward of our deeds; but this man has done nothing wrong.
> (Luke 23.40-41)

Devotional Thought: How do you respond to suffering and afflictions? I've heard it said that we know more about a person when they pass through the fire than when they rest on beds of ease.

As Jesus hung on the cross, he was "reviled by those around him." Yet there was one man, a stranger, who saw something different in this co-sufferer. His response changed as he observed Jesus on the cross.

I want to be like Jesus, don't you? I want other people to look at me and see that there is hope for them. The thief on the cross saw Jesus forgive his executioners. He witnessed Jesus as he cared for his mother and friend. He heard Jesus call upon God with his last breath. That had a powerful impact on this man who had lived his life full of sin and deceit. He finally saw the truth and called out to Jesus, the man who had done nothing wrong.

Christianity that condemns, faith that becomes bitter, religion that lashes out... Those things are all too prevalent. People want to see a faith that makes a difference. People, I believe, are hungry for something real. They want the talk and the walk to match. When they see that, they will sit up and take notice.

May God give us grace to love in the midst of hate, to forgive in response to hurt, and to trust when nothing is going right. Then, people will believe our testimonies about the Lord!

Prayer: Jesus, thank you for your example of love and faith in the midst of suffering. Help me to love my enemies and trust in God even when the pain runs deep. Amen.

Psalm of the Day: 145:1-9

Abide With Me

Daily Reading: Luke 24

> *They urged him strongly, saying, "Stay with us, for it is toward evening and the day is now far spent."* (Luke 24.29)

Devotional Thought: There is an old hymn I love. It's not one we think about typically at Christmas, but I think it points us to Emmanuel, God with us:
Abide with me! Fast falls the eventide; the darkness deepens; Lord, with me abide!

When other helpers fail and comforts flee, Help of the helpless, oh, abide with me...
I fear no foe, with Thee at hand to bless: Ills have no weight, and tears no bitterness:
Where is death's sting? Where, grave, thy victory? I triumph still, if Thou abide with me.
(Abide With Me, Henry Francis Lyte)

Jesus came on that first Christmas in order to be with us. The disciples on the road to Emmaus, longed for the hidden Jesus to remain with them. They felt the tug of night and desired the comfort of their unrecognized friend. "Stay with us, for it is toward evening..."

Our hearts still yearn for him, don't they? On this Christmas Eve, look to the heavens - as did the shepherds on the hillside - and hear the angel proclaim in the darkness: " Fear not, for behold, I bring you good news of great joy that will be for all the people. For unto you is born this day in the city of David a Savior, who is Christ the Lord. And this will be a sign for you: you will find a baby wrapped in swaddling cloths and lying in a manger" (Luke 2.10-12).

May you find The Baby on this most holy night!

Prayer: Jesus, thank you for revealing yourself to us. Give us eyes to see and hearts to feel your presence, O Emmanuel. Amen.

Psalm of the Day: 145:10-21

Merry Christmas!

Daily Reading: Luke 2.1-20

---

[1] *In those days a decree went out from Caesar Augustus that all the world should be registered.* [2] *This was the first registration when Quirinius was governor of Syria.* [3] *And all went to be registered, each to his own town.* [4] *And Joseph also went up from Galilee, from the town of Nazareth, to Judea, to the city of David, which is called Bethlehem, because he was of the house and lineage of David,* [5] *to be registered with Mary, his betrothed, who was with child.* [6] *And while they were there, the time came for her to give birth.* [7] *And she gave birth to her firstborn son and wrapped him in swaddling cloths and laid him in a manger, because there was no place for them in the inn.*

[8] *And in the same region there were shepherds out in the field, keeping watch over their flock by night.* [9] *And an angel of the Lord appeared to them, and the glory of the Lord shone around them, and they were filled with great fear.* [10] *And the angel said to them, "Fear not, for behold, I bring you good news of great joy that will be for all the people.* [11] *For unto you is born this day in the city of David a Savior, who is Christ the Lord.* [12] *And this will be a sign for you: you will find a baby wrapped in swaddling cloths and lying in a manger."*

[13] *And suddenly there was with the angel a multitude of the heavenly host praising God and saying,* [14] *"Glory to God in the highest, and on earth peace among those with whom he is pleased!"*

[15] *When the angels went away from them into heaven, the shepherds said to one another, "Let us go over to Bethlehem and see this thing that has happened, which the Lord has made known to us."* [16] *And they went with haste and found Mary and Joseph, and the baby lying in a manger.* [17] *And when they saw it, they made known the saying that had been told them concerning this child.* [18] *And all who heard it wondered at what the shepherds told them.*

[19] *But Mary treasured up all these things, pondering them in her heart.* [20] *And the shepherds returned, glorifying and praising God for all they had heard and seen, as it had been told them.*

Prayer: Jesus, on this Christmas Day, I kneel before you and wonder at the greatness of your love. Help me to glorify you today and always. Amen.

Psalm of the Day: 146:1-10

Claim Your Inheritance!
Daily Reading: Ephesians 1

In him we have obtained an inheritance... (Ephesians 1.11)

Devotional Thought: Have you ever received an inheritance? Many of us have. Some of us have inherited things we just as soon would not have! But, in Jesus, we have an inheritance that we can enjoy forever and ever! According to Ephesians 1...

Our inheritance is not accidental, but purposeful. "Obtained" here actually means we have been "chosen by lot..." According to the "counsel of his will" (v. 11), we have been chosen to receive this inheritance. I have ministered to families whose inheritance came about rather randomly - according to the courts and the statutes in effect. I have also ministered to those whose inheritance was purposeful and clear. That kind is by far the best to deal with!

Our inheritance must be claimed. Paul said that we have "heard... and believed... the message" (v. 13). An inheritance on the books is worthless. It is not until the heir claims it that it changes hands from the estate to the heir. God wants us to claim our inheritance in Jesus!

Wait, there's more!

Our inheritance is certain. It is "sealed and guaranteed..." (vv. 13-14).

Our inheritance brings honor to God. It is to the "Praise of his glory" (vv. 12, 14).

Our inheritance waits. It will be there "until we acquire possession of it..." (v. 14).

"Blessed be the God and Father of our Lord Jesus Christ! According to his great mercy, he has caused us to be born again to a living hope through the resurrection of Jesus Christ from the dead, to an inheritance that is imperishable, undefiled, and unfading, kept in heaven for you!" (1 Peter 1.3-4)

Prayer: Thank you, Father, for my inheritance: eternal life. Help me to claim it and live with the assurance that it shall be mine forever and ever in Jesus. Amen!

Psalm of the Day: 147:1-11

God's GPS

Daily Reading: Ephesians 2

Following the course of this world... (Ephesians 2.2)

Devotional Thought: Recently, I was going with my friend Matt to a mission project on the north side of Cincinnati. He was driving and we were following his GPS. At our exit, we got off on the right, just as I had done many times before at that particular exit. What we didn't know, however, and what the outdated GPS didn't 'know', was that the exit had changed. Instead of exiting right, we needed to exit left. We thought we were right - after all GPS is never wrong - but we were headed the wrong direction!

The Apostle Paul warned that "following the course of this world" was like that. When we walked that way, we didn't know where we were headed. "There is a way that seems right to a man, but its end is the way to death" (Proverbs 16.25). Spiritually dead people, following a spiritually dead course, may think that they are right, but are dead wrong. No matter how sincerely we believe a lie, it is a lie nonetheless.

Our world is full of different courses. We have so many options to choose from. We can find all manner of "truth" on the internet. But, the only reliable truth is found in the Word of God. Let's use God's GPS and make sure we reach the right destination!

Prayer: Thank you, Father, for your Word which shows us the way to life. Thank you that your Son is the Way, the Truth, and the Life. Help us to follow him and so to arrive at the proper destination. Amen.

Psalm of the Day: 147:12-20

Even Bigger!

Daily Reading: Ephesians 3

Now to him who is able to do far more abundantly than all that we ask or think, according to the power at work within us, to him be glory in the church and in Christ Jesus throughout all generations, forever and ever. Amen. (Ephesians 3.20-21)

Devotional Thought: Once when I was spreading mulch in my backyard, my pickup truck sank down in a soft place. No matter what I tried, I could not get it unstuck. I even tried to lift it by the back bumper. I only ended up tearing my tendon loose from my bicep. That hurt! I called my friend Phil who had a tractor. Pulling my truck from the mud was not a problem for him at all!

We get stuck in the mud sometimes, don't we? We try and try and try, but we are just not able to lift ourselves out by our own bootstraps. When we strain too much, we end up hurting ourselves. God, however is not limited. Consider what Paul says in these two verses:

God works. God is able to do. God is a doer. He is not passive, as the deist's "watchmaker God" who winds up the world and then goes on his way to let it run itself. No, God is involved in the workings of his world. He will never leave us or forsake us! Whatever you are going through, rest in the assurance that God is working!

God exceeds. God is able to do more than we ask or think. He exceeds our human powers. He even exceeds our human imaginations. He is not limited by anything!

God works in us. God is able to work in us. He is not limited by our humanity. As a matter of fact, Paul says in another place that his power is made perfect in our weakness! No problem, no deficiency, no obstacle can prevent him from working in you.

Are you stuck in the mud? Call God! He's got the biggest tractor you can imagine. Even bigger!

Prayer: Father, thank you that your power is not limited by anything. Lift me up from the miry clay, I pray. Amen.

Psalm of the Day: 148:1-6

Are You Resolute?

Daily Reading: Ephesians 4

> Let no corrupting talk come out of your mouths, but only such as is good for building up, as fits the occasion, that it may give grace to those who hear. (Ephesians 4:29)

Devotional Thought: Many Americans will start the day on January 1 determined to suddenly become a new person. New Years' resolutions will include many diet plans, exercise schedules, gym memberships, and refrigerator clean-outs. There will also be some promises for new behavior or routines, church attendance, quiet times, family devotions, or giving to the church. These resolutions in and of themselves are not bad, but I believe the motivation behind them should be examined.

Too many people approach what may be a positive change for the wrong reasons, or under the wrong power. Most of our resolutions turn into embarrassing memories two weeks later. The reality in our Christian lives is that our strength is not sufficient. Rather, the Lord uses our weaknesses to create dependence on him, the source of our true strength.

Paul has a lot to say in Ephesians about unity in the body of Christ, and living the new life of a believer. There are many imperatives in this chapter, directing believers in what they should and should not be doing. One of my personal favorites as a mother to three young girls comes from this chapter, in verse 29. "Let no corrupting talk come out of your mouths, but only such as is good for building up... that it may give grace to those who hear." That is wonderful advice for all of us! However, it cannot be accomplished through the sheer force of our will. It requires an acknowledgement of our own weakness and a complete dependence on the Lord and his power.

This year, instead of resolutions, take some time with the Lord and ask him to examine your heart, find any offensive way, and lead you in the way everlasting (Ps. 139:23-24).

Jenny

Prayer: Lord, we acknowledge that our own attempts to create any lasting, worthy change are weak and ineffectual. We are all prone to take control over our own lives, pridefully displaying our victories as our own. Help us to rely on your Spirit's work in our hearts, and to give all the glory to whom it belongs.

Psalm of the Day: 148:7-14

Such Love!

Daily Reading: Ephesians 5

as Christ loved the church... (Ephesians 5.25)

Devotional Thought: In Ephesians 5 we find a beautiful description of the love between a husband and wife. Enclosed within joyful self-surrender (mutual submission), marital love reveals the nature of Christ's love for his Church:

Christ's love is a...

Sacrificing love. Christ gave himself for the church. His love was so great that he died on the cross to redeem his bride. No demand was too high for Christ's love, no service too low. I ask prospective husbands: "You say you would die for your fiancé. Would you sweep the floors for her?" Christ's love is like that.

Sanctifying love. Christ desires a pure and holy bride. I like what one author wrote: "'Without spot or wrinkle' means without one trace of defilement or one mark of age." In the words of Robert Browning, "Grow old along with me! The best is yet to be, the last of life, for which the first was made." Over the years, Christ sets apart his bride as holy and precious.

Sustaining love. Just as we nourish and care for our bodies, we should also nourish and care for our spouses. Our love sustains our mates through the years. Christ's love is like that. He makes promises to us. He protects us. He provides for us.

Secret love. Paul spoke of the profound mystery of marital love, a love that goes within the bridal chamber and is shared intimately between a husband and wife. The love of Christ for the church is a "secret love" that is shared only within the bonds of Jesus. It is a mystery that awaits full revelation until the end.

Such love! Such wondrous love!

Prayer: Thank you, Jesus, for your wonderful love. I receive it with gladness of heart. Help me to love you in return with a sacrificing, sanctifying, sustaining, secret love. Amen.

Psalm of the Day: 149:1-9

Suit Up!

Daily Reading: Ephesians 6

Put on the whole armor of God. (Ephesians 6.11)

Devotional Thought: For our closing devotion, I would like to share a prayer I have written that helps me to "put on the whole armor of God."

Father, thank you for the armor of God. I put it on today, that I might stand firm in you and in the strength of your might; that I may be able to stand against the schemes of the devil.

I put on the **belt of truth** in order to recognize the light of the Kingdom and the lies of Satan.

I put on the **breastplate of righteousness** to protect my heart from all wrong affections, my head from all wrong attractions, and my hands from all wrong actions.

Make me ready – **having put on the shoes of readiness given by the gospel of peace**– to share Christ's love everywhere with everyone in every way. The gates of hell cannot prevail against your church!

I take up the **shield of faith**, for I know that my enemy – the devil – is like a roaring lion, seeking whom he may devour. But by faith in the name of Jesus, I shall overcome.

I put on the **helmet of salvation**. May it protect me from trusting in myself or in anybody or anything else besides you.

I pick up the **sword of the Spirit** – the very Word of God. May it become a part of my life. Change me by the power of your Word so that you may use me to change the world.

I commit to **pray in the Spirit** today, for all the saints with all kinds of prayers. Please help me to sense your presence and talk to you all day.

And finally, Lord, I **pray for my pastor** and for others in authority over the church that they may fearlessly make known the mystery of the gospel.

Amen.

Psalm of the Day: 150:1-6

Acknowledgments...

In addition to Pastor Scott, others have contributed devotional articles to *The Climb: Start Here.* Jenny Wade Powell, who is Scott and Lana's oldest daughter, has co-written with her father for over five years. Many of her articles from "A-Chapter-A-Day" - their daily email devotionals - have found their way into this book. Many other guest authors from those daily emails have graciously given permission to include them in this book.

I want to thank my wife, Lana, for editing and proof-reading the final manuscript. Also for her partnership in ministry!

My kids - Jenny, Eric, Emily, Aaron, Amy, and Evan - for pushing me to "get out of the boat" and focus on my writing.

Dale and the staff at One Stop Publications who were so helpful in getting this first devotional book published.

Al, Eric, Keith, and Steve - the board at Momentum Ministries - who encouraged me and helped me maintain momentum without overdoing it.

Kenny who organized a launch team and helped me promote this book.

All the folks who have subscribed to my daily devotional emails for 8 years!

Quotations from Beacon Bible Commentary, Beacon Hill Press of Kansas City, Kansas City, MO, are gratefully acknowledged as follows:
Ralph Earle in vol. 6 - Matthew; vol. 7 - Acts; vol. 10 - Revelation
Charles L. Childers in vol. 6 - Luke
Donald S. Metz in vol. 8 - I Corinthians
Frank G. Carver in vol. 8 - II Corinthians
J. Glenn Gould in vol. 9 - I and II Timothy
John B. Nielson in vol. 9 - Philemon
Richard S. Taylor in vol. 10 - Hebrews
Delbert R. Rose in vol. 10 - Jude

NOTES:

NOTES: